MORE PRAISE FOR WE KILL

'This chilling and comprehensive survey more than amply demonstrates that drone strikes are war crimes, and that this new technology is not only an effective device of mass murder at a distance, but that it also eliminates barriers for commanders to "prosecute wars at their caprice".'

Noam Chomsky

'By far the best book on drone warfare and the ethics of targeted assassinations to date. Powerful and eloquent, Laurie Calhoun elucidates a set of convincing arguments as to why drone killing is ethically indefensible and strategically counterproductive, but also why it is so seductive to our governments. It should be required reading for politicians, military planners and journalists.'

Richard Jackson, author of *Confessions of a Terrorist*

'A comprehensive and shocking survey of the dirty consequences of US drone strikes. Calhoun provides important information on civilian casualties, which puts the lie to the CIA's denial of such losses. This important work will be helpful in any re-examination of drone policy.'

Melvin A. Goodman, former CIA analyst and author of *National Insecurity: The Cost of American Militarism*

About the author

Laurie Calhoun is a philosopher and cultural critic with a special interest in film as a source of moral insight. She is the author of *War and Delusion: A Critical Examination* and *Philosophy Unmasked: A Skeptic's Critique*, in addition to dozens of essays on war, morality and politics.

WE KILL BECAUSE WE CAN

FROM SOLDIERING TO ASSASSINATION IN THE DRONE AGE

LAURIE CALHOUN

ZED

Zed Books

LONDON

For Mary 'Code' Calhoun

We Kill Because We Can: From Soldiering to Assassination in the Drone Age was first published in 2015 by Zed Books Ltd, The Foundry, 17 Oval Way, London SE11 5RR, UK.

This edition published 2016.

www.zedbooks.net

Typeset in ITC Galliard Std by seagulls.net
Cover design by Steven Marsden

A catalogue record for this book is available from the British Library.

ISBN 978-1-78360-547-7 pb
ISBN 978-1-78360-549-1 pdf
ISBN 978-1-78360-550-7 epub
ISBN 978-1-78360-551-4 mobi

CONTENTS

Foreword to the paperback edition   vii

Preface   xv

Introduction   1

PART I: FIND

1. Drone Nation   11
2. From Black Ops to Standard Operating Procedure   31
3. The Logic of Targeted Killing   53
4. Lethal Creep   77

PART II: FIX

5. Strike First, Suppress Questions Later   105
6. The New Banality of Killing   133
7. The Operators   155
8. From Conscience to Oblivion   179

PART III: FINISH

9. Death and Politics   207
10. Death and Taxes   231
11. The Death of Military Virtue   255
12. Tyrants Are as Tyrants Do   277

Conclusion   299

Postface   321

Appendix: Drone Killing and Just War Theory   325

Notes   335

Books Cited   365

Films Cited   371

Acronyms and Abbreviations   375

Acknowledgments   377

Index   381

FOREWORD TO THE PAPERBACK EDITION

It was bound to happen, and it did. In 2015, the ranks of the drone warriors began swiftly to swell. As the economic potential for remote-control killing capacity in the hands of political leaders all over the world became clear to players in the lethal drone industry, an elite club once numbering only two members, the governments of the United States and Israel, admitted many others. The most significant new inductee was surely Britain.

In August 2015, two British citizens were destroyed by remote-control under the authorization of Prime Minister David Cameron. After hundreds of strikes against terrorist suspects authorized by US President Barack Obama and reported by the mainstream media as acts of national defense in the Global War on Terror, the prime minister's action may have appeared to conform to the norm established by previous practice. Cameron's decision to kill British citizens using lethal drones served to strengthen the precedent set by Obama, under whose leadership US citizens were intentionally executed by remote control during the fall of 2011.

However, the British prime minister's targeted killing of compatriots was not merely an act of emulation or show of support for the US president, for it represented a significant and qualitative expansion of drone warfare. Capital punishment is prohibited by both British law and the EU Charter, but Cameron killed Reyaad Khan and Ruhul

Amin in Syria using missiles and labeling the executions acts of war. Like Obama before him, Cameron claimed that his elimination of citizens located abroad was a matter of national self-defense.

In both the United States and Britain, the assertion by the government of the right to kill citizens neither indicted nor tried for crimes – a radical expansion of executive power – was accepted by many people for the simple reason that it happened so far away. 'Taking the battle to the enemy' proved to be no less a palatable political proposition in Britain than it had been in the United States. Over a short period of time, the British government has acquired an impressive array of lethal drones, some of which Cameron christened 'Protectors', rather than 'Predators' or 'Reapers', to convey the impression that they are implements of defense, not tools of assassination.

Collaboration between the various drone warriors serves to reinforce the never-debated 'assassination as warfare' norm, while broadening the reach and increasing the frequency of remote-control killing. When in November 2015, using intelligence provided in part by Britain, the US government fired on British national Mohammed Emwazi, better known as Jihadi John, the post-strike reports were worded cautiously: '"Jihadi John" Probably Killed'; 'US "reasonably certain" strike killed IS militant'. Why the caution? Because, as in so many other cases, previous strikes aiming for Emwazi had killed other persons in his stead. Who were the victims? The taxpayers funding the drone program will never know. The case of Emwazi underscores how, in addition to claiming the right to kill suspects assumed to be guilty until proven innocent, the drone warriors are simultaneously asserting the right to destroy anyone, whatever their identity may be, who happens to be in any way associated with or located near a target, in any place on the planet labeled a 'battlefield' by those in charge.

Some of the strikes in 2015 missed their intended targets but killed persons who could not be facilely written off as Enemy Killed in Action, or EKIA, the label applied to the unnamed military-age males annihilated in drone strikes, according to classified US government documents made public by *The Intercept*. When acknowledged, the innocent victims continue to be written off as 'collateral damage', even when the missiles are fired on lands where there are no allied combat troops on the 'battlefield' to protect. Two persons taken hostage by Al-Qaeda, Italian citizen Giovanni Lo Porto and US citizen Warren Weinstein, were killed in a drone strike on 15 January 2015, along with two other Americans, Adam Gadahn and Ahmed Farouq, both of whom were believed to be associated with the radical Islamist group. But the drone warriors had no idea who any of the victims were until after the 'signature strike', carried out at a site believed by analysts to be frequented by Al-Qaeda operatives.

So much for 'near certainty', the epistemic criterion for drone strikes claimed in May 2013 by President Obama to be used in selecting targets. Were the deaths of the alleged Al-Qaeda members killed in these strikes more valuable than the lives of the innocent people killed at the same time or by mistake in their place? This question has arisen over and over again in the drone age but is ignored by the self-styled 'smart warriors'. The mores of Western civilization continue to erode as the destruction of potential future enemies is given higher priority than anything else, including what in centuries past was considered to be the sanctity of innocent life.

British national Junaid Hussain, killed in August 2015 by a US drone with the aid of British intelligence, was a twenty-one-year-old hacker and, therefore, a mere child at the time of the 2003 invasion of Iraq. His obliteration by a missile was further evidence of lethal creep, yet another qualitative leap for the drone warriors. The Pentagon had announced in 2011 that they would consider 'cyberterrorists' fair game for military attack. Before his annihilation, Hussain had served six months in a British prison for hacking the email of Tony Blair. By destroying this twenty-one-year-old suspect, described by one analyst as a 'nuisance', the remote-control killers expanded yet again the domain of allegedly legitimate military targets. 'The friend of my enemy is my enemy', so if propagandists and hackers express sympathy with radical jihadist groups, then they become fair game for summary execution without trial, even if they never fired a gun or planted a bomb.

For more than a decade, the US government declined to reply to inquiries regarding their killing of targets in countries such as Pakistan and Yemen, invoking 'State Secrets Privilege' under a national security pretext. As a result, the drone program could not be effectively criticized in the public square. The Stimson Center Task Force on Lethal Drone Policy, commissioned by the US government to assess the drone program, concluded in its February 2016 'report card' that next to no progress had been made on issues of accountability, transparency or the development of international norms. New threats, such as ISIS, continue to emerge, but policymakers have refused to face up to their role in generating and shaping these enemies, despite the testimony of the many radical Islamic jihadists who have inveighed against Western military intervention, not only Osama bin Laden, but also recently minted dissidents such as Junaid Hussain.

By 2016, at least nineteen countries already possessed or were about to acquire lethal drone technology, and UAVs (unmanned aerial vehicles) and their associated ammunitions were being produced and sold all over the world. As a result, leaders considerably less scrupulous than some believe Barack Obama to be now find themselves with their fingers on the buttons of machines prepared to kill at their caprice. Given the general tendency of political leaders to make use of the 'tools' ready at hand, it seems likely that the governments of other Western countries – Italy, Spain, France, Germany, Canada, et al. – which have already secured large contracts for drones and missiles, will follow Obama's and Cameron's example in the not-too-distant future. The new members of the drone killing club can be expected, too, to use bribed intelligence and electronic surveillance to locate some of their compatriots hiding out in remote war zones, with the aim, ultimately, of eliminating them by remote control in the name of national defense. As the leaders of more and more nations opt to follow the example set by Britain, Israel and the United States, the legitimacy of using drones to destroy persons suspected of complicity in possible future terrorist plots will become more and more difficult to contest in venues such as the International Criminal Court in The Hague.

In tandem with the global spread of the new technology, drone bases have proliferated as well, with UAVs flying out of places as diverse as Cameroon, Sicily, Jordan and the Seychelles. More bases imply more drones imply more operators imply longer kill lists. What have the drone warriors wrought? Given the US precedent, the only true constraints on the use of this technology will depend on the discretion of the local war-making authority. The drone base in Cameroon deserves special mention, for that country has been governed by a single leader, President Paul Biya, since 1982. Biya is renowned for creativity in electoral fraud, in addition to gross human rights violations. Nonetheless, the US government saw fit in 2015 to erect a drone base in that land and to provide some 300 US Special Forces to help train Cameroonian soldiers to kill.

The spirit of innovation is everywhere on display among the 'smart warriors', with smaller and more lethal drones being developed every day. Swarms of dozens of drones working in concert have been tested and will no doubt soon be deployed to conflict zones, further augmenting the lethal potential of remote-control technology. The goal of achieving fully automated unmanned aerial systems, with human operators removed from the 'kill chain', is also within reach. Israel's 'Hero' drone is small enough to be convenient for terrorist groups themselves to use, and in early 2016 the US Army was calling for bids on contracts for microdrones to be carried in deployed soldiers' kits. No matter how much work is done to develop means to defeat drones before they are misused, the potential for commandeering will never go away, because this technology requires an electronic network and, therefore, is hackable. It is only a matter of time before the military drones of states will be intercepted by non-state actors, who can be expected to append payloads with the message 'return to sender'.

Political leaders around the globe have been seduced by the concept of 'smart power' to believe that they can wage and win wars abroad without sacrificing any troops. Advocates of drone warfare appear not to recognize the paradox involved in claiming the right to kill in national self-defense persons located too far away to harm anyone in the homeland. But just as it was obvious that other governments would eventually follow the US example in using lethal drones to dispatch suspects, it is only a matter of time before leaders will begin to ask whether the geographical location of their targets is in fact relevant to the question whether they should be killed. Isn't an alleged terrorist much more dangerous to the people of Britain on British soil than he is thousands of miles away?

The governments of Nigeria and Pakistan affirmed as much in 2015; both executed nationals in the homeland using lethal drones. The Israeli government had already killed many Palestinian suspects by remote control, so Israel deserves some credit as a role model on this front. The summary execution without trial of suspected militants by the Nigerian and Pakistani governments – and by the Iraqi government as well – is hardly surprising, given the political climates of those lands. Others like them will surely follow suit, eliminating more and more political dissidents, now that lethal drone technology is readily available and can be purchased from China, Israel and other countries. Iran reportedly has a robust lethal drone development program underway, among other governments keen to obviate the need to meet any weapons import requirements whatsoever. Meanwhile the explosion of hobbyists suggests the potential for the use of drones by not only terrorists but also criminals more generally. The modularity of drones – the fact that they can be made deadly by snapping on some form of lethal delivery system – makes clear the potential for lawlessness and harm.

Lethal creep is in full evidence as the use of drones leads to the deployment of manned bombers in lands where war was never waged. The reported killing of more than 150 people in Somalia by the US government on 7 March 2016, using both drones and regular combat planes, was announced with little objection by anyone, having been made to seem to be just another event in the never-ending Global War on Terror. The 'light footprint' strategy favored by President Obama becomes heavier and heavier as the failure of the 'killing machine' to make anyone more secure becomes more and more difficult to deny, given the attacks on both Paris and San Bernardino in 2015, and on Brussels in 2016. The reigning chaos and insecurity throughout the Middle East ensures that there will be further blowback in Western lands as violent extremists continue to retaliate for what they view as a Global War on Islam.

As civil rights continue to be curtailed in tandem with the expansion of executive power, military drones have already begun to fly surveillance missions over US skies. The question is not whether but when Western leaders will begin to call for targeted killing in the homeland of suspects already under the government's watchful eyes.

PREFACE

I first became aware of the existence of weaponized drones shortly after the execution by the Central Intelligence Agency (CIA) of six persons driving down a road in Yemen on 3 November 2002. I watched footage of the aftermath of the attack in amazement, not that people could be pulverized to powder by such a mighty machine, but that the commentators on the event were unanimously praising it as a magnificent feat. There seemed to be no appreciation whatsoever of the maze of moral questions raised by the use of technology in this way.

Puzzled, I penned an essay, 'The Strange Case of Summary Execution by Predator Drone', which was published in the journal *Peace Review* in early 2003. Six years later, in January 2009, elated and relieved by the results of the 2008 election and the prospect of a peace-loving president, I sent a copy of my essay to Barack Obama. Against all hope for change, summary execution by Predator drone was not brought to a halt by the new administration. Even more surprisingly, targeted killing came swiftly to define US foreign policy, despite never having been subjected to public debate.

The use of sophisticated technology to 'find, fix, and finish' unarmed human beings located in faraway places and selected for annihilation through secretive deliberations by a small committee of bureaucrats represents a radical departure from the ways in which 'war' was fought in the past. Somehow all of this escaped the attention of nearly everyone in the United States until three Americans were 'taken out' by Predator drone strikes authorized by President Obama in the fall of 2011. One of them was a sixteen-year-old boy, Abdulrahman al-Awlaki, the son of Anwar al-Awlaki, who had been killed two weeks earlier and was an outspoken critic of what he characterized as the US government's criminal war on Islamists.

People are polarized by Predator drones. For every person appalled by the remote-control killing of terrorist suspects, there is someone else who praises the practice. As ghastly as anti-drone activists believe the summary execution of unarmed persons to be, the policymakers have satisfied themselves that there is a legal framework through which to understand the lethal actions as permissible forms of warfare. If that framework, involving substantive reinterpretations of such concepts as *imminent threat*, is deemed valid, then presumably it will be invoked by other leaders and governments in the future, and it should be applicable retrospectively, too. If the new standards are applied consistently to all perpetrators of political homicide, then much of history will need to be rewritten.

Far more important than the legal conventions governing warfare, which are subject to modification as new leaders emerge and societies transform over time, are the moral principles reflected even by practices currently deemed legal. The time has arrived to subject the drone program, and all that it entails, to moral scrutiny, to soberly assess whether we can in good conscience condone the clinical killing of unarmed persons by operators whose lives are not in any direct danger when they kill. Drones also present an unprecedented opportunity to consider in a more general way the practice of war in the modern world. Targeted killings strip away all else from war but the premeditated end deliberately sought: the death of human beings.

INTRODUCTION

Over the course of human history, military institutions have been incrementally removing 'the human factor' from warfare and increasing the distance between soldiers and the persons whom they kill. From bare hands and knives to arrows and spears, from one-shot rifles to rapid-fire machine guns capable of cutting an entire line of human beings in half, each successive generation of weapons has moved rival combatants farther and farther apart. Landmines are a form of automated technology, albeit crude, which were designed to impede the forward motion of enemy soldiers while allied soldiers lay in wait somewhere else. The invention of airplanes and bombs introduced not merely a quantitative but a qualitative change, making it possible to kill enemy troops from the sky. Atomic munitions exponentially increased the destructive force to be unleashed through the simple push of a button. In each of these cases, what began as an ingenious invention intended to minimize allied combatant casualties ended in the indiscriminate killing and maiming of civilians.

The most recent paradigm-shifting military innovation is the weaponized unmanned aerial vehicle (UAV), sometimes referred to as the unmanned combat aerial vehicle (UCAV). These aircraft are controlled by operators located thousands of miles away from the sites of their destruction. Armed with precision laser-guided missiles, UCAVs, the most prevalent of which is the Predator drone, are said by their advocates to make 'surgical strikes' against enemies possible while minimizing collateral damage and preserving allied soldiers'

1

lives. The use of unmanned aircraft for literal force protection in declared war zones may seem like a natural extension of the warrior's arm, not so different from the use of manned air support. For that purpose, drones were used after the US invasions of Afghanistan and Iraq, where occupying troops on the ground struggled daily with insurgent attacks on installations and on military vehicles attempting to travel from one place to another while patrolling areas of ferment.

Drones have proven, however, to be more than just another among many lethal weapons in the military's arsenal for use in wars already waged. Over the course of less than a decade, both the practice of and the propensity toward institutional killing have been transformed by this new technology. Drones introduced the possibility of waging what are in effect wars without incurring the risk of soldiers' death historically associated with calls to arms. In the past, the inevitable sacrifice of compatriot lives sometimes served to rein in bellicose leaders, who, before resorting to war, needed first persuasively to explain why the deployment – and likely loss – of troops had become necessary. With drones at their disposal, commanders have become freer to prosecute wars at their caprice – wars of choice – for they may do so without placing soldiers in harm's way.

Given the nearly complete absence of domestic debate over the use of drones before they were deployed in hundreds of strikes abroad in countries with which the United States is not officially at war, it seems safe to say that technology has guided policy, and not vice versa. But does possibility imply permissibility? Should the current state of technology dictate morality? Or should not antecedent moral values shape policies and drive decisions about how to develop and use technology? These and many other questions of ethics are raised by the targeted killing of specific persons, a practice formerly considered taboo and undertaken only covertly by US leaders.

The first clue that technology has driven policy, not the other way around, is the preponderance of neologisms used to defend the practice of targeted killing. 'Unlawful combatants' are said to be protected by neither the Geneva Conventions nor the laws of civil society. 'Imminent threats' need not imply immediacy. The category of combatants subject to targeting has been enlarged to include all military-age men (from sixteen to fifty) in hostile areas, where 'hostile', too, is defined by the killers. On its face, this all looks like a suspicious form of linguistic legerdemain designed precisely to render permissible the use of Predator drones to dispatch persons abroad. What cannot be denied is that language is public, so if these neologisms and redefinitions are upheld by some governments, then they become available to others as well.

Today, the summary execution without trial of suspects in lands far away is carried out overtly and unselfconsciously and has come to be regarded by US military and political elites as a standard operating procedure – apparently for no better reason than that it is now easier than ever to kill. Surely the rapid ascendance of targeted killing as a means of addressing conflict has much to do with the simple fact that UAV technology is being used most extensively by a nation with a military so vast as to preclude retaliation by other states. The Israeli government was the first to deploy weaponized drones to eliminate stigmatized political enemies, but the US government was the first to do so thousands of miles beyond the borders of its sovereign territory.

The United States set the precedent for nuclear warheads and other weapons of mass destruction (WMD) now shared by several states and sought by many others, and it seems likely that other nations will also follow suit in the case of drones. Swiftly proliferating remotely piloted aircraft (RPA) technology has radically altered the practice of war in the twenty-first century and promises to remove more and more soldiers from the 'battlefields' where they kill. At the same time, the very availability of drones affects decisions about how, when, where and against whom this new form of 'war' is fought.

As new technology continues to spread around the globe, the leaders of other governments will emulate the superpower in dispatching their declared enemies through the use of this advanced form of weaponry, propelled forward by the drone industry boom. They, too, will draw fine legal distinctions between *targeted killing* (which they do) and *assassination* (which they do not).[1] When the leaders of other nations begin to execute their avowed enemies using missile-equipped drones, they will invoke the very same rationalizations as their role model did: that by killing suspected terrorists they are preventing future harm to innocent people while circumventing the sacrifice of troops.

More than a decade has elapsed since the first publicly acknowledged use of a Predator drone to execute suspects located abroad, yet for several years very little sustained critique was aired. In the aftermath of the terrorist attacks of 11 September 2001, an exceptionally lax critical climate reigned in the United States. Accepting that 'we are at war', many newscasters deferred to the US president as concern with winning the 'Global War on Terror' (GWOT) gripped politicians, strategists and journalists alike. The populace docilely accepted liberty-restricting policies and legislation, such as the Patriot Act, under the assumption that certain sacrifices and compromises would be needed to keep the homeland safe. Many US citizens have rallied behind the government's assiduous efforts to 'take the battle to the enemy', and appear to believe that the low number of jihadist attacks on domestic soil in recent years illustrates the effectiveness of the government's many antiterrorism initiatives. That many more civilians have been victimized in these various efforts than were killed on 11 September 2001 has generally been ignored.

As the drone program has continued to grow, encompassing a larger and larger swath of territory in the Middle East, and seeping deeper and deeper into Africa, vociferous critics have slowly begun to emerge. Medea Benjamin, co-founder of the antiwar group CODEPINK, has staged a number of protests and even accessed a US presidential foreign policy address on 23 May 2013, during which she interrupted President Obama to lodge a variety of complaints. Among other things, Benjamin called for the release of the prisoners at Guantánamo Bay and demanded an apology to the 'thousands of Muslims' killed by drones 'on the basis of suspicious activities'. The activist was escorted out of the room, but not before the president pensively acknowledged, 'The voice of that woman is worth paying attention to,' revealing that even he recognizes, on some level, that there may be problems with his administration's policies.

The practice of targeted killing is truly controversial, even more so than war itself, which in the past appeared to many (not all) military supporters to be subject to 'rules' set out centuries ago by the early just war theorists and later incorporated in modern protocols such as the Geneva Conventions and the *Charter of the United Nations* (1945). The refusal to offer the suspects targeted by drones the possibility of continued survival should they agree to renounce their stand is but one of the glaring ways in which what remote-control killers do today bears nearly no resemblance to what soldiers did in the past. While sitting before computer screens, drone operators snipe unwitting targets who may have no idea that they have been spied on for days, weeks, even months, and are about to be annihilated, stripped even of the right to surrender enshrined in orthodox military protocols forged over centuries.

The people who vehemently oppose the use of weaponized drones, the self-proclaimed anti-drone activists, see a rupture between past and present military practices.[2] Last resort has become first resort. Courage has become cowardice. Black ops have become standard operating procedure. A former intelligence agency is now a killing machine.

Service to country has become crass opportunism. Self-defense has become naked aggression. Guilt beyond a reasonable doubt has become possible future potential for guilt. Voices of dissent have been irrevocably silenced. Just war has become blind slaughter. Respect for the enemy has given way to dehumanization. Patriots have been replaced by mercenaries. Human rights have been eclipsed by concern with the protection of soldiers' lives. The US war on terrorism is carried out using terrorist tactics. Wars of necessity have been replaced by ever-proliferating wars of choice.

Most disconcertingly of all, the United States of America, once arguably a beacon of hope to people around the globe, has become an eagle eye hovering above with extended claws, keen to 'project power without projecting vulnerability'. That slick sound bite, frequently intoned by US military spokespersons as they vaunt the alleged virtues of drones, masks a deleterious truth. What the US establishment has failed to process in its endeavor to 'project power without projecting vulnerability' is that nothing in the world is uglier than a tyrant, and practices which violate ordinary people's sense of fair play inspire anger and hatred, not respect. Public relations sound bites such as 'taking the battle to the enemy' may make Americans feel better about the actions of their government, but it is evident from interviews with bereft survivors on the ground that drones do not merely project power. They project terror, and induce fear and anxiety in precisely the manner of a cruel and capricious oppressor.

From the perspectives of some of the members of communities under siege, the hegemonic crimes alleged by Osama bin Laden and other Al-Qaeda leaders to have been the basis for the attacks on symbols of US power on 11 September 2001 have been repeated over and over again, with the toll of civilian casualties among Muslim communities mounting seemingly with no end in sight. The persons incensed at being subjected to the specter of drones lurking menacingly above their heads are sometimes persuaded to heed the call to jihad by groups such as Al-Qaeda and the Taliban. In this way, the use of UAVs to 'project power without projecting vulnerability' may prove in retrospect to have been an illusion, ultimately making the persons allegedly being protected more vulnerable than ever before.

Policy debates about drones have focused on factual matters such as: What proportion of the people killed have been civilians? Is it one-third, or is it one-half? Or perhaps only 20 percent of the victims have been innocent of any wrongdoing. False dichotomies also abound, as in bold assertions that Hellfire missiles launched by Predator drones should be deployed because they are more precise and discriminate than Tomahawk missiles. If the proverbial 'options on the table' are *either* to use weaponized drones *or* to launch Tomahawk missiles, then drones naturally win the debate, assuming that the goal is to 'take out' an individual or small group as opposed to an entire village.[3] However, by delving a bit deeper, beneath the superficial level of most discourse on this topic, the presumptions underlying policymakers' adoption of intentional, premeditated homicide as a standard operating procedure can be identified and assessed.

Grave concerns have been aired by scholars about the use of weaponized drones, above all whether the United States is not violating international law, committing war crimes, and essentially shredding both the *Universal Declaration of Human Rights* (1948) and the *Charter of the United Nations* (1945) through a concerted and wide-ranging program of assassination of suspects.[4] These are pressing questions, as are practical matters such as whether the drone program makes the citizens paying for it less, not more, safe and secure, by fomenting terrorist groups and inspiring people to sympathize with them or even to become active members themselves. Drones have surely been used to eliminate some terrorists, but critics maintain that they have created even more, and the statements of recently minted jihadists have corroborated this claim, for they explicitly cite the effects of previous drone strikes as the reason for their decision to attack.

When no soldier's life is directly on the line, then killing by remote control cannot be literally construed as legitimate self-defense – certainly not on its face. Whether the United States has violated international law in some of the most controversial cases – particularly in nations where war was never formally waged, and there are no soldiers on the ground to protect – continues to be the subject of heated debate.[5] What matters most at this point in history is that the world's sole military superpower has paved the normative way forward with targeted killing by Predator drone, setting a precedent to be followed by the leaders of other states – allies and enemies alike.

Some of the questions addressed in this book have been posed in one way or another in the press. I offer answers to those questions, but I also treat them as a springboard from which to address a variety of more complex issues such as: *What purposes, beyond self-defense, are served by the annihilation of human beings?* Along the way, I examine the implications of a variety of apparently radical transformations in policies and moral attitudes. The very fact that an officially acknowledged targeted killing program should ever have arisen reveals much about the worldview of those who opt to 'Kill don't capture', and highlights nagging inconsistencies within modern liberal democratic states. Procedures such as 'double tap', the use of a follow-up missile after a target has already been struck, raise vexing questions about legality and war crimes, as first-responders in no way even suspected of wrongdoing are often killed in the second strike. Such procedures also reveal something about the perpetrators' views of not only warfare but also the value and meaning of human life.

PART I
FIND

CHAPTER 1
DRONE NATION

'Very frankly, it's the only game in town.'

Leon Panetta, CIA Director, 2009–11;
US Secretary of Defense, 2011–13[6]

'The CIA gets what it wants.'

US President Barack Obama[7]

THE DRONE AGE effectively commenced on 3 November 2002, when the US Central Intelligence Agency (CIA) used a Hellfire missile-equipped unmanned aerial vehicle (UAV), the MQ-1 Predator drone, to obliterate the occupants of a vehicle driving down a dusty road in Yemen. The aftermath of the strike was internationally broadcast, but there was not much to see beyond a swirl of desert sand and some scrap metal remains. Yemeni authorities identified one of the men as Ali Qaed Sunian al-Harithi, 'Abu Ali', believed to be responsible for the bombing of the USS destroyer *Cole* on 12 October 2000. US authorities affirmed that the six men eliminated in the strike were evil terrorists, members of Al-Qaeda and, therefore, legitimate targets of attack. The event was widely touted as a triumph of technology, the use of a sophisticated machine to terminate with extreme prejudice the enemy while risking no harm to good soldiers fighting a just war, what had been christened the 'Global War on Terror' (GWOT), waged in response to the attacks of 11 September 2001.

There might have been a public outcry about the execution without trial by the US government of six persons on 3 November 2002, but there was not. In newspaper reports of the event, a focus on the innovative nature of the technology – by journalists apparently blinded by the science of the feat – eclipsed any serious consideration of the morality or legality of the action. Enthusiastic approval was expressed by the mainstream media, with praise for the orchestrators of the mission working to keep the homeland safe by stopping the terrorists before they had the chance to reach US shores. Following the media, most of the populace appeared to accept the action as both legitimate and laudable. Viewed from the perspective of those who planned the strike, the test was thus not only a tactical but also a political success. From that point forward, the use of drones to kill suspects located abroad became more and more frequent, until at last it was no longer an exceptional measure but a standard operating procedure. More than a decade elapsed before some people began to reflect upon the meaning of what was done in Yemen on that historic day. Many US citizens forgot all about it, having never considered the topic worthy of debate.

One of the most significant features of the use of military force by the CIA on 3 November 2002 was that the United States was not at war with Yemen. Indeed, such an encroachment on another country's sovereign territory looks on its face like a declaration of war. However, it swiftly emerged that permission for the action had been granted by the president of Yemen, Ali Abdullah Saleh, who was keen to demonstrate his solidarity with the United States in the wake of 9/11 so as to avoid being militarily chastened next, after the Taliban in Afghanistan. The strike had been permitted by Saleh on the condition that a cover story be used to explain what would be characterized as accidental deaths. When then-Deputy Defense Secretary Paul Wolfowitz revealed to the media that the action was carried out by the CIA under the auspices of the US government, Saleh's cover was blown.[8]

US President George W. Bush had proclaimed that any nation harboring or supporting terrorists would be fair game for military attack, and Yemen was known to have provided a safe haven to Al-Qaeda members in the past. President Saleh's worries were not, therefore, without reason, and he acted swiftly to demonstrate his willingness to collaborate with the superpower in a variety of essentially self-serving initiatives, including the use of warlords to rout out possible Al-Qaeda sympathizers. Both sticks and carrots were used in persuading Saleh to comply with US government requests to operate freely on Yemeni sovereign territory. The initial military aid and loan package offered by the Bush administration to Saleh for helping to 'take care of' (either arrest or kill) the persons in Yemen on the US government's list of wanted suspects was about $400 million.[9] As greedy and power-hungry rivals maneuvered to cash in on the hefty rewards being offered in exchange for the delivery of Al-Qaeda members – dead or alive – Islamists were rounded up and sometimes killed in the mercenary hope that they might possibly have something to do with Al-Qaeda. Needless to say, many entirely innocent people were erroneously incarcerated or executed in the process.[10]

Eventually it became clear that key figures in the Bush administration – Vice President Dick Cheney, Secretary of Defense Donald Rumsfeld and Deputy Defense Secretary Paul Wolfowitz, among others – had set their sights on not Yemen but Iraq and were scheming much earlier about how to rationalize the 2003 war for which 9/11 came to serve as a pretext.

A cavalier attitude toward the innocence of some terrorist suspects has been a constant feature in cases of targeted killing since the drone strike on 3 November 2002. The most obvious concern to arise in critical minds, of which there appear to have been precious few at the time, would be that the car's inhabitants may not have been terrorists after all. Detection mechanisms can be miscalibrated in many ways, and fallible human beings can misread even correctly calibrated machines. Furthermore, in the case in question – and in the hundreds of similar strikes to follow – the information leading to the deployment of Hellfire missiles against the alleged suspects was obtained through the use of bribes. It is a matter of common knowledge that desperately poor people may furnish ersatz 'intelligence' when sufficiently enticed. It is therefore entirely possible that the swirl of dust amidst scrap metal remains on that road in Yemen was really an innocent family traveling in the wrong vehicle, at the wrong time and in the wrong place. Could the CIA have made such a mistake?

After a drone strike, the same vehicle driven by the head of a family or the head of a terrorist cell would leave precisely the same scrap metal remains. The human bodies blown apart may not be identifiable at all. The crater left behind upon obliteration of a terrorist safe haven is indistinguishable from the crater left behind when a house filled with innocent people is targeted as a result of faulty intelligence. The only certainty at the time of the strike is that, whoever the victims were, and whatever their intentions for the future may have been – and whether or not they would ever have found the means and seen fit to undertake a journey to the United States to attempt to harm the inhabitants of that land – their deaths were effected by Predator drone.

An operative collected fragments of the bodily remains for DNA analysis after the November 2002 strike in Yemen. But we will never know who most of the people killed by drones were and whether they were indeed guilty of a capital offense and truly deserved to die, for none of the slain suspects has ever been tried in a court of law, nor even indicted for crimes. Prominent 'high value' targets have been identified in press releases touting GWOT victories against execrable enemies. Most of the dead remain unnamed. Time and time again, initial positive spins on strikes said by officials to have taken out 'evil terrorists' were later proven to be false by investigative reports conducted by brave journalists on the ground.

The US government is clearly capable of and willing to direct its most powerful institutions to lethal ends, but what does this killing accomplish, strategically speaking? All of the people intentionally targeted are thought to be guilty, in some sense, but this raises the question whether it would not be better to capture rather than kill them. Assume, for the sake of argument, that the people destroyed on 3 November 2002 were the people who the CIA said that they were, and that they had committed the crimes said to warrant their deaths. The very fact that Al-Qaeda operatives and associates should be snuffed out in this way raises vexing skeptical questions about those who plan and carry out the strikes. For either such actions kill bona fide Al-Qaeda members, or they do not. If the targets are truly Al-Qaeda operatives, genuinely guilty of capital crimes, then their annihilation constitutes at once the termination with extreme prejudice of many intelligence leads. Does it not?

At the time of the November 2002 strike, the location of Osama bin Laden was shrouded in secrecy. There had been indications that he was hiding out for some time in the Tora Bora mountain range of Afghanistan near the Pakistan border, but the Al-Qaeda leader craftily eluded the Special Forces on his trail. Some among his followers must have known where he was. Throughout the lengthy duration of his successful evasion of the many forces arrayed against him, Bin Laden communicated with the outside world through the use of couriers. Moreover, like all human beings, he could not have lived without the provision of food and water. How, then, could the CIA have annihilated potentially fruitful intelligence leads which might reveal where Bin Laden had taken refuge?

It is difficult to understand why a competent intelligence agency would destroy possible sources of intelligence, but it may be equally difficult to believe that they would dispatch persons whom they truly believed to be innocent. The CIA analysts who gather intelligence for and manage drone strikes probably do believe their targets to be guilty of crimes. But suspects are suspects, and belief is belief. It is therefore quite conceivable that the CIA analysts' tradecraft leading up to drone strikes is sometimes dead wrong, just as when they failed to read the writing on the wall which might have stopped the attacks of 9/11.[11]

The United States has long prided itself on being an open and free democratic society, and the government is not generally regarded by its citizens as a medieval-style monarch ruling with an iron fist. That is precisely why there was something highly disturbing about what transpired in Yemen on 3 November 2002, the first action of its kind and the precedent for hundreds more strikes further down the line, long after Bush and his entourage had receded from public life. The vehicle's passengers, driving down that ill-fated road in Yemen, were judged guilty without trial of crimes for which they were sentenced to death and executed.

The killers appointed themselves at once the police, the judge, the jurors and the executioners in a radical refashioning of procedural 'justice' paid for by the citizens of an ostensibly democratic nation, the most fundamental principles of which are transparency and due process, the rule of law. The judges, a group of anonymous analysts who deployed the Hellfire-missile equipped Predator drone, were and remain accountable to no one. In summarily executing those people, the CIA agents involved appear to have assumed that they could not possibly be wrong. Or perhaps they simply did not care. It is one thing accidentally to kill innocent persons located in a Third World nation ruled by an autocrat who in exchange for bribes of military aid permits the extrajudicial execution of the inhabitants of his land. It is quite another to hunt down and kill a US citizen. Or is it?

On 30 September 2011, less than a decade after the November 2002 drone strike in Yemen, the US government crossed over the line demarcating foreign enemies from US citizens by knowingly and deliberately targeting and assassinating Anwar al-Awlaki, whose name was on the government's hit list, and Samir Khan, also a US citizen, who was with the target at the time. Despite this intentional and premeditated execution without trial of US citizens, many Americans continue to support the use of drones to 'neutralize' enemies abroad, having bought into the prevailing rationalization that the use of this precision technology spares the lives of US troops and minimizes collateral damage.

It seems to be a matter of common sense to many people that if 'we are at war', and troops' lives can be preserved through the use of existent technologies, then they should obviously be employed.[12] Terrorists roaming at large, whatever their nationality, are by definition a threat to be addressed with the swiftest and surest of means – so the reasoning goes. In accepting even the liquidation of US citizens such as Anwar al-Awlaki – killed in a drone strike in Yemen a few months after Osama bin Laden had been executed by a team of Navy SEALs in Pakistan – many people have followed the Bush administration in conflating the categories of *terrorist suspects* and *terrorists*, as though every suspect were automatically guilty of capital crimes.

More sophisticated supporters of drone killing appear to be thinking along utilitarian lines. In *Utilitarianism*, a classic of nineteenth-century moral and political philosophy, John Stuart Mill championed the idea that the right action maximizes the positive outcome (utility or happiness) for the greatest number of people. The aim prescribed by utilitarianism is essentially 'the greater good', which may sometimes require the sacrifice of the interests of a few. Some advocates of the use of weaponized drones to dispatch suspected terrorists acknowledge that not all suspects are guilty, but they accept something akin to the utilitarian view according to which it becomes permissible to torture or kill some innocent people when this will make the world a safer place by protecting everyone else. As appealing as this sort of argument may be to self-styled 'realists' and other pragmatic types, it is faulty – and not only for its flat-out denial of universal human rights. Even assuming the soundness of utilitarianism, which implies that human rights are but convenient fictions, there is a mistaken premise in the argument: that the wrongs being committed under the guise of utilitarianism for the greater good make the world more, not less, safe and secure.

One clear example of a failure of the utilitarian rationale in the case of torture was that of Ibn al Sheikh al-Libbi, who, after being subjected to extensive 'enhanced interrogation techniques', eventually 'confessed' that there was a connection between Saddam Hussein and Al-Qaeda.[13] As a result in part of that forced confession of disinformation – which the victim later explained was made in order to avoid being tortured further – Iraq was invaded. Hundreds of thousands of Iraqis were killed, along with thousands of US troops. The utilitarianism argument fails in the case of Libbi because the premise, that the torture would produce sound intelligence, was false.[14]

The long history of the military practice of torture reveals that the victims who do not succumb before it is too late will eventually say whatever their interrogators want them to say – if they can figure out what that is – in order to prevent further harm and pain to themselves. Torture is an unreliable method of producing sound intelligence, first and foremost because some of the interrogees simply have no pertinent information to share. Despite the many historical demonstrations of this fact – in Nazi Germany; fascist Italy, Spain, Argentina and Chile; French-occupied Algeria; Vietnam; and in both Afghanistan and Iraq – champions of 'enhanced interrogation techniques' such as waterboarding continue to labor under the false belief that somehow utilitarianism sanctions torture, which they presume must be allowed in extreme circumstances of emergency, such as when 'we are at war'.

The 'enhanced' interrogators – and they can be found in nearly every war context throughout history – conduct themselves as though the more they torture a suspect, the more likely it is that he will 'give up' some useful information. In the case of Libbi, the 'information' coughed up did prove useful to those keen to craft a pretext for a war waged under a cluster of falsehoods, all of which were obtained through dubious means.[15] The 2003 invasion and occupation of Iraq, however, did not serve 'the greater good' under any reasonable interpretation of those words.

The folly of extended detention and mistreatment of suspects never charged with crimes (the evidence is insufficient, nearly always circumstantial, and based on hearsay and speculation) further highlights the strategic problem with the use of torture. Whenever suspects have been detained for years, months, or even weeks, whatever 'actionable intelligence' they may once have had becomes stale. In cases where information painfully extracted over a lengthy period of time is acted upon as though it were fresh, such coerced information may lead tragically to the apprehension or death of the wrong targets, not the persons sought. Even when the suspects are guilty and have been privy to plans for future terrorist plots, the longer they are detained, the less reliable the information provided by them becomes.[16]

Bribed intelligence, which is used in selecting targets for drone strikes, poses equally bad, if not worse, problems of reliability, for those who provide the information may or may not have an interest in the truth. They may be interested only in getting their hands on a thick wad of cash – and fast. In courts of law, such self-interested motives are kept in check by requiring all witnesses to be subject to cross-examination. In the drone program version of 'due process', informants may simply fabricate a credible story, then take the money and run. No small matter turns on the truth of the testimony: it is the very life of the suspects implicated. Whenever drone operators work from faulty intelligence – whether mistakes or lies – innocent persons are bound to be 'fixed and finished' in place of the terrorist suspects presumed guilty of capital crimes.

The expirable nature of intelligence in these cases adds an extra layer of fallibility to the process, for missile strikes are carried out when 'opportunities' arise. In reality, groups of people gather for many different reasons, most of which have nothing to do with devising nefarious plots against the United States. On 14 December 2009, in a strike approved by Pentagon attorney Jeh Johnson after a rushed review of the available intelligence, a Bedouin camp was mistaken for an Al-Qaeda training camp, and fifty-eight people were killed by cruise missiles.[17] On 17 March 2011, forty-two people who had gathered together for a *jirga* to settle a dispute over a chromite mine were slaughtered. The US administration claimed that all of the dead were militants; others investigating the event concluded that only four persons present were affiliated in any way with the Taliban.[18] On 12 December 2013, a group of fifteen civilians en route to a wedding in the central Al-Bayda province of Yemen were destroyed by a US drone, having been mistaken for an Al-Qaeda convoy.[19]

Terrorism experts have analyzed the comportment of groups such as Al-Qaeda in recent years and determined that they operate very secretively, sharing information only sparingly, on a strict 'need to know' basis, precisely in the manner of the intelligence agencies, including the CIA, of modern Western states. A lateral, decentralized structure appears to have supplanted the top-down hierarchical approach of Al-Qaeda in the years since 2001, as the high-level leaders were all on the run. Such strategic developments among factional terrorists have made the use of protracted detention and muscular attempts to extract secrets even less likely to succeed than they might initially have seemed, as there is little chance that even an ardent Al-Qaeda member will have much, if any, useful information to share. On rare occasions, suspects in possession of actionable intelligence have been 'broken' in a timely way by their interrogators, but in the case of a group as strategically savvy as Al-Qaeda, it is difficult to believe that they would not immediately alter any plans to which a captured prisoner had been privy. Email addresses, SIM cards and pseudonyms are all a dime a dozen. It's also a simple matter to change venues – whether for meetings or attacks – at the last minute.

After the disclosure of ignominious crimes at Abu Ghraib prison in Iraq, and Bagram in Afghanistan, the use of 'harsh interrogation techniques' in attempting to extract intelligence from suspects was sharply curtailed as politicians called for reform. Perhaps it was also in part a recognition of the inefficacy of long-term detention and torture as a source of sound intelligence which led the architects of counterterrorism initiatives to begin to focus more on killing than on capture. The reasoning behind the expansion of the Predator drone targeted killing policy may have been something like this:

If the captured suspects are never going to surrender any worthwhile information, no matter how long they are imprisoned, and no matter what is done to them, then why not just kill them instead?

'Kill don't capture' became a doctrine – the rule, not the exception – under US President Obama, after he signed executive orders banning torture and closing secret prisons. Part of the reason for the expanded kill campaign appears to have been the difficulty faced by the new administration in persuading congressmen to allow trials of suspected terrorists to take place in their own jurisdictions. Everyone feared retaliatory attacks.[20] But the practice of targeted killing commenced under George W. Bush, and it is difficult to see how it might have become a standard operating procedure if not as a result of something like the above sort of reasoning. In the drone age, the concept of 'reliable evidence' has been supplanted by 'actionable intelligence', which paradoxically enough is considered sufficient grounds for execution, although it likely would not hold up for conviction in a court of law, being circumstantial and largely based on hearsay.

In truth, there are two completely distinct possible explanations for a prisoner's inability to provide actionable intelligence. One is that, although he is a terrorist, he has not been made privy to any information which might be used to jeopardize the group or disrupt its activities. The other is that he is innocent and not a part of any plot against the people of the United States.

In *The Art of War*, the ancient Chinese military strategist Sun Tzu counsels warriors: 'Know thine enemy.' Sound martial policies rest on reasonable predictions about what the enemy will do should various courses of action be pursued. The consequences of antiterrorist initiatives – whether or not they promote the greater good – will depend ultimately on how other people react in response. Rather than make an effort to understand the shadowy enemy, the Bush administration chose to ignore the spokesmen for Al-Qaeda, preferring to explain the attacks of 9/11 as caused by the evil terrorists' 'hatred of our freedom'. When it became clear that the people of most other countries opposed the US plan to attack Iraq in 2003, the Bush administration abruptly withdrew a draft resolution at the United Nations and moved brazenly ahead with full-scale war plans in flagrant disregard of global opinion, including, significantly, that of the Muslim world.

Once the United States had invaded Iraq – what many people around the globe regarded as a war of aggression and a violation of international law[21] – jihadists from a variety of nations, heeding the call of Al-Qaeda, traveled to the occupied land to defend their brethren from what they took to be the Western heathens. Yemen history scholar Gregory Johnsen explains the urge suddenly felt by many Muslims to undertake jihad against the invaders of Iraq: 'It was a simple case: non-Muslim troops attacking Muslims in a Muslim country. Fighting the US wasn't simply permitted; it was required.'[22]

The slogan that 'they hate us because of our freedom' was saucily denied by Osama bin Laden himself in a short quip from a videotape released prior to the 2004 US presidential election: 'Contrary to what Bush says and claims, that we hate your freedom: if that were true, then let him explain why we did not attack Sweden.'[23] Despite compelling evidence to the contrary, including the virulent insurgency in postwar Iraq, the Bush administration sound bite that 'they hate us because of our freedom' remained firmly lodged in the minds of many Americans, along with the specious pretexts for the invasion, that Saddam Hussein possessed weapons of mass destruction (WMD) and was poised to use them against the United States, and that he was in cahoots with Al-Qaeda.[24]

The targeting of US symbols of power on 11 September 2001 appears to have been primarily designed to display the effects of military destruction to the citizens who finance interventions by their government abroad. Al-Qaeda explicitly took issue with the deaths of innocent people caused by the 1991 Gulf War and the establishment of US military bases in Muslim lands such as Saudi Arabia. This suggests that a rational response to the first foreign attack on US soil since Pearl Harbor would have been to stop doing what it was that led the perpetrators to react with their own version of 'shock and awe'. Instead, both Afghanistan and Iraq were invaded, and even more US military bases have been established abroad and equipped with Predator drones ready to prey on people suspected of possibly conspiring to commit possible future terrorist acts.

Whether or not one believes in the sacrifice of a few for 'the greater good', the question of justice in cases of targeted killing must, strategically speaking, be addressed sooner or later. The people who rise up to the point of allying themselves with terrorist factions do so because of what they interpret as flagrant acts of injustice perpetrated by the government which they oppose. Osama bin Laden, albeit a clever and charismatic leader, lost much of his power to harm the people of the United States during the decade when he was dodging Special Forces. On 2 May 2011, he was irrevocably silenced. But if Bin Laden was galvanized to foment acts of terrorism by the US government's military actions abroad, surely other, new leaders can be expected to emerge from the ashes of the 2003 invasion of Iraq, and the craters left behind by Hellfire missiles in Afghanistan, Pakistan, Yemen, Somalia, Libya, Syria and beyond.

Supporters of the drone program have balked at allegations that collateral damage has been excessive – only hundreds of people, some claim – but they fail to appreciate a much more profound question: whether innocent civilians should *ever* be put at risk of death when no soldier's life is at stake. According to those who oppose the use of Predator drones in countries such as Pakistan and Yemen, where no US war was ever officially waged, the practice is tantamount to killing within what is the victims' civil society while at the same time invoking the wartime concept of collateral damage to excuse the deaths of innocent people.

An important constraint on police operations within civil society is that innocent bystanders must not be harmed. When the swiftest and most feasible means by which to apprehend a criminal suspect will also kill a dozen children, the police are obliged to devise another scheme. Police officers, like orthodox soldiers, regularly risk their lives in attempting to protect their fellow citizens. This is not true of drone operators, who kill by remote control. Drone advocates reject the police force analogy, maintaining that 'the world is a battlefield', but a troubling question remains: *Why is this sort of targeted killing and attendant risk of death to innocent civilians deemed acceptable only within poor lands governed by autocrats*? Children killed through the use of military weapons in the United States are considered murder victims. Why not when they happen to be located abroad in Third World countries?

The targeted killing program is intended to neutralize terrorists before they find ways to wreak havoc in the United States à la 9/11. In reality, terrorist incubation chambers are potentially any- and everywhere, as journalist Michael Hastings astutely observed: 'A terrorist safe haven can be anywhere ... the September 11 attacks were planned in Hamburg, Florida, and San Diego, among other places.'[25]

By sheer force of habit, military officers view matters through the lens of lethality. When they are called upon to advise the commander in chief about the best means by which to address threats and resolve disputes, they naturally begin from the assumption that killing is a sound solution to conflict.[26] When the CIA began running a Predator drone targeted killing program, it essentially became an arm of the Pentagon, with fewer and fewer agents engaged in any form of long-term strategic analysis, and more and more agents focused on how to kill as swiftly and efficiently as possible. By 2011, an estimated 20 percent of CIA analysts were directly involved in 'kinetic operations', as they are euphemistically termed. Even more disturbingly, the CIA itself assesses the soundness and efficacy of its own targeted killing program.[27] Instead of being reined in by the CIA, which was established for the purpose of providing the US executive with the information needed to forge sound policy, the military approach has come to redefine the Agency and to dictate policy. What is missing from such a lethal-centric perspective is thoughtful analysis and prediction of the likely future consequences of practices such as 'Kill don't capture.'

The drone program administrators appear to believe that the more suspects they kill, the better off the larger group will be. But there are a few problems with the argument according to which GWOT, in which Predator drones have played a key role, has been a resounding success, as said to be evidenced by the small number of terrorist actions on US soil since 11 September 2001. First, it is simply false that human beings – or even Americans – as a group have been made more safe, because many thousands of people have been killed in Afghanistan, Iraq, Pakistan, Yemen, Libya and elsewhere. Nearly twice the number of US nationals killed on 9/11 were killed in Iraq alone, as the toll of soldier deaths during the occupation approached 6,000. That is not even to take into consideration the number of troops who were permanently maimed, or those who committed suicide upon returning home from active duty, their lives having been psychologically wrecked. If it is true, as some critics maintain, that the multi-day delay in responding to Hurricane Katrina in 2005 was a result of the fact that many of the local National Guardsmen had been called away to fight in Iraq, then at least some of the nearly 2,000 Katrina deaths should be counted as well.[28]

Second, orders of magnitude more non-nationals than US nationals have also been killed abroad. As a direct result of US-perpetrated deaths, anti-American sentiment – the very kind which gave rise to the crimes of 11 September 2001 – has swelled to unprecedented levels. By 2012, the United States had become the most reviled nation in the world by the people of Pakistan, considered even worse than the arch-rival and neighboring India.[29] This negative change in opinion was caused directly by US targeted killings in Pakistan, where Predator drones had pounded the northwestern provinces, said to harbor terrorists, hundreds of times.[30]

Finally, anti-American terrorist factions have coalesced specifically in response to the military behemoth which the US government has become. No state today can compete with the world's sole military superpower, so the only way to counter its incursions abroad militarily is to innovate, which is precisely what terrorist groups such as Al-Qaeda have done. They have conducted themselves as military strategists who exploit the weakness of the enemy. Because terrorism has become the only possible way to retaliate militarily against the actions of the US government, it can be said without hyperbole that the very size, wealth and power of the Department of Defense are what brought about anti-American factional terrorism in the first place. Large-scale, inter-state wars are now precluded by the sheer size of US arsenals, yet lawmakers have continued to lavish money upon the war makers whose incursions abroad gave rise to 9/11, according to the perpetrators themselves. The Predator drone program is the primary fruit of this profligacy.

CHAPTER 2
FROM BLACK OPS TO STANDARD OPERATING PROCEDURE

'What we need to do is optimize transparency on these issues, but at the same time, optimize secrecy.'

John Brennan, CIA Director (appointed in 2013)[31]

'What do you expect my son to do? There are missiles raining down on the village. He has to hide. But he is not hiding with Al-Qaeda; our tribe is protecting him right now ... He has been wrongly accused, it's unbelievable.'

Nasser al-Awlaki, speaking on CNN of his son, Anwar al-Awlaki, who was later killed by a US drone on 30 September 2011[32]

WAR HAS ALWAYS involved the intentional, premeditated killing of groups of people. Drone warfare is innovative in that it involves the intentional, premeditated killing of *specific* people, one by one. On its face, this activity looks indistinguishable from what in centuries past was labeled *assassination* or *extrajudicial execution*.[33] The tools have changed, but the aim is the same: the death of particular persons. US policymakers and supporters of the use of drones to dispatch enemies prefer the term *targeted killing*, which they maintain is legal, while *assassination* presumably remains illegal. One source of confusion arises from the fact that the Predator drone program in Pakistan, Yemen and elsewhere has been run by the CIA, not the US Department of Defense, which makes it difficult to understand how these targeted killings can be acts of *warfare*.[34]

Remotely piloted aircraft (RPA) missile strikes have been carried out by the United States in two distinct contexts. The skies above the declared war zones of Afghanistan and Iraq began to buzz with drones collecting information about insurgent redoubts. The second use of drones by the US government was not initially acknowledged and looks very much like the black op assassinations of the twentieth century. In places where there are no US troops on the ground to protect, reigning powers bow to pressure to permit such killing in exchange for generous provisions of military aid.

Viewed from the outside, this second use of drones, the physical activity of tracking a person with the aim of terminating his life, is indistinguishable from assassination. Drone program advocates and opponents part company on precisely the question whether this form of intentional and premeditated killing constitutes murder or not. Even some military supporters ask whether the use of drones in this way does not violate the Geneva Conventions prohibiting the summary execution of enemy soldiers. The people killed by drones are typically not armed. Whether they should be deemed active combatants, and therefore legitimate military targets, is a matter of considerable controversy.

Weaponized drones were first deployed to eliminate specific people by the US government during the Bush administration against Al-Qaeda terrorist suspects, and by the Israeli government against Palestinian terrorist suspects. Other varieties of intentional and premeditated homicide using diverse implements – guns, knives, poisons, exploding phones, etc. – have been carried out by human beings throughout history for many different reasons, often political. During the twentieth century, a number of US presidents undertook to track and kill individuals covertly, but never before was this practice freely admitted, much less vaunted, as it came to be under George W. Bush.

As in the case of drone killing by the CIA, 'extraordinary rendition' and 'enhanced interrogation techniques' (now acknowledged to have been torture) were openly avowed as official policies only after information about them had leaked out. The practices were then vociferously championed by figures such as US Vice President Dick Cheney, who claimed that such measures had become necessary, given the terrorist attacks of 11 September 2001. Drones were used in both Afghanistan and Iraq during and after the invasions, but the drone age arguably began with the CIA's remote-control killing of persons located where US war had not been formally waged. The first publicly acknowledged CIA drone strike, on 3 November 2002 in Yemen, was carried out under a cover story, but once the truth emerged, Predator drone killings began to proliferate. Like extraordinary rendition and enhanced interrogation, remote-control killing was touted as an essential tool in the war on terrorism.

President Bush boasted in his January 2003 State of the Union Address that thousands of suspected terrorists had been taken prisoner and that many others had 'met a different fate', to which he exultantly added: 'Let's put it this way: they are no longer a problem to the United States and our friends and allies.'[35] Bush's smug public pronouncement that his administration was now officially in the business of executing suspects without trial somewhat disturbingly prompted a standing ovation by many members of Congress. In this way, Bush set the stage, and the official rhetoric came to condone and even praise the homicidal content of the formerly hush-hush operations known as *black ops*.

Homicide used as a political tool in shaping foreign policy is nothing new. Such killing has generally been viewed as illegal and referred to as *assassination*. Before the dawning of the drone age, targeted killing was ordered and contracted behind closed doors and carried out by agents whose true identities were disguised. What is new in the twenty-first century is the widespread and overt use of targeted killing by a well-established modern Western democratic state with stable laws and institutions in place. In the past, the elimination of enemies through homicide was favored by tyrants and those who rose up against them, including small factions shut out from political processes by their government. Such groups maintain that they have been left with no alternative but to instigate acts of insurrection against the reigning powers. The logic of violent resistance was well illustrated by the Algerians under French occupation, the 'partisans' in Vichy

France under German occupation, and the Palestinians in Israel, to offer only a few of many possible examples.

Some have identified Michael Collins and Sinn Féin's Irish Republican Army (IRA) as the inventors of urban guerrilla warfare and mentors of sorts to the resistance fighters of World War II. Collins' group succeeded in securing some of its demands by targeting intelligence agents and thereby provoking the British government to retaliate. The Black and Tans went out on a shooting spree, which backfired when they massacred entirely innocent people, causing public support for the IRA to swell.[36] This tried-and-true provocation strategy has been used over and over again by factions such as the Kosovo Liberation Army (KLA) and terrorist organizations such as Al-Qaeda, who, too, spur their adversaries to overreact.

The very establishment of Special Forces and the use of black ops by formal governments appear, somewhat ironically, to have drawn inspiration from Michael Collins and the IRA. Consider how Mossad (Israel's equivalent of the CIA) retaliated against the Munich massacre of 1972. Munich was, essentially, Israel's 'Everything changed' moment. During the 1972 Olympics, what began as a hostage-taking gambit by the Palestinian Liberation Organization (PLO) for use as a bargaining chip in securing the release of prisoners ended in deadly disaster. All eleven Israeli hostages, along with most of the perpetrators, were killed. What happened in Munich catalyzed a radical transformation in Israel's approach, a dramatic move away from at least the nominal adherence to international law, just as the events of 11 September 2001 were pivotal to the United States, whose secret Bush-era prisons were similar to Israel's Facility 1391, said officially to be nonexistent.[37]

Immediately following the Munich massacre, Mossad enlisted some of its own personnel to renounce their official positions and all traceable ties to the organization only to work unofficially, as private contractors, under pseudonyms, in plausibly deniable operations to hunt down and kill the suspects on a government-produced hit list. That black op obviously saw the light of day, and Steven Spielberg's film *Munich* (2005) made the case a matter of common knowledge.[38] Spielberg's telescopic account looks at the effects of premeditated killing upon the perpetrators of the post-Munich Mossad black ops, who through a series of assassinations find themselves progressively more endangered and psychologically troubled by what they have done.

Special Forces, Delta Marines, Green Berets, and other soldiers already trained for challenging, dangerous and 'extraordinary' tasks, have often been enlisted in top-secret missions during wartime. In Vietnam, Afghanistan and Iraq, during publicly acknowledged wars, regular soldiers were enlisted to infiltrate the enemy not only to obtain intelligence in the manner of spies but also to exercise their prowess in 'silent killing'.[39] Throughout the twentieth century, deniable operators were deployed in many covert government initiatives beyond declared battlefields as well. Such agents, working for governments but under a cloak of secrecy, occupy a shadowy realm above the law and below the radar of official policy. Many black ops require a skill set unique to Special Forces and have been carried out by veterans afforded the opportunity to put back to use expertise acquired during their uniformed service. In other cases, regular soldiers have been 'borrowed' during an approved leave of absence in order to carry out black ops.[40]

Mercenary soldiers have existed since the earliest times of recorded military history, but in the twentieth century their use was often hidden from view, with the high-level administrators of governments erecting a moral and legal façade before the taxpayers funding war. Behind the scenes, strategists pursued their own realpolitik policies, justified in their minds as exigencies of national defense. The perpetrators of black ops during the Cold War were scrupulously hidden from public view through complex machinations devised to camouflage their connections to the governments for which they were contracted privately to work. Black operators and their weapons did not exist, according to the official documents of formal governments, although their deeds certainly had tangible and sometimes dire effects for the people of other lands, especially in Latin America and Africa, hotly contested territories during the US–USSR standoff.

During the Cold War, spies were rife, and covert operators were sent out on secret missions to influence policy all over the world, enlisted by communists and capitalists alike. The leaders on both sides were attempting to contain the seepage of their arch adversary into new territories but without making open declarations of war. The neutralization of perceived threats to national interests – including what proved to be ineffective US-installed puppet leaders such as South Vietnam's Ngo Dinh Diem – was planned and carried out by the CIA, often to the detriment of the people ruled by recipients of US military aid.[41] Many of the black ops undertaken throughout the twentieth century by the US government failed, but not for want of the desire to destroy the intended targets. Among the thwarted schemes were the Kennedy administration's repeated attempts to assassinate Cuban leader Fidel Castro using means as varied as poisoned food and cigars rigged with explosives – essentially improvised explosive devices (IEDs).[42]

Most black ops from the twentieth century remain secret, the true stories of what transpired having been buried with the victims, and sometimes the perpetrators as well, whose deaths were ascribed to accidents or natural causes. Such missions are made possible by 'black budgets' placed at the discretionary use of unaccountable individuals, under the pretext that national security requires top secrecy. The people who conceive, organize and execute such schemes are human beings no less vulnerable to the forces of corruption and temptation than anyone else – indeed, perhaps more so, given the provision to them of what is tantamount to Plato's Ring of Gyges, the magical device which permits its wearer to commit crimes invisibly.

Recent depictions of intelligence agents in television series such as *Homeland*, *MI5* (*Spooks* in the UK) and *The Americans*, and films such as *Zero Dark Thirty*, *Breach*, *Syriana*, *Safe House* and *The Bourne Identity*, offer telling glimpses into the human fallibility of the persons who hold high-level security clearances. These fictional works are based on real-world scenarios and provide helpful reminders of how the persons in such positions are moved by emotions, vulnerable to temptation, and subject to corruption no less than anyone else. To express skepticism about the wisdom of granting human beings the power to kill with impunity is not necessarily to question their motives. Many agents involved in secret kill programs may well have the best of intentions, wishing only to defend the nation. The question becomes whether their activities actually help or instead hinder the realization of that aim, by inflaming potential new enemies abroad.

In addition to the inevitable mistakes of well-intentioned but fallible human beings, the potential for abuse in secretive kill programs can scarcely be denied. We know of the existence of 'a few bad apples' from atrocious crimes committed by enlisted soldiers in Afghanistan and Iraq, and cases such as My Lai in Vietnam. But what about the 'bad apples' involved in black ops and secret kill programs? Uniformed soldiers who commit murder are subject to court-martial. In contrast, the personnel granted access to 'black' funds, plausibly deniable operators and untraceable arms can do with them as they see fit, for none of them even exists, according to the official story. Adding more names to hit lists is simple to do, given that they are penned in invisible ink, and there is no procedure by which to take to task those who draft such lists in secret meetings.

On occasion, the direct perpetrators of black ops abroad have been exposed and indicted for crimes – and left to their own devices, given the lack of any traceable connection to the contracting government. In one such case, Ahmed Bouchiki, a Moroccan waiter, was mistakenly killed in 1973 by an undercover, plausibly deniable Mossad assassination team operating in Norway. Five of the perpetrators were convicted of murder under the Norwegian justice system.[43] More recently, the CIA-contracted abductors of Osama Mustafa Hassan Nasr – who was transferred in 2003 from Milan to Egypt, where he was tortured – were tried and convicted *in absentia* in an Italian court in 2009 after the story came to light.[44]

The use of clandestinely hired private operators throughout the twentieth century provided high-level government administrators with the capacity to carry out 'sensitive' missions deemed necessary while evading public scrutiny. The fact that black-op killing depends on sketchy intelligence obtained from shadowy figures appears to be cursorily brushed aside by many of the perpetrators, some of whom conduct themselves with such enthusiasm that they may view themselves as somehow divinely ordained. Others are empirically indistinguishable from garden-variety hitmen, who will kill anyone at the request of anyone, provided only that the price is right. A third group includes assassins who seize such contracts as opportunities to do some target practice, as did a group operating in Angola in 1975 – and elsewhere as well, including, some have alleged, Afghanistan and Iraq.[45]

There are limits to the credulity of even the most enthusiastic patriots when it comes to actions offensive to ordinary people's basic sense of decency and justice. For those times, administrators continue to opt for covert actions or black ops, protecting themselves through the complex apparatus of secrecy built directly into intelligence institutions. Black ops appear generally to be conceived and implemented by well-meaning people who regard themselves as better situated and informed to make policy than are legislators. In a nation such as the United States, the legislative and executive branches are together to assess the need for war. Black ops provide the executive with the power to wage what are effectively microwars without the advice and consent of Congress required by the US Constitution for full-scale military engagement. However, the possibility for black ops is preserved and affirmed by the very existence of the black budget, which *is* approved by Congress and fully funded by US taxpayers. By financing the black budget, citizens grant administrators permission to kill beyond the boundaries of the land – and 'beyond the pale'.

Like torture, the use of black ops has always been justified in the minds of those who devise and orchestrate the missions as tactically necessary whenever 'ordinary' (legal) means alone seem unlikely to effect the desired outcome, which, it is assumed, must be achieved. The potential for abuse is patent. According to Tony Geraghty, 'Much of the history of Special Forces – anyone's Special Forces – is a story of dirty, morally reprehensible – if effective – work.'[46] The operative notion of 'effective' here, as in the official stories proffered by formal militaries, is *lethal*. The covert team sent by Mossad to Europe after the Munich massacre did indeed wipe out most of the people on its hit list, and so was *effective* in that sense. The conflict between the Israeli government and the Palestinians, needless to say, raged on unabated, and was perhaps even exacerbated by the Mossad-instigated murders.

The recent declassification of many thousands of CIA documents revealed that, despite common misconceptions, George W. Bush was not the first president in the history of the United States to flout international law. In the 1970s, a congressional investigation headed by Senator Frank Church was undertaken in order to rein in what came to be viewed as gross executive abuses of power during the Vietnam war era.[47] The Church Committee took the CIA sternly to task and a moratorium was placed on political assassination once and for all – or so it seemed, until Osama bin Laden arrived on the scene.

'Everything changed' on 11 September 2001 in some ways, but in other ways nothing changed, for George W. Bush was not unprecedented in invoking executive privilege to undertake covert operations abroad with the intention of terminating the lives of individuals never indicted for crimes. In addition to spearheading the 1999 NATO intervention in Kosovo, the Clinton administration bombed both Iraq and Sudan. President Clinton also initiated the use of extraordinary rendition, a practice often mistakenly presumed to have been dreamt up by the Bush administration's 'dark side' neoconservatives.[48] It was Clinton, too, who lifted the post-Church Committee assassination ban by issuing a presidential finding to authorize the pursuit and targeting of Osama bin Laden.[49]

With the George W. Bush administration, a new level of transparency was achieved, but not because foreign affairs suddenly came to reflect the lofty moral rhetoric and carefully cleansed official stories proffered by spokespersons for the Pentagon. Instead, the president himself, with the support of the US Congress, came overtly to champion practices previously regarded by many as at least unmentionable, if not unthinkable, including summary execution without trial.

According to the Geneva Conventions, unarmed combatants must be taken as prisoners of war, not lined up before a firing squad and mowed down at the caprice of the platoon leader. This protocol, grounded in the just war tradition, reflects the longstanding view that, even in wartime, there are limits on the killing of combatants. To 'take no prisoners' is to flout the conventional wisdom on the proper conduct of war. The persons obliterated by Hellfire missiles while driving down a road or sitting in their home surrounded by friends or family members are not engaged in acts of war. Critics therefore ask: *How can their summary execution be anything else but a crime?*

The Bush administration notoriously derided the Geneva Conventions as 'quaint', but they also crafted innovative briefs to 'legalize' formerly illegal policies. Locutions such as 'unlawful combatant' began to pepper official documents, allowing policy advocates to deny the very applicability of the Geneva Conventions (even if valid) to the persons either indefinitely detained or killed by Predator drone. Arguably the most jarring change in policy was the explicit conflation of *offense* and *defense* so as to rationalize proactive or 'preemptive' war. This new approach was expressed in the most unequivocal of terms in the *National Security Strategy of the United States of America* issued in September 2002: 'We recognize that our best defense is a good offense.'[50]

'Everything changed' when President Bush, Vice President Cheney, Secretary of Defense Rumsfeld and their colleagues saw fit to 'take off the gloves' in dealing with the elusive global terrorist threat, and to do so ruthlessly, with scant regard for the many innocent human lives to be lost in the process. The Wild West placard slogan, 'Wanted Dead or Alive', was applied to Osama bin Laden, and anyone deemed his ally became fair game, it was claimed, as Bush infamously intoned: 'You're either with us or against us in the fight against terror.'[51] 'Everything changed' was precisely the sound bite parroted by a few foreign leaders as well. British Prime Minister Tony Blair, despite initial behind-closed-doors reservations, came eventually to embrace and enthusiastically to promote the 2003 invasion of Iraq.

Targeted killing as acknowledged US policy began with George W. Bush, but Barack Obama demonstrated extraordinary zeal in ordering hundreds of Predator drone strikes in at least six different countries, thereby dramatically surpassing his predecessor on this front. Obama tracked down and killed Osama bin Laden, but also thousands of other human beings – some of whom had apparently never even heard of 9/11 – and the targeted killing program continues on, long after Bin Laden's demise.[52] The most obvious strategic problem with the practice of targeted killing (setting aside for the moment the legal and moral problems) is that mistakes really are made, and when innocent people are 'taken out' in lieu of the 'evil terrorists' intended, this serves to fuel the fire of groups such as Al-Qaeda, causing previously neutral persons to flock to their cause.

There are more theoretical problems as well. Any person killed in a black op during the twentieth century might have been killed by a Predator drone, had the technology existed at the time. How would the use of a Predator drone-delivered Hellfire missile have affected the interpretation of a case such as that of Ahmed Bouchiki, the Moroccan waiter killed in 1973 by an undercover Mossad assassination team later convicted of murder? Suppose that Mossad had used a Predator drone to take out its target. How would the story have changed?

One obvious difference would be the production of collateral damage. If Bouchiki had been 'employed on' (to use one of the many euphemisms for drone killing) in the restaurant where he worked, then everyone else present would likely have died as well. All of the people killed, including Bouchiki, would be officially classified as collateral damage, since even Bouchiki was mistakenly targeted (presumably on the basis of faulty intelligence). Or would they? Would the Norwegian government have refrained from charging the assassins with murder if they had adamantly claimed to be fighting a 'just war' such as the 'Global War on Terror'? Can an impermissible act of assassination become a permissible act of war by linguistic decree?

The problem for the killers in the Bouchiki case, whatever weapon they might have used, is that the target was not located in a land governed by a leader such as President Saleh in Yemen. The government of Norway had not granted permission to the government of Israel to dispatch its declared enemies on Norwegian soil, and that is why the members of the plausibly deniable Mossad team were indicted, tried and convicted of murder. Do the residents of Norway have more rights than those of Yemen, Pakistan and Somalia, where US drones have been used in ostensibly similar acts of targeted killing?

The oddity of labeling what appears to be good old-fashioned assassination as an act of *war* is that it seems to change nothing about the homicide itself. It serves the purpose, instead, of making collateral damage possible where it was not before. The irony, then, is that more people, even known to be innocent, become subject to slaughter when an act of assassination is rebranded as an act of war, despite the fact that the other distinctive features of warfare are conspicuously absent. Among other things, to say that collateral damage is 'unavoidable' during wartime is to assert that the use of deadly force is a last resort, as in a case of legitimate self-defense. But there is no sense in which an unarmed person poses an immediate threat to his killers in cases involving Predator drones deployed in lands where there are no soldiers on the ground. Through a suspicious linguistic device, the operators come to benefit from the proverbial 'fog of war' permitting even innocent persons to be harmed foreseeably – so long as it was not intended but a side effect – despite the fact that those who order the strikes and launch the weapons do not face the risks historically associated with war.

Do targeted killings by Predator drone differ in moral essence from assassination or extrajudicial killing? One thing is clear: if neologism and redefinition can change the morality of an act of killing, then they do so in every relevantly similar case. Were all of the assassinations instigated in the twentieth century legitimate acts of war? What about all other acts of intentional, premeditated killing (commonly referred to as *murder*) committed by individuals against their own avowed enemies?

In cases of targeted killing of alleged criminals, moral legitimacy turns on the reliability of the facts purported to be true – and the credibility of those who float them as facts. The CIA claims to know that the people whom it obliterates using Predator drones are evil terrorists who must be eliminated. History attests that the CIA has often been wrong. Skepticism about the reliability of CIA judgments is not a matter of conspiracy mongering; it is firmly grounded in facts and has been documented by a number of authors independently, including *New York Times* journalist Timothy Weiner, whose eye-opening history of the CIA, *Legacy of Ashes*, is based on 'the family jewels', thousands of formerly classified documents made public in 2007.

Among other notorious failings, the CIA grossly exaggerated the Soviet threat throughout the Cold War, directly causing the proliferation and spread of weapons, including weapons of mass destruction (WMD), around the world. In *Failure of Intelligence* (2008), Melvin Goodman, a veteran CIA officer, provides an insider's look at the extreme politicization of the reports prepared for presidents by CIA analysts. The directors were often more concerned with supporting the incumbent executive's policies than with providing the accurate information needed for the revision or abandonment of ill-conceived initiatives such as the catastrophic escalation of the war between North and South Vietnam.[53]

More recently, and most spectacularly, the CIA utterly failed in its mission to provide any inkling of the events of 11 September 2001, despite a variety of signs pointing toward the intention of Al-Qaeda to attack targets in the United States using commercial airliners. In terms of tactical blunders, much closer to the sorts of facts relevant to the November 2002 strike and hundreds of others in the years to follow, the CIA provided erroneous coordinates to NATO pilots during the 1999 bombing of Kosovo, which resulted in the obliteration of the Chinese embassy in Belgrade. Also during the Clinton administration, an aspirin factory in Sudan was bombed on the basis of unconfirmed evidence (provided by the CIA) that it was producing chemical weapons.[54] Under President George H. W. Bush, during Operation Desert Storm, a shelter harboring more than 400 innocent civilians was destroyed on 13 February 1991 – again, based on CIA-sourced coordinates.[55]

Far more devastating than one-off examples of erroneous grid coordinates, the CIA instigated or supported coups throughout the twentieth century, often deposing democratically elected leaders and propping up right-wing military dictators who went on to commit countless human rights violations against civilians. The CIA also failed to forecast the fall of the Berlin Wall in 1989 and the invasion of Kuwait by Saddam Hussein in 1990, among many other historic events. Under intense political pressure, the CIA provided the US administration with a spurious pretext for the 2003 invasion of Iraq, which led to the deaths of hundreds of thousands of people, including thousands of US troops. The number of troops who came home maimed was much greater than the number slain, and a disturbing percentage of veterans have taken their own lives since.[56] The CIA was also in charge of a misguided 'enhanced interrogation' program from 2001 to 2006, which was denounced in a scathing

Senate Intelligence Committee report as not only brutal but also ineffective and deceptive. In this CIA-managed program, more than 100 prisoners were tortured, 26 of whom were later revealed to have been mistakenly detained.[57]

The fallibility of the CIA has been amply demonstrated and raises the question of how an official targeted killing program could have been placed under Agency control. In the light of all of the manifest failures of intelligence on the part of the institution whose very *raison d'être* is none other than to provide reliable information and analysis for the purpose of forging sound policy, it is not at all far-fetched to conclude that CIA assessments of who does and does not deserve to be sentenced to death and destroyed by Predator drone can only be undependable, at best. The reliability of the CIA can hardly have improved in the twenty-first century while persons with no intelligence background whatsoever (such as former congressman Leon Panetta and General David Petraeus) have been appointed directors of the Agency.

The summary execution by Predator drone of suspects in non-Western, non-democratic states located far from the US homeland bears similarities to the support of right-wing dictatorships during the Cold War, the difference being that the 'evil enemy' is no longer *communism* but fluid and shadowy *terrorism*. The primary difference between the pre-Church commission period of the CIA and the post-9/11 period is that the sort of targeted killing once carried out only through black ops has become official policy and a standard operating procedure. Hit lists of targets to be assassinated are regularly drawn up by the CIA, whose ranks have been bolstered by a significant contingent of privately contracted workers. The case of Edward Snowden somewhat ironically illustrates that, with the privatization of many aspects of intelligence work, the floodgates have been flung open to basically any- and everything.

Some of the private contractors (such as Snowden) may demur from US policy; others may believe in their heart of hearts that 'everything is permitted'. Just as during the twentieth century some of the deniable operators sent to fledgling democracies in Africa were excessive in their quest to 'find, fix, and finish' suspects, there may well be such individuals today helping to draw up the US government's hit lists. All sight of accountability has been lost, and perpetrators even of flagrant crimes are protected by a thick – indeed impenetrable – wall of secrecy under a national security pretext.

Congressional oversight committees have been ineffective since 9/11 because the persons on them are politicians, who tend toward worst-case scenarios in calculating which policies to support. In effect, they hedge their bets. This political force was in full evidence in October 2002, when Congress granted George W. Bush carte blanche to wage war on his own timetable and according to his own perception of the need. By renouncing their war powers, the members of Congress who supported the open-ended resolution could blame the president if things went badly – and they did.

The very same concern with retaining their positions explains why members of Congress have thrown so much money at the very agencies which failed to protect the people of the United States on 11 September 2001. Politicians paint themselves as strong on defense by funding any and every initiative said to be a part of the war against violent extremists. If the initiatives fail, then the explanation becomes that the agencies need even more support. Once drones had been designated the tool of choice in combating terrorism, the US fleet grew rapidly. Even when politicians are wary of drone proliferation, they may be hesitant to agitate for a reduction of the fleet, reasoning that any terrorist attack on US soil will be interpreted by some voters as a result of wavering or weakness on national defense.

* * *

Despite the helpful leaks in recent years of hundreds of thousands of classified documents, which have provided US citizens with some glimpse into what precisely their government is doing in their name and with their money, the secrecy of the procedures and criteria used to select targets for Predator drone killing remains firmly in place. At the same time, the aims of the program – to kill terrorists, one by one – are not hidden and denied but vaunted. Whether or not one trusts the CIA in the light of all of its many documented failures, the practice in which its agents and associates have been engaged – the summary execution without trial of suspects – was until recently considered unlawful among Western democratic states.

Nations which continue to execute even convicted capital criminals are excluded from admission to the European Union (EU). The recognition of fundamental human rights is required of all EU member states, and the practice of capital punishment raises serious concerns about such rights, given the undeniable potential for both error and abuse. Either capital punishment is just, or it is not. But in every case the conviction and sentencing to death of a human being for a capital crime leaves open the possibility for error. This is one of the primary reasons why opponents of the death penalty insist that the practice must come to an end.

Whether or not, in a world graced with perfect institutions, it would be just to execute those who have in fact committed capital crimes, we live in an imperfect world replete with error. 'To err is human,' and the purpose of due process, one of the hallmarks of modern democratic societies, is to minimize the occurrence of the grossest form of injustice, the infliction of irrevocable penalties upon people for crimes which they did not commit. Given human fallibility, it is clear that, just as in the black ops of the twentieth century, some of the persons intentionally destroyed by Predator drone have been innocent – in addition to obvious cases of collateral damage, such as the children slain. As a matter of rhetoric, in the mainstream media, the elimination of a *suspect* now cements him in public discourse as a *terrorist*: he had to be guilty, in order to be killed!

Democracy requires the possibility of dissent. Yet it is not possible to contest the US government's interpretation of what transpired in Yemen on 3 November 2002, or in any of the many drone strikes to follow, most of which were approved by Barack Obama. During his first presidential election campaign, Obama vigorously criticized the Bush administration's 2003 invasion of Iraq. What Obama failed to grasp as he went on to expand the drone program is that preemptive war and summary execution of suspects are two sides of the same tyrannical coin. Summary execution by Predator drone is triply protected by secrecy, for neither the perpetrators nor most of the victims can be identified, and the procedures used to produce target lists are not subject to critique. US presidents throughout the twentieth century evinced a willingness to go 'above and beyond the call of duty' by invoking executive privilege to carry out covert actions in the name of national defense. If the execution without trial of individual persons located abroad – even US citizens – is now embraced by the president as a standard operating procedure, one can only surmise what the new black ops might comprise.

Targeted killing is no longer a black op, because it is acknowledged as public policy, but the Predator drone program remains morally gray. The life-or-death decisions being made by anonymous analysts remain opaque, under cover of national security. Even when the Obama administration received a court order in 2014 to release the memos said to justify the execution of US citizen Anwar al-Awlaki without trial, the documents were redacted to exclude the evidential basis for the killing.[58] The official version of these events remains in place, for it cannot even in principle be refuted by people denied access to the evidence leading up to a strike. The killers may be dressed up in republican clothes, but the summary execution of persons by a small committee of president-appointed bureaucrats, with no provision for appeal of what are in effect death sentences, smacks of simple tyranny.

After years of denying the very existence of the targeted killing program, US officials today acknowledge drone strikes, painting them as acts of war intended to keep the homeland safe. The operators who recognize that some of their victims were innocent may lament 'the fog of war'. But to call the execution without trial of an unarmed person in a land thousands of miles away an 'act of war' is to alter the concept of combatant beyond all recognition, permitting the obliteration of any person deemed by the killer to be worthy of death. Terrorists, too, indulge in creative reconceptualization, defining civilians as guilty by association of the crimes committed by their government.

The forty-third president of the United States and his entourage were always careful to 'lawyer up' – as former Secretary of Defense Donald Rumsfeld would say – before stripping suspects of their right to do the same. But Obama's primary method of dealing with terrorist suspects, to kill rather than capture them, has been even more draconian than Bush's 'extraordinary rendition' and 'enhanced interrogation' in secret prisons located in torture-friendly countries. In the drone age under Obama, suspects are no less deprived of legal representation than they were under Bush, but that is because in the aftermath of a deadly drone strike there is nothing left of them to represent.

CHAPTER 3
THE LOGIC OF TARGETED KILLING

'The Army? Ain't nothing like the army. The Army is:
Some guy you don't know sends you out to whack
some other guy you don't know. Army.'

Benjamin 'Lefty' Ruggiero, *Donnie Brasco*[59]

'The only type of killing that's safe is when a stranger kills a
stranger. No motive. Nothing to link the victim to the execution.
Now why would a stranger kill a stranger? Because somebody's
willing to pay. It's a business. Same as any other business.'

Claude, *Murder by Contract*[60]

REMOTE-CONTROL KILLING is new in history, which is why as people attempt to understand this practice, they naturally draw comparisons with more familiar forms of homicide. The two most common analogies – to conventional acts of war or premeditated murder – are generally regarded as either permissible or forbidden, with no real gray area in between.

In principle, one might accept the use of remote-control killing but criticize the procedure and criteria by which targets are currently being selected for execution. However, since the decisions are made in secret, with no disclosure of the evidential basis for placing names on the US government's hit lists, supporters of the program are simply trusting those in charge to be judicious in their selection process. Needless to say, opponents to the Predator drone program find it preposterous that anyone should support such executions without knowledge of the procedures being used to determine whom to kill and why, and with no provision for revisiting the decisions in the event of intelligence analysis and tradecraft gone awry.

The informants on the ground who identify targets for destruction also report back after a strike. This confirmation bias explains what is often claimed to be the resplendent success of the drone killing campaign – praised by many authors who blithely accept the reports without any apparent recognition that there is no independent verification taking place. Bryan Glyn Williams, the author of *Predators: The CIA's Drone War on al Qaeda* (2013), is a typical example of this tendency. He spends entire chapters 'proving' that drone strikes do not kill civilians, without acknowledging that the *suspects* who have been identified by informants are reported as the *terrorists* or *militants* killed after a strike.[61] Williams ignores altogether the vexing categorization of all military-age men as fair game for execution by drones, and he accepts that 'Arabs' in the territories where missiles are launched can safely be assumed to be jihadists.[62]

In areas where there are no intelligence agents on the ground, it is not even possible to confirm that the intended targets were hit, as Shuja Nawaz of the Atlantic Council explains: 'We know fairly well how many strikes are occurring. What we don't know is the details, who the targets were, whether they were actually eliminated, or whether some other people were killed, because verification is very difficult.'[63]

The need for a thorough review of targeting criteria seems especially pressing in view of the fact that many of the detainees held indefinitely at Guantánamo Bay were eventually cleared of any and all complicity in alleged terrorist activities. What if they had been killed instead? The historical record, written by their killers, would have characterized them as evil terrorists, not erroneously targeted suspects. In all such cases, suspected terrorists are first and foremost suspects, which implies that they may not be plotting any act of violence against anyone. Even if they despise the US government, they may lack the means and the wherewithal to harm citizens of the United States. Is anti-American sentiment now a capital offense?

Innocent suspects erroneously believed to be guilty as a result of stale or otherwise faulty intelligence are not the only persons endangered by drones. Whenever UCAVs are deployed, bystanders not even suspected of hatching evil schemes are at risk of death. The 'modest' magnitude of civilian casualties from the drone program is trumpeted by its advocates as a virtue because they view targeted killing as a legitimate form of warfare. The number – whether thousands or 'only' hundreds of obviously innocent people (such as children) destroyed – is small when compared with the casualties of full-scale wars such as in Iraq and Vietnam, or World War II, where hundreds of thousands or even millions of noncombatants died. Drones are said by their advocates to 'project power without projecting vulnerability' and to permit 'surgical strikes' against persons identified as the enemy while minimizing collateral damage and preventing the sacrifice of troops. *How could any of this be wrong?* ask those who hail the dawning of the drone age.

Those who protest the very same number of civilian casualties (hundreds or thousands) are thinking in terms of murder. If an individual who intentionally and premeditatedly slays thirteen people – as did Nidal Hasan at Fort Hood military base on 5 November 2009 – is a monster, then what about someone who orders the execution of thousands of people? What if, instead of commencing from the assumption that drone killing is a form of warfare, one begins with the bare act of killing by remote control, the termination of a human being's life, and moves in the opposite direction? Rather than 'extend the warrior's arm', what if one closes up the distance between the operator and his target, until at last the killer stands before his victim and shoots him in the head, point-blank and in cold blood. Would that not constitute an act of murder, whether the killer was in uniform or civilian dress? The victim is unarmed and not posing a threat to his killer. His back is turned (targets of drone strikes do not know that they are about to die), and he is shot at close range in the back of the head (there is virtually no chance that he will survive).

Such an action looks to critics like a paradigmatic case of murder, for there is no plausible pretext of legitimate self-defense available. Certainly, if a policeman killed a person on the street in this manner, he would be charged with murder. But if such a one-on-one, face-to-face act of cold-blooded killing would obviously be murder, then how can the same act carried out by someone who is not even in principle capable of being harmed by the target be morally permissible? What anti-drone activists regard as intrinsically evil in this scenario is the premeditated and intentional annihilation of a human being, a center of consciousness, as though the killer were Almighty God.

Both the pro-drone and the anti-drone perspectives may seem on their face to be based on sound reasoning, which explains why people hold their respective positions so forcefully. Moving in toward the victim appears to imply that such execution is indisputably wrong – an act of cold-blooded murder. Moving out, in the opposite direction, away from the battlefield, extending the arm of the warrior, appears to imply that killing by remote control is an acceptable form of warfare. From the policymakers' perspective, the use of drones to neutralize enemy forces is no more and no less than a lengthening of the warrior's arm. Proponents of the drone program may even contend that such killing is more humane than traditional military killing, because the victims do not hear the missile coming before it destroys them.

Some critics oppose specifically the use of unmanned – but not manned – aerial vehicles to kill people in lands far away, pointing to what they take to be a crucial difference between the two cases: if human pilots are on board, and they are being targeted from the ground, then they can construe what they do as a form of self-defense. Drone killings are not acts of *literal* self-defense, for the people who sit in offices at Creech Air Force Base in Nevada and 'employ on' targets by remote control are not in any danger and therefore are not defending their own lives by doing so. In a case of legitimate self-defense, a person attempts to protect herself from an armed aggressor who is in the process of attacking her. What is absent from the mind of the target in a drone strike is the clear and present intention to harm another human being *at the moment when the target is destroyed*. But the positive intention to kill *is* present among the personnel attempting to 'light up' terrorist suspects who are entirely unaware of their imminent demise. How different is this practice, logically speaking, from the notorious killing campaigns of simple tyrants?

Institutional killing involves a formal apparatus absent in cases of legitimate self-defense by individuals. When paranoid leaders – Ugandan president Idi Amin was arguably one example, and there have been others – carry out systematic, bureaucratic killing, snuffing out any and every potential threat to their power, they invariably conceive of what they are doing as 'self-defense'.[64] What remains to be shown is how the new Predator drone program of premeditated and intentional, *institutional* homicide differs from the outrageous mass murders perpetrated by the tyrants of the past. Such leaders ordered summary executions under the aegis of the government and in the name of national defense.

Following the Obama administration's Department of Justice White Paper (released in June 2010), drone advocates will retort that Al-Qaeda is incessantly planning attacks against the United States, and so, against all appearances, drone operators are in fact defending their own lives, along with those of their compatriots. The problem with this line of reasoning is that it redefines 'self-defense' so broadly as to permit any killer to claim that he acted out of fear that his victim might possibly, some day, even in the remote future, undertake to harm him.

If incrementally diminishing the distance between the drone operator and his victim would imply the permissibility of homicide committed by paranoid killers who claim to be defending themselves by dispatching persons designated as *enemies*, then the 'act of war' analogy may be faulty after all, despite its superficial plausibility. If one begins with a permissible act of war and increases the distance to the point where the soldier is no longer in any immediate danger, then perhaps it is precisely the removal of *simultaneous risk* from the equation which changes, too, the morality of this form of homicide.[65] There is another suspicious problem with the blanket assumption that Predator drone killing is permissible as a form of warfare. It does not seem possible to come up with an example where murder has ever been committed by a drone operator. By definition, the victims are either legitimate targets or collateral damage, and yet the killer was never in any direct or immediate danger of bodily harm when he fired missiles to obliterate them.

Consider the plight of Mamana Bibi, a sixty-eight-year-old grandmother who was 'taken out' by Predator drone on 24 October 2012 while picking okra all alone in a large field in Ghundi Kala village, Pakistan. Clearly something went awry – were the killers not at the very least culpably negligent? Amnesty International investigated the case and has asked the US government to clarify the events of that day.[66] The killers may or may not ever comply, but if they do, they will in all likelihood plead collateral damage and exculpate themselves by citing a faulty GPS coordinate.

To staunch opponents of what they take to be assassination (who reject the nuanced distinction between *assassination* and *targeted killing*), it does not matter whether acts of remote-control killing are considered a form of warfare or not. Even if they are a part of war, drone strikes are war crimes, in direct violation of the Geneva Conventions, according to which unarmed enemies must be taken prisoner, not executed point-blank. Moreover, war crimes do not excuse collateral damage, which is deemed permissible only in cases of justified acts of war. When unarmed persons are summarily executed, even though they are not engaged actively in hostilities and do not directly threaten their killers, then they have simply been murdered.

It is true that, before the drone age, during formal military conflicts between rival groups on a well-defined battlefield, it was generally thought that soldiers could be lawfully neutralized up until the moment when the war had come to an end. In other words, surprise attacks on battalions during an ongoing war were not thought to violate the Geneva Conventions.[67] However, in the case of the drone killing campaign, there are no boundaries – whether temporal or geographical – as the US government has decreed any and every territory fair game. More than three years after Osama bin Laden had been eliminated, President Obama reaffirmed the idea in these terms: 'I have made it clear that we will hunt down terrorists who threaten our country, wherever they are.'[68] The problem with drone 'warfare' in unoccupied lands is that the killers are simply labeling villages and cities as battlefields, and interpreting the persons present there as soldiers to be slain, even though the targets are not and have never been engaged in physical combat with their eventual killers.

International protocols such as the *Charter of the United Nations* (1945), the *Universal Declaration of Human Rights* (1948) and the Geneva Conventions are brushed aside by advocates of remote-control killing, who maintain that because their targets are 'unlawful combatants', they do not enjoy the protections codified in such documents. At the same time, the active program participants appear to believe that, in ordering and carrying out the strikes, they are doing no more than extending an act of war to its logical limit, or perhaps distilling war to its essence. International law is accepted by some advocates of drone warfare but said not to apply to this particular enemy: the members of virulent terrorist groups. The question then must be posed: *To whom* do *the protocols apply in the twenty-first century, now that interstate wars with the United States are precluded by the sheer size and formidable wealth of its military?*

Article 11 of the *Universal Declaration of Human Rights* states: 'Everyone charged with a penal offence has the right to be presumed innocent until proved guilty according to law in a public trial at which he has had all the guarantees necessary for his defence.' The only persons to whom such a provision meaningfully applies are *suspects*, which is precisely the status of the persons intentionally and premeditatedly obliterated by Predator drone-delivered Hellfire missiles. Some of the people being killed – above all, the *innocent* suspects – have no idea that they have made their way onto a hit list of targets to be eliminated should the opportunity arise. How could they defend themselves, when they have never been charged with a crime? Anyone whose name makes it onto a kill list was presumably first on the US government's terrorist watch list. But according to the March 2013 *Watchlisting Guidance* manual: 'The general policy of the U.S. Government is to neither confirm nor deny an individual's watchlist status.'[69]

Many persons were demonstrated to have been mistakenly incarcerated in the prison at Guantánamo Bay, having been swept up and spirited away for reasons deriving from the very same types of intelligence and analysis used to produce Predator drone hit lists. Often these people were located in hostile territories, essentially 'in the wrong place at the wrong time'. The prisoners cleared for release from Guantánamo Bay were captured and contained as terrorist suspects. Years later, they were determined not to have been terrorists at all. It seems reasonable to infer, therefore, that approximately the same percentage of innocent persons incarcerated should be found among the suspects being dispatched by drone.

It may be countered that more care is taken in constructing the hit lists, but this is clearly false in 'crowd killing' or 'signature strikes', where multiple unidentified individuals are targeted on the basis of their apparently suspicious association with other apparently suspicious persons. The innocent victims in such cases, like the wrongly interned persons at Guantánamo Bay, have been singled out for punishment for being 'in the wrong place at the wrong time'. In the case of drone strikes, the sanction is irrevocable.

The open-ended notion of self-defense assumed to be valid by the executors of the drone program has always been embraced by dictators, who crush even the faintest uprising against their regimes. It can be seen within Western liberal democratic societies as well, among certain criminal organizations. In some ways, the Predator drone program looks disturbingly similar to the activities of Mafia bosses, who, too, draw up hit lists of enemies to be neutralized. The difference is that the US government may make recourse to the police force in addressing unacceptable behavior, as in the case of Timothy McVeigh, who was charged and convicted of murder and sentenced to death for killing 168 people by igniting a bomb at the Federal Building in Oklahoma City on 19 April 1995. In stark contrast, the Bush administration chose to characterize the terrorist attacks of 11 September 2001 as acts of war, not crime, and retaliated against entire nations.

Like the executors of the drone program, Mafia bosses conceive of their conflicts as 'wars'. It is not possible to analyze in detail what goes on behind closed doors as secret hit lists are drawn up, but the activities of contract killers or 'technicians' are rather well understood, thanks to the garrulousness of a few. Hitmen study their targets, surreptitiously watching them for a period of time in order to ascertain their habits, their schedules and their haunts. In this way, the killers can arrive at plans of action which will minimize the probability of accidentally harming other people.

The paramount concern for the hitman is to get the job done without being detected and without leaving any evidence behind which might implicate the killer or his boss in the murder. With these prudential constraints in mind, a hitman may observe his target for several days, weeks, or even months before striking. While studying the target, the hitman lurks in the shadows and takes great pains to avoid being noticed by the person whom he intends to kill. When at last he strikes, it is done with no warning to the victim, who has nearly no chance of survival, being entirely unaware that someone somewhere has paid to see that he die.[70]

These dynamics, the lurking and striking without warning, are common to drone operators and make their profession look not unlike that of the hitman. Professional hitmen, like drone operators, intentionally and premeditatedly kill victims against whom they can harbor no personal rancor, given that they are strangers. Typically, someone who wishes to eliminate another human being for personal reasons hires a hitman who knows nothing about the person. The malice aforethought inheres in the person who pays the hitman to kill, not in the hitman himself.

It is not without reason that crime syndicates refer to their low-level operatives as *soldiers*, for their role in such organizations is analogous to that of the soldiers, including the drone operators, of formal military institutions. In both cases, the killers have agreed through accepting their position to terminate the lives of human beings at the behest of their commanders and without raising questions as to the justice or legitimacy of those acts of killing. An essential part of the soldier's station, regardless of who his leader may be – whether Winston Churchill or Adolf Hitler, George Bush or Saddam Hussein,

Lucky Luciano or John Gotti – is to follow orders received from on high without posing questions or airing skepticism about the wisdom of what they have been called upon to do.

Modern Western society has a fascination with the glamorized depiction of the culture of organized crime in films such as *The Godfather*, directed by Francis Ford Coppola. In this saga, Michael Corleone (played by Al Pacino) conveys a sense of strength and a desire to defend his family (in both senses) and his honor by ordering that threats to his power be squelched. The hitmen enlisted to carry out the murders are not depicted nearly so favorably, for they simply follow orders to kill anyone whom their boss wants eliminated – for whatever reason. The appeal of such figures derives from their risk-taking behavior, which requires courage whenever their own lives are jeopardized by their activities, as is the case during the commission of high-level crimes.

In recent decades, the traditional honor code of the Mafia has fallen by the wayside, with many criminals engaging in treacherous behavior in order to save themselves or to cash in on best-selling memoirs. In the process, images of gangsters have become correspondingly less glamorous. In *Donnie Brasco*, a film based on the true story of 'Lefty', a hitman from New York City, the killer boasts of having 'clipped the wings' of twenty-six men over the course of his career, but it is clear that he is no more than a tool and has no real power in the criminal underworld. Twenty-six may sound like a lot of murders, but the number is quite low compared with the number of persons whose deaths are directly caused or facilitated by Predator drone operators (who track targets and launch missiles) and sensors (who guide missiles using laser technology). Upon retiring from the profession after five years, Brandon Bryant was presented with a 'scorecard' informing him that he had contributed to the deaths of 1,626 human beings.[71]

Law-abiding citizens are shocked to learn of the existence of career contract killers such as Richard Kuklinski, a New Jersey hitman who admitted to having dispatched some 100 people in exchange for five-digit sums of cash.[72] Yet the structural parallels between the modern military and organized crime are palpable. In both cases, deadly force is being opted for in lieu of non-violent means of persuasion. In both cases, 'soldiers' agree to kill at the behest of their leader and without questioning the grounds for such action. In remote-control killing, as in illegal contract killing, the targets to be eliminated have been determined from behind closed doors to be mortal enemies worthy of death. Drone operators work under far less stringent practical constraints (prudence) than either combat soldiers or hitmen, for they risk neither physical danger nor punishment by the government for their mistakes. Instead, they work as protected employees of the state. Moreover, at the sites where strikes are carried out, there is no locally accessible evidence linking the individual remote-control killer as a specific perpetrator of the deaths caused by him. In contrast, the hitman may be caught in the act or leave traces behind (fingerprints, a strand of hair, etc.) which can potentially link him to the homicide. Occasionally, a contract killer's dirty deed is captured on tape.

In *The Godfather: Part II*, Michael Corleone's solicitor, Tom Hagen, attempts to dissuade his boss from getting carried away in ordering the execution of people who do not really need to die. He asks: 'Is it worth it? I mean, you've won. You want to wipe everybody out?' The Godfather replies: 'I don't feel I have to wipe everybody out, Tom. Just my enemies. That's all.' This scenario is relevant to the real world because in it the US president continues to approve lethal hits on persons even loosely associated with Al-Qaeda and long after Osama bin Laden and most of the other planners and perpetrators of the 9/11 attacks have been eliminated. From bringing the persons responsible for 9/11 to justice, the targeted killing campaign expanded to include 'associates', under some form of 'the friend of my enemy is my enemy' logic.

The problem with this construction is well illustrated by the insurgents who fled Afghanistan to Pakistan and sought refuge among local tribes, who in some cases knew nothing about the people to whom they had offered safe haven. According to Akbar Ahmed, former Pakistani ambassador to the UK and an anthropologist by training, within these peripheral tribes: 'The code's paramount principle is the law of hospitality pertaining to the welcoming and protection of guests, which is said to reflect the honor of the host. Even a stranger seeking refuge, whatever his background, will find shelter among those adhering to the code.'[73] When unwitting hosts are obliterated along with guests suspected of terrorism, gestures of humanity are perversely contorted into capital crimes.

At the same time that killing by a stable, First World nation has become a first rather than a last resort – with the capture of enemies essentially defined as 'infeasible' – other previously clear-cut concepts have become blurred, including the distinction between regular and mercenary soldiers or private contractees. In the twentieth century, private operators working under false identities were enlisted to carry out deniable black ops. In the drone age, the private operators working in collaboration with the military or the CIA and participating in the 'kill chain' of the targeting program have authentic faces and names, and are paid by US taxpayers through funds accounted for in officially approved contracts.

The similarities between the military and organized crime have become more and more visible with the advent of the private military company (PMC), whose operatives are motivated by financial incentives no less than the widely maligned mercenary soldiers of centuries past. The US government's decision to enlist such companies to fill gaps in its 'kill chain' reveals that there is no essential difference between what the uniformed soldiers of a nation do and what surrogate private operators or 'guns for hire' do. There is, of course, a sense in which even the voluntary soldiers of Western societies can be accurately described as *mercenary*, whenever their sole or primary reason for enlisting is to earn a salary and receive other employment benefits.[74] Nonetheless, regular military personnel continue, by and large, to enjoy their culturally habituated reputation as patriotic, honorable and noble, in contrast to the mercenaries of earlier times, who were regarded as untrustworthy and dishonorable – obviously capable of being bribed and, if sufficiently enticed, prepared to switch sides.[75] During the Cold War, double agents were discovered even among spies with high-level security clearance.

The military retains the favor of the populace, and the type of 'financial persuasion' involved in the legal recruitment of regular soldiers and their privately contracted colleagues is not generally viewed as unscrupulous or morally dubious in any way. The longstanding approval of the military, conjoined with a firm belief among Americans in the virtues of capitalism, has given rise to an accommodating attitude toward war profiteers more generally, as is reflected by the profligate contracting practices of the government, most spectacularly displayed in Iraq beginning in 2003. Financial scandals involving firms such as Halliburton were exposed but swiftly forgotten by a populace inclined to support any and every initiative labeled *defense*, and fully prepared to forgive mistakes made by the war architects and their collaborators.[76]

The high rates of success vaunted by Predator drone program administrators with financial interests and careers at stake appear to have a great deal to do with the fact that the very people who finger targets – sometimes planting *pathrai* (computer chip) GPS locators on them – report back on the success of the strikes. In truth, what such a 'successful' mission shows is not that a guilty person was slain, but that the suspect identified as guilty by a paid informant was slain. The ambiguity here trades on the conflation of *terrorist suspects* and *terrorists*, which are not one and the same.

The question of guilt is the most important factor but it receives no judicial consideration whatsoever, and once the suspect has been killed, he becomes in public discourse a 'dead terrorist', when only moments earlier he was still a suspect. He is convicted, in effect, through state execution. In the deniable missions of the twentieth century, government-contracted killers acting under assumed identities were protected from the consequences of their mistakes by a cloak of secrecy. In the drone age, the analysts and killers are protected for the time being by a bureaucratic cloak of anonymity. Discoveries of bad intel are tragically post-mortem – too late for the victims wrongly obliterated.

Morally speaking, the intentional hunting down and killing of human beings, which is precisely what drone strikes are, appears to be indistinguishable from premeditated murder. The goal is not to incapacitate but to kill, as is illustrated in a most grisly way by the 'double tap' strikes intended to wipe out even the wounded survivors of an initial strike.[77] What makes first-degree murder so reprehensible is the positive intention to erase the existence of another human being, to destroy a center of consciousness. What critics of remote-control killing find even worse than revenge killing is that the grounds for execution may have nearly nothing to do with the actions of the person himself. As this form of homicide has gained acceptance among US bureaucrats as a means of warfare, the hit lists have grown lengthier, with unnamed persons being targeted solely on the basis of the people with whom they appear to associate.

The military requirement of strict obedience to orders, which mandates that soldiers perform their duties unflinchingly and without questioning the objectives or soundness of what they have been told to do, has its origins in legitimate self-defense. In centuries past, the disobedience of a single soldier had the potential to endanger an entire platoon and jeopardize the larger mission under way, and ultimately the outcome of the war. In the drone age, however, it is difficult to see how the extermination of individuals one by one can be rationalized under the same pretext, particularly in places where there are no soldiers on the ground to protect.

During wartime, there are always rules of engagement (ROE) applicable on the battlefield. However, ROE are specified by commanders, who may at their caprice decide to define the enemy in whatever way they like.[78] The dependence of ROE on commanders' opinions was unforgettably demonstrated in Fallujah (Iraq) in November 2004, when all remaining residents of the city were defined as 'fair game' before the city was razed.[79] Commanders may, as has happened in the expansive drone program, simply stipulate that all males from the ages of sixteen to fifty located in a certain place are 'combatants' and therefore legitimate targets of attack.[80] In the US government's 'signature strikes', unnamed persons are destroyed because their 'pattern of life movements' are said to match a profile (a 'disposition matrix'[81]) believed to be typical of terrorists. In Western Pakistan, the blanket assumption that 'Arabs' located in remote tribal areas are always jihadists has served as the basis for many strikes. Places thought to be frequented by terrorists may instead harbor political dissidents with no international aspirations whatsoever, least of all the intention to travel abroad to harm the people of the United States.

The operators of weaponized drones, like their civilian commander in chief and his advisers, do not kill in *self-defense* or as a *last resort* in any meaningful sense of those words. Yet the notion of collateral damage has not been reconsidered or revised with the transformation of soldiers to operators who kill without risking their personal demise. Instead, 'collateral damage' is simply assumed to be permissible even though the former grounds for its alleged permissibility have evaporated into thin air.

In many official reports of drone killing, military spokespersons have either flatly denied that noncombatants were destroyed by the strikes, or else omitted any mention of the victims while trumpeting the 'evil terrorists' slain. In some of these cases, the initial 'official' assessments were later emended when journalists, antiwar activists and non-governmental organization (NGO) personnel traveled to the sites to investigate the extent of the damage done. Whatever the percentage may be – and this will vary greatly depending upon whether one denies the conceptual possibility of a 'military-age male civilian' – significant numbers of innocent people have been annihilated or maimed, and many others have been left bereft of their loved ones and homes.[82] A further ill of war – one which is particularly acute in the drone age and altogether omitted from the official story – is the anxiety caused to the people under surveillance. Having seen how Hellfire missiles rip human bodies asunder unpredictably and without warning (when they are not fully incinerated), some of the physical survivors become psychological and emotional casualties, never knowing whether they may be the next in line to die – by mistake or by design. Others who witness the carnage vow to seek revenge.

What is noteworthy in the cases of Obama's targeted killing program and the actions taken by both Nidal Hasan at Fort Hood and Humam al-Balawi at Camp Chapman is that all of the killers believed themselves to be eliminating culprits guilty of crimes and to be preventing further future harm to innocent persons. In Al-Balawi's videotaped suicide note made before blowing himself up along with seven CIA agents (some of whom were private contractors) on 30 December 2009, the Jordanian doctor said: 'This jihadi attack will be the first of the revenge operations against the Americans and their drone teams.'[83] In March 2009, when the Tehrik-e-Taliban Pakistan attacked a cricket match in Sri Lanka and the police academy in Lahore, Baitullah Mehsud explained: 'We did it as a retaliation for US missile strikes off drones inside the Pakistan territory.'[84] If what they say is taken at face value, these killers genuinely believed that the military actions of the United States were unjust, and they undertook to stop the perpetrators from killing even more. Had the United States not been fighting wars in Afghanistan and Iraq, and destroying people in Pakistan and Yemen as well, then these men might never have sought revenge. The US campaigns were, needless to say, direct responses to the crimes of 9/11.

In the wars of the twentieth century, ground troops confronted their enemy face to face. In the targeting of suspects by Predator drone, the killers are ordered to liquidate targets who pose no direct threat to the operators themselves. Supporters of the program are apt to claim that 'Everything changed' on 11 September 2001, and insist that many terrorist attacks have been thwarted through the use of drones. In the light of cases such as Nidal Hasan, Humam al-Balawi and Baitullah Mehsud, the question remains: *Have more terrorist acts been prevented or inspired by Predator drones?* The fleet of UAVs has rapidly expanded in the twenty-first century in an assiduous effort by US administrators to contain global terrorism. But is that because targeted killing campaigns create terrorists?

* * *

Lethal centrism – the focus on how to kill ever-more swiftly and efficiently – has always been a defining feature of the military, but it has become far more manifest in the drone age as unarmed persons are summarily executed. The victims are denied the right to surrender and have no opportunity to demonstrate that the actionable intelligence leading to the decision to strip them of their lives is faulty. 'Kill don't capture' policy represents lethal centrism in its purest form, admitting as 'actionable intelligence' what is generally considered to be judicially inadmissible evidence within civil society. In a court of law, hearsay and circumstantial evidence do not suffice for a first-degree murder conviction because they leave open the possibility of reasonable doubt about the defendant's guilt. In the drone killing of alleged suspects in remote tribal territories, hearsay and circumstantial evidence are used exhaustively and exclusively to select targets deemed worthy of death without the possibility of judicial review.

Extrajudicial killing has taken place in one form or another since time immemorial, but the surprise in the drone age has been that an ostensibly democratic government, complete with a republican constitution, a sophisticated court system and stable institutions dedicated to fighting crime should adopt the policy 'Kill don't capture' even when suspects are not armed and dangerous at the time when they are fired on. Crime organizations such as the Mafia concern themselves with efficient killing primarily as a means to protect themselves against prosecution for criminal activities, or else to expand the reach of power by eliminating competitors. Mafia hits serve, too, as a warning to those who might consider serving as witnesses against members of the syndicate.

The terror instilled in communities where persons suspected of associating with the killers' enemies are snuffed out – as occurs both in Mafia domains and at drone strike sites – has a muffling effect. In such circumstances, the local residents grow fearful of the consequences of speaking out or even meeting with other persons in their communities, for fear that they may be mistaken as a 'friend of the enemy'. Amnesty International has reported on the oppressive effects of the Predator drone program in communities where people avoid interacting with others, even in ordinary places such as markets, for fear that they might be pegged as suspicious 'associates' while browsing in the produce section. Witnesses and survivors of drone strikes are also afraid to discuss the events because they have received threats from unknown persons warning them not to speak.[85]

In homicides committed by groups such as the Mafia, the primary aim, aside from revenge, is the consolidation and expansion of power, a fact which they do not attempt to hide through the use of hypocritical moral pablum about global justice. A syndicate boss does not claim that he will make the world a better place for all of humanity by ordering that rivals and threats to his freedom be expunged from the face of the earth. Instead, he usurps the resources of competitors and secures the ability to live and work at large by ordering such hits. At the same time, such murders – conceived of by the boss himself as acts of self-defense – serve to protect himself from the possibility of other threats, by warning potential traitors in no uncertain terms what to expect should they betray him in any way. In criminal organizations, as in the domains of petty despots more generally, the purpose of killing witnesses is not to obliterate them but to prevent them from implicating the killers in previous crimes, thereby imperiling their power.

Just as drone operators bear similarities to contract killers, war profiteers might be usefully compared with the bosses of organized crime, for it is through the death of human beings that they amass wealth, influence and power. When wars promise to enrich some corporate players, then the support by those who stand to profit is obviously tainted by ulterior motives. In the drone age, as many former and current military officers serve on the boards of directors of major weapons and military service companies, the patent conflict of interest should be of serious concern to anyone who believes in the sanctity of human life.

The Predator drone program–Mafia analogy has not been widely explored or embraced, but the parallels are clear and were strongly suggested by the revelation that President Obama himself was an active member of the 'kill committee' which convened on 'Terror Tuesdays' to determine whom to target after watching PowerPoint presentations and considering 'flash cards' about the 'nominees'.[86] Supporters of the drone program will reflexively reject the Mafia analogy, but perhaps it will begin to gain traction and be applied seriously when the dictators of lands not aided and abetted by the US government (as in Yemen and Pakistan) begin to use drone technology to stifle political dissent after their own behind-closed-doors deliberations regarding suitable targets for annihilation.

The crucial assumption of the Justice Department's White Paper, which was penned with the intention of elucidating the supposed presidential authority to kill even US citizens abroad, is that 'We are at war with Al-Qaeda.' The threat posed by terrorists is said to justify any and all actions against members of that group or their broadly interpreted *associates*, the drone advocate's perspective being that the enemy has evolved, expanded and dispersed over the years since 9/11. If, however, the latest wave of terrorists is reacting specifically to the consequences of the drone program itself, then this constitutes a vivid illustration that 'violence breeds violence' in a vicious vortex of moral corruption.

CHAPTER 4
LETHAL CREEP

'There's a concept, "the banality of evil". When you start doing it *en masse*, 200, 300 people die because of the idea of "targeted assassination". Suddenly the processes become a kind of conveyor belt. You ask yourself less and less where to stop.'

Ami Ayalon, Head of Shin Bet, 1996–2000[87]

'You start out with a target list, and maybe you've got 50 guys on it, maybe you've got 200 guys on it, but you can work your way through those 50 or 200 guys, and then suddenly at the end of that target list you've got a new target list of 3,000 people on it.'

Andrew Exum, former US Army Ranger[88]

BEFORE THE INVENTION of aerial means of transport in the early twentieth century, the defense of a nation was equivalent to securing the physical perimeters of a territory. With the development of airplanes, national defense became more complex, as suddenly it was possible to attack countries from above, in the interior parts of their land. In all of the flurry of World War II, the concept of national defense evolved so quickly and so thoroughly that it began to be seen by US strategists as essentially something to be carried out somewhere else, far from the homeland. Crossing that threshold and reconceptualizing national defense as the application of military force far from the borders of the nation said to be defended, a matter of 'taking the battle to the enemy', led perhaps inevitably to the current practice of executing persons located abroad without trial – even US nationals suspected of treason – despite the fact that doing so gravely imperils other, entirely innocent, people.

After World War II and the devastation wrought by nations through the use of weapons of mass destruction – both 'conventional' and atomic bombs – limits on the use of deadly force by governments were explicitly incorporated in the 1945 *Charter of the United Nations.* The intention of the new conventions between states was to limit the capricious resort to war on the part of bellicose leaders by requiring that they seek out and receive the approval of the UN Security Council before wielding deadly force abroad.

In 2003, the George W. Bush administration ignored world opinion and acted for all intents and purposes unilaterally, as though the UN *Charter* had never been drafted. Paradoxically, those agitating for war claimed both that Saddam Hussein's violation of prior UN resolutions (relating to the 1991 Gulf War) justified the invasion of Iraq in 2003, and that the United States had no need for a 'permission slip' from the Security Council in order to proceed. Promoters of the invasion called the United Nations a 'debate team' and brandished the creative category of *unlawful combatant*, to which conventions governing war and civil society were said not to apply. These legal and linguistic maneuvers paved the way for the Obama administration's controversial implementation of a robust program of targeted killing in lands where war was never formally waged.

On its face, targeted killing conflicts radically with the self-professed values and principles of modern Western liberal democratic states. Under domestic law, premeditated homicide is a capital offense because of what is regarded as the sanctity of human life. In civil society, only literal self-defense justifies the killing of another human being, and only when there is no other way to prevent that person from harming someone else. Drone program supporters already accept the practice of military intervention abroad, including the bombing of territories inhabited by civilians, and find the case against the use of weaponized drones weak because they view the strikes as acts of war, which invariably risk collateral damage.[89]

Necessity is supposed to be the only reason why soldiers may be placed in harm's way and permitted to die. During wartime, troops are deployed by commanders who send them out to counter enemy fire. The very same reason of necessity is what is supposed to forgive so-called collateral damage, when noncombatants are unintentionally killed by soldiers attempting to achieve a military objective. Whether or not the twentieth-century wars in which the United States participated were necessary is open to debate, but they were always said by their promoters to be last resorts. Drone strikes are claimed by their advocates to be necessary, but they are carried out when an opportunity to eliminate a suspect arises. The targets are stalked before they are killed – sometimes for months or even years.

An equally important distinction between orthodox acts of warfare and drone killing is that the targets are not warned and extended the opportunity to surrender before they are slain. There is no sense in which the persons destroyed by drone strikes can be said to be respected as human beings, for they have essentially been sentenced to death with no possibility of appeal. Given the demographics involved – some of the able-bodied males targeted are adolescents located in 'hostile' territories – it seems likely that at least some of the suspects would be willing to surrender, were they made aware that the alternative is death. Certainly, it stretches credulity to claim that impressionable teenagers are 'evil terrorists' worthy of annihilation. These persons – many so vaguely suspected that their bodies have not even been connected to a name – are eliminated on the mere suspicion that they may possibly decide in the future to attempt to undertake to harm the people of the United States.

The 'Global War on Terror' was waged in response to the attacks of 11 September 2001, but some of the intended victims of targeted killing campaigns were toddlers at that time and so could not even in principle be guilty of complicity in that crime. Judging by their words, the new burgeoning terrorist class appears primarily to comprise persons outraged by the US wars in Afghanistan and Iraq, and wherever JSOC (Joint Special Operations Command) and drones have been sent out to 'find, fix, and finish' the enemy broadly construed. Under Obama, US military missions have spread throughout more than a hundred countries.[90]

Lawrence B. Wilkerson, former chief of staff to Secretary of State Colin Powell, explains the perspective problem and why the ranks of terrorist groups continue to swell in the drone age: 'From their point of view, this is not war, this is murder, and that's the way they look at it. It [drone killing] is recruiting terrorists all over the world. It's making young men and young women make the decision that the United States is their enemy and therefore worthy of their jihad.'[91]

Anwar al-Awlaki warned about this danger in an interview with *National Geographic News* on 28 September 2001, a decade before he was destroyed by a drone:

> My worry is that because of this conflict, the views of Osama bin Laden will become appealing to some of the population of the Muslim world. Never in the past were there any demonstrations raising the picture of Osama bin Laden – it has just happened now. So Osama bin Laden, who was considered to be an extremist, radical in his views, could end up becoming mainstream. That's a very frightening thing, so the US needs to be very careful and not have itself perceived as an enemy of Islam.[92]

During the conventional wars of the twentieth century, many of the soldiers slain were essentially innocent by virtue of the terms of their service. In the 1991 Gulf War, for example, the soldiers who fought for Iraqi dictator Saddam Hussein – under threat of death for refusal to do so – were clearly coerced, and yet thousands of them were slaughtered, some while attempting to retreat.[93] In the new practice of drone warfare, different but equally troubling moral problems arise, analogous to false conviction and vigilante killing within civil society. In drone strikes, targets can be misidentified, and crimes can be erroneously ascribed to innocent persons. These are not negligible matters, given that much of what is taken to be 'actionable intelligence' is acquired through the bribery of manifestly desperate people and mercenary bounty hunters.

In cases where troop protection is not at issue, the practice of targeted killing is even more worrisome, morally speaking, whether or not the suspected terrorist or militant has ever killed anyone or is planning to do so. Even if suspects are guilty of their alleged crimes, there does not seem to be any excuse for deploying drones – which invariably risk the deaths of entirely innocent bystanders – when this is not a side effect of attempting to save the lives of people on the ground. In truth, if occupying troops are in a land as a result of an illegally waged war, then they have no right to be there in the first place. To prioritize foreign soldiers' safety over that of innocent locals – exemplified by the bastion-like Green Zone in Baghdad during the US occupation – constitutes a moral farce of sorts.

Perhaps it was in part a transfer of the deadly practices prevalent in occupied Iraq which gave rise to the notion that it would be perfectly acceptable to target suspects in other lands as a standard operating procedure, even in places where the United States had never officially declared war – not even on dubious grounds. In occupied Iraq, innocent persons were routinely killed at checkpoints for refusing to obey the orders of soldiers speaking in English. Other victims failed to heed the instructions written on placards. Many of those killed, being illiterate, simply misunderstood what they were instructed to do. In addition, suspects in Iraq were regularly rounded up in night raids and sometimes killed in the process.

As misguided as the 2003 invasion of Iraq may have been, once the war had been waged, there were US troops on the ground to be protected by air cover. In contrast, in lands where no troops are being protected, there is no plausible sense in which the obliteration of a house or vehicle can be understood as an unavoidable act of war, for if those persons can be pinpointed, then surely they can be captured. What is missing is only the will to do so. Military dictators have always executed their suspected enemies without trial. Meanwhile, US leaders claim that their Predator drone program is an important part of national defense and a legitimate military practice. But in order for the alleged distinction between extrajudicial execution or assassination and targeted killing to make any sense, there must be a contrast class.

The case of Osama bin Laden is telling in this regard. Heavily armed Navy SEALs accessed his compound in Abbottabad, Pakistan. They shot and killed the unarmed Al-Qaeda leader in cold blood. This is a clear case (and there are others) where the killers 'found and fixed' a target and elected to 'finish', not capture, him, even though capture was possible. Bin Laden might have been shot using a tranquilizer gun, rather than bullets, in which case his unconscious body could have been removed from the scene just as his corpse was. The question which arises, then, is this: *What would constitute an instance of* assassination, *if every act of killing ordered by President Obama, up to and including the execution of the unarmed Osama bin Laden, is an instance of* targeted killing?

To those who would classify the Bin Laden execution as exceptional, given his preeminent role in the attacks of 11 September 2001, the case of Anwar al-Awlaki remains, given that he had been captured and held without charge in Yemen at the US government's request for more than a year. Upon his release from prison, Al-Awlaki was hunted down and killed by Predator drone. There are further problems with the official story of Al-Awlaki. The alleged grounds for his execution include what was claimed to be his complicity in the attempt by Umar Farouk to blow up an airliner above Detroit. But a drone strike aiming for Al-Awlaki was carried out on 24 December 2009, the day before Farouk's action.[94]

Among the administrators of the Predator drone program, all sight appears to have been lost of the original rationale behind killing as a last resort and in legitimate self-defense. Innocent people and suspects are killed by drone-delivered missiles as a supposed means of saving other innocent people from future possible harm, although none of the victims in unoccupied lands – whether intended targets or collateral damage – is posing a direct and immediate physical threat to anyone at the time of their deaths.

The concept of *imminence* was drained of all meaning by the Obama administration's White Paper, in emulation of the Bush administration's penchant for preemption. A true test for genuine (not Orwellian) imminence would be to answer this question: *What act of murder would immediately ensue if this suspect were not killed?* In the vast majority of cases, the answer is: *None whatsoever.* What all of this linguistic innovation ultimately reveals is that the lethal focus of the military has now seeped into the government more generally, with human life dramatically devalued in the process.

As the targeted killing campaigns have proliferated and spread throughout many lands, with hit lists growing ever lengthier, it has become a frighteningly surreal yet common practice for suspects located thousands of miles away from the US homeland to be executed because some unaccountable, anonymous person somewhere has labeled them potentially dangerous terrorists. The criterion for conviction and state execution has been weakened from 'guilty beyond a reasonable doubt of first-degree murder' to 'possibly guilty of harboring terrorist thoughts'. The suspects are deemed guilty until proven innocent, but it is impossible for them to prove their innocence, for they are not apprised of the fact that they are about to be killed. The White Paper expresses the operative inversion of the burden of proof in these terms: 'The US government may not be aware of all al-Qa'ida plots as they are developing and thus cannot be confident that none is about to occur.'

There are two sources of intelligence used in the selection of targets: HUMINT (human intelligence), usually obtained through bribery; and SIGINT (signals intelligence), which derives in part from observation and interpretation of the video footage transmitted from drones sent out to prowl. A further source of SIGINT was reported in 2014: the use of metadata siphoned from cell phone SIM card usage by suspects.[95] HUMINT is obviously vulnerable to corruption; SIGINT involves inference on the part of operators and analysts who labor under a confirmation bias, having commenced from the assumption that the area which they have been directed to watch is a site of 'suspicious' activity. The use of easily switchable and replaceable SIM cards to track suspects is, needless to say, highly fallible as well.

The 'conviction' in these cases can only be as strong as the HUMINT, which, however, is extremely weak, and nothing short of Kafkaesque when the 'crime' in question is a possible future terrorist act, which the suspect may or may not ever have decided to undertake, were he permitted to live. Perhaps targeted killing became 'the only game in town', as CIA Director Leon Panetta put it, because analysts finally recognized how undependable the testimony of persons paid to name the perpetrators of potential future crimes truly is. By killing the suspects, instead of permitting them to 'lawyer up' as they languished in prison, those in charge of defending the nation magically transformed suspects into terrorists in the public eye. This is an astonishing use of sleight of hand. It has also been the modus operandi of military dictators and totalitarian regimes throughout history.

At some point, the executors of the Predator drone program adopted a much broader criterion for targeting, that suspects 'act as terrorists might'. Such 'signature strikes', as they came to be termed, have been used to kill not 'high-value targets' but unnamed persons, who obviously have not been connected to any specific crimes, because their names are not even known. In this way, just as the discovery that torture did not yield reliable intelligence inclined administrators to adopt targeted killing as a preferred alternative to extraordinary rendition and prolonged detention without charge, signature strikes may have arisen from the realization that the HUMINT being used wasn't all that good in the case of named persons, so unnamed persons became targets as well.

Another factor in the ascendance of remote-control killing appears to have been the general conflation of criminal justice with military procedures. The thinking among some administrators may have been something like this: *During wartime, soldiers do not know the names of the rival soldiers whom they kill, so why should 'drone warriors' know the names of their targets?* The ambiguity between 'fighting crime' and 'military combat' in dealing with politically driven enemies serves to augment what is said to be the legitimate theater of killing. The terrorist suspects are only suspects until they are killed, at which point they are transformed in the official story to 'enemy soldiers'. Meanwhile, the innocent bystanders destroyed are written off as collateral damage, just as though the strike were part of an orthodox war.

The process by which *assassination* was rebranded as a legitimate military practice – now labeled *targeted killing* – involved a series of remarkable linguistic maneuvers, especially disconcerting in view of the fact that Obama had overtly denounced the Bush administration's policies which, too, traded on neologism. 'State Secrets Privilege' was adduced by the Bush administration in defense of its most egregious initiatives, including extraordinary rendition of suspects to lands where they were tortured by local security agents, and the use by the CIA and its affiliates of 'enhanced interrogation techniques' at Bagram, Abu Ghraib, Guantánamo Bay and beyond.

'State Secrets Privilege' was invoked also by the Obama administration when it refused to elucidate an arguably even worse policy: the summary execution of suspects by an institutional apparatus of homicide, aptly termed by some a 'killing machine'.[96] The Obama administration has persistently refused to offer any insight into the process by which targets are selected for elimination. It took several years for officials even to acknowledge that drone strikes were being carried out in Pakistan. Eventually the policy became undeniable, given the magnitude of independently documented harm, both physical and psychological, caused to the people of the northwestern provinces.[97]

A key factor in the elevation of death as an end in itself is the conservative nature of not only already implemented practices such as 'shoot first, ask questions later' in Iraq, but also stable institutions more generally. Institutional figureheads generally defend and extend current practices as part of the status quo, a tendency well illustrated by President Obama's adoption of the targeted killing program instigated under George W. Bush. Upon election to the office of president, Obama, being new to foreign affairs, deferred to and heeded the advice of the top brass at the Pentagon and the high-level administrators of the CIA without any apparent recognition of the role that institutional conservatism plays in narrowly delimiting what is said to be the acceptable range of 'options on the table'.[98]

On 23 January 2009, within three days of assuming the presidency, Obama had authorized a strike in Pakistan in which Fahim Qureshi was severely injured and the rest of his family destroyed. A second CIA strike on that same day killed several more people. All of the victims were civilians, but they were identified by their killers as 'militants' in the initial reports.[99] Rather than pause to reconsider the CIA's targeted killing program, the new president increased the pace of the

Predator drone strikes. A cynic might surmise that Obama felt the need to rack up some dead terrorists as quickly as possible in order to improve his tally.

One thing is clear: career administrators reach naturally for the tools familiar and readily available to them – already a part of their arsenal – and they conceptualize wars along the lines of the ones with which they are personally familiar. Institutional conservatism operates simultaneously across diverse domains, but always favors the retention of current practices, if not an expansion of their reach, in what becomes a way of demonstrating that the practices were sound all along. In the case of targeted killing, the policy preceded the debate by more than a decade, time enough to ensure that all of the figures currently in advisory positions to the president are champions of the practice. For obvious reasons, calling for a radical revision of high-level policies is not going to be welcomed with open arms by the architects of those very policies who still occupy high-level positions in the administration.

Over time, institutions undergo homogenization as they attract supporters of the policies currently in place and repel those who demur from them. Internally, within the organization itself, the culling of conscience is bound to result as persons with scruples about killing their fellow human beings will naturally avoid enlistment in or employment by what has been tellingly labeled a 'killing machine'. Moreover, the persons who ascend to leadership roles in such an institution are precisely those who prove themselves to be not only willing but also able and even enthusiastic about 'lighting up' the enemy wherever they may be found.[100]

On their face, drone strikes in lands where no US troops are on the ground to protect are no more and no less than extrajudicial executions of persons suspected of crimes – or not, as became graphic in the case of Anwar al-Awlaki's son, Abdulrahman, who was at a barbecue with some of his teenage friends when they were all destroyed by a Predator drone-delivered missile. Why did this happen? The once slick and simple answer has begun to wear thin: 'We are at war.' *When, exactly, did the United States declare war on Yemen?* A formal declaration of war would have served as a warning to persons such as Abdulrahman not to travel to that land.[101] Furthermore, civilians in nations under military attack take all possible precautions to shelter themselves from harm, and to the best of their ability they avoid active war zones.

The underlying problem here, the lethal centrism in full evidence among twenty-first-century US policymakers, derives in part from the compartmentalization of government. The military's job is to fight and kill when it is called upon to do so. Therefore, no one in the military itself is spending time and energy thinking about how to diminish the need for war. On the contrary, military personnel actively seek out opportunities to exercise their prowess at prosecuting wars. The proverbial 'options on the table' for military officers are exhausted by the various ways in which people and structures can be destroyed. When asked to draw up plans for the commander in chief during times of conflict, veterans of earlier wars are naturally inclined to offer alternatives such as 'Tomahawk missiles or Predator drones'. Veteran CIA analyst Melvin Goodman diagnoses the problem as follows:

> Military officers have never been known for distinguishing themselves in long-term geopolitical thinking or in solving problems of strategic intelligence ... the absence of an independent civilian counter to the power of military intelligence threatens civilian control of the decision to use military power and makes it more likely that intelligence will be tailored to suit the purposes of the Pentagon.[102]

At the same time, given the hierarchical structure of the military, with the commander in chief at the top, even the highest-level officers are soldiers in the sense that they are required to follow orders regarding where and when to deploy. The expression of skepticism about the wisdom of a commander's decrees amounts to an act of insubordination in this framework and subculture. When General Eric Shinseki testified in February 2003 that a successful stabilization of Iraq would likely require multiple times the number of troops projected by Secretary of Defense Donald Rumsfeld, Shinseki lost his job. Needless to say, the disastrous occupation vindicated General Shinseki's assessment.[103]

What might be termed 'the lethal turn' in US foreign policy, the decision actively to pursue death as an end in itself, perhaps began when military officers were tapped not only to advise the executive on issues of national defense but also to play key roles in the intelligence agencies. Since what military men know best is how to kill, they understandably sought to kill rather than garner and analyze information. Stated starkly, the CIA transmogrified into 'one hell of a killing machine' because it was being run by killers.[104] Targeted killing is all tactic and no strategy: there is no endpoint in sight beyond the death of human beings. It is not possible for the parties to the dispute to sign an armistice, or for the enemy to surrender. A formal institution of homicide elevates death to an end in itself.

To suggest that policies should be revisited – for example, a top military adviser's insistence that more deadly JSOC night raids are needed in Afghanistan (as was the considered opinion of General Stanley McChrystal, appointed by Obama to lead the US effort in that land) – would be to question that expert's alleged expertise. As Af-Pak, the crossing over the Afghanistan border into Pakistan to chase down fleeing insurgents, became a hard policy, the military's legitimization (to itself, if no one else) of the use of Predator drone missile strikes in hundreds of places began to weaken the initial restrictions more and more, until finally the people being killed had never fled Afghanistan at all. Now they were simply residing in an area of Pakistan, the Federally Administered Tribal Areas, said to harbor terrorists.

Suspects and terrorists had long been conflated by the Bush administration, and this confusion continued seamlessly under Obama, despite the fact that he holds a law degree (a Juris Doctor from Harvard University) and presumably understands the concept of *suspect*. Under Obama, the conflations began to proliferate and the hit lists to lengthen. All military-age men in areas designated 'hostile' were defined as combatants, a group previously defined as 'unlawful combatants' by the Bush team, thus stripping the targets of all rights under international law or the Geneva Conventions. The incredible report by John Brennan on 29 June 2011, according to which not a single civilian had been slain by the United States during the previous year's drone campaign, was finally clarified upon the revelation that, in fact, simply *being a male capable of taking up arms* in a territory deemed 'hostile' sufficed in the minds of the drone program administrators to dispatch the suspect and label the homicide an 'act of war'.[105]

The 'Kill don't capture' policy expanded to encompass several other lands, with significant initiatives being run simultaneously in Yemen, Somalia, Mali, Libya, the Philippines and, beginning in 2014, Syria as well. Somewhere along the line, the sanctity of human life – the once widespread idea, even among military personnel, that people should never be slain unless there is no possible way to avoid such a drastic measure – was forgotten by the persons penning US policy and those who authorized it, including President Obama.

About 3,000 civilians were killed on 11 September 2001. Since then, hundreds of thousands more innocent people have been killed in initiatives ostensibly intended to demonstrate that it was wrong for

Al-Qaeda to have killed innocent people. With the advent of weaponized drones, it has become possible to kill without sacrificing troops, but the focus on lethality remains the same. All sight appears to have been lost of why it was ever deemed permissible to resort to deadly force in the first place: because there was no alternative – or so it was claimed – until the drone age.

As killing became a policy aim, analysts and operators began working diligently to 'find, fix, and finish' as many suspects as possible. By early 2014, the Obama administration was reportedly 'weighing the possibility' of dispatching another US citizen by Predator drone, this time in Pakistan. The concern was whether they could meet their new, more stringent standards, including that the target present 'a continuing, imminent threat to Americans'.[106] In discussing the case, an aide relayed that 'the Defense Department was initially reluctant to place the individual on the targeting list, questioning whether he met the new standards that Mr. Obama laid out in May. But eventually the Pentagon came around.'[107] What is odd about this report is that the CIA sought to kill a US citizen and had to *persuade* the Pentagon to agree. In other words, summary execution without trial had become not a last resort but a desired outcome.[108]

The profound irony of the Predator drone program emerges when one recalls how GWOT began. The outrage against the terrorist attacks of 11 September 2001 was grounded in two separate features of the killings. First, most of the victims were civilians, not soldiers, much less armed combatants. Second, the unarmed persons were targeted in a surprise attack, making it impossible for them to defend and protect themselves. The result was a death toll of thousands of people who not only never threatened their killers but had no idea who they were. Before 9/11, the US military paid lip service to the just war tradition, including the requirements of public declaration and last resort, and the restriction on intentional killing to the active soldiers on the enemy side, with everyone else said to be protected by what is termed *noncombatant immunity*. The terrorists of 9/11 violated all of these requirements and were vehemently condemned for doing so.

Given Osama bin Laden's remarks on this matter, the perpetrators probably did conceive of the workers in the World Trade Center and the Pentagon as complicit in the crimes committed by the US military. Moreover, they may well have thought themselves to be acting as a last resort, lacking other means to address what they took to be those crimes, given the unassailability of the US military behemoth. But there is no way to interpret their surprise attack as not having violated the requirements of public declaration and the provision to the so-called soldiers (or collaborators) of the opportunity to surrender. Of course, no one ever supposed that Al-Qaeda was schooled in or claimed to champion the just war tradition. Among other things, subnational and transnational factions reject the intrinsic conservatism of the just war paradigm enshrined in the concept of 'legitimate authority', which appears to restrict 'just wars' to those waged by formal states.

What has ensued since 9/11 is a progressive wearing away of what was formerly the official policy of military institutions, to observe – or at the very least pretend to observe – those same requirements. The very labeling of the crimes of 11 September 2001 as acts of war prefigured the reconceptualization of targeted killings as retaliatory acts of war. Through the summary execution of suspects located thousands of miles away, the US government has effectively followed the lead of the killers of 9/11, modeling what has become largely unquestioned protocol on their crimes. The perpetrators of the 9/11 attacks targeted people in another land without telling them that they were being targeted, using invisible weapons camouflaged as passenger airliners to strike without warning. In seeming emulation of their avowed enemy, the US government now targets people in other lands without telling them that they are being targeted, using invisible weapons, Predator drones, which stalk and strike without warning.

The hijackers of 9/11 executed human beings for complicity in crimes of which they were deemed guilty by the killers themselves. Among those alleged crimes were the hundreds of thousands of innocent people who died as a result of the 1991 Gulf War, and the establishment of permanent US military bases in the Middle East.[109] Likewise, the suspects executed by Predator drone are deemed guilty by their killers of crimes for which they are neither indicted nor brought to trial. These stark similarities suggest that the shadowy terrorist enemy has essentially created its adversary in its image.

In view of this development – that the practice of stealth targeted killing has become a standard operating procedure on the part of a government previously said to be constrained by orthodox rules of war – it is plausible that the US military's apparent adherence to 'the rules' was never more than a rhetorical ploy designed to garner and retain public support for intervention abroad. Among other glaring evidence, the sounds bites 'all options are on the table' and 'last resort' were parroted throughout the twentieth century by war makers, long before the drone age, in apparent incognizance of the inherent contradiction between the two.

At this point in history, 'last resort' has come to mean that the administration has decided to wield deadly force – end of story. To pronounce that 'all options are on the table' is to acknowledge that the use of military means is not a last resort. *Last resort* is but a metaphor in the mouths of the leaders of First World nations capable of exerting influence in a variety of other, nonlethal ways.[110] Just war rhetoric, rich as it is in propaganda value, in this way set the stage for the era of remote-control killing. The CIA became the primary executor of the program in countries where Congress had not previously authorized military intervention – presumably in order to avoid potential legal tangles. But the *moral* authority to kill was assumed by Bush, and after him by Obama, as a result of the widespread and uncritical acceptance of the just war tradition's concept of 'legitimate authority'. Not only does hawkish just war rhetoric lead to military action, but the very availability of deadly weapons inclines administrators to reach for them as 'tools'. A leader concerned with shoring up his image as 'strong' may playact what he believes people think brave leaders should do, drawing on examples from earlier eras. Whenever the possibility of a war is floated, some among the populace accept the very first rationalizations proffered, reasoning along the lines of former Secretary of State Madeleine Albright in a remark to Colin Powell: 'What's the point of having this superb military that you're always talking about if we can't use it?'[111]

As things stand, war – and now targeted killing, having been rebranded by policymakers as a part of war – has been normalized to the point where it is thought of by political leaders first, rather than last. It suffices to interpret 'last' metaphorically to defend such wars as 'just', exactly as was done in the past. In deciding to wield the mighty weapons of war, including Hellfire missile-equipped Predator drones, due consideration is virtually never given to the long-term consequences with which any rational policymaker should be concerned. This is because 'unintended consequences', including blowback, are forgiven as permissible 'collateral damage' in military orthodoxy.[112] Abstract conceptions of justice and short-term consequences guide the thinking of leaders who wage war – in whatever guise – and those who support them.

The president's advisers comprise a homogeneous cross-section of people who *already believe* that what they are doing is good, and therefore that more of the same is automatically better. These institutional dynamics help to explain the in some ways baffling case of Barack Obama, who persistently pledged on the campaign trail before being elected president that he would reverse many of the Bush policies but instead dramatically expanded the Predator drone program. The new president may have halfheartedly rejected torture (while declining to prosecute the Bush-era torturers), but he substituted summary execution in its stead. As his own rhetoric began to parrot famously alliterative Pentagon-speak, the influence of the military on Obama's policy became more and more patent: 'We will continue to use every element of our national power to disrupt, to dismantle, and defeat the violent extremists who threaten us.'[113]

The very names of the Predator and Reaper aircraft convey a switch in focus from defense to death. Lethal centrism has reached a new acme – or nadir – in the drone age, arguably as a result of the very fact that the CIA, an institution formerly concerned with gathering and analyzing information, has been militarized. As Mark Lowenthal, a former CIA official, explains: 'There's a huge cultural and generational issue at stake here. A lot of the people hired since 9/11 have done nothing but tactical work for the past 12 years, and intellectually it's very difficult to go from a tactical approach to seeing things more strategically.'[114] The 'tactical work' in question is none other than targeted killing, the focus of the Agency over more than a decade of the twenty-first century, during which the CIA has been staffed and even headed up at crucial turning points by former military officers. All of this makes it difficult to see how the black ops rebranded as standard operating procedure might be reined in, given the tendency of institutions toward conservatism.

Under the advice and direction of military officers, the intelligence establishment came to share the Pentagon's longstanding focus on lethality, with much more effort and energy invested in the tactical means to kill than in strategic analysis. The finest, most sophisticated implements of homicide have been developed to use against individual suspects by a military behemoth. At the same time, extreme risk aversion has given rise to 'wars' being fought with no immediate danger to any allied combatant's life, while non-national civilians continue to be destroyed as the so-called collateral damage of remote-control killing missions. All of this intentional homicide is carried out under the further assumption that the persons identified as 'insurgents' or 'militants' are doing anything more than defending their community or rising up against a despotic central regime.

Over the course of less than a decade, the US government developed an extensive Predator drone program to penetrate large swaths of land where villagers previously lived in peace – certainly with no fear of Hellfire missiles raining down upon them. In the notorious turf wars between the Department of Defense (DoD) and the CIA, the military won out, ideologically speaking, perhaps for no better reason than that it is easier to kill than it is to persuade people to change their views or to divine their intentions. The job of the military is to kill, and they do it very well. The original mission of the CIA was to provide sound intelligence, which they have failed to do time and time again. If Predator drone targeted killing became 'the only game in town', that was *only* because the CIA failed to devise any other 'game' for dealing with Al-Qaeda. The abject failure of the CIA may explain why suddenly a military officer, General David Petraeus, was tapped by Obama to lead the CIA in 2011: because he had been successful. Military officers, who rise in the ranks in part for their obedience, generally do what they are told to do well. But there is a profound problem here: the skills needed to be a commander of killers are very different from the skills needed to head up a competent intelligence agency. In some ways, the CIA was effectively shuttered, becoming tantamount to a branch of the DoD to be enlisted to kill suspects in places where war had never officially been waged.

At various points, 'troop surge' proposals were floated in both Iraq and Afghanistan. Occasionally, 'hearts and minds' rhetoric has been recycled. In truth, the creative initiative of military officers is always constrained by the walls of the lethality box. The choices are basically to increase troop presence and ramp up the application of deadly force, or else to retreat. In order to appear strong, military leaders may focus on how to devise ways to kill more people – and to do so faster – with body counts as the measure of success. As the CIA came to embrace and promote a military mindset, the 'actionable intelligence' permitting the execution of a perceived potential enemy proved to be much easier to come by than the sort of evidence which would be needed for conviction of a criminal in a court of law.

One might expect civilian institutions to make every effort to protect innocent human life. The CIA has instead championed the practice of summary execution of suspects. 'Kill don't capture' policy inverts the burden of proof, assuming that, far from having an inviolable right to life, human beings have no rights at all – provided only that they happen to reside in a land governed by a petty despot willing to cede his compatriots' rights (as if they were his own) in exchange for military aid. The killers, operating from their secure bunkers in Nevada, or in drone stations now dotting the globe, continue to act as did the obedient soldiers of centuries past. The 'killing machine' is fortified by the self-image of uniform-clad operators as soldiers, who follow orders unflinchingly, but the reason for this military exigency (to avoid endangering fellow troops) has evaporated away. The operators do not act as analysts, for they have no means by which to assess the value of the intelligence provided to them. Instead, obeying their superior officers, just as good soldiers have always done, they accept orders to kill, on the basis of intelligence assumed to be valid.

The US government proudly vaunts the terrorists (suspects) stopped in their tracks. However, human rights groups have compiled the names of many civilians also destroyed. According to the Bureau of Investigative Journalism, by January 2014, the Obama administration had killed at least 2,400 people, in 390 strikes, with a minimum of 273 victims known to be civilians.[115] The estimates vary greatly, however, depending on the source. Reprieve, a UK-based human rights organization, estimated the toll of drone deaths by 2014 to be about 4,700. The sheer vagueness of terms such as 'militant', 'insurgent' and 'associate', and the vast disparities between the different statistics reported, suggest that no one really knows how many noncombatants have found themselves at the receiving end of a Hellfire missile. In many cases, the successful elimination of named high-value targets such as Anwar al-Awlaki and Baitullah Mehsud was preceded by multiple failed attempts. Who were the nameless people killed in their stead?[116]

By 2009, many members of the Taliban and Al-Qaeda had already been killed or had fled Afghanistan. Many thousands more people lost their lives in Iraq, and both countries were rendered dysfunctional when the US invaders failed to quell postwar chaos.[117] Next to the hundreds of thousands of people destroyed in the Bush-waged wars in Afghanistan and Iraq, the death toll of the Obama administration policies may appear modest. But the expansive Predator drone program is far more insidious, given the potential for adoption by governments all over the world, in emulation of the US executive. The power-hungry leaders of small countries could never invade and occupy sovereign nations, but they surely can hold their own versions of 'Terror Tuesdays' and select political enemies for elimination by Predator drone. In order to gain generous US military support for such a purge, an unscrupulous leader needs only to characterize his adversaries in sufficiently Al-Qaeda-esque terms.

PART II
FIX

PART II

CHAPTER 5
STRIKE FIRST, SUPPRESS QUESTIONS LATER

'If America continues to attack the innocent people of the tribal areas then we are forced to attack America. We will make new plans to attack them. You prepare for jihad and this is the time of jihad.'

Hakimullah Mehsud, Tehrik-i-Taliban Pakistan
leader from 2009 to 2013[118]

'Indefinite detention is pretty tame compared
to being destroyed by a drone.'

US Senator Rand Paul[119]

IMAGINE:

On a clear spring day you return home from work to find that the house next door has disappeared. In its place lies a deep crater. It's as though a spaceship homed in from above, engulfed the building along with the inhabitants, and then flew away. Scattered rubble marks the peripheries of a property which once was a hub of life.

Upon opening your front door, you see that whatever demolished your neighbors' former place of residence – and whoever may have been there at the time – also created a general mess of everything you own. All of the glasses and plates are broken. Bent picture frames and shards of ceramic vases are strewn about the floor. The refrigerator lies on its side, and much of the furniture is mangled.

Everyone in your family was away when the event took place, so you are able to breathe a sigh of relief that no one close to you was hurt by what must have been a forceful impact indeed. You pick up the phone, hands trembling, to call the police and find out what's going on, but discover that it's out of order. The electricity and water have been disrupted as well. You reach for your cell phone only to find that it, too, no longer works. You peer out the window anxiously, now afraid for your own safety. There is not a single soul in sight. Eventually you steel yourself to go back outside and get to the bottom of this.

You see no one for blocks and blocks, but upon arriving at a cluster of stores a mile or so away, you learn from the small group assembled there that a military strike has been carried out against suspected terrorists. This news comes as a real shock to you, as your neighbors are all upstanding, law-abiding citizens, at least as far as you know. In fact, the couple who lived in the now nonexistent house next to yours were retired workers living on a pension. Their grandchildren sometimes came over to play in the yard, and everyone seemed perfectly normal to you.

However, you are swiftly apprised by the local authorities that the son of the couple was one of the suspects. He had been pegged as a member of a radical Muslim jihadist movement associated with Al-Qaeda, and the strike was intended to take him out. According to the latest intelligence, he was planning to visit his parents that afternoon. It turned out, instead, that his wife decided to take the children to pay a surprise visit to their grandparents. They arrived with a picnic lunch in the suspected jihadist's car at about noon. Shortly thereafter, all of them were obliterated – the mother, the children and the grandparents – by a Hellfire missile delivered by Predator drone.

That night you awaken abruptly in a cold sweat while dreaming about a neighborhood party you attended last summer. Suddenly you recall that you exchanged business cards with the suspected jihadist back when you first shook hands.

The above scenario might seem farfetched to some, but it is more or less what has been transpiring for years now in several countries on the other side of the planet. In places most Americans could not locate on a map, the US government conducts deadly Predator drone strikes against targets identified as hostile threats to the homeland by spies bribed to provide 'actionable intelligence'. The very same practice carried out within the borders of the United States would be a violation of domestic criminal law. The primary reason why the above thought experiment rarely rises to the level of consciousness in the minds of supporters of US wars abroad may simply be that they know that no other nation currently in existence could get away with that sort of action in their own neighborhood. But is this not a capitulation to 'might makes right'? Would the same people be willing to accept Germany's killing machine, if only the Nazis had won World War II?

Within civil society, the execution without trial of suspects – vigilante killing – is illegal. *Why, then,* drone activists want to know, *is the US executive being permitted this practice abroad?* If extrajudicial killing is wrong within US borders, then how can it be right to do this to people located in other lands? Perhaps the more important question is: *How is this being allowed to happen in places thousands of miles away?* Most of the people living under lethal drones lack the means to make their way to the United States, even if they happen to hate the US government, which more and more of them surely do in the drone age. As one survivor in Waziristan explains: 'Drone strikes have turned all of Waziristan into enemies. We were not their enemy before the drone attack, but now they have made us their enemy by killing us with drones.'[120]

During Barack Obama's first term as president, there was very little audible outcry against drone strikes to quell in the United States, in large part because the existence of the targeted killing program was not officially acknowledged, and civilian casualties were systematically denied. Note that in Nazi Germany, too, the institution of homicide was initially a carefully guarded state secret. History has a way, eventually, of bringing the sordid details of institutional carnage and complicity to light.[121] In the case of the US government's targeted killing program, the intentional assassination by executive order of US citizens marked a turning point. 'Everything changed', according to civil libertarians, not on 11 September 2001, but a decade later, on 30 September 2011, when Anwar al-Awlaki, a US citizen, was deliberately tracked down and executed without trial by his own government, in an action smacking of tyranny. Even some military supporters who accept that 'war is hell' and do not balk at the resultant collateral damage when non-national threats to the US republic are targeted, were given pause by the use of drones by President Obama to impose the death sentence upon citizens without trial.

Perhaps Obama, in authorizing the elimination of US citizen Anwar al-Awlaki, and possibly his son as well, was giddy in the aftermath of his 'call' on 2 May 2011 to kill Osama bin Laden rather than take him alive. Perhaps the president was simply jockeying to maximize short-term political gains by painting himself as strong on defense so that he would win his upcoming re-election campaign. Al-Awlaki was portrayed as a high-level, operational AQAP (Al-Qaeda on the Arabian Peninsula) leader and destroyed by 'drone warrior' Obama, who had been widely praised for hunting down and killing Osama bin Laden, despite the fact that the Al-Qaeda leader was unarmed at the time of his death. As the jubilant celebrations in the streets of US cities attested, many Americans viewed the point-blank execution of Bin Laden at his compound in Abbottabad, Pakistan, as an act of just retribution.

Only some form of utilitarian reasoning might yield a conclusion to the effect that a US citizen should be summarily executed without trial by his very own government, as was Anwar al-Awlaki, who had publicly condemned the attacks of 11 September 2001. The Obama administration offered a controversial legal pretext in explaining its quest to kill Al-Awlaki. What constitutes 'due process' is, according to the White Paper, essentially up to the president to decide and does not require any form of judicial involvement whatsoever. The underlying assumption is utilitarian in spirit: that violations of civil rights in a few cases are outweighed by the greater good.

Not all Americans buy the utilitarian or 'greater good' argument when it comes to the targeting and summary execution of US citizens suspected of complicity in terrorism. Treason is a crime, for which suspected traitors must be indicted and stand trial. Under the US Constitution, citizens have rights to life, liberty and the pursuit of happiness, in addition to more specific rights such as freedom of expression and a fair trial, all protected by codified laws. Extrajudicial killings conducted by the executive, whose power and authority to act on behalf of the people are predicated on the president's vow to uphold the Constitution, raise pressing questions about the proper role and limits of government. Can the executive branch of a democratic government of the people, by the people, and for the people be used to strip *those very people* of their most fundamental rights, including the right to dissent from their government's policies?

Anwar al-Awlaki was said by the US government to be linked to various terrorist actions, having served as a 'spiritual adviser' to the perpetrators. Outspoken skeptics, including his father, have asked whether the propagandist and Islamist cleric ever committed a crime himself or directly facilitated anyone else's commission of a crime. Was the extent of Al-Awlaki's complicity his vocal expression of dissent from the practices of the US military and his praise of the jihadists resisting the US occupations and attempting (in their view) to defend Islam from the hegemon in other parts of the world? Can the mere fact that various terrorists have cited Al-Awlaki's sermons and harsh criticisms of US military policy as a source of inspiration implicate him in acts of terrorism? A sober consideration of the details of the case – to the extent to which they can be ascertained – suggests that government officials appear above all to have wanted the preacher to stop talking, which was why they silenced him for good.[122]

The lines between free speech and terrorism seem to have been effaced in this case, but without a judicial review of the evidence alleged to demonstrate Al-Awlaki's guilt, we are left only with the narrative penned by his killers, according to whom he was an evil terrorist. His father, Nasser al-Awlaki, filed lawsuits in which a conflicting narrative was put forth: that his son had been unjustly targeted and executed in a flagrant and inexcusable violation of the US Constitution. Calling this homicide an 'act of war' does not seem to help matters, for Al-Awlaki was not attempting to kill anyone when he was slain. Moreover, he was tracked for a lengthy period of time, which strongly suggests that it would have been possible to capture him and make him stand trial for whatever crimes he was believed to have committed.

The US Department of Justice's White Paper was composed to explain and defend the government's assiduous pursuit of Al-Awlaki. In the document, intuitively comprehensible concepts such as 'imminence' have been redefined so that it is unclear whether any act of murder would be excluded by any killer claiming to wish to defend himself from a future potential act of aggression.[123] Indeed, the reasoning of the White Paper would seem to apply equally well, *mutatis mutandis*, to the case of Nidal Hasan, the former army psychiatrist who shot to death thirteen people and injured thirty more at Fort Hood military base in Texas on 5 November 2009. Hasan regarded himself as engaged in a war against an evil enemy (the US government) and claimed that he wished to stop those who became his victims from deploying to Afghanistan, where they would contribute to crimes against Islamic people. The killer was convicted of all charges and sentenced to death, and the Obama legal team would obviously deny that the terms of their White Paper are applicable in his case. But the legal framework embodies a moral framework, which appears to have been Nidal Hasan's own, provided only that the identity of the enemy be changed from 'Al-Qaeda' to 'the US military', and the geographies in danger to drone strike sites:

> *By its nature, therefore, the threat posed by the US military and its associated forces demands a broader concept of imminence in judging when a person continually planning drone attacks presents an imminent threat, making the use of force appropriate. In this context, imminence must incorporate considerations of the relevant window of opportunity, the possibility of reducing collateral damage to civilians, and the likelihood of heading off future disastrous attacks on the inhabitants of Pakistan, Yemen, Somalia, Afghanistan and Iraq.*

The Bush administration legal team invoked the concept of 'unlawful combatant' in order to evade legal tangles over both lawful combatants taken prisoner, who would be protected by the Geneva Conventions, and civilians taken prisoner, who would be protected by the laws of civil society. The Obama administration, too, conceived of 'terrorist suspects' as devoid of rights, and declined to prosecute Bush administration officials for their role in the rendering, incarceration, torture and, in some cases, killing of so-called unlawful combatants. Many of the prisoners were innocent and cleared for release yet remain locked up at Guantánamo Bay to this day. It appears (though we cannot know, given the secrecy of the procedure used to 'convict' him) that Anwar al-Awlaki was deemed an 'unlawful combatant' by the powers that be, making him fair game, they believed, for targeted killing (which looks indistinguishable from summary execution without trial), despite the fact that he was born in the United States and may have committed the 'crime' of serving as a source of inspiration to some active terrorists.

Is the geographical location of a US citizen relevant to whether he may be deprived of his very life without being so much as charged with a crime, much less tried before being sentenced to death? The branches of the US government were purposely segregated by the nation's founders precisely in order to prevent the worst threat to democracy: the potential for tyranny in the executive branch. With the executive serving as the police, the judge, the jury and the executioner in cases of targeted killing of US citizens, a disturbing conflation of the formerly separate branches of government has arisen in the drone age.

These concerns were broached unforgettably in the halls of Congress on 6 March 2013, when US Senator Rand Paul staged a thirteen-hour filibuster in opposition to the appointment of John Brennan as the director of the CIA. Paul was not specifically alleging that the killing of Anwar al-Awlaki was illegal. Instead, he was demanding that the government elucidate its criteria for placing the names of US citizens on its 'hit list'. The Kentucky senator and other civil libertarians and staunch defenders of the Constitution are concerned about the prospect of drone strikes being used to execute US citizens in the homeland. Can persons suspected of complicity in terrorism be obliterated without warning by a drone strike as they sip a latte in Starbucks? Both the president and the attorney general, Eric Holder, were evasive on this issue, suggesting that, although they had not done so yet, they 'might' target US citizen suspects such as Anwar al-Awlaki not only abroad but also within US sovereign territory.

Eventually the administration acceded to Senator Paul's request, explicitly acknowledging that the US president does not possess the authority to kill a noncombatant citizen on US soil. The day after the filibuster, Attorney General Holder wrote to Senator Paul: 'Does the president have the authority to use a weaponized drone to kill an American not engaged in combat on American soil? The answer is no.'[124] Liberty lovers expelled a collective sigh of relief, but the reason for the administration's months of reticence and resistance to address Senator Paul's question, even as John Brennan's confirmation as CIA director hung in the balance, emerges upon recognition that the answer leads directly to another, far more vexing, question: *Was not the unarmed Al-Awlaki a noncombatant when he was killed in Yemen?* If he was a noncombatant on Yemeni soil, why would he be subject to execution there but not on US soil? If the administration owns, as it seems to have done, thanks to Senator Paul's filibuster, that Al-Awlaki could not have been legally executed without trial on US soil, then why and how was this permissible in Yemen? Is geographical location at all relevant to a person's legal status and civil rights? Can relocation alone, the mere crossing over the line demarcating a border, transform a noncombatant into an unlawful combatant to be taken out by Predator drone? This implication is unintuitive, to put it mildly, and does not cohere with international conventions. Anwar al-Awlaki was not executed by the Yemeni but by the US government on Yemeni soil.

The claim is frequently made by drone program advocates, echoing the reasoning of the White Paper, that when capture is 'infeasible', killing becomes permissible. The targeting of Al-Awlaki, then, is supposed to be a case where a Predator drone strike was carried out because of the 'infeasibility' of capture. However, critics have rightly observed that Al-Awlaki was tracked for a lengthy period of time before being killed. He was, in fact, incarcerated in a Yemeni prison, at the US government's request, for more than a year, which alone shows that it was possible to capture him. Anwar al-Awlaki was killed in Yemen despite the feasibility of capturing him, as demonstrated by the fact that he had been taken into custody before. The US government *chose* to execute a US citizen rather than indict him for treason and allow him to stand trial.

Feasibility is one of the many wiggle words of the White Paper, along with *imminent threat* and *associate*. All of these terms are open to a wide range of interpretation and are intentionally vague, apparently so as to permit whichever instances of execution the 'kill committee' decides on, and to justify *ex post facto* the acts of homicide carried out by operators under order. Attorney General Holder's sloppily written response to Senator Paul further illustrates the potential for ambiguity inherent to bureaucratically crafted rules of engagement (ROE). The wording of the question and answer – written by the highest authority at the US Department of Justice – can reasonably be interpreted to mean that 'no American may be killed *unless he is engaged in combat on American soil*'. The White Paper, of course, asserts the contrary, claiming the right of the executive to kill a US citizen such as Anwar al-Awlaki while located abroad.

The foundation of modern democratic societies is the rule of law, including such principles as habeas corpus, the right to be explicitly charged with a crime before being taken away, imprisoned and, above all, executed. The case of Anwar al-Awlaki raises not minor concerns or mere niceties but major problems for any ostensibly democratic nation claiming to champion liberty and civil rights. The persons who attain the status of president of a constitutional democracy have been elected by the populace, but they are obviously no less fallible than the human beings who selected them as their leader.

The purpose of 'checks and balances' is to circumvent to the greatest possible extent disastrously unjust outcomes on the part of institutions designed and erected to serve justice itself. In some domestic criminal court cases, guilty convictions are eventually over-turned when it emerges that somewhere along the line – for example, in the laboratory analysis of DNA – something went awry.[125] In other cases, the detective-gathered evidence said to demonstrate the defendant's guilt later proves to have been dubious. Sometimes concern with professional advancement exerts an influence on an ambitious officer's work.[126] Tragically, convicted capital criminals have on occasion been exonerated only after their state execution. In all of these sorts of cases, mistakes were made. Some were errors of judgment, others a matter of individual corruption or co-option.

No one can reasonably deny that human beings are fallible and subject to manipulation and corruption, and there is no reason for excluding the same possibility in cases involving the military and intelligence analysts who single out suspects for annihilation by Predator drone hits abroad. These cases are exceptional only in that the perpetrators are protected by an impenetrable shield of secrecy said to be necessary for reasons of 'national security'. In truth, this alleged pretext for secrecy serves above all to protect the perpetrators against allegations of having wrongfully killed. Notorious cases in both Afghanistan and Iraq, where either enlisted soldiers or privately contracted security forces deliberately killed civilians, suffice to show that the personnel involved in war theaters are every bit as subject to immorality and criminality as are people in civil society.[127]

It is impossible to check the tradecraft of the analysts who designate names for the US government's official hit lists, of which there appear to be three: one at the National Security Council, one at the CIA, and one at the Department of Defense (DoD). PBS reports that a hodgepodge of rules and criteria have been used, and the authority to 'make the call' has been spread out among multiple command strata:

Permission to kill also was granted variously, depending on the agency involved and the location of the person targeted … Some individuals could be killed on the say-so of tactical commanders without approval from above, while others could not be killed without senior military or even cabinet-level approval; still others could not be killed without presidential approval. Until July 2009, the military's lethal drones targeted individuals in Iraq and Afghanistan, and now most of the kills take place in Afghanistan; the CIA's drones, on the other hand, killed people in countries where US forces were not conducting military operations, including Yemen, Somalia, and Pakistan. Presidential approval was absolutely required to operate in these countries. In Somalia, where there was no effective government, once the White House approved the overall mission, all that was needed were multiple CIA or JSOC confirmations of the target's location – so the wrong person wouldn't be killed. In Yemen, where the government of Ali Abdullah Saleh had agreed to allow the CIA and JSOC to operate, authority was delegated to commanders in the region. In Pakistan, however, in August 2010, after a number of civilians had died in drone attacks and the public there began to grow more vocal in its opposition to them, CIA director Leon Panetta announced that he would personally approve every drone strike. The director's input had not been required since the first year after 9/11.[128]

As a result of the incessantly invoked 'State Secrets Privilege' under a national security pretext, the populace paying for these executions has no idea what the evidential basis for the 'convictions' might be. How does one's name end up on a 'hit list'? Once mistakenly placed there, how could it ever be removed?[129] As the wars in Afghanistan and Iraq dragged on, not only operational terrorists but also the financial supporters of anti-American groups came to be regarded as suitable targets for execution. Were outspoken propagandists considered fair game as well?

No one denies that Anwar al-Awlaki emitted 'fighting words'. Did he do anything else, or is outspoken dissent and the public praise of jihadists now a capital crime? This controversial case suggests that the US government has stepped onto a slippery slope, conflating antiwar dissent and factional terrorism, and threatening the very free speech essential to a flourishing democracy.[130] Was Al-Awlaki the 'Bin Laden of the internet'? If the Fort Hood killer was inspired by Al-Awlaki, the fact remains: Nidal Hasan *chose* to fire his gun at those who became his victims. Words are not bullets, and blogposts are not bombs.

The execution by Predator drone of Anwar al-Awlaki has received far more attention than any other drone strike treated in the press for the simple reason that he was an intentionally targeted US citizen.[131] But the very same doubts raised by critics in this case apply to every other person alleged to be a 'collaborator' or 'supporter' or 'associate' of violent terrorists, many of whom may simply have been protesting against what they took to be US war crimes. There are important conceptual distinctions between suspects and terrorists, and between dissenters and killers. The US government appears to have lost all sight of these distinctions, perhaps as a result of the militarization of its intelligence agencies.

In drone strikes, the victims – both the guilty and the innocent – are stripped of all rights, even the most basic, the right to life. The persons suspected of wrongdoing are not simply incarcerated without indictment and left to rot in prison cells (the fate suffered by many detainees since 11 September 2001) but *annihilated* in what amounts to the shortest of all possible stays on death row, with no provision for appeal or re-examination of the evidence which led to the 'conviction'. Yet it is well known that suspects charged with capital crimes within civil society are often acquitted, as the evidence proves unconvincing to a jury of their peers. Jurors in US criminal trials are sternly instructed by the court that a verdict of guilty must be established *beyond a reasonable doubt*. The slick technological apparatus sustaining drone strikes serves as a red herring, diverting attention from what matters more than anything else: whether it is true that the persons about to be killed are guilty of capital crimes, and deserve to die.

The consequences of drone strikes are irrevocable. Yet even in places where the United States is not officially at war, and there are no troops on the ground to protect, the emphasis is on the killing, with little if any attention given to the fundamentally dubious basis – usually paid 'testimony' – of the intelligence leading up to remote-control homicides. What appears to have happened in these cases is that the martial law of lands under occupation (in Afghanistan and Iraq) has been applied in places where there is no occupation, and so there are no corresponding troops to support. The targeted killings are labeled *acts of war* as though there were some sort of urgency which precluded any other action. But viewed from the ground, the deaths look indistinguishable from unlawful assassination, and they overlap with acts of war *only* in the effective impunity of the killers.

In fact, remote-control killers are granted a blanket power to kill not shared by soldiers on the ground during an occupation, who are required to observe certain conventions, such as the provision to enemy soldiers of the opportunity to surrender, should they be willing to lay down their arms. The persons killed in most drone strikes do not bear any arms. They are assumed to be intrinsically incapable of surrendering, having been christened *metaphysical terrorists* by their killers. In reality, the targets are suspects. But the verification problem is far more profound than the mere lack of gumshoes on the ground. For what might constitute a 'verification' of conviction by hearsay? To make matters worse, when analysts are rewarded for producing names for hit lists, and risk professional censure for failing to do so, their 'qualifying reasons' may become flimsier and flimsier, until at last unnamed 'suspects' are being killed. Indeed, this is precisely what has come to pass in so-called signature strikes.

Over a short period of time, the criteria used to determine whom to add to the US government's hit lists (once said to feature 'high-value targets') expanded to encompass such 'crimes' as being located in the northwestern provinces of Pakistan and carrying a rifle, or riding around in a truck 'in the manner of insurgents'. Surely the most egregious 'criterion' to date is that of simply *being* a military-age male situated in a so-called hostile territory, what is tantamount to racial profiling and gross injustice whenever an innocent person is slain. Anyone who does not immediately recognize the injustice involved in the use of such a standard for signature strikes should pause to consider whether foreign journalists of military age who happen to be male and happen to be reporting on events in territories deemed hostile – and who obviously are not terrorists – would not also be acceptable targets according to the same ROE. Clearly, this pseudo-judicial structure does not promote but undermines freedom – above all, freedom of speech, which entails the freedom to dissent from unjust practices.

The eeriness of what is being done with weaponized drones emerges in real-time films of the strikes, many of which have been posted on YouTube. The persons 'employed on' are splotches on a screen, with no identifying markers beyond the fact that someone somewhere, whether salaried analyst or bribed informant, has fingered them as terrorists. The 'kill committee', a group of bureaucrats – including, remarkably, the US president – deems in secret deliberations behind closed doors which reasons are sufficient for adding a name to a hit list. The human intelligence is what locates the targets, but in every case it is the weakest link in the 'kill chain', for the persons paid to provide and produce actionable intelligence may or may not be concerned with avoiding harm to innocent people, much less with telling the truth.

Even in cases where the precise identity of the persons killed has been ascertained, there are entirely rational grounds for doubt about the 'actionable intelligence' allegedly demonstrating guilt whenever it is being provided by bounty hunters, whose primary concern is to earn as much money as they can, and as quickly as possible. The historical record attests that in previous episodes where similar 'rounding up' and bounty-hunting practices were carried out, some of the informants were shameless mercenaries, while others merely selected for execution people against whom they held grudges or whom they wished to see eliminated for one reason or another. It happened in Nazi Germany and Vichy France, and it happened in Afghanistan and Iraq.

According to Akbar Ahmed, some of the informants in Pakistan have capitalized on the opportunity to seek revenge against personal enemies: 'Tribesmen serving as paid CIA informants were directing American drones against their rivals, falsely claiming that these individuals were terror targets.'[132] There is no worse injustice than to execute innocent persons, which is bound to happen when 'bad guys' such as warlords are rewarded for furnishing the names of other 'bad guys'. Why is such gross injustice permitted in Predator drone cases but not in domestic disputes? The answer seems reflexively to be: 'This is war.' However, the pretext of needing to protect soldiers does not apply in unoccupied territories such as Yemen and Pakistan.

Could a single terrorist suspect pose a serious threat to the very existence of a nation state? Even Osama bin Laden was rendered impotent the moment Navy SEALs took over his compound, and he would have been equally incapable of masterminding further terrorist acts had he been placed in solitary confinement rather than killed. The disproportionate attention and massive resources allocated to stopping a single person whose activities led to the deaths of, at most, several thousand people, is put into proper relief only by comparing the civilian casualty toll of US military campaigns in places such as Vietnam, Afghanistan and Iraq. Tragically, the long shadow cast by Bin Laden and others identified as evil terrorists has served to rationalize in the minds of military supporters large-scale policies of destruction and death.

A glaring problem with the pretext of national self-defense is the vast power asymmetry between a single supposedly threatening individual and the state itself. The assumption on the part of the killers is that drone strikes are a means by which to secure the homeland, so the more killing the better. Judging by the anti-American protests in places such as Pakistan, the practice has proven to degrade the security of the very people paying for these practices, as every drone strike creates more outrage against what is perceived to be the despicable and ignoble US hegemon, precisely the sort of anger which gave rise to the terrorist attacks of 11 September 2001.

The targeted killing of suspects abroad is accepted as part of fighting a 'just war' by many US military supporters, but would they regard as permissible the delivery of a Hellfire missile via Predator drone to their neighbor's home? Despite the explicit rejection of racism and sexism in modern Western societies, the age-old prejudices inherent to war linger on. Non-threatening non-nationals are treated according to a different set of moral standards, and they do not enjoy the same protections as 'outsider' civilians. To accept this wartime division is to deny outright the *Universal Declaration of Human Rights*. Some people are more equal than others.

Even if it is true that people are subject to and protected by only the laws of the land where they reside, what remains to be explained is how the elected officials of one nation might have any rights over the residents of another, as is presumed in Predator drone targeted killings abroad. Virtually no one in the United States would accept that a suspect regarded as a threat to another nation but located on US soil could be freely assassinated – along with anyone else who happened to be around at the time. Not even Israel would be openly permitted to carry out such an act in the United States, one surmises.

Whistleblowers such as Private Bradley Edward Manning (whose name was legally changed to Chelsea Elizabeth Manning in 2013) and former National Security Agency employee Edward Snowden who step forward to reveal crimes committed by the US government to the citizens paying for them are branded by officials as *traitors*, and thereby arrayed in the same category as Anwar al-Awlaki. But to reinterpret non-violent dissidence as a form of treachery is to step onto a continuum at the end of which only totalitarianism lies. Under fascist regimes, those who sympathize with dissenters come to be branded as traitors by extension. The concept of *associate*, crucial to the White Paper, is notoriously vague, and does not bode well for the future of an open society. It is precisely through this sort of bureaucratic neologism that governments initially supported by the populace can devolve into dictatorships, as happened throughout postcolonial Africa and Latin America during the Cold War.

Those who would suppress dissent from all US policies, even when they are demonstrably criminal, fail to recognize that the laws of democratic societies have progressed morally only as a result of the willingness of some people to stand up for what they believe to be right and to protest against what they believe to be wrong. Is it even conceptually possible, in a genuine democracy, to decry as 'enemies of the state' persons who oppose US military practice, when it is the right of every citizen to have opinions and to express them? Dissidents such as Manning and Snowden – and soldiers such as Camilo Mejía who refuse to redeploy to what they have come to believe are criminal wars – are cast as traitors not for their potential or intention to kill US nationals but because they supposedly 'inspire' others to do so, just as Anwar al-Awlaki did.

When the soldiers of formal military institutions demur from the campaigns in which they have been deployed, as did Private Manning, who disseminated hundreds of thousands of classified cables and video footage documenting war crimes, they are castigated as criminals by those who perpetrated the very crimes illuminated. Manning was not executed but sentenced to thirty-five years in prison for attempting to reveal to US taxpayers what their money was being used to fund. The fact that the revelations painted the US government in a negative, even evil, light was perversely blamed upon the whistleblower, when in fact the fault lies only with those complicit in the scandals exposed.

With millions of persons holding high-level security clearances in the private-contracting age of the military, there is no way to guarantee that state secrets will be kept, as was demonstrated unforgettably by the disclosures of Edward Snowden in June 2013.[133] Surely another dissident will pop up again in the not-too-distant future out of the many people potentially capable of accessing and sharing classified documents. Aggressive covert foreign policy initiatives are shortsighted and misguided in that they commence from the assumption that no one will ever find out – or if they do, they won't care. But the people on the ground, the victims, find out immediately, and the bereft survivors do care, and some among them decide to retaliate violently against what they take to be crimes.

Assuming that these mass exposures of the dark side of US foreign policy will continue on the current schedule (every two years or so), the US government would do better to change its ways than to lock up the whistleblowers and throw away the key. Such dissidents are easily replaced – as readily as insurgents and fledgling terrorists – whenever the galvanizing war crimes persist. The sentencing of Private Manning to thirty-five years in prison will not deter dissenters from taking action in the future. Instead, they may follow the lead of Edward Snowden and seek political asylum in other lands rather than face discreditation and indictment by the perpetrators whose much worse crimes have been brought to light. Ultimately, all 'state secrets' in a democracy will be declassified, after which the ugly truth of what was done will become a matter of common knowledge. Invoking 'State Secrets Privilege' protects the wrongdoers from the disgrace of what they have done only in the short term. If one of the 'kill committee' members suffers a crisis of conscience (as did former US Secretary of Defense Robert S. McNamara many years after the Vietnam war[134]), then perhaps among the revelations of the future will be the guidelines used and the evidential bases for adding names to the US government's hit lists.

The blame in all cases where war crimes are finally exposed falls squarely on the shoulders of the perpetrators: had they done nothing wrong, there would be nothing to air. The only way to contain fallout over the secrets revealed is to avoid committing what are widely regarded as crimes. The claim so often made by patriots in defending mass surveillance – that no law-abiding citizen should worry that they are being watched and their communications sifted through – applies equally well to the governments whose activities are made public by whistleblowers. Plato observed more than two thousand years ago that the best way to achieve the reputation of a moral person is to act as a moral person would. The same sage advice is no less applicable to government administrators.

Drone strikes are one example; cyberattacks are another. Cyber-terrorists, too, can look to the United States for normative guidance, just as nations clamoring for nuclear weapons have always done. It is impossible to take seriously the denunciation by US spokespersons of hackers such as Snowden when behind the scenes, in covert operations, the US government has undertaken not only spying but pernicious attacks against other regimes, as when a computer worm was introduced to destroy centrifuges in Iran with the intention of preventing that government's production of a nuclear bomb.[135] The hypocrisy in that case is multidimensional, given that it is the United States' own possession – and use in 1945 – of nuclear warheads which motivates other states to acquire such weapons in order to have some chance of repelling a preemptive attack (as in Iraq in 2003) through deterrence.

If crimes are not committed, then they cannot be exposed. Whether or not whistleblowers unveil the crimes to the populace on the other side of the world who pay for them, the local people directly affected are all too aware of what happens on the ground. The opinions of the residents of communities under siege are shaped by what actually transpires, by what they witness with their own eyes, not the official story of administrators already confirmed as liars. Americans may have believed Obama's targeted killing program director John Brennan when he claimed in 2011 that no civilians were killed by US drones in Pakistan during the previous year. However, the people living there who have witnessed the cratering of homes in their neighborhoods know the truth, and some among them join forces with violent terrorist groups in response to what they take to be the evil US regime.

The profoundest irony of all in allegations that Private Manning and Edward Snowden 'aid and abet the enemy' is that the true inspiration for not only their acts of dissidence but also the vast majority of recent terrorist attacks are the homicides committed by the US government. In reality, the US government would seem to be the most significant 'spiritual supporter' of its very own enemies, if this reasoning is followed to its logical limit. Manning and Snowden have done no more than reveal to Americans what precisely they are paying for when they file their federal taxes each year. The drone killing program remained an official secret for years, but as ignorant as Americans may have been about the crimes committed in their name and paid for by them, the 'top secret' missions were all too familiar to the victims abroad and their bereft survivors, in addition to the international journalists and NGOs who investigate allegations of war crimes.

Withholding the facts from the US citizens who pay for drone attacks serves no purpose beyond short-term political expediency: to protect those in office so that they can retain their current positions. Far worse, such secrecy positively endangers Americans, who may have no idea why they should be in peril if they embark on journeys abroad to places where US policies have angered locals. Private Manning was charged with, but not convicted of, 'aiding and abetting' the enemy. The high-level policymakers such as George W. Bush, Barack Obama and their delegates, whose authorizations led to the killing of innocent people located in so-called hostile territories, are surely the principal parties guilty of aiding and abetting the enemy, for they, more than anyone else, have inspired people to join forces with terrorist groups in retaliatory quests for revenge.

Case in point: Anwar al-Awlaki vociferously opposed the policies of the US government, including its violent incursions in lands abroad. He eventually became radicalized to the point where he applauded terrorist actions and enjoined those outraged by US policies to take up the jihadist cause. The case of this US citizen, whose guilt appears to inhere primarily in his having served as a source of inspiration to a variety of terrorists who did commit violent crimes, raises the far more troubling question whether, by extension, antiwar critics might also become fair game for summary execution. Yemeni journalist Abdalilah Shaya investigated US drone strikes, including the massacre at Majala on 17 December 2009 in which innocent civilians were claimed by their killers to have been militants.[136] The journalist was branded an Al-Qaeda media front and thrown in prison. Just as he was about to be set free, President Obama called President Saleh to express concern over the journalist's imminent release.[137]

In helping further to expose the US government's 'dark side', Private Manning violated US law, but is it a crime even to decry war crimes? Should Noam Chomsky and Medea Benjamin be 'taken out' by Predator drone, if some hapless terrorist straps explosives to his torso and claims to have been inspired by them? What about journalists who challenge the government's official stories, as Michael Hastings and Jeremy Scahill have done?[138] Perhaps it was only a coincidence, but after having been explicitly threatened with death by US military personnel, Hastings, who was working on an exposé of newly appointed CIA Director John Brennan, died in a single-car automobile accident on 18 June 2013.[139] Is Jeremy Scahill, the author of *Dirty Wars: The World is a Battlefield* (2013), a 'traitor' for investigating what happened to Anwar al-Awlaki?[140]

What about readers who find Scahill's accounts plausible? Is merely having a negative opinion of the government's policies treasonous, too? Or must one articulate one's dissent – say, in a blog article or comment posted on the internet – in order to become branded an 'enemy sympathizer' or 'associate' and therefore 'fair game' for execution by Predator drone? Does one's right to a fair trial end the moment one is imprudent enough to set foot in Yemen or some other place ruled by a petty despot who accepts bribes of military aid for granting permission to execute without trial the people located there?

The case of Anwar al-Awlaki remains something of a mystery, as the versions of the story offered by his assailants (the US government) and his family and apologists vary radically. In fact, Al-Awlaki publicly denounced the attacks of 11 September 2001, and his doing so was captured for posterity on film:

> Our position needs to be reiterated, and needs to be very clear. The fact that the US has administered the death and homicide of over 1 million civilians in Iraq, the fact that the US is supporting the deaths and killing of thousands of Palestinians, does not justify the killing of one US civilian in New York City or Washington, DC.[141]

Whether Al-Awlaki himself ever perpetrated any violent act against any other human being may never be known, but, under US law, he should have been considered innocent until proven guilty beyond a reasonable doubt as concluded by a jury of his peers. The very fact that there should be such a compelling counternarrative strongly suggests that the strict US criminal court criterion, *guilty beyond a reasonable doubt*, would not have been met in a trial by jury. Disconcertingly, this makes it seem far more likely that Anwar al-Awlaki was killed rather than captured precisely because the evidence of his guilt was insufficient to ensure a conviction in a court of law.

The summary execution without trial of citizens is well known to be a standard operating procedure of tyrants, who kill their adversaries for threatening the status quo power structure, having first vilified the victims as criminals. Dictators conceive of their elimination of dissidents in terms of self-defense, but despots do not champion freedom of speech, as do modern Western democracies – at least nominally. The use of drones by the Obama administration to execute even US citizens situated abroad appears to violate a variety of constitutional rights, and it is difficult to comprehend how the notion of 'imminence' put forth in the White Paper might have two different meanings, depending upon the person's geographical location.

Either the threat allegedly posed by a person to be taken out by Predator drone is imminent, or it is not. But physical threats, such as an armed madman shooting persons from the top of a skyscraper, may be countered with physical force on US soil, and that is the same reason, presumably, why the killing of a combatant on a battlefield becomes permissible. The problem with the US government's institutional killing program is that the targets are a direct menace to neither their killers nor their compatriots at the moment when they are killed. A puzzle arises: *How can suspects be* more *dangerous abroad – and hence fair game for killing – than they are on US soil?* Indeed, the case for the use of deadly force against an alleged physical threat would seem to grow weaker and weaker the farther from US territory the suspect is located, reaching the limit of impermissibility when there is no immediate physical danger to any other person present, as in cases where there are not even any troops on the ground to protect. This suggests a strong basis for rejecting the targeted killing of not only US citizens located abroad, but also any person who is not directly threatening other people with death.

CHAPTER 6
THE NEW BANALITY OF KILLING

'The death of Trayvon Martin was a tragedy. Not just for his family, or for any one community, but for America. I know this case has elicited strong passions. And in the wake of the verdict, I know those passions may be running even higher. But we are a nation of laws, and a jury has spoken.'

US President Barack Obama, 14 July 2013[142]

'"Due process" and "judicial process" are not one and the same, particularly when it comes to national security. The Constitution guarantees due process, not judicial process.'

US Attorney General Eric Holder, 2009–14[143]

ONLY LEGITIMATE SELF-DEFENSE exonerates a killer within civil society. Consider the controversial case of George Zimmerman, who was acquitted in a Florida criminal court on all charges of wrongdoing in the death of Trayvon Martin, an unarmed black adolescent shot dead during a fight with the defendant on 26 February 2012. The details of the case were hazy – whether Zimmerman had pursued and provoked Martin, which then led to a scuffle that culminated in Zimmerman's firing of his gun.

Whatever errors of judgment Zimmerman may have made in the moments leading up to the death, the ultimate question for the jurors came down to this: *Did Zimmerman intend to kill Martin, or was he acting only in self-defense?* Zimmerman was working as a neighborhood watch patrolman, out on the prowl for suspicious activities. Recent perpetrators of crimes in the area had reportedly been young black males. The family and supporters of Trayvon Martin portrayed him as an entirely innocent teenager who was not violating the law in any way but only walking home from a store. The defense attorneys maintained that Martin attacked Zimmerman, and the ensuing fight resulted in the tragic drawing of the killer's gun to shoot the victim. By following Martin and getting out of his vehicle to confront him, Zimmerman disobeyed the police, who had instructed the neighborhood watch scout to stay put, as they were on their way. By the time the police arrived on the scene, Martin was already dead, and Zimmerman's head was dripping with blood. Who was at fault in this case?

The overwhelming fogginess of what transpired on the day of Trayvon Martin's death is precisely why the jury returned a not guilty verdict. A murder suspect tried in a US criminal court is not to be sentenced unless his culpability has been established in all of the jurors' minds beyond a reasonable doubt. There were open, unanswered questions in the Zimmerman case. Photographs showed that the defendant had suffered head injuries, presumably caused by what became his victim. There have been cases in history where killers inflicted injury upon themselves in order to establish a pretext for a plea of self-defense. Barring that possibility, only the survivor's version of the story remained, which appeared to be confirmed by the physical evidence. According to Zimmerman, Martin bashed his head against the concrete ground. It can hardly be denied that the physical fight between the two young men was made possible by Zimmerman's decision to leave his truck rather than wait for the police to arrive. Nonetheless, the defendant's plea of not guilty and the explanation given for his use of deadly force in self-defense were accepted by the jurors after weighing all available evidence.

The 'Stand Your Ground' policy said to justify Zimmerman's use of a gun in the state of Florida bears some similarity to the *felony murder rule*. If a policeman mistakenly shoots an innocent bystander during an armed robbery, then the criminal, not the policeman, is said to be responsible for the death. If the robber had not been in the process of committing a crime, then the policeman would never have reached for his gun. The Trayvon Martin case was highly controversial because the victim was not committing any crime, but his pursuer *suspected* that he might be, given reports of recent thefts in the area. To many people, Zimmerman's behavior smacked of racial profiling, a notorious problem for African Americans, as they have often been singled out for special scrutiny solely on the basis of the color of their skin.

In the aftermath of the acquittal of George Zimmerman, President Barack Obama soberly observed to the American people that 'Trayvon Martin could have been me thirty-five years ago.'[144] What the US president appears not to have recognized is that he might also have been the son of Anwar al-Awlaki, Abdulrahman al-Awlaki, who was killed under Obama's authority by a Predator drone-delivered missile on 14 October 2011. Both slain teenagers had brown skin, and they were about the same age – Abdulrahman was sixteen years old; Trayvon was seventeen. At the time of his death, Anwar al-Awlaki's son was with a group of friends at an open-air barbecue in Shabwah, Yemen. All of them were obliterated. Why did this happen?

When asked about the killing of Abdulrahman al-Awlaki, Obama's press secretary, Robert Gibbs, blurted out: 'I would suggest that you should have a far more responsible father if they are truly concerned about the well-being of their children. I don't think becoming an Al-Qaeda jihadist terrorist is the best way to go about doing your business.'[145] This glib and in some ways nonsensical response well illustrates what has become the banality of killing inherent to the Predator drone program. Gibbs' reply seemed to imply that the crimes of the elder Al-Awlaki were the reason for the killing of his son. Would the reason, then, for the deaths of the others present at the time be, according to Gibbs, that they should have chosen a friend who had chosen a more responsible father? Several innocent, unarmed, brown-skinned teenagers were destroyed by a Predator drone-delivered missile as they prepared to eat their dinner. Any one of those adolescents might have been Barack Hussein Obama.

Various theories about the case of Abdulrahman al-Awlaki have been floated. Unfortunately, the most plausible is simply that Obama's secret 'kill committee' – the small group of men who convened behind closed doors on 'Terror Tuesdays' for meetings chaired by targeted killing 'czar' John Brennan to watch PowerPoint presentations on 'nominees' to the US government hit list – decided to squelch a possible burgeoning terrorist before he had the chance to become one.[146] Abdulrahman's father had recently been hunted down and killed by the CIA, and if anything can drive formerly non-violent young men into the arms of anti-American groups such as Al-Qaeda, it is their personal experience of having lost a close friend or family member to a US missile. The young Al-Awlaki had only just turned sixteen years of age at the time of his death. Was this coincidental? Or was Al-Awlaki's son deemed fair game for targeting, having suddenly come of military age, as stipulated by his killers? What explains the silence of Barack Obama on the fate of brown-skinned Abdulrahman al-Awlaki, when it was every bit as tragic as the death of Trayvon Martin?

In truth, it is difficult to imagine why a committee capable of defining all males from the ages of sixteen to fifty in 'hostile' territories as combatants worthy of summary execution might harbor any scruples about snuffing out the progeny of men long on the government's hit list. That the Predator drone program administrators may have intentionally assassinated the son of Anwar al-Awlaki becomes even more plausible in view of the fact that Khalid, the unarmed son of Osama bin Laden, was executed along with his father during the May 2011 raid on the Bin Laden compound in Abbottabad, Pakistan. No attempt was made to capture Bin Laden's son, nor to incapacitate him.[147] Was Bin Laden's son guilty of any crimes? The world may never know. He was 'guilty' of being Osama bin Laden's son, just as Abdulrahman al-Awlaki was 'guilty' of being Anwar al-Awlaki's son. One thing is certain: neither son had anything whatsoever to do with what transpired on 11 September 2001, as both were children at the time.

The George Zimmerman–Trayvon Martin case is an apt metaphor for both preemptive war and targeted killing, for the latter is essentially micro-preemptive war. Zimmerman's explanation for having fired his gun on the unarmed Martin was that he was afraid that Martin would reach for and use the gun. If Zimmerman, a neighborhood scout in a Florida program designed to counter local crime, had not been in possession of a loaded gun, then Martin would not have been killed on that day. Likewise, if not for the advent of a new technology, the Predator drone, the son of Anwar al-Awlaki and his friends in Yemen would not have been slain. Would any of them ever have developed the desire and found the means to attack the people of the United States? It seems unlikely and is a matter of pure conjecture. The vast majority of people who dissent from US military practices never end up wielding deadly violence against any other human being, whether American or not.

President Obama did not devise the policy of 'signature strikes', which involves ending the lives of persons who fit the criteria of a 'disposition matrix'. In 'crowd killing', all military-age males in 'hostile' areas are defined as fair game for targeting. What is surprising is that Obama, a brown-skinned male very familiar with the problem of racial profiling in the United States, somehow failed to recognize that signature strikes and crowd killing are essentially forms of racial profiling. The signature strike practice was developed by the CIA near the end of the Bush administration, but Obama accepted and proceeded vastly to expand the Predator drone killing program. Under Obama's leadership, thousands of people were destroyed by Hellfire missiles. The morally dubious definition of all military-age males as *combatants* in designated areas of the world – persons who happen also to have brown skin – may not have achieved the magnitude of a full-scale genocide, but the logic bears an eerie resemblance to that of genocidal killers.

To see the parallels between signature strikes and racial genocide, it suffices to consider how a Nazi administrator such as Adolf Eichmann might take the reasoning of the US Department of Justice White Paper to 'justify' the annihilation of the Jewish people. Simply substitute 'the Jews' for 'Al-Qaeda' and 'Germany' for 'the United States', and a 'legal pretext' for the Holocaust emerges:

> *Der Führer has authority to respond to the imminent threat posed by the Jews and their associated forces, arising from his constitutional responsibility to protect the country, the inherent right of the German state to national self-defense under international law ... As detailed in this White Paper, in defined circumstances, a targeted killing of a German citizen who is a Jew or collaborates with the Jews would be lawful under German and international law. Targeting a member of an enemy force who poses an imminent threat of violent attack to Germany is not unlawful. It is a lawful act of national self-defense. Nor would it violate otherwise applicable federal laws barring unlawful killings ... Moreover, a lethal operation in a foreign nation would be consistent with international legal principles of sovereignty and neutrality if it were conducted, for example, with the consent of the host nation's government or after a determination that the host nation is unable or unwilling to suppress the threat posed by the individual targeted.*
>
> *Were the target of a lethal operation a German citizen who may have rights under the German Constitution, that individual's citizenship would not immunize him from a lethal operation.*

All of the justificatory work in the White Paper is underpinned by the assumption that the evil enemy is hatching schemes to destroy the nation claiming the right to self-defense. The 'imminent threat' is an idea in the mind of administrators and not subject to denial. The Nazis denigrated the Jews as wicked threats to their nation and the German people. If such a Nazi reading of the White Paper would not legitimate the Holocaust, then the pretext is equally bogus for the extermination of brown-skinned suspects who 'behave' as terrorists might.

Genocide involves defining entire classes of people as worthy of execution not for anything which they themselves have done, but because of identifying properties which they share. Obama's short-term political success at appearing 'strong on national defense' by expanding the Predator drone program can be expected to serve as a long-term precedent to be invoked by leaders even more thorough and determined than the current US administration to 'wipe out' their enemies as defined by themselves. If the world is a battlefield, as advocates of targeted killing maintain, then why not eliminate all Islamists between the ages of sixteen and fifty? Why stop with the males? Do not brown-skinned females in that same age group give birth to all of these evil terrorists?[148] And why focus only on the people of Third World nations? What about Canadian and European Islamists? What about American Islamists? Most of those people have brown skin.

The rebranding by the Obama administration of assassination as a military practice (dubbed 'targeted killing') was undoubtedly intended as part of the new president's endeavor to avoid the sorts of full-scale wars in which his predecessor had embroiled the nation, particularly in Iraq. The 'light footprint' strategy has been seen by commentators in Obama's decision to use drones in hundreds of cases to kill rather than capture suspected terrorists. The long-term, global consequences of this policy will eventually become clear when other nations and groups point to the US example in executing without trial their avowed enemies one by one. Among the burgeoning non-US drone warriors, heads of state will follow their role model in insisting that such killing is permitted by the 'self-defense' clause of the *Charter of the United Nations.*

Perhaps the biggest surprise of all is that no one in the US administration appears to have recognized that normalizing a practice formerly considered to be taboo – and prohibited by international law according to two successive United Nations Special Rapporteurs on extrajudicial executions, Philip Alston and Christof Heyns – will embolden and fortify factions and 'lone wolf' operators much more than military states.[149] Subnational and transnational factions have access to neither state-supported military institutions nor formal judicial systems. By transmitting the message that assassination has suddenly become morally permissible, a part of 'just war', it seems quite likely that jihadists, too, will be spurred on to conduct themselves more along the lines of assassins than soldiers. If even the soldiers of well-established, formal military institutions have become snipers at a distance, hiding in the shadows and dispatching their victims without warning and with no provision for the possibility of surrender, then there would no longer seem to be any distinction between those killers and the sorts of persons who undertake to assassinate heads of state.

If the most militarily powerful nation on the planet is permitted to have its 'Terror Tuesdays', it is difficult to see why the leaders of non-democratic nations and dissenting factions might refrain from doing the same. The apparent short-term tactical success of the Predator drone program is likely to prove illusory and may well lead to long-term strategic failure, just as has happened in Israel, where targeted killing was also normalized by the government.

Without formal declarations of war, the targeted killings perpetrated in several different lands could not have taken place in the twentieth century – at least not according to the official story of what the US government does. Assassinations of leaders regarded as hostile to US interests were attempted before the drone age, but under a cloak of secrecy in deniable missions or black ops. The rebranding of assassination as a standard military practice has resulted in untoward side effects far transcending the execution without trial of persons mistakenly believed by their killers to be guilty of capital crimes. In Yemen, Pakistan, Somalia, Libya and other countries with which the United States is not officially at war, the lives of other people, known to be innocent, have been ruined – the so-called collateral damage inevitable during wartime – despite the fact that they do not inhabit declared war zones.

The category of *collateral damage* has been at once expanded and contracted by a technological development conjoined with linguistic artifice. As the wars in Afghanistan and Iraq dragged on, and 'high-value targets' became more and more scarce, the drone program executors began working with yet another new definition. This time, *civilian* was defined to exclude males from the ages of sixteen to fifty. The very fact that the killers themselves should redefine a term integral to the concept of collateral damage so as to exculpate themselves from wrongdoing suggests that the concept of *collateral damage*, invoked in military reports of the deaths of innocent people, may itself have been suspect all along.

In reality, there are two forms of collateral damage: first-order collateral damage, which destroys innocent people; and second-order collateral damage, which is the resultant harm to survivors on the ground.[150] The Predator drone killing program is said by its promoters to 'project power without projecting vulnerability', but the true price paid in blood spilled can be measured in the perspectives of those who survive the drone attacks but are deprived of their loved ones and community members. By 2012, 74 percent of Pakistanis surveyed described the United States as their enemy.[151] The northwestern provinces have been beset by hundreds of missiles delivered by drones which lurk menacingly above the homes of suspects and innocent persons alike.

In terms of their deleterious psychological effects, Predator drones offer the same pseudo-discrimination as other weapons of war. According to Usama Khilji:

> Drones produce a monotonous buzz, almost like the sound of a generator, which together with the uncertainty that comes with the perpetual fear of missile strikes have had an immense psychological impact on the population ... Local doctors have declared many adults mentally unfit due to the effect drones have had on them.[152]

Even if they are not eventually going to be killed by them, all of the people on the ground are terrorized by drones. Some among the survivors will find violent outlets for their sorrow, fear and rage.

The case of Pakistan is in some ways even more perplexing than Afghanistan and Iraq, because there are no US troops on the ground (wrongly or not) who can be said to require the protection provided by weaponized Predator drones. There appears to be no recognition among US leaders (whether military or political, which were conflated in both the Bush and the Obama administrations) that what supposedly made killing in war, including collateral damage, permissible was that it had become – or at the very least seemed to be – a *last resort*. Killing men in possession of firearms in lands far away, men who pose no direct threat to US citizens and who in fact share the American belief in the right to bear arms, is hypocritical to say the least.

The Trayvon Martin–George Zimmerman case is relevant in this regard as well. Far from strengthening potential victims' state of security, 'Stand Your Ground' policies expand what is said to be the reasonable use of deadly force in every case where a gun is present and the person who fires the weapon feels in some sense threatened. The policy ends by inverting the burden of proof while simultaneously endangering unarmed and innocent people. Rather than having to demonstrate that he was justified in wielding deadly force, the defendant needs only to demonstrate that he lacked the intention to murder his victim. The burden of proof favors the killer, since it is much more difficult to establish an intention to murder than to prove that the use of deadly force was not unreasonable from the shooter's perspective, invariably skewed by the state of fear in which he was laboring, as evidenced by the very fact that he drew his gun.

Policies such as 'Stand Your Ground' reveal that the military's lethal centrism has seeped into domestic law, transforming the criteria for what constitutes the justifiable use of deadly force even within civil society. Any doubts about what might be termed the 'military turn' in law enforcement were put to rest by the events in Ferguson, Missouri, after the shooting of another young black male, Michael Brown, by a white police officer on 9 August 2014. Massive protests were met by a police force empirically indistinguishable from a military corps.[153] Police departments all over the United States have been the recipients of equipment fit for the 'boots on the ground' battles so unpalatable to Americans, including President Obama. With drones at the commander in chief's disposal, and a willingness to dispatch suspects anywhere at any time, the hardware of ground warfare, such as armored tanks and grenade launchers, has become less and less necessary, if not irrelevant, to most conflicts abroad. As a result, much of this battle-ready equipment has been transferred to local police departments for their use in maintaining law and order in the homeland. Martial law is very different from domestic criminal law.

Police officers dressed and equipped as combat soldiers may come to conduct themselves as though fighting on a battlefield, not protecting the citizenry – and all the more when some among the force happen also to be veterans, as they often are.

Just as in drone strikes, in a domestic case such as that of Trayvon Martin, what comes to matter is not the reality of who the person was, but the *perception of him by his killer.* Zimmerman accosted Martin under the assumption that he was a criminal, when in fact he was nothing of the kind. But because this was Zimmerman's belief at the time when he fired his gun, he was acquitted of wrongful killing. His legal team succeeded in persuading the jury that the defendant had acted not with malicious intent but out of fear for his own life. True, he might have shot Martin in the foot, not the chest, but the fearful state in which Zimmerman acted is said to explain that faulty judgment, too.

A wave of anger spread across the United States in response to the not guilty verdict in Zimmerman's trial because Trayvon Martin was not a robber at all, nor was he armed. Had Martin been engaged in violent criminal activities, then any death caused, including his own, would have been his fault, following the felony murder rule. Instead, Trayvon Martin was just a teenager walking peacefully down the street. In the absence of witnesses with competing narratives, the survivor's, not the victim's, version of the story prevails, just as in warfare: *the victors write history.* A neighborhood watch program which results in the slaughter of innocent residents has reflections also in the deaths of civilians caused by blowback retaliation against military practices abroad, such as occurred on 11 September 2001. It can be reasonably predicted that further such crimes will arrive later on down the line as a direct result of the Predator drone program applied with such ruthlessness and zeal in places thousands of miles away from the US homeland.

* * *

Legal processes aspire to knowledge and truth, and although they may fall short of that mark, jurors and judges in US criminal trials are strenuously instructed never to convict on the considerably less demanding criterion of probability alone. In order for an unarmed suspect to be legally executed within US borders, it would need first to be established not only that the person was who the killers claimed him to be, but also that he had in fact committed a capital crime. The guilt of the suspect would need to be concluded by the judicial, not the executive, branch of government.

Within civil society, corrupt judges and police officers, bribed jurors and witnesses who commit perjury are sometimes exposed. Adjustments to the outcomes of trials are made in cases in which corrupt or otherwise false evidence is demonstrated to have played a key role. In contrast, there is no remedy, even in principle, for the problem of faulty evidence and testimony in the summary execution of suspects by Predator drone. No 'conviction' is ever overturned, because the killers write the history of the events of the day. When children, who are obviously innocent, are destroyed, their deaths, when acknowledged, are explained away by the killers as regrettable mistakes: collateral damage. The strikes are conceived of by the perpetrators as acts of war, which is why the category of collateral damage on 'the battlefield' is said to apply. During wartime, the killers, not the victims, issue the last word on what transpired when they eliminate some human beings from the face of the earth – provided only that the killers win the war. The glaring problem with this picture is that the civil societies of some of the lands being fired on by Predator drones have simply been *stipulated* as war zones – again, by the killers themselves – in order to broaden their license to kill.

Supporters of the use of drones to 'project power without projecting vulnerability' do not generally appear to distinguish deployments by the CIA in countries such as Yemen and Pakistan from deployments by the Department of Defense in Afghanistan and Iraq during the occupations. The wars waged by US President George W. Bush left troops on the ground to protect as they attempted to restore some semblance of order to the lands after the central government had been deposed. Critics of the use of drones to kill in countries with which the United States is not formally at war object that the practice is unlawful and tantamount to what in the twentieth century was known as 'extrajudicial execution'. No amount of linguistic contortionism and rebranding – defining *assassination* as *high-value targeted killing*, stigmatizing targets as *unlawful combatants*, and denying the very possibility of military-age male *civilians* in areas labeled *hostile* by the killers themselves – is going to change the basic morality of premeditated, intentional acts of homicide.

When the apparently disparate applications of deadly force in occupied versus unoccupied lands are examined more closely, it emerges that the use of drone-delivered missiles in Yemen, Libya, Somalia and Pakistan may not be so different from what transpired in Iraq after all. If the invasion of Iraq in 2003 was a violation of international law, then the acts of killing committed by occupying troops are analogous to the acts of killing committed by German soldiers in Vichy France during World War II. Iraq was invaded offensively, despite massive global protests and without the approval of the UN Security Council. If any comparison holds between Iraq and Germany, it is that the US troops were closer to the German invaders than to the liberators of France. US military supporters often ignore the distinctive features of these cases, as though 'our troops' are always on the side of what is right. But the roles of the United States during World War II and in the 2003 invasion and occupation of Iraq are the opposite of one another.

During World War II, the US military traveled across the ocean to free the French people, whose land had been invaded and occupied by the Germans. Rushing to the defense of an ally is quite different from initiating a war, as occurred in Iraq in 2003. France was at peace, and Iraq was at peace. Both countries were abruptly and violently invaded by a foreign military power. Suddenly bombs were going off and people were being killed. Who was to blame? Who else but the invaders? Once the weapons of mass destruction (WMD) pretext for the invasion of Iraq had been debunked, military supporters switched to new rationalizations: the liberation of the Iraqi people from a dictator, and the importance of spreading democracy. Those were not, however, the reasons why the war was waged. Instead, they were desperate, ad hoc attempts to confer legitimacy upon what most of the people of the world regarded as an illegitimate invasion in violation of international law, which, perversely enough, came to be reimagined by some war advocates as a *humanitarian intervention*.[154]

If the 2003 invasion of Iraq was a violation of international law, then every person killed in the conflict was the victim of a war crime, and no one should have supported the US occupation any more than they should have supported the German occupation of France. The two cases are much closer to one another than Americans are willing to admit, although antiwar activists and some intellectuals have made the connection. It seems quite likely that a good portion of the supposedly 'evil' insurgents destroyed during the occupation were Iraqis who viewed their country as under attack by a foreign army – which, of course, it was. Many others were members of the Ba'ath party or the Iraqi army, all of whom were dismissed from their positions by the Coalition Provisional Authority and blacklisted – effectively excluded from further legal employment in the land.

Viewed in this light, the much-maligned insurgents were in some cases not so different from the partisans in France under German occupation during World War II, the ranks of which, too, included some criminal elements. Postwar chaos gave rise to much opportunistic looting and other forms of crime. At the same time, Iraq became a 'breeding ground' and a magnet for the very terrorists whom the invasion was said to be intended to repel, supposedly by preventing the transfer to them by the Iraqi dictator of his (nonexistent) WMD.

All of that folly aside, the central point remains: some among those who resisted the US occupation of Iraq were protesting the illegal invasion, just as the partisans had done in German-occupied France. The use of drones to eliminate insurgents who were attempting to expel the invaders from their land cannot be construed as literal self-defense if the troops being protected had no right to be there. When those same drones killed entirely innocent people, then the deaths would be the responsibility not of the insurgents (as the US administration invariably maintains) but of the occupiers. Had Iraq never been invaded, then the insurgents would never have acted so as to repel the invaders. Were the occupiers not situated in Iraq, there would be no pretext of ground troop self-defense to rationalize the use of weaponized Predator drones in the first place.

During World War II, US soldiers did in fact kill some innocent French citizens while attempting to dislodge the occupying German forces from France. Those collateral damage casualties seem closer to accidental killings or, if analogous to domestic cases, then the blame for the deaths would fall on the Germans, who were prosecuting a criminal war without which US troops would not have been in the position of wielding deadly weapons in France. According to the felony murder rule applied in domestic contexts, a criminal is responsible for the deaths that occur during his commission of a crime, even if he does not kill other people and had no intention of doing such a thing, and even if his heartfelt desire was only to feed his family.

After the 2003 invasion of Iraq, which had been based on faulty and fabricated intelligence, the occupying soldiers had no more right to be in that land than did the Germans in France.[155] All of this implies that the drone strikes intended to protect soldiers on the ground in Iraq were really no different in moral essence from drone strikes used to kill suspected terrorists in countries with which the United States is not even at war. The closer one examines the situation in Iraq, the more the cases start to seem alike, and this may help to explain why many supporters of the use of drones do not distinguish between the two ostensibly distinct deployments, within countries with which the United States is or is not officially at war. However, rather than it being the case that both uses are legitimate, it seems more plausible that neither is.

'The world is a battlefield,' US military supporters retort, enthusiastically endorsing the Bush administration's claim – and the Obama administration's continuation of the same – to be at war with terrorists all over the globe and willing to hunt down and kill suspected enemies wherever they may hide. By their account, every act of killing committed by the US government and its agents (including the CIA) is now an act of self-defense. But does this make any sense? In Yemen, the permission to use drones to kill people was granted by President Ali Abdullah Saleh. In the storied tradition of the petty despots of many a Third World nation throughout the Cold War and since, Saleh accepted large amounts of military aid as payment for effectively ceding his country's sovereignty to the United States. The question, then, is this: *Do such leaders have the right to trade away the lives of their compatriots in order to shore up their own power?*

In the deployment of weaponized drones against the inhabitants of other lands, what is starkly absent is the urgency involved in the use of lethal means by killers whose lives are directly at risk – and *who have the right to be where they are at the time.* If acts of war are to be legitimated by the standard line – according to which killing is a last resort, and all other avenues have been blocked and all other options exhausted – then it is difficult to see how any of these missile strikes might be regarded as legitimate. In contrast, the attempt to shoot down drones threatening death from above seems to be a perfectly rational and morally acceptable practice. The story, then, was inverted in Iraq. The persons attempting to defend themselves from menacing planes and drones above, or from the troops on the ground who conducted violent raids – often killing innocent people or spiriting them away – were exercising their right to legitimate self-defense. When someone invades our home or neighborhood, we have the right to defend ourselves from them, do we not? If so, do not the people of other lands have the same right?

What began as yet another Bush administration excess – the summary execution of unarmed suspects by Predator drone – has come to be a preferred 'tool' in the seemingly interminable 'Global War on Terror'. To the surprise and consternation of the antiwar activists who labored diligently to elect Barack Obama in 2008, the new president's solution to the Bush administration policies of extraordinary rendition and enhanced interrogation techniques, censured by human rights advocates the world over, was to step up the drone killing program, essentially eliminating the problem of human rights abuses by defining the executed suspects as guilty. These people have been 'convicted' and executed by the US government on the basis of bribed hearsay, in most cases for possible future terrorist acts.

By now, targeted killing, through sheer repetition, has become normalized to such an extent that most Americans are inured to the practice and appear not even to have entertained the possibility that there might be something morally awry with the execution of suspects without trial, even though the practice blatantly violates every principle for which the United States presumably stands. Due process and transparency, and the necessity of establishing guilt beyond a reasonable doubt before punishing (much less executing) a suspect have all been abandoned. Americans ask only that they be protected from harm on US soil, and if that requires executing scores of persons abroad who might possibly one day consider traveling to the United States to attempt to undertake jihad, then so be it, they say.

The stated policy goal for a time was to decimate Al-Qaeda, to win the war by attrition of the enemy's forces, and to bring the perpetrators of 9/11 to justice. When Osama bin Laden was finally located, Obama 'made the call', ordering the summary execution of the Al-Qaeda leader, which was carried out by a Special Forces team under his command. Bin Laden was not assassinated by drone, but in cold blood by a group of Navy SEALs acting on information gleaned through the use of a drone. By killing rather than capturing Bin Laden, did the United States defeat the person said to be most directly responsible for the crimes of 11 September 2001? Or did the infamous international terrorist ironically succeed in creating his sworn enemy in his image?

After the Al-Qaeda mastermind's execution, the drone strikes in Pakistan and beyond continued with frightening regularity, despite claims by administration figures, including both President Obama and Secretary of State John Kerry, that the program would be curtailed. The official implementation of a 'Kill don't capture' policy has ultimately revealed not only that *collateral damage* was a rhetorical trope all along, but that the notion of *last resort* no longer has any relevance in what is claimed to be modern warfare, notwithstanding the just war rhetoric parroted from centuries past. Those who view Predator drone targeted killing as a form of warfare perhaps recognize, on some level, that war, like black ops, has *always* promoted the tyrannical agenda embraced by terrorist factions. Political killers are united in their belief that a small number of human beings possess the right to decide who must die and what would be an acceptable price to pay in *other* people's lives in the quest for a sought-after goal.

The grandest irony of all is that twenty-first-century war as conducted by a First World nation has become asymmetrical and irregular, in seeming emulation of the architects of 9/11. Rather than pursue and prosecute the criminals within the bounds of the law, the Bush administration essentially adopted the modus operandi of post-Munich Mossad, while attempting simultaneously to sail along on its post-World War II laurels, as though no one would notice how in occupied Iraq the US soldiers looked much more like the Germans than the Allied troops. Prisoners were 'rendered' and tortured, and suspects identified as such on the basis of bribes were sniped – along with anyone else unfortunate enough to be by their side. Under Obama, the World War II parallels remain in place, and in some ways have grown even worse. Killing campaigns have ramified throughout several countries beyond Afghanistan and Iraq, degrading the security of people throughout the Middle East and Africa as well. In the drone strikes authorized by Obama on 'no boots battlefields' in Pakistan, Yemen, Somalia, Libya and Syria, human beings have been denied the right to surrender and executed point-blank and in cold blood, not for threatening US soldiers on the ground (there are none), but for being members of a group defined by the killers themselves as intrinsically evil.

CHAPTER 7
THE OPERATORS

'It's a very, very strong tug of war inside a pilot, that he has to think about employing this against someone that he really would probably like sitting in a bar with and having a drink. Pilots all love flying, that's what they love more than anything else. They don't love killing.'

Jeffrey L. Ethell, former military pilot[156]

'Insurgents were like having a house infested with rats; the more of them you killed, it seemed, the more they bred.'

US Lieutenant Colonel Matthew J. Martin, drone operator[157]

Dᴜʀɪɴɢ Wᴏʀʟᴅ Wᴀʀ II, fighter pilots earned a reputation for being the crème de la crème among enlisted men. Survival in that theater necessitated quick wits, unflappable composure under extraordinarily stressful conditions, and technical savvy at maneuvering a very complicated machine while dodging bullets from all sides. Many pilots sent out on sorties never returned, and those who did were lauded as certified heroes, their sheer survival serving as the proof of their prowess. In World War I, the vocation of the military pilot required perhaps even more daring, as the technology being used was so new.[158] The men who flew out to joust with fighters from the other side in what were tantamount to duels in the sky were esteemed as the best – the boldest and the bravest – in the military. Many of the combatant pilots during World Wars I and II may have been killed in spite of their talent and keen powers of perception, but one thing is clear: those who survived managed to beat not only the odds but also their rivals on the enemy side.[159]

The heroic image of wartime pilots continues to inform people's attitudes toward the military in the twenty-first century, long after such conflicts have receded into the annals of history. For decades now, modern wars have not involved such duel-like combat in the air between the soldiers of two adversarial nations. Instead, the wars waged by technologically advanced states have become very one-sided affairs, with the people on the ground, mainly civilians, subject to massive bombing as pilots above attempt to weaken the forces of the enemy below. Stores of weapons and enemy headquarters are typically located in civilian-populated areas (often urban), with the result that fighting what is depicted as a 'just war' against an 'evil enemy' may result in the slaughter primarily of innocent people who happen to reside in the vicinity of military targets.

The positive image of fighter pilots who fire massively destructive munitions remains nonetheless firmly etched in the minds of war supporters. To those who view the 1945 atomic bombings of Japan as having been permissible or even necessary, Paul Tibbets and Kermit Beahan, who piloted the planes used to destroy the cities of Hiroshima and Nagasaki, were heroes. Knowing that their planes might be shot down, the pilots flew over Japan to let loose the most destructive bombs in existence to that point in history. To those who view the razing of civilian population centers in Japan as excessive, the pilots who delivered the bombs to the cities may look more like war criminals. No one, however, denies that fighter pilots exhibit courage, for they risk their lives by flying above territories equipped with anti-aircraft defense systems.

With the advent of the UCAV, a thick wedge has been driven between the myth and the reality of those who maneuver military aircraft. Today, much of the bombing and reconnaissance essential to planning on the ground is being conducted by machines capable of absorbing all of the risk formerly incurred by human pilots. Predator drones and other UCAVs transmit information to and receive instructions from operators sitting in offices thousands of miles from the site of conflict. During World Wars I and II, troops had to persist in makeshift trenches in extreme weather conditions while being deprived for weeks or even months on end of all creature comforts, unable to bathe or change their clothes for long periods of time and subsisting on minimal rations. The stench of death hung in the air, a constant reminder of the fragility of the troops' existence. In stark contrast, 'office warriors' firing on a twenty-first-century 'battlefield' on the other side of the planet can run out for a Dunkin' Donuts break between their various point-and-click killing missions and return to their homes for a hot meal at the end of the day.

At first glance, it may seem beyond dispute that new technology which takes pilots completely out of harm's way is a positive development. But the effect of this technological capacity on the very concept of war and warriors should not be ignored. The courage and composure so important to military personnel in the past have become less and less necessary, not only for the commander in chief sequestered behind an impenetrable bastion, but also for these so-called warriors themselves. In the twenty-first century, commanders and operators watch war on a big screen, in the manner of a sporting spectacle, not a threat to their ongoing existence. This radical change in the conduct of war is a concern not only among antiwar critics and pacifists who view remote-control killing as murder. When the US Department of Defense drew up plans to offer a medal of valor to drone operators, combat veterans protested so vehemently that the award was scrapped.[160] Veterans who survived potentially lethal missions and witnessed some of their comrades die recognize that both courage and soldierly sacrifice have been deleted from the drone operator's job description.

Before the dawning of the drone age, the changes in what continues to be termed 'warfare' were quantitative in nature. The distance between troops and the enemy was increased through the invention of more and more powerful weapons to be fired from greater and greater distances, but soldiers still risked death through deployment. As technology advanced over the course of the twentieth century, the vocation of the pilot became progressively less dangerous, requiring a person correspondingly less courageous to fill that role. At the same time, risk aversion among commanders and politicians increased dramatically in tandem with the more and more formidable lethality of weapons.

During the 1999 NATO bombing of Kosovo, pilots flew high above their targets so as to avoid combatant casualties, even at the cost of mistakes on the ground. The risk intolerance witnessed during that intervention was undoubtedly an effort to avoid the political consequences of soldierly sacrifice after the 1993 'Black Hawk Down' catastrophe in Somalia, when the bodies of slain US marines were dragged through the streets of Mogadishu as rebel forces jeered and cheered. To avoid another such unsavory scenario, US President Bill Clinton and Secretary of State Madeleine Albright intervened in Kosovo but without deploying ground troops. Not a single US soldier died in the 1999 intervention, but it was still physically possible, in principle, for the pilots to be shot down by enemy forces. When modern pilots flying thousands of feet above their targets face the specter of death in combat – however improbable that may be – it remains possible to believe that they are akin to the heroic warriors of the past.

Persons dressed in military attire, but who no longer bear the risks key to the very concept of the soldier, would seem to be engaged in an altogether different sort of task. There is no sense in which a drone operator's individual instances of killing constitute *literal* acts of self-defense, as was the case in former times whenever soldiers confronted armed adversaries directly – whether on the ground or in the air. Before the drone age, soldiers often found themselves in the position of having to kill or be killed. In stark contrast, point-and-click killers do not risk death should they miss or decline to shoot their targets. Nimble-fingered desktop warriors may be adept video game players, but the game in which they are engaged is unilaterally deadly. If UCAV operators and their associated analysts fail to perform competently, then the people who pay for their mistakes are civilians on the ground.

When the killers formerly known as 'soldiers' are taken completely out of harm's way, then the 'sacrifice' made by commanders becomes *only* the people on the ground – whoever they may be. UCAVs have reduced the physical danger to their pilots to nothing more serious than the carpal tunnel syndrome to which modern office workers in general are vulnerable. Drone operators depress buttons to kill without incurring any risk to their person should they place an arrow on the wrong image or hit the space bar by mistake. There is, on the other hand, significant risk to the inhabitants of the land in which such missions take place. Not only one errant click, but one piece of bad or expired intel, one false address, one misidentification, one erroneous set of GPS coordinates means the difference between neutralizing a cluster of suspected Al-Qaeda operatives and blowing up a wedding party, human limbs strewn far and wide.[161]

A lengthy kill chain is only as strong as its weakest link. From the perspective of those concerned by the many mistakes made – assuming that the tragic weddings-turned-funerals were not intentionally targeted – the large number of persons involved in the drone killing program introduces the possibility of layers and layers of literally fatal error. Military administrators take great pains to vaunt the superior precision of their latest arms, but the high frequency of friendly fire incidents in Afghanistan and Iraq revealed that, however 'smart' weapons may be, they are still wielded by all-too-human operators. One telling example of friendly fire drone killing was that of Navy Hospitalman Benjamin Rast and Marine Staff Sergeant Jeremy Smith, who on 6 April 2011 were misidentified as Taliban and 'taken out', essentially for being military-age men in a hostile territory.[162] On

9 June 2014, again in Afghanistan, five US soldiers were killed by their own comrades. A military investigation concluded that the incident was 'the result of poor communication, inadequate planning and several other mistakes'.[163] Had the victims been not US soldiers but unnamed 'terrorist suspects', then no investigation would have taken place, and the deaths would have served as proof of their guilt in the official story proffered to the people who paid for the strikes.

Nowhere was the fallibility of the CIA and its associates more spectacularly displayed than at Camp Chapman on 30 December 2009, when government analysts and private contractors were blown up in a suicide bombing by a double agent who had tricked high-level personnel into believing that he was on their side. Just as the Pentagon, the institution charged with defending the United States against physical attack, proved incapable even of protecting the perimeters of its own buildings on 11 September 2001, the CIA, the agency charged with generating and analyzing intelligence, was hoodwinked into serving up some of its own to Al-Qaeda.

Supporters of the targeted killing program tend to ignore the disturbing implications of such mistakes and gullibly assume that the 'militants' and 'insurgents' reportedly slain in missile strikes were guilty, not innocent, suspects. However, the documented destruction of obviously innocent children by the US government in Pakistan, Yemen, Somalia and Libya reveals that the civilian occupants of lands under weaponized drone surveillance are at continuous risk of the arbitrary termination of their lives. This is a particularly sinister type of moral harm to the innocent persons terrorized by the prospect of their imminent demise and the impossibility of protecting themselves from the menacing drones hovering above in the sky.

A further, and in some ways more insidious, moral wrong is being done at the same time to the communities where strikes are carried out. Persons terrified of being marked as *associates* begin to draw into themselves as social gatherings become increasingly dangerous for their potential to be misinterpreted as terrorist retreats. Once people are killed by missiles thundering down from above, militants on the ground round up and execute persons whom they believe to be treacherous collaborators with the perpetrators of the drone strikes. David Rohde, an American journalist who was held in captivity for months by the Taliban, relays one such incident: 'Several days later, we hear that foreign militants have arrested a local man. After the militants disemboweled the local man and chopped off his leg, he purportedly "confessed" to being a spy. Then the militants decapitated him and hung his body in the town bazaar as a warning to the local population.'[164]

In this way, entire communities come under siege as trust and interpersonal relationships are destroyed along with intended individual targets (suspects who may or may not be guilty of capital crimes) and the unintended victims. Qadir Khan, a Waziristan civil servant, illuminates the stressful conditions of the people living in the peripheral areas under attack:

> Innocent people are being killed day in and day out. Some are killed by militants to terrorize people, branding them as American spies and friends of Pakistan army; others are killed by Pak army for violating so-called lawful orders or branding them as conspirators and friends of the militants and yet others are killed by drone attacks of the Americans. They are all killing innocent civilians without a fair trial, without a chance to prove their innocence. They are all together in the kill for different reasons.[165]

Some drone operators appear to be insulated from the moral questions raised by their vocation and may even delight in the production of 'bug splats' and 'splashes' using joy sticks familiar to them from video games played during childhood.[166] They may gleefully pursue the 'squirters', the fleeing survivors of an initial strike who run desperately away in an attempt to evade annihilation by a follow-up missile. Other operators have denied that they kill their targets mechanically, as though in a video game. Chad, an RPA operator interviewed in the documentary *Rise of the Drones*, staidly reports: 'It's not like a video game at all. There's no reset button. There's no turning it off. You have to stay there ... and stay focused on the destruction that you just caused, from your aircraft.'[167]

Operators sometimes become troubled to the point where they develop PTSD (post-traumatic stress disorder) and abandon the profession, although they never personally risked any physical danger as they killed.[168] Such cases reveal that, more than trauma from the fear of death, moral consequences such as guilt may weigh heavily on an institutional killer's conscience. Drone operators may track their targets over lengthy periods of time before killing them, watching them interact with their family, eat meals and engage in other normal human activities. After a target is taken out, the drone operator monitors what happens as people rush to the scene. When a strike victim does not die instantly, the operator watches him slowly bleed to death, as the infrared heat signature of a living body fades from the screen, and the person 'splashed' eventually blends in with the ground.

Given the fluid context of factional terrorism and the malleable selection criteria and ROE more generally, reports of drone operators who suffer compunction for what they have been asked and have agreed to do should come as no surprise. Nor is the high burnout rate of persons in this profession difficult to comprehend.[169] The most fundamental ROE of a uniformed soldier, that his very life or his comrades' lives should be in immediate danger before he wields deadly force, has been altogether dispensed with in contexts where there are no soldiers on the ground to protect. This situation naturally evokes critical questions in some operators' minds regarding what precisely they are doing and why. Will they be condemned as murderers later on down the line? Even if they are not, they must live with the knowledge of what they have done.

Some of these 'soldiers' no doubt recognize that a 'rule' according to which males between the ages of sixteen and fifty are fair game for targeting is arbitrary – and perhaps even deeply unjust. The notion that a person should be erased from existence for the 'crime' of carrying a weapon in a country such as Pakistan, which is not even under US occupation, is equally preposterous, and all the more so in view of the fact that Americans generally affirm their right to bear arms as a means of self-defense. The young operators (often recruited directly out of high school) asked to kill fellow human beings in accordance with such ROE may appreciate that they themselves would have been branded as terrorists and fair game for execution, if only they had been unfortunate enough to come of military age in a territory identified as 'hostile' by the Predator drone program administrators. The ROE have become more and more lax as definitions and concepts are modified in order, apparently, to maximize the number of targets killed. Such killings can then be claimed as successes in the seemingly endless war against violent extremists, accruing political capital to the commander in chief and high-ranking officials at the expense of the innocent persons terrorized and destroyed.[170]

Seasoned professionals may occasionally feel pangs of compunction about their acts of killing, even when they are convinced that the persons whom they eliminated were guilty of crimes. Such operators may not abandon the vocation but still perceive on some level that there is something vaguely disturbing about the practice in which they are engaged. Yuval Diskin was the head of Israel's Shin Bet from 2005 to 2011, the period during which targeted killing came to be a standard operating procedure as a result of the advent of drones. About this practice, he reflects:

> Sometimes it's a super-clean operation. No one was hurt except the terrorists. Even then, later, life stops, at night, in the day, when you're shaving. We all have our moments. On vacation … You say, 'Okay, I made a decision and X number of people were killed. They were definitely about to launch a big attack. No one near them was hurt. It was as sterile as possible.' Yet you still say, 'There's something unnatural about it.' What's unnatural is the power you have to take three people, terrorists, and take their lives in an instant.[171]

Drone strikes are viewed by advocates as legitimate acts of war but by opponents as the point-blank annihilation of either a soldier denied the right to surrender or a suspect denied the right to appeal his extrajudicial conviction. Predictably enough, given these diametrically opposed ways of viewing remote-control killing, there are essentially two types of operators: those who become plagued by what they do, to the point where they abandon the profession, and those who rise in the ranks to become commanders.

Brandon Bryant is an example of the burnout operator. In reflecting on his experience he laments: 'I saw men, women and children die during that time. I never thought I would kill that many people. In fact, I thought I couldn't kill anyone at all.'[172] Only those operators who are able to process this practice as morally permissible, and even worthy, will come to occupy command and control positions in the future. They will naturally promote and perpetuate the Predator drone program, in part as a way of demonstrating that what they have already done was right all along.

Predator (2010), the memoir of drone operator Matthew J. Martin, who killed targets in both Afghanistan and Iraq, disturbingly reveals that 'well-adjusted' personnel (not suffering from PTSD) may regard their victims as subhuman – he refers to them variously as 'rats', 'mice' and 'rabbits' – while also knowing that their anger has been provoked by the US military itself. The most obvious problem with Martin's rat analogy (aside from its denial of the humanity of the persons 'exterminated') is that, in occupied lands such as Afghanistan and Iraq, where Martin pursued and killed insurgents, the 'house infested with rats' was owned by the 'rats', not their killers. The hegemonic presumption that the United States has the right to occupy any land on the planet is in fact what has directly motivated much, if not most, anti-American terrorism.

Occasionally Martin evinces short blips of awareness of what critics might find to be wrong with his role as a remote-control killer, executing people in lands far away when his own life is not in any direct danger at all. In reflecting on the 'unreal' nature of his involvement in wartime operations when he flew from Virginia to Nevada to kill people, Martin writes: 'I flew nearly 3,000 miles to climb into a stationary cockpit and fly an unmanned warplane 7,500 miles away to find some angry poor people and kill them. Then I caught a commercial air carrier to go 3,000 miles back home to have breakfast with my wife.'[173]

Throughout his first-person account of life as a drone operator, Martin repeatedly ridicules the radical Islamists for believing that they will be rewarded with seventy-two virgins in heaven for their sacrifice. Probably the worst part of this frank but unselfconsciously disconcerting account is Martin's smug sense of superiority.[174] In addition to denigrating in a rather xenophobic way nearly everything and everyone non-American, he repeatedly refers to himself as 'the professor', even while failing to understand the most basic problems with the war in which he is killing. 'The professor's' account of why he is killing Iraqis is that 'the United States invaded Iraq on the grounds of "weapons of mass destruction" and Saddam Hussein's alleged support of Al-Qaeda terrorism'.[175] That those pretexts were entirely spurious is swiftly ignored or forgotten throughout the rest of the book, as Martin delights in deriding Saddam Hussein and everyone else labeled by him as 'the bad guys'. But if the 2003 invasion of Iraq was illegal, then every single person killed in the conflict was the victim of a war crime – including those targeted by Martin – an implication which escapes him entirely.

The author repeatedly refers to his task as 'hunting', and in several different passages equates his quarry with rodents. The hunting analogy is quite apt, for the radical power disparity between the hunters and the quarry in drone killing is patent. Animals pursued in the wild by men with big guns are obviously at a marked disadvantage. The flouting of any conception of fair play leads people on the ground to despise the US government for its Predator drones, denouncing the killers as ignoble cowards who hide in their trailers in Nevada while they snipe unwitting suspects, some of whom are entirely innocent of any wrongdoing.

The sound bite that drones 'project power without projecting vulnerability' leaves out their most important and intensely emotional effect upon some among the bereft survivors: to inspire hatred. Precisely such hatred gives rise to factional terrorism in what the perpetrators regard as just retaliation for war crimes. Faisal Shahzad, who plotted to bomb Times Square in New York City, testified at his trial: 'The drones, when they hit, they don't see children. They don't see anybody. They kill women, children, they kill everybody.'[176]

A mild-mannered Yemeni lawyer expressed a related concern and strategic warning on Twitter: 'Dear Obama, when a US drone missile kills a child in Yemen, the father will go to war with you, guaranteed. Nothing to do with Al-Qaeda.'[177]

Predator offers an unsettling but eye-opening record of a drone operator's way of processing a war in which he annihilates from thousands of miles away people who pose no immediate threat to him when they are killed. Above all, Martin's account reveals the mental gymnastics needed to be able to live with oneself in carrying out such a vocation. Martin occasionally seems vaguely to grasp what is wrong with the practice in which he is engaged, but he then moves quickly to dispel this impression. The epilogue to the book is an unequivocal declaration of Martin's belief in the rightness of what he is doing, which leads one to suspect that the text may have been appended at the behest of his commanding officers.

Martin's actions contributed to the ever-expanding class of enemies in the 'house of rats' which the invaded lands became as angry poor people (by his own characterization) teamed up with terrorist factions in direct response to what they took to be war crimes committed by the US government. Yet the drone operator proceeds to forget all of this when he writes: 'Sometimes it didn't make a lot of sense, fighting the Global War by killing one or two guys at a time. Still, I supposed if we kept at it long enough and killed enough of them, the violence would eventually subside to the point that our rebuilding efforts could gain traction and we'd be on our way to bringing some sort of stability, if not prosperity, to the country.'[178] This sort of reasoning on the part of higher-level military officers and analysts may have been what gave rise to the administration's labeling of all military-age men in hostile areas as combatants and legitimate targets, not only in places such as Fallujah but also, later, in the northwestern provinces of Pakistan.

In what has become a frenzy of killing, all sight has been lost of the human nature of the victims. 'Towel heads' and '*hadjis*' were reviled by the US ground troops who faced an unremitting threat of death as they patrolled occupied territories, but their rage blinded them to the causal mechanism – the concrete factors – which gave rise to so many incensed insurgents in the first place. Killers create killers who create more and more vicious killers, and after a few iterations of this senseless cycle of violence it becomes impossible for either side to regard the other as human beings. The enemy is cast as loathsome and evil, irremediably unjust and immoral. They must be wiped from the face of the earth in order, the killers claim, for peace and justice to be able to reign once again. But there is a glaring problem with this approach: insurgents and terrorists are not born; they are made.

During the US occupation of Iraq, Secretary of Defense Donald Rumsfeld, to his credit, at one point posed a surprisingly incisive question: 'Are we capturing, killing, or deterring and dissuading more terrorists every day than the madrassas and the radical clerics are recruiting, training, and deploying against [our forces]?'[179] Rumsfeld did not, however, go on to connect the dots. He somehow failed to process the direct causal connection between the commission of war crimes by agents of the US government and the increased propensity of young Islamic men to join the ranks of the insurgents retaliating violently against such acts. Insurgents and terrorists do not simply pop into existence *ex nihilo*. They are formed in cultural contexts from children (usually boys), and have often witnessed the consequences of military campaigns.

When young persons observe the brutal effects of bombing and night raids, this serves to confirm in their minds what insurgent and terrorist leaders have already claimed in efforts to galvanize support for their cause to defeat the enemy through jihad. General Stanley McChrystal reportedly coined the phrase 'insurgent math' to explain how killing two members of a group of ten insurgents would not leave eight behind, but perhaps twenty, because: 'Those two that were killed, their relatives don't understand that they're doing bad things. Okay, a foreigner killed my brother, I got to fight them.'[180] Admiral Michael Mullen offered a related warning: 'Each time an errant bomb or a bomb accurately aimed but against the wrong target kills or hurts civilians, we risk setting our strategy back months, if not years.'[181]

Unfortunately, the essentially self-defensive logic of much of the insurgency in Iraq appears to have escaped those who ordered the disruptive patrols and night raids throughout that land. Had the patrols not been carried out in the way in which they were, had military-age men not been rounded up like cattle, taken away for months at a time and subjected to 'enhanced interrogation techniques' until they 'divulged' what they may or may not have known, then in all likelihood the insurgency would never have grown to the unwieldy extent to which it did. As the State Department itself owned, the global incidence of terrorism increased markedly subsequent to the 2003 invasion of Iraq. The Bush administration averred that during the occupation Iraq became a 'magnet' for aspirant terrorists, who traveled to the country and in some cases martyred themselves for the opportunity to kill US troops.

Some war supporters spun the 'magnet effect' as good in the sense that the military was 'taking the battle to the enemy' and drawing terrorists to a centralized place where they could be hunted down and obliterated rather than allowed to attack the US homeland as on 11 September 2001. This view, which gained a following among many people in the United States, mistakenly assumed a constant, finite number of terrorists who could be drawn to the magnet and then dispersed like iron filings in the wind. In truth, the practices of the US military and its associates were largely responsible for the rapid and continuous augmentation of the ranks of the insurgents.

In thinly veiled efforts to rationalize their actions above all to themselves, Matthew Martin and other drone operators invoke episodes from the past, especially World War II, drawing analogies between what they do and what enlisted men before them did. The analogy to World War II falls apart the moment one recognizes that the US troops in Iraq were more like the Germans than the Allied forces in France. As far as their general role as 'soldiers' is concerned, the drone operators who report to work in combat uniform to spend the day in secluded trailers far from the bloody fray and impervious to any form of threat are not unlike George W. Bush, who, too, dressed up in combat pilot gear, pretending to be a warrior in a staged appearance on an aircraft carrier to announce 'Mission Accomplished' after the 2003 invasion of Iraq. All of this might be laughable if it were not so devastating for the victims and the survivors left bereft in the wake of missile strikes and terrified by the prospect of being next in the line of fire.

The suicide hijackers of 11 September 2001, despite having been willing to march directly to their deaths in defending their 'cause', were decried as 'craven' and 'cowardly' by many Americans, including the president and other government officials, and this depiction was further promoted by patriotic pundits in the mainstream media. In fact, a closer look at the criminal actions of terrorist factions reveals that they have done no more than to devise innovative strategies with the aim of defeating an adversary whose orthodox military means vastly exceed their own. Al-Qaeda and its affiliates were not the first groups in history to have adopted this ploy.

During World War II, members of the French resistance operated covertly, in civilian attire, using guerrilla warfare tactics to sabotage the operations of occupying German troops. Helmuth Tausend, a former captain in the German army who was stationed during the occupation in Clermont-Ferrand, recounts one such episode during an interview in Marcel Ophüls' film *Le chagrin et la pitié* (*The Sorrow and the Pity*) (1969):

> A detachment of our troops near Clermont passed in front of twenty-odd peasants digging up potatoes. Suddenly they all dropped their hoes, dashed toward their guns, and proceeded to shoot fourteen of our men dead. Do you consider that a partisan war? For me, partisans are people who wear armbands, helmets and the like. What happened in that potato field was assassination. You must admit that we were obliged to react. I'd even say that it was our duty, as officers, to demand security measures for our troops.

By denouncing in no uncertain terms what he takes to be this outrage, the German captain appeals to the 'rule of war' according to which soldiers, even 'partisans', must identify themselves as combatants by wearing uniforms or, at the very least, some form of visible insignia on their arms, in order to distinguish themselves from noncombatant civilians. What the German officer appears not to understand – although it is difficult to see how that could be – is that to have done so would have made the French resisters immediate targets for execution by the occupying troops. Not only would identifying themselves as dissenters have been suicidal, even more importantly it would have utterly sabotaged their own mission to defeat the Germans. The desperate underdogs in these conflicts are often willing to die for their cause, but they are not willing to die for no reason at all. In this regard, they do not differ from regular, uniformed soldiers, who fight only until it becomes obvious that there is no hope, at which point they lay down their arms before the more powerful force.

Matthew Martin goes out of his way to relay his experiences on site in Afghanistan and Iraq, where he was sent to train other operators, and specifically his sense of fear when his living quarters came under attack from enemy fire. However, he fails altogether to recognize that when, as a drone operator, he labored to protect troops on the ground in occupied Iraq, he was much closer to German soldier Helmuth Tausend than to any US soldier sent to Europe during World War II. From Martin's first-person perspective, of course, his life is in danger. But because the land had been wrongly invaded, the occupiers had no legitimate cause for complaint when the local people retaliated violently. That Iraq went on to become a meeting ground and recruiting camp for Al-Qaeda jihadists in the region was simply the grandest consequence of the many strategic follies of an ill-advised war against another nation at peace, followed by an inept occupation.

Reading *Predator*, the published first-person account of a drone operator whose self-proclaimed mission is to 'hunt and kill' persons deemed worthy of death by anonymous analysts, does not provide much reason for believing that those who fire the missiles are any less fallible or ignorant than the employees of Blackwater, some of whom were reported to have indulged in 'target shooting' of innocent people while working in Iraq.[182] Here is a typical example revealing Martin's basic ignorance of history, specifically regarding how Saddam Hussein became a dictator: 'I flew missions over Baghdad, looked down upon where he was confined, and puzzled over the depravity of human nature that spawned sadistic men like him and allowed them to attain such power'.[183] Martin, 'the professor', appears to be entirely unaware that his own government empowered Saddam Hussein by furnishing him with military aid and technology throughout his vicious eight-year war with Iran.

The significance of this account is not merely anecdotal. Given that the author is an active-duty officer of the US military – indeed, a lieutenant colonel – his work must have been vetted by the powers that be. Martin's is not just some outlier piece of screed scrawled by a 'bad apple' or low-level grunt soon to be court-martialed, unemployed and perhaps even homeless. *Predator* is a book-length account which has been approved by some of the very administrators who decide when and where other people should die. The operator's ignorance of basic facts of history, and his unbridled disdain for the cultures of the people slain, screams out from every page. The fact that his memoir was even published reveals that Martin's commanders, too, see nothing wrong with characterizing the victims of drone strikes as vermin, 'rats' and 'mice' to be hunted down and exterminated.

At one point, Martin explains the criterion used for deciding to kill a person posing no physical threat to him: 'A target was fair game as long as he [the ground commander] could demonstrate a hostile act or hostile intent.'[184] But 'hostile intent' is entirely a matter of interpretation. Is yelling out in rage against the US occupation a demonstration of 'hostile intent'? Apparently so. Journalist Michael Hastings learned from discussions with military personnel that 'pilots gauge enemy and friendly areas by the reaction of the Afghans they fly over. Friendlies wave and smile. Enemies throw rocks and show the bottoms of the soles of their feet, an insult in the Muslim world.'[185]

In his resignation letter lamenting the disastrous mission in Afghanistan, former US Foreign Service Officer Matthew Hoh wrote: 'I have observed that the bulk of the insurgency fights not for the white banner of the Taliban, but rather against the presence of foreign soldiers.'[186] Matters only become worse when there are no commanders on the ground and no troops below to protect, as in countries such as Pakistan and Yemen, with which the United States is not even at war. At this point in history, the right to 'make the call' has been dispersed across many commanders as the web of US targeted killing has expanded and the hit lists and line items have multiplied, increasing the opportunities for abuse by personnel who for one reason or another wish to kill with impunity, as they are now able to do. The use of the vague criterion of 'hostility' in determining whom to execute is furthermore grounded in an erroneous understanding of the enemy as bent on attacking the United States. In reality, the intentions of most insurgents are far more local. GWOT has been seized upon by many a corrupt foreign leader to enlist the US government to aid and abet their campaigns to neutralize political enemies and people living on the periphery long regarded as troublesome.[187]

Martin occasionally exhibits some awareness of how people opposed to the practice of remote-control killing view what he does. Here is how he caricatures their puzzlement: 'Some people would look at me strangely. "Let me get this right," they might say, and I knew what was coming. "You're out there on the air force base killing innocent people on the other side of the world while they can't shoot back at you?"' Yet the operator does nothing to dispel the dark cloud hanging over his vocation: 'I tried to contain my temper, I truly tried. Not always successfully. Sometimes I broke down my response to a few words: "You have no idea what you're talking about."'[188]

The burden of proof of moral permissibility lies with the person who would kill other human beings when his own life is not immediately – or even remotely – threatened, not with the person who expresses surprise and consternation that anyone should agree to do such a thing. Matthew Martin and all of the weaponized drone operators and sensors like him are, setting euphemisms to one side, professional killers. They are not soldiers in the traditional sense, and until what they are doing has been explained and justified to the people at direct risk of death, those who are regularly terrorized by drones flying above their heads, it will continue to look an awful lot like murder.

The proudest professional accomplishment of Matthew Martin, as described in *Predator*, and apparently the grounds for his promotion to the rank of lieutenant colonel, is to have shortened the 'kill chain', making it easier for operators to destroy targets without first getting higher-level clearance. The drone operator begins from the assumption that what he is doing must be right, and then maneuvers and negotiates so that he and his coworkers will be permitted to kill more people faster. What needs to be examined is why and how anyone – whether military supporter or not – should believe that killing persons located thousands of miles away who are not engaged in combat is a noble vocation. Isn't that precisely what Osama bin Laden did on 11 September 2001?

The scenario on the twenty-first-century 'battlefield' fired on by drone operators bears scant resemblance to the history of human sacrifice during the wars of centuries past. The persons directly threatened with annihilation by military weapons have become less and less likely to be soldiers themselves. Civilians may not be the targets, but they are sometimes the victims, and even when they survive, they have been and continue to be terrorized by the ominous threat of death. The diminished physical risk on the part of drone operators is accompanied by increased risk – both physical and psychological – to the innocent people on the ground. If terrorism is the arbitrary threat of death against innocent people, then there is no denying that the hovering overhead of weaponized drones is terrorism, plain and simple. It is not recognized as such by the perpetrators only because the practice of targeting killing grew slowly, step by step, out of what were construed to be acts of just war.

More than anything else, *Predator* succeeds in illustrating how remote-control killers, who face no physical danger while annihilating human beings on the other side of the planet, are able to sleep at night. Whenever conscience begins to stir, it must be suppressed, by all means necessary, in order to rationalize killing 'angry poor people' abroad. The insider perspective shared by Martin goes a great distance toward explaining the antipathy of the people of lands besieged by US missiles. Indeed, it seems safe to say that this memoir could be used as yet another recruitment tool by Al-Qaeda, revealing, as they would interpret it, the ignobility of the enemy.

From the perspective of the victims, what drone operators do seems much closer to what a professional hitman does than what the soldiers of World War II did in confronting an enemy bent upon killing them. This enormously important strategic point has been lost on those who run the Predator drone program: *The people on the ground base their future actions on their own interpretations, not those of the operators who killed their loved ones and cratered their homes.* Drone operators kill vastly more people than do soldiers in conventional combat, and the sheer magnitude of their carnage takes its psychological toll in some cases. Certainly, it seems safe to say that no soldier on the ground has personally killed or facilitated the execution of 1,626 human beings, as Brandon Bryant did.[189] Is he a hero, or is he a mass murderer?

CHAPTER 8
FROM CONSCIENCE TO OBLIVION

'I was kind of freaked out. My whole body was shaking. It was something that was completely different. The first time doing it, it feels bad almost. It's not easy to take another person's life. It's tough to think about. A lot of guys were congratulating me, telling me, "You protected them; you did your job. That's what you are trained to do, supposed to do," so that was good reinforcement. But it's still tough.'

A drone pilot reminiscing on his first kill[190]

'In the early days, for our consciences we wanted to know who we were killing before anyone pulled the trigger. Now we're lighting these people up all over the place.'

Richard Blee, former Head of CIA Alec Station[191]

THE NUMBER OF PERSONS destroyed by Predator drone is reported perfunctorily, with an emphasis on the 'evil terrorists' slain and no mention of the survivors left bereft or maimed. The innocent civilians (such as children) injured or killed collaterally are invariably omitted from initial reports. The administration's official account of 'successful' strikes captures the attention of the media's current news cycle and is the only version of the story which most Americans ever hear. In the twentieth century, too, the military downplayed when it did not flatly deny collateral damage – as though the nameless, faceless noncombatants killed had neither moral value nor human rights. In the drone age, the class of *combatants*, individuals fair game for intentional targeting, has been enlarged to include all able-bodied male persons unfortunate enough to be located in areas where terrorists are thought by anonymous analysts to be hiding out.

Given the military focus on lethality, taken up also by the CIA in the twenty-first century, it is not terribly surprising that some of the soldiers and private contractors on the ground in Afghanistan and Iraq became target shooters looking to 'get some', sniping people whom they claimed to be justified in killing even when the pretext of self-defense stretched credulity. In Iraq, the number of 'dead *hadjis*' became a measure of success and to some soldiers a source of pride.[192] A similar dynamic was witnessed in Vietnam, when draftees attempted to rack up as many dead Vietcong as they could, having been encouraged to do so by their commanding officers.[193]

Perhaps, then, it was inevitable that assassination, once carried out by stable governments only through black ops, would eventually become an official and publicly acknowledged policy. What began as an amalgamated law enforcement–military effort to track down and bring to justice the perpetrators of the terrorist attacks of 11 September 2001 led to the generation of ever-lengthier lists of targets, including unnamed persons whose activities on the ground were said to match behavior patterns regarded as 'typical' of terrorists. There are obviously exceptions to every tendency, and the observation of shadowy figures on a computer monitor does not and cannot reveal the beliefs and intentions of the persons 'employed on' by drone operators.

As a graphic illustration of lethal centrism reflected in the outlook and comportment of troops, consider the widely disseminated YouTube video of a massacre in the suburb of New Baghdad, Iraq, on 12 July 2007. On that day, several civilians were 'neutralized', including Reuters employees carrying cameras misidentified as AK-47s and RPGs (rocket propelled grenades) by trigger-ready shooters hovering ominously above in a helicopter, and ready and willing to fire the moment they could claim that the person was armed. The videotape made of the mission from the Apache helicopter was furnished to WikiLeaks by Private Manning and published online under the provocative title 'Collateral Murder'.

The stomach-wrenching footage of the 'Collateral Murder' incident shows a wounded journalist attempting to drag himself away from the scene after the initial spray of artillery. One of the shooters cheers him on: 'Come on, buddy. All you gotta do is pick up a weapon.' The speaker is anxiously awaiting the moment when the already-wounded and obviously incapacitated man will reach for anything interpretable as a weapon, thereby granting the shooter the right to finish him off and be able to claim that he killed in accordance with military protocol.

When a van drives up to save one of the injured survivors of the initial salvo, it, too, is blown away. The two children inside the vehicle are deemed collateral damage, and their presence is blamed upon the allegedly evil terrorists (in reality, camera-toting journalists) who made the mistake, the soldiers assure one another, of bringing children into a firefight. The audio of the soldiers who carried out the series of killings documented in 'Collateral Murder' reveals what must be their own interpretations of what they have done, if they are to sleep at night. Upon insistence by Reuters, two of whose employees were shown executed in the film, the US military investigated the incident but concluded that the soldiers had acted in accordance with standard operating procedure and correctly followed their ROE.

What the short film unforgettably displays is that even regular soldiers who risk nothing, no personal harm whatsoever, shooting as they are from a distance, may literally seek out opportunities to kill. This tendency has obviously been enhanced in the drone age by the enlistment of young adults to train essentially as assassins, whose primary vocation is to hunt down and destroy suspects from thousands of miles away. *What do you do for a living?* The answer of a UCAV operator is clear: *I kill people.* There is no other way of glossing the reality. Bureaucratic euphemisms aside, weaponized drone operators are professional killers. The measure of their vocational competence becomes the number of successful hits which they carry out or facilitate. Accordingly, they are galvanized to seize opportunities to kill in order to advance professionally. Just as writers 'score' book deals, killers 'score' hits. Drone operator Matthew Martin, who was promoted for his service in Afghanistan and Iraq, devised ways by which to shorten the 'kill chain', with more authority accorded to the operators themselves to 'engage targets' and 'do kinetic' as opportunities arise.

Scenarios such as 'Collateral Murder' reveal that some regular soldiers have reached the point where they literally seek out targets to kill. Upon completion of their enlistment term, recent veterans were prime candidates to accept civilian positions working for PMCs, not only because they would command generous salaries relative to what they earned as uniformed soldiers, but also because they did not have to demonstrate to anyone that they observed, even nominally, proper protocol (ROE) before discharging their weapons. As civilians operating in a foreign land, they were permitted to kill in self-defense and granted maximum discretion in interpreting what that meant. Paul Bremer's Coalition Provisional Authority Order 17 explicitly provided civilian contractees with legal immunity in their use of lethal force, what author Tony Geraghty describes as a 'licence to kill'.[194] The trigger-ready tendencies of regular soldiers and Special Forces in chaotic urban warfare settings certainly cannot be said to have been tempered by their collaboration with private military contractees operating in what in Iraq was literally a law-free zone.

'Collateral Murder' also provides a broader illustration of why administrators who have already participated in targeted killing must, for their own state of equanimity, convince others that the practice is sound. Just as the killers of the Reuters employees in New Baghdad consoled themselves that the 'evil terrorists' were to blame for bringing children into a firefight, bureaucrats will argue vigorously and enthusiastically for the continuation of a program through which they themselves have already authorized homicide. When the incumbent Predator drone program administrators persuaded newly elected President Barack Obama to embrace the practice, they succeeded in perpetuating and even expanding the program. At the same time, they confirmed in all of the killers' minds that what they had already done was, in fact, legally and morally sound. Personnel who strongly demur from the prevailing 'conventional wisdom' handed down by their superiors cannot rise in the ranks, and some eventually renounce their positions, leaving only enthusiasts behind.

Not all institutional killers are able to maintain a sunny disposition having once recognized what they have been lured into doing. A disproportionately high number (relative to earlier conflicts) of the surviving soldiers of the wars in Afghanistan and Iraq committed suicide, apparently unable to bear what they had seen and what they had done, and knowing, deep down inside, how far the official story diverged from the truth. Supporters of the use of weaponized drones generally assume that this technology spares the lives of soldiers, and it is true that the operators are situated physically far from the battlefield. However, the persons effectively enlisted to serve as executioners at a distance sometimes have difficulty reconciling what they do at the office with what they do when they return home, interacting with their family after having spent the work day destroying other families abroad. One operator explains:

> We watched him wake up in the morning; we watched him leave for work in his vehicle; we tracked him to where he was building these weapons; we watched him eat lunch; we watched him go home and play soccer in his yard with his family – with his two little girls ... We watched him live with his wife; we watched him sleep; we watched him get up in the middle of the night, go to the back of his house and build weapons.[195]

Even when they are convinced that their targets are up to no good, the killers are also aware that the targets are often somebody's husband, father, son and brother.

As confused as many jihadists may be, those who join up with groups such as the Taliban and Al-Qaeda believe in what they are doing. The drone operators themselves may or may not believe in the justice of the remote-control killing of suspects – some no doubt view what they do solely as a felicitous employment opportunity. Drone operator starting salaries range from $50,000 to $100,000. Some operators are reported to earn as much as $200,000.[196] When Brandon Bryant decided to renounce his position, he was offered an enticing $109,000 bonus to stay. Bryant declined, having reached the point where he could no longer do what he was being asked to do in good conscience.

Functionally speaking, there are two very different types of drone operator: the well-adjusted, such as Matthew Martin, and the mal-adjusted, such as Brandon Bryant. The former was promoted for his service; the latter, who suffered agonizing bouts of regret for the more than 1,600 kills in which he participated, was diagnosed with post-traumatic stress disorder (PTSD) and suffers nightmares for having contributed to so much carnage. Bryant abandoned the Air Force after five years of service, from 2006 to 2011, having enlisted in order to avoid accumulating college debt.

As the military's campaign to maximize lethality marches inexorably ahead, institutional inertia protects, perpetuates and expands current practices. At the same time, the Pentagon's public relations wing focuses on justifying, promoting and cleansing its wars for domestic public consumption. Part of the war-marketing enterprise involves dismissing or silencing naysayers, war critics of all stripes, including soldiers racked with guilt and gripped by regret for what they have done under the aegis of the military. A related twenty-first-century development, the liberal dispensation of drugs to both active-duty soldiers and veterans, calls out for scrutiny. Like the drone program, the use of drugs to assuage soldiers' anxiety about what they are being asked to do has its origins in technological advances made in recent years and driven by the unremitting quest for enhanced lethality.[197]

In the twenty-first century, many veterans were plagued by PTSD after multiple deployments to Afghanistan and Iraq, and the proportion of suicides among troops reached the highest level ever in US military history, exceeding even that of the Vietnam era. This combatant death toll impugns the alleged effectiveness of GWOT, the notion that antiterrorist measures have increased the security of the US populace. If, as the Veterans Administration (VA) reported in 2012, 8,000 soldiers are killing themselves each year, deaths which result directly from their service, then it cannot be said that the US populace has been made more secure by its government's counterterrorism practices.[198] Instead, human beings as a group, and Americans more specifically, have been harmed, because thousands more US citizens who would otherwise be alive today have died since the government opted to paint the crimes of 11 September 2001 as acts of war and 'take the battle to the enemy'.

The soldiers sent out on patrols in Iraq lived in a state of nearly continuous danger, undoubtedly the source of many of their psychological troubles, including insomnia. There is no true antidote for what some of these soldiers have been made to endure, having committed or witnessed tragic and irrevocable acts. Some well-meaning troops mistakenly destroyed civilians who failed to stop at checkpoints because they did not understand what they were being told to do by the soldiers speaking in English; others were ordered to roll right through women and children who had been sent by insurgents to stand before convoys to impede their forward motion.[199]

The treatment provided to the twenty-first-century troops who suffer compunction and distress as a result of harrowing wartime experiences has been primarily pharmaceutical. Drugs are doled out liberally as a cost-effective means of dealing with the ever-more prevalent cases of anxiety experienced by both active-duty soldiers and veterans. But the doubts arising in some combatants' minds are perfectly rational and legitimate skeptical questions about what they have been asked to do. They are, after all, expected to kill people whom they have never met and about whom they know nothing beyond the information provided by the very commanders ordering them to kill.[200] This condition is shared by drone operators, who are not privy to the analysis of the HUMINT leading up to the designation of persons as legitimate targets. Such decisions are made by bureaucrats behind closed doors.

In a mission such as the 2003 invasion of Iraq, which was widely criticized even by US citizens who generally support military incursions abroad, inchoate skeptical doubts in soldiers' minds are likely to be magnified by the fact that so many people – not only pacifists – are opposed to the war. Nonetheless, those soldiers in full possession of their mental faculties who dare to demur from the official policy wind up criminalized by the institution, essentially for refusing to talk the 'just war' talk and promote the company line – whatever that may require, up to and including lies.[201] Examples of notorious cover-ups include the attempt to depict former NFL (National Football League) player Pat Tillman as a courageous warrior who died in combat against an evil enemy, when in fact he was killed in a friendly fire incident.[202]

Not all soldiers are as compliant as Lieutenant Colonel Matthew J. Martin. Instead of penning memoirs which support the military institution, some soldiers have protested against what they regard as war crimes, such as the grisly killing of civilians and journalists unforgettably captured in the short film 'Collateral Murder'. Whether a soldier is defended by the military establishment or decried and criminalized, as in the case of Private Manning, depends entirely upon the effect of his actions on the institution's public image. US Staff Sergeant Camilo Mejía, some of whose vocal protests against the Iraq war echoed outrage among the populace over the treatment of prisoners at Abu Ghraib, was discredited through criminalization by the Pentagon for refusing to redeploy to Iraq.[203]

In every war, some combatants evolve into war opponents as a result of their experiences, having directly witnessed the disparity between 'the official story' and the reality of what is being done. Howard Zinn, the author of *A People's History of the United States*, flew combat sorties in World War II. After having bombed a village in France with napalm, Zinn's entire view of the military enterprise was transformed to the point where he became an outspoken war opponent and advocate of peace, dedicating the rest of his life to the cause of social justice.[204]

Military critics are often denounced by patriots as traitors, particularly when their views have been transformed by their own participation in war. Sergeant Mejía and Private Manning had twentieth-century predecessors who were far more effectively silenced than they. In World War I, many conscripted soldiers found the conditions and terms of their deployment so intolerable that they inflicted injuries upon themselves in the hope of securing an honorable discharge.[205] Because at that time desertion was a crime punishable by execution, all of the soldiers who mutilated themselves knowingly risked death by doing so, and some of them were court-martialed and convicted by military tribunals before being killed by comrades under order, on pain of death for disobedience. Tragically, the soldiers executed as traitors opposed not their country but the war in which they had been embroiled against their will. Some World War I soldiers succeeded in securing honorable discharges after self-mutilation, but they were no less effectively silenced, since they could not reveal the true reasons for their discharge (their willful desire to desert) without risking prosecution, ignominy and death.

Over the course of the twentieth century, Western society became much more liberal, one effect of which was a loosening of the grasp of the once strict tyranny of the military over enlistees. The hierarchical structure of the military remains autocratic, with the commander in chief – 'The Decider', as George W. Bush so aptly put it – at the pinnacle. However, the means by which to impose that structure have been significantly weakened in modern liberal states because the punishments meted out to refractory soldiers have become less severe. In the past, it was possible to keep most soldiers in line through the threat of execution for disobedience or desertion. But Western society's attitudes toward capital punishment have changed. In many nations – including all members of the European Union – the death penalty has been outlawed even in cases of convicted first-degree murder. Needless to say, the United States has yet to abolish capital punishment, but the US military no longer possesses the power to threaten soldiers with death for desertion. What are deemed more serious crimes, such as 'aiding and abetting the enemy', with which Private Manning was charged, may carry the death penalty.

Unlike Manning and Mejía, most morally troubled soldiers do not join antiwar movements and find positive political outlets for their discontent. On 17 August 2010, veteran National Guardsman Matthew Magdzas shot and killed his wife, April, their daughter, Lila, the family's three dogs, and then himself. For his PTSD symptoms, including recurrent nightmares, Magdzas had been prescribed Lexapro, Ultram and clonazepam. At least 112 other National Guardsmen took their lives in 2010 as well, the rate of suicide among that group having increased by 450 percent since 2004.[206] Reported statistics on troop suicides do not include accidental self-killings (such as drug over-doses) and are conservative estimates. Some suicides are interpreted or portrayed by families as natural or accidental deaths, whether to shield the fallen soldier from disgrace or to collect on insurance policies, which do not pay in the event of intentional self-killing.

The National Guardsmen were deployed unexpectedly abroad, but record numbers (and percentages) of the regular, full-time veterans of the wars in Afghanistan and Iraq have also committed suicide. Many of the soldiers who have taken their own lives, like Magdzas, were prescribed a battery of medications intended to address their PTSD symptoms.[207] Some of the antidepressant drugs being provided to soldiers are known to increase violent and, specifically, suicidal tendencies, as is printed in the contraindications accompanying the prescription medications. The number of veterans who took their own lives continued to grow throughout the occupation of Iraq, but also in its aftermath, even when soldiers knew that they would not be redeployed for combat to that theater.

The problem of soldier alienation has existed for as long as wars have been fought overseas, but it appears to have become much worse in the twenty-first century than it was in the past, judging by the record percentages of troops who have taken their own lives. Rather than examine the role of drugs in the decisions of so many able-bodied young veterans to destroy themselves after having survived life-threatening tours of duty, the emphasis in reporting on these incidents is on the lack of an adequate support system for veterans upon their return to civil society.

The symptoms for which psychiatric medications are prescribed include suicidal tendencies, thus providing an ironclad defense against any allegation to the effect that the drugs themselves may have contributed to the soldiers' demise. This curiously impervious logic is equally applicable to and helps to explain the trend within society more generally toward the more and more frequent use of prescription drugs in lieu of analysis and nonmedicinal therapies in treating persons who seek professional help with their psychological concerns. The pro-med trend has been accelerated by recent changes in insurance policies to cover drugs but not 'talk therapy', which obviously inclines psychiatrists to medicate their patients. When drugs are covered by a patient's health plan but dialogue is not, many doctors will write prescriptions rather than lose a client.[208]

In the case of veteran suicides, rather than acknowledge that the disorientation caused by an overload of prescription drugs in the system – or even a modest dose of what are mind-altering agents – may have led soldiers to take their own lives, advocates of pharmaceutical therapy are apt to argue that, in fact, they have prevented even more tragic deaths from occurring. This is a difficult hypothesis to refute, the counterfactual claim being that, were fewer soldiers to take the drugs, then there would be even more suicides. Any attempt to test such a hypothesis, by withdrawing drugs from the persons currently being medicated, would be interpreted by the drugs' advocates as irresponsibly placing the patients in even greater danger of seeking a solution to their trauma and anxiety through self-inflicted death.

However, there have been cases where it cannot be denied that the drugs themselves physically caused soldiers' deaths. Marine veteran Andrew White died in his sleep on 12 February 2008 of a prescription medication overdose. The potential interaction effects of the 'multi-med cocktails' being increasingly prescribed (as in White's case) are unpredictable and sometimes prove to be deadly.[209] Despite such disturbing stories, drugs continue to be regarded as 'the answer' by the VA and have been made available to ill-at-ease soldiers even preemptively, before going to war.

During the occupation of Iraq, 20 percent of the soldiers on active duty, serving in the war theater, were taking medications such as Seroquel, among more than 100 other psychotropic drugs listed in the CENTCOM (United States Central Command) formulary. Even highly addictive substances such as Valium and Xanax are offered to soldiers who manifest anxiety – a perfectly normal reaction to the extraordinary nature of their experience – before, during and after their service. As a result of the VA's liberal dispensation policies, soldiers can become long-term users of drugs to which they may otherwise never have had access, what amounts to a financial windfall for the firms involved. Billions of dollars are at stake in decisions about where, when and how to prescribe medications to soldiers and veterans.[210] Compounding the perverse potential for pharmaceutical firm profits arising from GWOT, people living under drones in places such as Pakistan are increasingly being prescribed psychotropic medications as a means of coping with depression and stress.[211]

Drugs have been dispensed to US soldiers at unprecedented levels in the twenty-first century, and are now provided upon request, but the 'medication' of troops also took place during the US engagement in Vietnam. The difference is that the free-flowing drugs in Vietnam were not secured through Pentagon contracts and furnished by the VA. Still, the popular drugs of that era – the years of the hippie movement – were readily available to soldiers, including marijuana, LSD (lysergic acid diethylamide) and heroin. In Vietnam, the Pentagon's anti-marijuana policy had the effect of promoting the use of highly addictive heroin, which could be procured in pure form for a pittance. As a result, many veterans returned home with a serious addiction to a hard drug, having smoked the opiate during their service in an effort to make their experience more bearable.[212]

* * *

The rate of suicide among US soldiers from 2005 to 2011 was estimated to be double that of the general population.[213] Why have so many troops who fought tooth and nail to preserve their lives while deployed turned guns upon themselves once safely back at home? Part of the solution to this puzzle may lie in the distinction between civilians and active-duty soldiers in an open, liberal democratic society. During the term of their active service, soldiers must unflinchingly carry out the specific orders issued by their superior officers. Skeptical doubts about the terms of their deployment are not tolerated among soldiers within the military hierarchy. It is not the role of soldiers to assess the need for war, nor whether war is the only or even the best solution to the conflict in which they have been called up to serve.

The institution of the military has not varied in this respect throughout the entire history of warfare, regardless of the nature of the leader, group or society being defended by recourse to deadly force. The requirement of strict obedience is justified by traditional military protocol as a measure to maximize the probability of both survival and victory. Combat soldiers work in complex, highly dangerous and extremely stressful contexts. The coordinated movements of a platoon may be disrupted by an individual soldier's hesitation to act, with potentially dire consequences for the entire group.

In its hierarchical structure, the subculture of the military is similar to a tyrannical regime: the laws are handed down from on high, and all subjects must obey, from small orders issued by one's direct supervising officer all the way up to the commander in chief, who decrees when and where the troops are to be deployed and whom they are to kill. Strict obedience to authority is required, and any deviation from orders deemed lawful constitutes an indictable crime.

In nations under despotic rule, there is no schism between the military and civil society. Dissent is prohibited in both. Under a tyrannical regime, the requirements upon soldiers are no different from those of civilians. Both are required to heed the dictates of their leader – whatever they may be – on pain of severe punishment (usually death) for failure to do so. A society governed by a despot may not be an easy one for critical thinkers to survive in, but it is a consistent one: soldiers and civilians alike are prohibited from expressing dissent, and the requirements imposed upon soldiers do not change at the end of a war.

The soldiers of Western liberal states, in contrast, are not only asked to don a helmet during the period of their military service, they are expected to inhabit an entirely different world from that in which they were raised. The two worlds – off-duty and on-duty – of the soldier defending a free society such as the United States may be difficult to reconcile because, having already achieved adulthood, enlistees are accustomed to an open, questioning environment in which criticism and debate are valued. While on active duty, the soldier finds himself in the position of not being able to do what has been permitted throughout his life up to this point: to air questions and moral concerns, and to engage in dialogues with others over differences of opinion about policy. Habits die hard, and while soldiers may stifle their puzzlement regarding the terms and conditions of their deployment and what they are asked to do, in certain contexts, nagging questions will begin nonetheless to take shape in their minds.

The rampant use of mind-altering substances by soldiers is symptomatic of a much deeper problem, as is the incidence of suicide among troops – whether or not they take their own lives under the influence of drugs. Soldiers find it necessary to numb their critical faculties and to anesthetize themselves emotionally in order to accept what they are being asked to do, and to live with what they have witnessed and done. When they do not succeed in rendering their experience surreal enough to be tolerable, they sometimes take their own lives.

For those soldiers who survive their tour of duty to return to civilian life in liberal democratic society, critical thinking becomes officially permissible again. At this point, veterans of war may agonize over the death and destruction of human beings which they themselves helped to perpetrate under a false pretext (in Iraq, the nonexistent WMD; in Vietnam, the grossly exaggerated communist threat), during what they may now believe in their heart of hearts was neither a just nor a necessary war. Drone operators may be safe from physical harm, but they are peculiarly vulnerable in this regard – shuffling back and forth as they do between the office and their home – which helps to explain the new phenomenon of 'drone operator burnout'.[214]

Remote-control killers may become plagued by the shunting between their office hours, during which they kill human beings, and the rest of the day, in civilian society, where homicide is strictly forbidden. When it becomes obvious from what the operators have directly witnessed that they are destroying people who do not truly deserve to die, the killers may become overwhelmed by emotions such as guilt. They may regret having believed the rhetoric used to motivate them to engage targets, obliterating not only suspects but also innocent bystanders caught in the deadly missile's radius of effect. The killers may suffer compunction for having acted against their conscience in some cases.

Both combat soldiers and drone operators and sensors may find themselves questioning the motives behind the missions in which they have served as tools. They may be haunted by misgivings to such a degree that they never recover from having mistakenly (they now believe) agreed to kill on command their fellow human beings. Sensor operators such as Brandon Bryant, who aided and abetted what they later came to believe were crimes, may suffer severe anguish for their complicity in the victims' demise.

The liberal dispensation of drugs to active-duty soldiers and veterans alike might seem to be merely one manifestation of a much more general cultural phenomenon, with more and more psychiatrists prescribing medication in lieu of other forms of therapy.[215] The dominant psychiatric medication trend, with drugs being widely prescribed for what were formerly considered minor and entirely normal levels of anxiety associated with everyday life in human society, surely has much to do with massive marketing efforts by pharmaceutical firms.[216] However, other dynamics, peculiar to the modern military, have contributed as well. The Pentagon, being an institution, has its own reasons of self-preservation for supporting the increased use of drugs by soldiers before, during and after their service. Self-doubt among soldiers who have yet to deploy is diagnosed by military physicians as a medical condition, pathological anxiety, to be treated by drugs.

Drones may offer, more than anything else, the latest and greatest solution to the problem of how to get men (and now women as well) to kill complete strangers on command. The quest for increased lethality generated Predator drones, which make it possible to engage targets without jeopardizing the lives of allied combatants. When soldiers who wield deadly weapons are at no risk of physical harm, and when they come into contact with the consequences of their homicidal actions only through surreal video images, it may become much easier for them to kill – and all the more so when this is accomplished through an action as trivial and familiar as the clicking of a computer mouse or the pressing of a button in a comfortable office setting. The same physical movements used to shop online and check email are now used by drone operators to destroy human beings.

The introduction of vast distances between institutional killers and their victims appears to have the effect of making war as surreal to some of those who push the buttons as it is to policymakers. Operators 'engage' and 'employ on' their targets, 'lighting up' human beings to produce 'splashes' and 'bug splat' on the video screen. Watching YouTube videos of UCAV killings, referred to by some as 'Predator porn', has become a pastime of some military supporters. Live streaming of people being killed began in military and CIA headquarters as 'Kill TV' and bears disturbing similarities to 'snuff' films, which are not just *about* murder but also depict scenes *of* murder.[217] The greater the distance between them, the less humanly connected the killers and viewers alike become to the victims, including the nameless collateral damage unintentionally produced in attempts to extinguish whoever has been designated the enemy.

In view of longstanding and assiduous efforts to increase the lethality of troops, the widespread use of drugs contracted for by the Pentagon and prescribed by VA physicians can be understood, too, as a part of this same chronology: the ongoing quest to make soldiers more willing and able to kill.[218] When twenty-first-century enlistees raised in a liberal democratic society begin to experience compunction or express doubts about what they have been called upon to do, the time becomes ripe to iron out their anxiety through the use of medication. Drugs can be used to muffle the opinions of soldiers who find themselves disagreeing with the official stories of glorious war proffered by smiling, jovial secretaries of defense such as Robert S. McNamara and Donald Rumsfeld.[219] Philosophical concerns such as whether killing is a genuine solution to conflict, or whether a particular war is in fact just, may be facilely brushed aside and effectively invalidated by diagnosing the soldiers in which they arise as maladjusted. Once medicated, soldiers may no longer feel the need to articulate their concerns because they have melted away in a drug-induced haze. At the same time, some of the substances currently being prescribed to troops are known to lower the threshold for violence, making it easier to kill and to do so without compunction.[220]

Multiple factors have conspired to give rise to the rampant medication of soldiers, including the now formidable economic forces exerted by pharmaceutical firms not only upon the insurance industry (which inclines physicians to opt for drug therapy) but also in shaping Pentagon prescription policy. A further contributing factor is the conservative nature of policies once implemented, and institutions, more generally. Administrators naturally tend to defend and maintain the current practices as part of the status quo, the acceptance of which was a prerequisite to their appointment. To criticize the Pentagon's preemptive drug policy implemented to increase troops' lethality would be to question current leaders' expertise, including VA hospital administrators and those to whom they answer.

The conservative nature of institutions and the resultant homogenization of administrators and practices are especially evident in the case of the US targeted killing program. Over eight years, George W. Bush used drone strikes fifty-two times; by the end of his first term, Barack Obama had already authorized hundreds of drone strikes, and was killing Muslims in several different lands simultaneously. The tactic of remote-control killing, having snuck in the back door as a necessary counterterrorism practice, was never examined or defended, but became a standard operating procedure by sheer dint of repetition. When Obama retained Bush administration officials in key national security positions and enlisted as his advisers men who had already mistreated or destroyed scores of people, he thereby ensured a seamless continuation of some of the same policies, including that of targeted killing.

Given the modern military institution's ever-more challenging task to keep soldiers 'on message' with the official story of the war, but without the threat of death for disobedience, the preemptive prescription of drugs intended to alleviate self-doubt and anxiety would seem to serve, first and foremost, a public relations purpose. The Pentagon's drug policy may have been initially implemented as part of the general campaign for increased lethality, but one of the unforeseen and felicitous consequences of that policy for the public relations wing of the military apparatus is to decrease the incidence of dissent among troops.

Pathologizing anxiety and medicating otherwise normal people as they attempt to cope with the stresses of battle eliminates credible criticism of the official rationale or the justice of the war or, more specifically, what troops are asked to do. A liberal drug dispensation policy minimizes the emergence of figures such as Sergeant Mejía and Private Manning, but also apostate drone operators and sensors such as Brandon Bryant. Soldiers and drone operators who have been medicated to the point where they are no longer bothered by the concerns aired by outspoken veterans have been effectively silenced. The soldiers who anesthetize their minds fall into line, precisely as the Pentagon's policy prescribes. The promiscuous provision of psychotropic drugs to troops prevents the persons best situated to offer critiques of a war – the soldiers who directly witness the nature and extent of the death and destruction caused – from being able to pose credible opposition to the institution's version of the story.

The drone program naturally attracts only certain types of employees, who are predisposed to believe that the killing by remote control of persons located thousands of miles away is morally permissible. This suggests that most of the killers will be unlikely to find themselves afflicted with PTSD as a result of what they have done, especially given the ready availability of 'war porn' videos. Judging by the comments online, the viewers of these YouTube clips cheer on the assassination of virtual representations of human beings as though the operators were playing Pac-Man or some other video game. The utter surreality of this form of warfare can only make it easier to kill more people faster, just as Matthew Martin endeavored to do, under the assumption that increased lethality is a positive thing.

As the existence of outspoken civilian war critics – who cannot be written off as victims of PTSD – attests, legitimate questions can be raised about the summary execution of persons based on circumstantial and hearsay evidence obtained through bribery. But critics within the 'kill chain' can be muted by writing them off as 'criminal' or 'sick' – even when they have perfectly valid and rational concerns about what they have witnessed and been asked to do. The use of Predator drones streamlines and sterilizes the killing process, removing soldiers from the battlefields where they kill, making it as easy for some (not all) as playing a video game. But anyone who has serious qualms about the practice will not become a drone operator in the first place. The discontents will abandon the profession, leaving only willful executioners to rise in the ranks, ensuring a continuation and expansion of the same policy in the future. Former operators who experience regret about what they agreed to do can be facilely diagnosed with PTSD and 'treated' accordingly.

Whatever misgivings drone operators may harbor about destroying human beings identified as legitimate targets on the basis of intelligence provided by unknown analysts and spies on the ground, they do not have to endure the stench of rotting corpses in trenches, as did many twentieth-century troops. Still, some operators may occasionally feel compunction, as even Matthew Martin did when he realized that he had pushed the button of an irretrievable missile only to watch two young boys on bicycles ride up to the target. But what about cases such as Abdulrahman al-Awlaki, the brown-skinned sixteen-year-old (no different in moral essence from Trayvon Martin) who was killed along with several of his friends while preparing to eat dinner? Who pushed the button? Did the operator believe himself to have suppressed the activities of several future terrorists simultaneously? If the action was not intentional, then perhaps the operator will feel regret for his part in the bloodbath, in which case he may seek out assistance from the VA, to be dispensed in the form of pills, thereby squelching any potential for effective dissent.

The official stories of war are written by the institution, not the fallen soldiers, the civilian casualties, the marginalized victims of PTSD, nor the heroic patriots who attempt to reveal the extent of war crimes committed by their government, as did Private Manning. Such soldiers' stories are effectively erased as the speaker is either destroyed or marginalized and criminalized. The spokespersons for the Pentagon and the CIA defend not the nation but their own institution, minimizing or even ignoring the tragic effects of their policies upon the victims.[221] Military administrators distance themselves from the soldiers who commit what are undeniably crimes (for example, at Bagram and Abu Ghraib prisons), even when the practices in which the troops engaged were approved at the highest level of the government.[222]

When soldiers and operators are met with skeptical glances in response to acts of killing carried out in the name of the nation, this may catalyze an introspective process, leaving the killers despondent and depressed. Some troops may conclude that they were horribly duped. They may decide that they have mistakenly submitted to authority and contributed to acts which, with the benefit of hindsight, seem tantamount to ghastly crimes. It is entirely normal for a person to experience guilt and regret after having committed a moral wrong, and there is no worse crime than the annihilation of another human being. That is what soldiers and drone operators have been lured into doing, and, among those who suffer from PTSD, that is the primary source of their psychological and emotional pain.

Reflective drone operators no doubt recognize that suspects are suspects. Of the persons identified as legitimate targets, some, like many of the unfortunate detainees at Guantánamo Bay, are innocent of the crimes for which they are being punished. Like the prisoners cleared for release from Guantánamo Bay, some of the persons 'taken out' by Predator drone may simply have been in the wrong place at the wrong time. Having once awakened to this fact, the killers may conclude that they misjudged the wisdom of enlistment, lacking a full understanding of what it would entail.

To give due credence to the voices of discontents such as Brandon Bryant would be to admit that society wronged these young people by enticing them to become professional killers, which they would otherwise never have done. The veritable epidemic of PTSD and soldier suicides in the twenty-first century reveals that there is something seriously awry with an institution which places human beings in the essentially corruptive situation of being required to kill on command, no questions asked. In the drone age, persons with no prior disposition to commit homicide are persuaded to execute unarmed suspects who do not directly threaten them. The operators are told that the targets wish to murder people, but such allegedly evil intentions cannot be read from silhouettes on a computer screen.

PART III
FINISH

CHAPTER 9
DEATH AND POLITICS

'The CIA can neither confirm nor deny the existence or nonexistence of responsive records because the existence or nonexistence of any such records is a currently and properly classified fact that is exempt from release.'

Mary Cole, CIA
Information Review Officer[223]

'Drones have not caused a huge number of civilian casualties ... It's not a bunch of folks in a room somewhere just making decisions, and it is also part and parcel of our overall authority when it comes to battling Al-Qaeda.'

US President Barack Obama[224]

Mᴜᴄʜ CONTROVERSY SURROUNDED the results of the US presidential election at the turn of the century, but the Supreme Court ruled George W. Bush, not Al Gore, the winner of the contest. A greater percentage of the electorate voted for Bush in 2004 than in 2000, and he was re-elected despite revelations that the weapons of mass destruction (WMD) serving as the primary pretext for the 2003 war on Iraq did not exist. The terrorist attacks of 11 September 2001 were undoubtedly one factor, but Bush appears also to have benefited to some extent from his waging of the war on Iraq, for many voters were persuaded in 2004 that the president should be permitted to 'finish' what he had begun. Viewed in a broader historical context, the re-election of Bush was not that surprising. The waging of war tends to buoy political leaders, even in societies where citizens are able to express dissent at the polls. During wartime, the populace is inclined to line up behind their leader in a parade of patriotism. 'Support our troops' becomes the rhetorical order of the day once war has been waged.

First World leaders do not endanger themselves by waging war. They do, however, succeed in promoting images of themselves as strong by flexing military muscle. President George H. W. Bush dispelled to some extent his image as a wimpy bureaucrat by ordering the invasion of Panama in 1989 in response to a relatively minor and localized scuffle involving a US military officer and his wife, hardly a matter warranting the mobilization of the military corps. Two years later, in 1991, while preparing the nation for a full-scale war to expel Saddam Hussein's forces from Kuwait, Bush proclaimed: 'nor will there be any negotiation. Principle cannot be compromised.'[225]

It is difficult to imagine, in either of those cases, that Bush Sr would have called for war had he been commanding the troops on the ground and putting his own life at stake. Yet these sorts of moves by leaders do, opinion polls attest, temporarily boost politicians' popularity, as though the willingness to sacrifice other people's lives evidenced leaders' own courage. Presidents are also able deftly to divert attention from domestic woes by waging wars abroad, as did Bill Clinton, who was embroiled in a sensational tabloid-worthy sex scandal in 1999. The moment the NATO bombing of Kosovo commenced on 24 March 1999, the focus of the media and the populace turned from the infamous 'blue dress' to the military campaign, with even some of Clinton's most outspoken detractors siding with the president in a show of solidarity.[226]

By sheer force of habit, people generally accept the history of warfare as a seamless tradition comprising a long sequence of courageous leaders, up to and including the current commander in chief. Aware of the impact of images on the public reception of leaders, the speech writers and advisers to George W. Bush hatched the scheme to dress him up in a combat pilot's uniform for his appearance on an aircraft carrier after the invasion of Iraq in 2003. The triumphant president stood at a podium in front of a huge banner emblazoned with the words 'Mission Accomplished'. He was met with the rousing applause of cheering troops. In truth, the entire theatrical production was a charade, for the costume-clad commander never risked so much as having his hair mussed up in the 'victory' – vaunted prematurely, it shortly thereafter emerged. To this day, Iraq remains in shambles as a direct result of the US invasion in 2003. What's more, a new global threat, ISIS (self-styled fighters for the Islamic State in Iraq and Al-Sham) was created directly by the US invasion and occupation of Iraq.

In addition to waging a preemptive war, Bush Jr brazenly taunted terrorists intent upon destabilizing Iraq. 'Bring 'em on!' he exclaimed, as though such a provocation were an expression of his own courage and strength. Bush's invitation both falsely suggested that he was courageous, and served positively to endanger the troops under his command. Jihadis continued to flock to the land (as they had already been doing), and thousands of US troops were sacrificed as the insurgency redoubled its efforts to defeat the invaders. Many more of the surviving soldiers were permanently maimed or committed suicide. Nonetheless, Bush was somehow confirmed through this fiasco – a full-scale war waged on false pretenses and a disastrously bungled occupation – as a strong leader in the minds of military supporters.

Conversely, when Barack Obama threatened missile strikes against Syria in August 2013 and then abruptly recanted in the face of international and domestic resistance to his plan, he was derided by critics as weak. Obama had claimed a year earlier that the use of chemical weapons was a 'red line' not to be crossed, so suddenly his credibility, along with that of the nation, was said to be at stake. However, it was entirely unclear what effect an intervention might have beyond terrorizing civilians who would be placed at further risk of death by the imminent military campaign. It was also unclear whether the Assad regime was solely responsible or the rebel forces themselves had used chemical weapons in an effort to provoke intervention.[227]

That missile strikes would not help and would likely harm the already suffering civilian population of Syria did not seem to carry much weight. But the British Parliament refused to support Obama's proposal for military action against Syria in 2013, heeding the lesson indelibly etched on their minds by the Iraq war, which had been based on faulty intelligence furnished by the CIA. As a result, Obama's war plans were delayed. He turned to Congress for support, which proved difficult to secure, given that some of the motley assortment of rebels to be aided by the action were Al-Qaeda affiliates.[228] When Obama backed down in the face of political opposition to his threatened air strikes against the Assad regime, he was ridiculed by hawkish pundits. Obama's warmongering critics were disappointed that the same president who had vastly expanded the Predator drone program and succeeded in hunting down and killing Osama bin Laden was now wavering in the face of dissent. In the end, the use of chemical weapons in Syria was addressed through the United Nations, as it should have been from the start.

Whether political leaders follow through on their threats or not, in the modern world they themselves are heavily protected throughout the duration of wars carried out by other people, most of whom are situated on the lower rungs of the military ladder. Curiously enough, when the leaders of enemy factions and terrorist groups emulate Western political leaders by sending soldiers out to kill and die in their stead, they are branded as cowards. Throughout the decade when he was being pursued, Osama bin Laden was often portrayed as a sort of mole or rat hiding in caves, a man too craven to face his enemy. The fact that he should have sent other persons to carry out the attacks of 11 September 2001, too, was depicted as a despicable display of pusillanimity.

Even more oddly, immediately after the 9/11 attacks, it became popular in the media to denounce the direct perpetrators – those who died along with the people whom they killed – as cowards. It is possible that some of those involved were unaware that they would die in the missions, but at least one person per plane must have known.

Deluded though he may be, there is no plausible sense in which a person who sacrifices his life for a cause in which he truly believes is a coward. When a few people attempted to point out these obvious facts, they were denigrated by pundits as enemy sympathizers. In reality, Al-Qaeda's modus operandi, with Bin Laden as 'commander in chief', conformed perfectly with the standard practice of modern military states. The top-level administrators decide when and where to wage war but watch what transpires on video screens in impenetrable command centers far from the bloody fray. In the drone age, a new breed of 'soldier', the UCAV operator, does the same.

Along with George W. Bush, the commander of two full-scale wars (and failed occupations), many of the policies implemented in response to the terrorist attacks of 11 September 2001 were supported by voters in 2004. Not everyone agreed with the Patriot Act, the Foreign Intelligence Surveillance Act, the practice of extraordinary rendition, the detention of suspects without charge at Guantánamo Bay, and the other dubious initiatives implemented by the Bush administration, but enough citizens were made to feel sufficiently safe by the absence of any attack on US soil in the period following 9/11 that they opted to re-elect the president.

Rather than fault government institutions for failing to protect the homeland, lawmakers lavished billions of dollars more upon them in the aftermath of 9/11, under the assumption that the explanation for the lapses was insufficient funding. Throwing money at the problem seemed like the patriotic thing to do, but in reality it degraded the security of not only non-threatening civilians in Afghanistan, Iraq and Pakistan, but also the people of the United States, given that thousands of US nationals (mostly soldiers) were killed during the first decade after 9/11. All of the deaths in combat, permanent disabilities and soldier suicides were direct consequences of GWOT.

By 2008, the US populace had grown war-weary, to put it mildly, and Barack Obama was elected as the 'peace candidate' who had vociferously opposed the 2003 invasion of Iraq. Obama derided the Iraq intervention as a 'stupid' war and vowed to bring US troops home. He also pledged that, as president, he would return to the original mission of the intervention in Afghanistan: to bring Osama bin Laden to justice. While a candidate, Obama decried many of the Bush policies, but upon assuming the presidency he immediately made Predator drone targeted killing the centerpiece of his foreign policy. Obama's promised 'change' amounted only to this: suspects began to be killed as a matter of course rather than rendered to secret prisons for the extraction of 'actionable intelligence' through the use of 'enhanced interrogation'. Obama called a halt to torture and closed most of the secret prisons, but he sent out scores of Predator drones in their stead, to kill rather than capture thousands of suspects in several different lands.

Only three days into Obama's presidency, on 23 January 2009, missiles were fired from drones at five different targets in Pakistan, provoking a mass protest in Islamabad.[229] In 2011, Obama ousted Muammar Gaddafi from Libya in a regime change as total as had been the removal of Saddam Hussein from Iraq, but he did so without ever officially waging a war. Predictably, many Libyans were killed by the hundreds of Hellfire missiles delivered by Predator drone.[230] In the ensuing chaos, the US ambassador and three other personnel were killed as a direct result of Obama's decision to depose Gaddafi. The anomie in post-Gaddafi Libya was not unlike that of postwar Iraq, but since the 'no boots' bombing of Libya was conceived of by its architects not as a war but as a rescue mission of sorts, the president perfunctorily ignored the potential for Libya to become a fertile ground for terrorist groups.

The ability of a leader to intervene militarily without sacrificing the lives of soldiers is a relatively new development in the history of warfare and constitutes a genuine revolution in military affairs.[231] As war has come to require progressively less sacrifice of compatriot lives, US leaders have exhibited a greater willingness to wield deadly force in cases where war is neither the last nor the best resort. The very fact that Obama considered launching missile strikes against the Assad regime in Syria after chemical weapons were used in August 2013 revealed that the military option appeals to leaders even when there is no strategic benefit to be gleaned, and even when the recourse to deadly force might well exacerbate what is already a bloody mess. Obama was rebuffed by both the US Congress and the British Parliament in 2013. Had the US president 'taken out' the Assad regime in 2013, then insurgent groups would likely have rushed in to fill the power vacuum, just as happened in both Libya and Iraq after the removal of secular dictators.

Remarkably, nearly one year to the day after having called for war against the government of Syria, Obama took to the stage once again to promote a new 'no boots' military campaign. This time he set his sights on some of the insurgents (the 'unvetted radical rebels') attempting to topple Assad. On 10 September 2014, Obama announced that he would be ordering air strikes against the dictator's most fearsome enemies on the ground, the members of ISIL (the Islamic State in Iraq and the Levant, also known as ISIS). The decision to bomb the 'radical rebels' in Syria, while providing 'appropriately vetted moderate rebels' with more military aid (weapons and training), was precipitated by the gruesome beheadings of journalists Steven Sotloff and James Foley. The tried-and-true provocation ploy worked yet again, for when the rebels disseminated video footage of the executions across the internet, they succeeded in luring the US government back into the sectarian Shiite–Sunni war raging in the Middle East. Obama ominously warned:

> While *we have not yet detected specific plotting against our homeland*, ISIL leaders have threatened America and our allies. Our Intelligence Community believes that thousands of foreigners – including Europeans and some Americans – have joined them in Syria and Iraq. Trained and battle-hardened, these fighters *could* try to return to their home countries and carry out deadly attacks.[232] [emphasis added]

In this way, Obama carried on in the preemptive war tradition of George W. Bush – as he had already done in the many drone strikes against persons deemed possibly capable of launching future terrorist attacks. Obama touted his targeted killing campaigns in Yemen and Somalia as templates for what he intended to do in Syria, with no apparent awareness that the drone wars had served to intensify anti-American sentiment throughout the region and indeed best explained the upsurge in ISIS strength. A further contributing factor was the covert provision by the CIA of 600 tons of weapons to 'appropriately vetted moderate rebels' during 2013.[233]

While publicly praising his missions in Yemen and Somalia as models of what he intended to do in Syria, Obama referred to the collaborating governments in those lands. But the US president's new war seemed closer to what he had done in Libya, for he launched missiles on Syrian sovereign territory without first securing the permission of the central government. Within months of having called for war against ISIL, Obama's 'success story' in Yemen proved to be altogether fictional. President Saleh's successor, Abd Rabu Mansour Hadi, who had also permitted the US government to operate freely on Yemeni soil in exchange for military aid, was deposed in a coup mounted by angry dissidents.[234]

As the US president attempted to drum up support from Congress and the populace for his proposed air strikes against the regime of Bashar al-Assad in 2013, and then again against ISIS in 2014, he repeatedly insisted that there would be 'no boots on the ground', as though this were a selling point for war. In June 2014, as the conditions in Iraq and Syria degenerated, Obama began flying drones over both lands without seeking legislative approval, just as he had done in Libya before. Later, when ISIS disseminated the video footage of journalists being beheaded, Secretary of State John Kerry recited Obama's 'no boots' mantra:

> We need to do kinetic, we need to attack them in ways that prevent them from taking over territory, that bolster the Iraqi security forces, others in the region who are prepared to take them on, without committing troops of our own, obviously. I think that's a red line for everybody here, no boots on the ground.[235]

When Obama began bombing Syria without getting a 'permission slip' from anyone (again, in the tradition of Bush), he reiterated that there would be 'no boots on the ground'. He opted to join in on the brutal civil war raging in Syria, waging a massive military campaign designed to destroy ISIS/ISIL, even while knowing that ISIS was the strongest opposing force to the Assad regime.[236] During his promotional pitch, President Obama, whose CIA had transmogrified under his leadership into a 'killing machine', ironically characterized ISIS as a 'network of death'. He garnered support for aerial bombing from undemocratic regimes in the region: Jordan, Bahrain, Saudi Arabia, Qatar and

United Arab Emirates, a coalition of governments concerned above all to shore up their own power against domestic dissidents with democratic aspirations.

For the leaders of militarily powerful states, war has always been one of the proverbial 'options on the table' so often spoken of by government officials whenever international disputes arise. With the greater and greater availability of RPA, and because the human costs appear from afar to be minimal, remote-control killing can be expected to continue to increase in frequency. Predator drone warfare does have lethal consequences, but collateral damage is either flatly denied or sanitized to the point where it seems to be completely nonexistent to the people who pay for it. The only discernible effect from the perspective of the vast majority of citizens who fund drone warfare is a drain on the budget, with nonmilitary programs eviscerated. Such fiscal sacrifices are deemed acceptable by those who believe in the efficacy of 'taking the battle to the enemy'.

Where before war was a major event, claimed to be undertaken only when the alternative would be catastrophic for the people paying for it, in the future military action may be opted for whenever and wherever it seems feasible. Certainly 'feasibility' appears to have supplanted 'necessity' as the key decision-making criterion in the Obama administration. The Department of Justice White Paper asserts the right to continuous, ubiquitous killing of anyone anywhere, because *imminent threat* is an idea in the mind of the Predator drone program administrators. In early 2014, the US government was reportedly debating the possibility of a strike on another US citizen located abroad, this time in Pakistan.[237] Why? Because it was possible to do so. Having already hunted down and killed Anwar al-Awlaki, the Obama administration now embraced the execution of US citizens without trial as one of the proverbial 'options on the table'. Executing another citizen would reinforce the norm according to which the targeting of Al-Awlaki was perfectly legitimate.

'War' reimagined in this way, as a list of suspects to be dispatched, is open-ended, metaphysical, and impervious to facts – precisely the model championed by the Bush administration, which famously insisted that Saddam Hussein 'prove' that his WMD were nonexistent. Signature strikes are arguably worse than the invasion of Iraq from a justificatory standpoint, because Saddam Hussein was at least believed (albeit erroneously) to possess WMD. The people being killed in the Predator drone program are often executed on the basis of what is claimed to be 'suspicious' behavior, including their association with people previously identified as 'suspicious'.

Part of the explanation for the uncritical acceptance of the 'Kill don't capture' policy is purely political: US congressmen mounted vigorous opposition to the housing of terrorist suspects in their voting jurisdictions. Politicians took great pains to prevent the trials of notorious figures such as Khalid Sheikh Mohammed from being held in local cities, under the assumption that such public spectacles would increase the likelihood of retaliatory terrorist attacks nearby.[238] Lawmakers garner reputations for being strong by supporting the elimination of proclaimed enemies of the state, which is one reason why they so frequently advocate war. Politicians also engage in complex, albeit short-term, calculations about how to protect themselves when policies do not deliver on their promises or have other untoward effects.

The best way to prevent being blamed for terrorist attacks provoked in the immediate future by civilian court trials, many congressmen appear to have reasoned, would be to ensure that such trials not take place anywhere near their electorate. In this way, the structure of modern Western politics – that, in order to keep their jobs, officials in a democracy must earn the favor of their constituents in the short term – explains why so little attention is paid to longer-term effects, including the blowback likely to result from current military policies. Missions judged to be sound in the short term for reasons of political expediency may prove in the long term to be disastrous, but leaders are subject to electoral redress for only so long as they hold office.

A new techno-tool, the weaponized Predator drone, provided the 'peace candidate' elected president the propitious opportunity both to wage war and to seem not to wage war – at least from the perspective of the people of the United States. Residents of Pakistan have a quite different view of the matter, as Malala Yousafzai attempted to explain to President Obama on 11 October 2013: 'Drone attacks are fueling terrorism. Innocent victims are killed in these acts, and they lead to resentment among the Pakistan people.'[239]

Judging by the number of angry protests in areas under assault by weaponized drones, with the burning of American flags and effigies of its leaders, the enemies of the United States grew vastly in number in the period after 11 September 2001, beginning with the wars in Afghanistan and Iraq. In the ensuing years, the map of hostile territories continued to enlarge as the targeted killing program came to be embraced with surprising enthusiasm by the president elected by war-weary Americans. 'Drone warrior' Obama championed the new technology of UCAVs as a 'smart' way to contend with the threat of terrorism without risking the lives of soldiers. By taking this tack, Obama succeeded in minimizing domestic dissent.

Needless to say, the people of Pakistan and Yemen do not vote in US elections. As in the case of George W. Bush, US voters re-elected Obama for a second term. The president's first-term performance was validated by the electorate, especially his success at hunting down and killing Osama bin Laden, but also his aggressive Predator drone program, which was finally made public by the president himself in advance of the 2012 election. The fact that, in the long term, Predator drone targeted killing and brutal JSOC raids – also stepped up by Obama – may well have the opposite effect, destabilizing rather than securing the nation, appears to be beyond the capability of either the president or his tacticians to entertain. Officials and politicians remain myopically focused on the current window of time and the number of 'kills' carried out, crossing names off ever-lengthening hit lists.

In the run-up to the 2012 presidential election, as Barack Obama sought to woo voters once again, he emphasized to audiences on the campaign trail that he had 'made the call' to kill rather than capture Osama bin Laden, and bragged of having wiped out the majority of the top Al-Qaeda leaders. The message played rather well to voters, and military supporters in particular lauded Obama's decision to kill rather than capture Bin Laden. But to say that Obama eliminated most of the top Al-Qaeda leaders is a deceptive characterization of what he has done, given the hydra-like structure of terrorist organizations. Cases in point (among others): Al-Shabaab in Somalia and ISIS in Iraq and Syria. 'Top Al-Qaeda leaders' are a dime a dozen. Pop off as many as you like, and new ones will always emerge from below to become the latest 'top Al-Qaeda leaders'. Osama bin Laden, after all, was not born but became an enemy of the United States. After having fought with the mujahedin funded by the US government during the war in Afghanistan against Soviet invaders, Bin Laden changed his tune, eventually coming to believe that the US military was his arch enemy. Bin Laden was obviously not alone in having been turned against the US government by its very own military policies.

Strikingly, even some people who spoke out publicly against the crimes of 11 September 2001, as Anwar al-Awlaki did, eventually came to praise jihad undertaken in retaliation against the US military's killing campaigns. To suppose that it is desirable or even possible to eliminate every person who may emerge from below as an Al-Qaeda leader is a losing proposition, because terrorist suspects are not all guilty of crimes. Moreover, entirely innocent people, not even suspected by anyone of wrongdoing, are sometimes destroyed alongside intended targets, causing anti-American sentiment around the globe to swell. Even if Obama were to root out every self-proclaimed Al-Qaeda member on the planet, he would have left in the process plenty of other enemies behind. They may call themselves 'Al-Qaeda', or they may call themselves something else (ISIS, ISIL, etc.). Many Al-Qaeda and Taliban sympathizers, like many of the insurgents in Iraq, have been no more and no less than the bereft survivors of US killing campaigns. Some of them were radicalized to the point of becoming jihadis.

Did killing Bin Laden show that Obama was a strong leader? To some, this may be the natural conclusion, and it was one reason why people voted to re-elect him in 2012. Others selected the incumbent president as a known entity and the likely lesser of two evils. 'No boots' drone warrior Obama appealed more to voters than did his opponent, but to suppose that ordering the execution of Bin Laden demonstrated Obama's strength is to fall prey to a mythic picture of leaders. Modern political leaders risk nothing personally by killing people abroad. Yet they elevate themselves in the eyes of those who infer from history that 'great leaders' are ready and willing to take their nations to war and to slay evil enemies.

The primary effect of killing rather than capturing Bin Laden was not to carry out a heroic act of justice but to prevent the Al-Qaeda leader from ever speaking again. What would Bin Laden and his lawyers have said, had Obama not made 'the call' to kill him, thereby silencing him forever? In all likelihood, Bin Laden would have continued to criticize US military policy, just as he had done before and continued to do after the terrorist attacks of 11 September 2001, which were depicted by Al-Qaeda as just retaliation for US military incursions abroad.

No reasonable person believes that the attacks of 11 September 2001 against civilians in their workplaces were acts of justice, but by killing Bin Laden, Obama silenced the Al-Qaeda leader and suppressed debate and soul-searching among administrators about US military policy. When Bin Laden was finally found and finished off, many people in the United States celebrated in the streets, having by then perhaps come to hold the Al-Qaeda leader responsible for not only 9/11 but also the costly wars in both Afghanistan and Iraq. Converts to violent jihadist groups have been persuaded to believe that Osama bin Laden spoke the truth, but his criticisms of US military policy were muffled by President Obama's decision to kill rather than capture the notorious Al-Qaeda mastermind.

The administration's treatment of whistleblowers such as Private Manning and Edward Snowden evinces a similar and concerted effort to mute dissent. The problem is not merely moral; it is strategic as well. Without knowing what they are actually paying for, US citizens will continue to be complicit in the very crimes exposed by dissidents. By hiding and denying its practices abroad, the US government endangers the very people whom it is charged to protect.[240] In fact, because policymakers have access to enhanced security not available to average citizens, the persons most likely to suffer the blowback of bad policies are civilians, not government leaders.

Assiduous attempts to suppress whistleblowers such as Manning and Snowden would be less surprising in a monarchy, but the United States has long prided itself on being a beacon of human rights and liberty. As the military gained power over the executive during the period spanning the terms of George W. Bush and Barack Obama, it came to dictate policy by sharply limiting the proverbial options on the table presented to the president by his advisers. Drones have paved the path to profligate military incursion in the affairs of other nations by creating a chasm between the people and the policies implemented abroad in their name.

On the campaign trail back in 2007 and 2008, Barack Obama repudiated many of the Bush administration practices and called for change. Once elected president, Obama embraced the most sweeping Bush-era innovations, most fundamentally the inversion of the burden of proof and the notion of 'offensive defense'. Just as the Bush administration had depended on the concept of 'unlawful combatant' in denying suspects any and all rights, the Obama administration deployed a variety of linguistic devices in sharply escalating the use of drone strikes, asserting the right to kill anyone anywhere identified by the killers themselves as 'associated' with Al-Qaeda – or simply 'evil', as in the case of ISIS.

The Obama legal team pronounced that all military-age males in territories designated 'hostile' are 'combatants' suitable for targeting, and the 'imminent' threat which they pose need not be 'immediate'. The crucial first step in this series of redefinitions was to characterize the terrorist attacks of 11 September 2001 as *acts of war* rather than *crimes*. From there, all of the subsequent conceptual innovations were designed to dispel impressions that what was being done in response to those crimes might be criminal as well. Apparently unaware of the implications of his targeted killing policy, Obama has inadvertently upheld the Bush administration's concept of preemptive war, albeit one missile at a time. Obama has also denied that there are any geographical or temporal limits on the use of drone warfare, and he has repeatedly sidestepped US law – most obviously in Libya – according to which the commander in chief is to confer with the sitting Congress before, not after, wielding military force.

The very same inversion of the burden of proof binds the policies of these presidents together over sixteen years of US history. George W. Bush insisted that Saddam Hussein prove that he had no WMD, and when UN weapons inspector Hans Blix reported that no evidence of a reconstituted WMD program had been found in Iraq, the Bush administration replied by shutting down the inspection process and waging war. In truth, no one can demonstrate the nonexistence of a thing through the presentation of positive evidence. Similarly, the military-age males executed by the Obama administration are 'guilty' of being potentially dangerous. How could persons defend themselves from such a charge? The simple answer is that they cannot, because everyone of sound body is *potentially* dangerous.

Needless to say, the impunity being asserted by the US executive escapes many military supporters. Whenever a new occasion for the application of military force arises, many people climb on the band wagon again, adding their little tambourine to the cacophonous group banging their drums for war. Some are true believers; others are war profiteers. Essentially the same script is rehearsed each time. First, war is claimed to be necessary and just. Doomsday tapestries are woven about what will transpire should the nation 'fail' to deploy deadly force. Legislators concerned with shoring up credentials as 'strong' leaders rally in favor of war. Politicians often have as constituents people whose source of gainful employment depends upon the flourishing of military industry. As a result, the representatives are doubly motivated to get behind the war effort, as their electoral future rides on it. The support of war may be for many individuals reasoning at a purely prudential level a matter of economic self-defense.

The diminution of risk to leaders, soldiers and the civilians of the killing nation has been accompanied by a diminution of responsibility. Without risk and responsibility, war runs rampant, unchecked, as no one is deterred by fear of death, and no one is deterred by fear of guilt. In such a world, people may kill with physical, legal and psychological impunity. At the macro level, too, there is no penalty for failure, for the price of drone warfare is paid, at least in the short term, in the lives of people other than those who execute them. There is as little reason for a leader to refrain from wielding the weapons with which his arsenals are stocked as there is for a person to stop gambling somebody else's money away. The person squandering the funds does not pay for his mistakes in any way, and least of all politically. Blowback, such as occurred spectacularly on 11 September 2001, arrives later on down the line.

When wars such as those in Vietnam, Afghanistan and Iraq, and smaller missions, such as in Yemen, Somalia and Libya, backfire, the officials who enlisted troops to kill effectively disappear – recede into the background, return to private life – leaving behind the messes they made for others to inherit and clean up as best they can, or simply to ignore. In the United States, where a president can serve only two consecutive terms, a commander in chief is rewarded politically for flexing military muscle with no concern for what will ensue once his tenure has come to an end. Political responsibility has been effaced from the war picture alongside risk in the drone age, so that neither serves as a deterrent to the use of military force abroad.

After essentially destroying Iraq, killing many thousands of innocent people, and causing the exodus of millions of native inhabitants of that land, George W. Bush has enjoyed his retirement painting portraits at his ranch in Texas. By the time the negative consequences of Obama's policies blow back in the form of future terrorist attacks, he, too, will be long gone, perhaps penning bestselling memoirs and playing golf on Martha's Vineyard. Future leaders, both in the United States and abroad, will contend with the long-range effects of these presidents' killing campaigns.

In terms of pure politics, Obama's decision to expand the drone program was not unlike the push by Dick Cheney and Donald Rumsfeld (during the George W. Bush administration) for the program of 'extraordinary rendition'. Rather than hold the previous administration responsible for its excesses and seeming violations of both international and domestic law, Obama opted in effect to 'let bygones be bygones'. The decision to overlook the crimes of the past leaves torture as an 'option on the table' for future US leaders, while also setting a dangerous precedent for the petty despots dotting the globe.[241] Obama's full-scale program of assassination can itself be viewed as the most extreme of all possible means by which to prevent the 'lawyering up' of suspects.

Appointed officials are protected in this system as well. When institutions such as the CIA fail miserably in what is ostensibly their role – to keep the nation secure by apprising the executive of genuine (not merely metaphysical) threats – they are not chastened for their incompetence but rewarded with ever-more generous allocations of funds, on the assumption that they must not have had enough before. Ten years after its most flagrant failure to date, when the CIA finally located Osama bin Laden, the Agency was praised as great, with no apparent memory of the fact that, if the analysts working at the time had been even marginally competent, then the attacks of 9/11 would never have taken place.

Crediting the government with the near absence of terrorist attacks on US soil since 9/11 is rather like crediting a physician with keeping a healthy person alive. The normal and natural state of the body is health, and the natural state of a republic is peace, safety and security. When a republic is assaulted, it has not been properly protected, just as when a patient falls ill and dies under the care of a physician who misdiagnoses and treats the wrong disease. The lavishing of funds upon an inept government agency is comparable to rewarding a physician for malpractice.

In cases where the physician not only missed the obvious signs and so failed to treat the symptoms in time to save the patient, but also administered deadly drugs and thereby directly killed him, no one would say that the physician deserves praise – or even a raise! But that is precisely analogous to what happened in the case of 9/11. The very reason stated by the architects of those crimes was none other than the US government's incursions in other lands abroad and its victimization of innocent people. Had the United States not caused the deaths of hundreds of thousands of people in Iraq (in the 1991 Gulf War and its aftermath), then the attacks of 9/11 would in all likelihood not have been planned and carried out. Rather than resolve not to repeat the mistakes of the past, by inflaming Islamist radicals and inspiring them to kill even more Americans, the government responded to the attacks of 9/11 with more of the same, making it entirely predictable that another such attack will eventually transpire.

The political response in September 2014 to ISIS in Syria is telling in this regard. In the immediate aftermath of the beheading of the two journalists whose videotaped executions provoked the new military campaign, an unscripted remark by Obama, 'We don't have a strategy yet', unwittingly revealed a sobering truth. The US administration moved ahead with a new campaign of military aggression despite the fact that the various rival factions – moderate and radical alike – were united under the 'rebel' banner against the central regime of Bashar al-Assad. In reality, the groups involved are so diverse and cleave along so many different lines that no one can reasonably claim to be able to predict how or whether the quagmire might eventually be resolved.[242]

Showing their truly expedient colors, the US Congress agreed in September 2014 vaguely to support Obama's 'appropriately vetted moderate rebels' in Syria while putting off a vote on the wisdom of the war until after the November 2014 midterm elections. It's a win–win situation for the politicians who agree to fund killing campaigns abroad, for they foster risk-free the image of strength and nobility associated with courageous leaders from history. In those instances where the war effort succeeds to some degree, they take credit. Failures are written off to other causes. In Iraq, the reconstruction debacle was not blamed on the bungled and inept planning of the Coalition Provisional Authority, nor on the false assumption of the secretary of defense (among others) that Iraq would be able to run on autopilot once Saddam Hussein had been deposed. The simple removal of a dictator is obviously not sufficient for the flourishing of democracy. Still, the postwar chaos was blamed not on poor planning but on the difficulty of securing a land where ethnic factions had been at each other's throats for centuries.

The technological means for targeted killing in the hands of leaders who risk harm to neither themselves nor their troops, protected in the short term as they all are far from the death and destruction, and shielded by time from the future blowback of their policies, makes it likely that the use of military force will become more and more frequent. The many drone strikes carried out in several different countries have been facilely painted as *necessary* when in fact they were chosen because they were *feasible*. Indeed, in the drone age, *last resort* has become code for *feasible*, which in turn means *possible* and *worth the price* in *other people's lives* which missile-lobbing leaders are willing to pay.

Adding insult to injury, the same structure makes it plausible that, in order to benefit from the image of courage and nobility of leaders past, current leaders may and probably do wield military force in order to burnish their own lackluster, bureaucratic images. The willingness to sacrifice other people's lives continues to be regarded, oddly enough, as a sign of courage and strength. With the advent of Predator drone warfare, fewer and fewer killers are sacrificed, but at the expense of civilians on the ground and erroneously targeted suspects who have been victims of faulty intelligence and secretive analysis on the part of people who stand to profit from what has become an industry of killing.

CHAPTER 10
DEATH
AND TAXES

'Ultimately, DARPA's mission is the creation
and prevention of strategic surprise.'

Paul Eremenko, Deputy Director, Tactical Technology Office,
Defense Advanced Research Projects Agency (DARPA)[243]

'Countries have an insatiable appetite for drones.'

James Pitts, Northrop Grumman executive[244]

ONE MIGHT REASONABLY suppose that UCAVs are more economical to deploy than manned aircraft, given that they do not require a live pilot in the cockpit. In truth, drone strikes as conducted by the US government are rather expensive, for they involve a more extensive support staff than do manned aerial strikes. By some estimates, about 200 different people contribute in one way or another to each launch. In addition, the Hellfire missile expended in a Predator drone strike against an individual or small group costs about $70,000.[245]

Compared with the cost of shooting a person point-blank in the back of the head, this all may sound rather expensive. According to drone program supporters, the proper comparison is not to individual acts of contract killing within civil society but to other forms of warfare. The large number of persons involved in each drone strike, including the analysts who assess the intelligence (obtained through human sources and electronic surveillance), is touted as evidence of the care with which the program is conducted by the US government, in what is depicted as a heartfelt effort to minimize the possibility of innocent people being erroneously slain.

On 23 May 2013, President Obama acknowledged the 'wide gap' between US government assessments of civilian casualties and those of other organizations. He nonetheless insisted that 'before any strike is taken, there must be near-certainty that no civilians will be killed or injured – the highest standard we can set'.[246] The meaning of *near-certainty* is left to the drone program managers to decide, along with *imminent, associate, feasible* and *combatant.* Whatever may be the level of care taken to avoid collateral damage, it in no way diminishes the psychological effects of the very real threat of death to the persons over whom Predator drones hover. The fear and anxiety induced by the humming of drones are particularly acute in the residents of places such as Waziristan who have already witnessed the brutal outcome of strikes nearby and may know the victims personally.

The missiles used in remote-control killing are destroyed by the strike and so, as in the case of all fired arms, they must be replenished if the practice is to proceed. Those who applaud the use of weaponized drones to 'engage' terrorist suspects are prone to draw comparisons with Tomahawk missiles, which cost on the order of $1.4 million (in 2011) and are equally lost through their one-time use. Tomahawk missiles are also massively more destructive and less discriminating in who and what gets destroyed. These may seem to be cogent arguments in favor of the use of Hellfire missile-equipped Predator drones. The comparison with Tomahawk missiles is faulty, however, for the only reason why the targets of drone strikes are taken out is because it has become possible to kill by remote control. Before this technology existed, potentially threatening individuals – 'angry poor people' – located thousands of miles away could not be eliminated by an outside government without waging a full-scale war. No one denies that weaponry has become more sophisticated, but has Western civilization progressed, or has it regressed?

A consideration of the counterfactual scenario, had weaponized drones never been developed, reveals that they make killing more, not less, possible, in perfect conformity with the military's longstanding quest for maximum lethality. 'No boots' wars, such as the interventions by the US president in Libya and Syria, were simply inconceivable until quite recently in history. The military worldview has won out in the sense that more people are killed who would not have been killed, were there no Predator drones. Not only the military but also the US government has become more lethal, as its targeted killing program was implemented only because of technology developed to expand the capacity of the military to do what was not possible prior to the drone age. The means to kill by remote control was sought by the Pentagon in association with DARPA but then adopted for use by the CIA, which became the primary executor of the Predator drone program in countries where war had never been waged.

Advocates of targeted killing balk at the suggestion that lethal centrism has infected the executive branch of government. As evidence, they cite the low level of collateral damage relative to that of full-scale wars. They further maintain that the use of Predator drones abroad can be credited with the near absence of terrorist attacks on the US homeland since 9/11. Whether the targeted killing program has diminished the incidence of domestic terrorism in the United States is open to debate, but global terrorism was reported in 2007 to have increased sevenfold since the 2003 invasion of Iraq.[247] Groups such as ISIS/ISIL and Al-Shabaab have emerged and grown in direct response to US military aggression abroad. Moreover, some of the persons killed by drones in places such as Yemen and Somalia, being dirt poor, would in all likelihood never have made it to US shores. Their deaths may well incite the ire of people residing in Western states, some of whom will choose to retaliate in attacks on major cosmopolitan cities far from the forsaken places where US missiles leave corpses and craters in their wake.

Which perspective more closely reflects the truth? Will drones increase or decrease the total number of dead people? The evidence can be marshaled in either direction, depending upon one's sympathies. It seems a matter of common sense that terrorists are sometimes formed in response to what they take to be war crimes. Each time innocent children are stripped of their lives, their family and other community members may become more sympathetic to groups such as Al-Qaeda and the Taliban whose primary propaganda line is to decry what they view as murder perpetrated by the US government.

What cannot be denied is that the most obvious examples of attempted terrorist acts on US soil since 9/11 were carried out by killers who, like Osama bin Laden, explicitly protested US military practice abroad. Najibullah Zazi (who plotted to attack the New York subway system) and Faisal Shahzad (who attempted to bomb Times Square) both claimed to be retaliating against the Predator drone program.[248] Nidal Hasan (the former army psychiatrist who opened fire at Fort Hood) and Dzhokhar Tsarnaev (who planted bombs at the Boston marathon in 2013) also took issue with the US government's use of Predator drones to kill people in lands far away.[249]

An important factor in what comes to be the perpetual motion of an institutional killing machine is that the use of military weapons leads to the production of more of the same. This purely economic force does not support peace efforts in the least, as weapons are disseminated all over the world through the capitalized weapons trade. Not killing people does not cost any money, nor does it generate any profit. Deploying thousands of Hellfire missiles leads to their assembly-line replenishment, along with a fleet of drones to deliver them to their targets. From the existence of drones and missiles follows the 'need' to hire and train personnel to manage and carry out killing campaigns so that the tools can be used. Over the first decade of the twenty-first century, the number of US government drones expanded from a handful to many thousands. This trend can be expected to continue as new applications are proposed wherever terrorists are said to emerge. At the same time, other countries have acquired or are clamoring for drones.

In the twentieth century, many a right-wing military junta secured the economic and logistical support of the US government by claiming that their political opponents were 'communists'. In the twenty-first century, the latest crop of foreign political opportunists identify their adversaries as associates of Al-Qaeda, although in many cases the conflict in question is purely domestic, with little potential for spilling out beyond the borders of the land.[250] The capacity for remote-control killing by governments is spreading rapidly around the globe as power-hungry leaders follow Yemeni president Saleh's lead in capitalizing on what they characterize as the Al-Qaeda threat in their own lands, what has been facetiously described as 'the gift that keeps on giving'.[251] Generous military aid packages are available to leaders who cooperate with the US government and label their political enemies 'radical Islamist militants'. In Iraq, the Sunni rebels were identified by the Shiite government in power as Al-Qaeda affiliates. In Egypt, after a military coup and the removal of the democratically elected government, the Muslim Brotherhood were officially denounced as 'terrorists' as well, and hundreds, if not thousands, have already been sentenced to death.

Short-term expediency has blinded US administrators to the reality that the Predator drone program serves both as a precedent and as a template for leaders all over the globe to dispatch their political opponents with no due process whatsoever and a blanket denial of human rights. In July 2014, President Obama began flying drones again above Iraq and agreed to sell 5,000 Hellfire missiles to the Iraqi government.[252] Needless to say, it is the prerogative of the importing government to specify how much care should be taken when such munitions are deployed.

* * *

In 1961, US President Dwight D. Eisenhower issued a stern warning about the dangers of capitalized war. He coined the phrase 'military-industrial complex' and expressed concern that the profit motive – a virtue under capitalism – would impel weapons companies to exert an insalubrious influence over politicians. The most obvious level of war profiteering involves deadly weapons and platforms for their delivery. In order to justify the production of more missiles, they must be depleted in one way or another. They may be deployed in wars, or they may be sold to other parties so that they can do the same.

The decades following World War II witnessed a near purge of 'dovish' elements from US politics, above all because of Cold War concerns. Over the same period, the war enterprise grew into an enormous business conglomerate, the most significant recent entrepreneurial undertaking of which was masterminded by former US Vice President Dick Cheney, who privatized many aspects of the military. By outsourcing military logistics to firms such as Halliburton and its subsidiary KBR (Kellogg Brown & Root), Cheney erected an enormous military service apparatus and ushered in a rash of new private security and logistics companies such as Blackwater and Aegis. These firms have flourished in the twenty-first century alongside more orthodox suppliers of weapons and transport systems, and a multilayered maze of apparently nonmilitary subcontractors.[253]

Of the many men throughout history who have made their fortunes from wars, Cheney stands unrivaled for having created the services contracting system which gave rise to a proliferation of PMCs during the occupation of Iraq.[254] Cheney's entrepreneurial innovation, known as LOGCAP (Logistics Civil Augmentation Program), was the idea that wars could be prosecuted using large numbers of nonmilitary personnel working for the Pentagon indirectly through private contracting arrangements. Cheney sold this idea as a way of saving taxpayer money.

Despite the wealth of the US military, its manpower was inadequate to prosecute two simultaneous wars, in both Afghanistan and Iraq. Gaps were filled with a significant contingent of freelancers once the second war had been waged. For the first time in US military history, private operators were enlisted in large numbers to carry out a variety of 'unsavory' tasks, ranging from serving as bodyguards in incredibly dangerous contexts to driving supply trucks along roads studded with improvised explosive devices (IEDs), or conducting 'harsh interrogation' of prisoners at facilities such as Bagram and Abu Ghraib prisons. No longer were private operators, as in centuries past, made to lurk in the shadows, acting under assumed names and contracted in secret arrangements behind closed doors. These 'freelancers' were deployed openly and officially by those whose authority it was to award contracts, including the former CEO of Halliburton, Dick Cheney.

It is no secret that many 'voluntary' soldiers enlist as a means to gainful, legal employment and in order to access benefits otherwise beyond their reach. These dynamics are not unique to the United States. Tony Geraghty reports: 'Soldiering in Britain has long been advertised by the Ministry of Defence not as a patriotic vocation, but as a good career move.'[255] As a result of the privatization of logistics and many services, the military now has to compete with the very private companies which LOGCAP helped to create. As a result, uniformed soldiering at the lower ranks may attract only the least competitive of candidates, with savvier prospective employees naturally seeking and securing much better offers from the private sector. The true reason for enlistment emerges in every twenty-first-century case in which a soldier has completed his required term of active duty and retired, only to accept a lucrative position working for a private company under contract with the US military.

In Iraq, the contractees were extraordinarily well paid, relative to the salary of enlisted men and women serving in analogous capacities, but they were also legally protected from prosecution for whatever they might do. This combination proved enticing to soldiers nearing the end of their initial term of uniformed service, some of whom saw fit not to re-enlist but to sell their services to the highest bidder. US taxpayers, who footed the bill for the lucrative and often 'no-bid' contracts to PMCs, also paid for the crimes committed by the 'soldiers of fortune' enlisted in their name. When 'off-the-leash' freelancers misbehaved, they were taken by locals to represent the US government no less than the uniformed soldiers. The result was an ever-more virulent insurgency bent on destroying not only uniformed military personnel, but also some of the better-behaved persons in civilian dress, including UN staff, humanitarian aid workers and journalists.[256]

Some of the freelancers were simple mercenaries who acted with complete disregard for the rights of the local people. Scandals involving Blackwater, Aegis and other PMCs naturally confirmed suspicions that the entire war was a matter of imperial conquest and insatiable thirst for oil, notwithstanding the rhetoric spouted by US officials about freedom and democracy. The use of such 'no-holds-barred' freelancers – some of whom were recruited from the battle-hardened militias of Third World countries – appears to have contributed significantly to the ever-degenerating security situation in Iraq. The locals became more and more suspicious of the occupiers' intentions upon witnessing innocent people wronged by employees of the US government.

A culture of impunity arose as a result of the peculiar legal status of the privately contracted operatives, who were subject to neither the restrictions governing military personnel (who risk court-martial for disobedience) nor US law, working as they were beyond US borders. Aside from revenge killing by incensed Iraqis and foreign insurgents, the only tangible sanction faced by the freelancers was the loss of their current job. There were plenty of other companies prepared to hire them, however, so even mercenaries who had violated protocol or acted in ways that reflected poorly upon their employer were able to carry on as before.

The PMC contracting explosion in the early twenty-first century expanded the terms of the military-industrial complex yet again, this time through the introduction of a substantial force of hired guns. The private workforce in Iraq was characterized by complex subcontracting arrangements, with primary contractors often enlisting other companies to carry out some of their tasks. These dynamics produced a double-dipping system of profiteering. As a result, no one ever knew exactly how many mercenary operators were on the ground during the occupation. According to reliable estimates, the number of private contractees exceeded the number of military personnel in Iraq.[257] A profound conflict of interest has long co-opted the weapons supply industry, leading to the award of extraordinarily lucrative contracts to firms with direct financial ties to persons in the military and other government agencies, including lawmakers.[258] But LOGCAP created the entire military service industry, which became poised to usurp more and more of what would formerly have been the military's operational turf, up to and including the Predator drone targeted killing program.

The haughty disdain for the rule of law witnessed in Iraq helps to explain the rapid expansion of the Predator drone targeted killing program, as human life was cheapened in the eyes of some of the very people whose profession it became to 'make the call', to decide who may live and who should die. The flippancy with which persons involved in the Predator drone program dismiss the possibility of mistakes having been made is seen in some of their public statements in response to critics' claims in the aftermath of strikes that innocent persons have been slain. Regarding 'signature strikes' and 'crowd killing', where clusters of unnamed targets are destroyed, one anonymous analyst compared the strike sites to the strip club in the HBO series *The Sopranos*: 'It's like watching *The Sopranos*. You know what's going on in the Bada Bing.'[259] In denying that dozens of innocent civilians were killed during a March 2011 *jirga* meeting in Datta Khel disrupted by US missiles, another analyst observed: 'These people weren't gathering for a bake sale. They were terrorists.'[260] In reality, most of the victims killed on that day were not connected in any way to the Taliban or other militant groups.

Some among the 'off-the-leash' hired guns in Iraq exhibited little respect for human life. Meanwhile, uniformed soldiers were placed in extraordinarily difficult and dangerous situations where 'shoot first, ask questions later' became a matter literally of self-defense, with devastating consequences for victims later determined to have been ordinary civilians posing no threat to anyone. In some ways, remote-control killing is the ultimate logical extension of 'shoot first, ask questions later', but what is missing is the very real danger of death should the operator decline to launch a missile. Thousands of operators have agreed to destroy suspects preemptively in a program which has origins in habits of thought formed in Iraq. These state executioners have been taught to accept remote-control killing as a legitimate form of warfare and lured to enlist by the prospect of generous salary and benefits packages. The number of new drone operators trained in the United States quadrupled between 2008 and 2013, and now surpasses the number of pilots being trained to fly manned aerial vehicles.[261] So long as no US nationals are sacrificed, most Americans can be expected to continue to ignore the effects on civilians abroad of the US government's use of deadly force. At the same time, the continuous deployment of the war-making apparatus will be supported by those who profit economically from the killing campaigns.

Under the prevailing assumption on the part of the US administration that the Predator drone program is a sound approach to national defense, the more missiles used, the more will be produced. The very availability of the weapons will then incline future US presidents to follow suit. The hardware alone of the drone program is a huge contract generator. As of 2013, the drone contracts for major weapons manufacturers were already at these figures: Boeing $1.8 billion; Northrop Grumman $10.9 billion; General Atomics $6.6 billion; and Raytheon $648 million.[262]

When President Obama threatened missile strikes against Syria in 2013 in response to the use of chemical weapons in that land, the value of Raytheon stock jumped by 20 percent over a matter of days.[263] But do people really support war as a means of making money? Some of them undoubtedly do, and weapons manufacturers have strong lobbies in Washington, DC, working to ensure that their companies win and retain lucrative Pentagon contracts. The members of Congress courted by such companies continue to fund the production of expensive weapons systems with the approval of each year's military budget. All of the people who profit from the replenishment of expended munitions obviously have self-interested reasons for promoting targeted killing and adding more and more names to the hit lists.

The administrators of PMCs are often former soldiers, and such veterans may consult both for the Pentagon and for private corporations whose success depends on the continuation of wars in progress and the waging of new ones whenever the opportunity can be said to arise.[264] These forces conspire to perpetuate institutional homicide under the confused assumption that the 'options on the table' are either to snipe suspects using RPAs or to destroy them and everyone around them using manned bombers.

With the advent of PMCs, 'contracting creep' has seeped into the area of personnel, with profit as a motive for promotion of and participation in war through the provision not only of weapons but also of manpower. This service-based potential for profit automatically inclines toward more interventions, since without them, companies in this sector cannot remain solvent. By their very nature, PMCs are flexible, ready and willing to innovate and expand their capacities in order to prove their usefulness and secure future contracts. Erik Prince's venture Blackwater – renamed Xe Services in 2009, then Academi in 2011 – is a case in point.[265] Even as four former Blackwater employees were on trial for murdering a slew of Iraqi civilians, Erik Prince was out on the media circuit floating yet another entrepreneurial scheme: that privately contracted soldiers be enlisted as the 'boots on the ground' in Obama's new 'no boots' campaign in Syria.[266]

The participation of private companies in the targeted killing of suspects abroad does not seem to be coincidentally related to the lengthening of the US government's hit lists (there are at least three). When private companies were invited to participate in the rapidly expanding targeted killing program of the Obama administration, they needed to generate actionable intelligence in order to be able to add names to the hit lists of suspects to be dispatched by Predator drone.

The problem is not merely that mercenaries – 'guns for hire' – may be more willing to kill, although that is a possibly relevant consideration as well. Even worse, in the targeted killing program, analysts have *financial incentives* for locating actionable intelligence, in order to demonstrate that they are proficient at their job and therefore deserve to remain gainfully employed. This point is well illustrated in the 2012 film directed by Kathryn Bigelow, *Zero Dark Thirty*, which reenacts the hunt for and execution of Osama bin Laden. A high-level CIA administrator, in frustration and anger at the staff of the Bin Laden unit for their failure to make any progress in tracking down the Al-Qaeda leader, exclaims: '*I want targets.* Do your fucking jobs: *Bring me people to kill!*' Among other problems, the desire to be able to do something – to do anything – renders US administrators subject to manipulation by foreign governments and bounty hunters seeking some of the generous provision of funds readily available for the asking. The leaders of even undemocratic, monarchic regimes whose own governance regularly flouts enlightened views on human rights need only to describe their enemies as 'evil terrorists' in order to tap into US military aid.

After the occupation debacles in both Afghanistan and Iraq, the 'new' counterinsurgency gospel of winning over 'hearts and minds' saw a brief revival as the shock-and-awe warriors acknowledged that superior lethality alone is insufficient to achieve political aims. But the short-lived effort at securing the peace by nonlethal means in Afghanistan proved to be less than successful, which explains in part the decision to focus on the elimination of suspects through Predator drone-delivered missiles. The measure of success became how many 'terrorists' (in reality, terrorist *suspects*) were killed, a quantity which can be objectified by administrators. Postwar stability, in contrast, is difficult to gauge and remains elusive, judging by the violent attacks with which both Afghanistan and Iraq continue to be plagued.

A literally *fatal* conflict of interest arises whenever a worker is rewarded for quantity rather than quality of output, and the nature of the work is deadly to begin with. When the primary measure of professional success is the number of 'dead terrorists' (again, terrorist *suspects*), then employees keen to keep their jobs will work to 'improve' their tally. Both contractors mining for 'actionable intelligence' and those producing deadly weapons have financial motives for finding opportunities to kill. An increase in state-inflicted homicide is predictable when persons with no qualms against killing and a self-interested financial incentive for racking up as many 'bug splats' and 'splashes' as possible are granted the authority to determine who should die. Thousands of human beings have been slain by US drones; many of the victims' identities are unknown.

A hearty skepticism about motives is warranted also in the case of the persons 'contracted' in more informal arrangements, whenever money is exchanged for information leading to the designation of targets. The layers of secrecy involved in the Predator drone program serve to protect its administrators from allegations of wrongdoing, but we can learn something about the analogous use of informants by career FBI (Federal Bureau of Investigation) officers in the US homeland. In *Terror Factory: Inside the FBI's Manufactured War on Terrorism* (2013), journalist Trevor Aaronson reveals that the scorecard mentality seen in the targeted killing program being run by the CIA pervades the FBI as well. In its quest for terrorist convictions, the Bureau has resorted to tactics in the US homeland which in pre-GWOT times would arguably have been considered entrapment. These efforts have culminated in the conviction of hundreds of 'terrorists' who have come in contact *only* with FBI agents and informants posing as terrorists – not real Al-Qaeda members – and without whose financial and logistical support the targets stung would never have become operational.

Not all informants are bribed. In many FBI terrorism investigations, domestic informants lacking legal immigration status have been coerced to spy on community members, on pain of deportation for refusal to comply. Some of the 15,000 FBI informants in the United States have been granted immunity for their own crimes, with the knowledge that if they fail to 'deliver' in sting operations, then they (the informants) will become subject to prosecution. Disturbingly, some of the informants used serially by the FBI appear to be career criminals and con artists. Such informants are further motivated by the enticement of a post-conviction 'performance incentive' once a target has been snared.[267]

What do we know about the informants abroad used by the CIA in places where deadly drone strikes are carried out? Bounty hunters in tribal areas who wish to shore up their own territorial power – including the warlords so often paid to collaborate with agents of the US government – have clear motives for 'handing over' suspects or providing the so-called actionable intelligence needed to 'find, fix, and finish' targets through the use of Predator drones. Corrupt but cooperative central governments are also able to become more entrenched through the use of 'the enemy of my enemy is my friend' ploy.

Domestically, financial incentives conjoined with the capitalization of the means needed to conduct killing campaigns lead naturally to more killing as the number of persons who stand to profit from the enterprise continues to grow. Successful politicians nearly always support the specific military installations and affiliated companies in their jurisdiction, for such enterprises keep some among their local constituents (the electorate) gainfully employed. These political and economic dynamics help to explain the maintenance of a Cold War-magnitude military budget long after the fall of the Soviet Union. The coordinated industry of companies such as Boeing, Lockheed Martin and General Electric, whose contracts with the US Department of Defense are continuously renewed and augmented, ensures the maintenance of enormous arsenals. The ready availability of the weapons then predisposes leaders to use them when the opportunity arises.

Even worse, in what is tantamount to a perverse form of Ponzi scheme, many a dictator's implements of murder, including those of Saddam Hussein, were first researched and developed in the United States and paid for by US taxpayers. Preposterously, in Afghanistan, an estimated 10 percent of the cash provided to contractors ended up in the hands of the very insurgents being fought.[268] An estimated $18 billion of the $70 billion of aid provided to Afghanistan 'went missing', and it seems likely that some of it, too, served to fuel, not combat, the insurgency.[269] In Syria, when 600 tons of weapons were furnished covertly to the 'appropriately vetted moderate rebels' in 2013, the result was a sudden takeover of territories by ISIS, the 'unvetted radical rebels'. Rather than terminate the weapons allocation and training program, the US Congress voted in 2014 to expand the operations and make them overt.

Americans may have no difficulty believing that German industrial leaders were capable of complicity in mass murder for the economic benefits envisioned through the 'redistribution' of the wealth of Jewish people made to 'disappear' during the reign of the Third Reich. However, US military supporters find it inordinately difficult to entertain the possibility that some of their own political leaders might promote unnecessary wars out of sheer greed. In truth, war entrepreneurs such as Dick Cheney do not merely profit from wars already in progress, as did the many corporate scions who cultivated relationships with the leadership of the Third Reich. Far worse, bona fide war entrepreneurs actively promote the initiation of wars yet to be waged, and incubate opportunities for the use of munitions such as the Hellfire missiles of the Predator drone program in what is claimed to be 'national defense'.

* * *

War architects and entrepreneurs adduce every marketing tool at their disposal, including just war rhetoric. Since the populace needs only to be told that a cause is 'just' and 'necessary' to throw their weight behind a military initiative, just war theory proves to be the hawk's most powerful propaganda tool. In defending his unorthodox drone wars, Obama has repeatedly made reference to the orthodox concepts of the just war paradigm: 'We are at war with an organization that right now would kill as many Americans as they could if we did not stop them first. So this is a just war – a war waged proportionally, in last resort, and in self-defense.'[270] To the surprise of the antiwar activists who helped to elect him in 2008, Obama even used his Nobel Peace Prize acceptance speech to talk about just war theory and promote the use of deadly force abroad.[271] War-exporter societies such as the United States develop, produce and disseminate deadly weapons, but equally important is their pro-war ideology and 'just war' rhetoric, which, along with arms, are taken up by rebel factions and postwar insurgents alike (see Appendix).

Through the brutal use of Predator drones to obliterate terrorist suspects, the US government offers a deleterious example of how to resolve conflict. People are constrained by law within the perimeters of modern liberal democratic societies to sort out differences in civilized ways. Enemies abroad, however, are invariably painted as beyond the reach of reason and worthy of annihilation, even when it is obvious that their ranks have swelled as a direct result of war makers' own policies, such as the ill-advised de-Ba'athization and dismissal of the entire army in post-Saddam Hussein Iraq, or the support of the Ethiopian invasion of Somalia, or the provision of tons of weapons to 'the rebels' in Syria. The list goes on and on ...

Blinded by what has become a full-fledged lethal obsession, military strategists look only forward, not back, in devising the ever-more deadly means to address future possible threats. The persons charged with defending the homeland seek out new opportunities to flex military muscle, even as they leave multiple societies – in Afghanistan, Iraq, Libya, Somalia, Yemen and beyond – in shambles. Focused as they are on short-term lethality, the policymakers who advocate war as the solution to virtually every conflict abroad appear to be utterly oblivious to the fact that they themselves, in preparing for future enemies, helped to create the last one whom they were called upon to defeat.

New weapons systems are continuously produced in a dizzying flurry of research and development. When the previous generation's weapons become passé, they are exported for use in the conflicts of less-developed nations devoid of military industry. As a result of the global arms trade, government and corporate leaders end by shaping the very enemies who will be identified in the future as necessary to contain, just as happened in the case of Saddam Hussein. The cycle of producing ever-more lethal weapons which eventually end up in the hands of despotic leaders, who then predictably deploy them so as to provoke a belligerent response, has been repeated over and over again.

Technological innovations spread rapidly around the world under free-market capitalism. As a result of a proactive, lethal-centric military conjoined with profit-driven industry, the taxpayers of countries such as the United States support both sides of everyone's wars, allies and enemies alike. They do this, first, by pouring money into DARPA for the creation of more and more lethal and innovative means of destruction and, second, by permitting weapons developed at home for the purpose of self-defense to be sold abroad. By 2011, the Obama administration had already approved the exportation of Northrop-manufactured Predator drones to South Korea.[272] By 2015, the sale of lethal drones to US allies more generally was under way.[273]

The curious notion advanced in Max Boot's *War Made New* (2006) and embraced by many political and military leaders, that the United States must continually struggle to set the pace of lethal technologies so as to maintain its status as sole superpower, is grounded in the same selective amnesia which permits administrators unwittingly to arm future adversaries who appear to be stable allies at the time of their empowerment. Later on down the line, some years after the provision of aid to what were formerly allies, the military is summoned to depose tyrants run amok. Gordon Adams has observed that the United States is 'in an arms race with itself', but that is not quite right.[274] The US government is in an arms race with enemies which it also *creates* by pushing forward with the invention and production of new means of homicide powerful enough to defeat the previous generation of weapons. In the case of drones, the semi-automatic quality is currently being researched away, with the aim, one day, of taking even fallible human operators out of the loop.[275]

Depictions of apocalyptic robotic warfare in films such as *The Terminator* series notwithstanding, the problem of target selection being carried out by computer is not really any worse than target selection by a small committee of anonymous bureaucrats operating behind closed doors according to their own secretive criteria and wholly insulated from critique. It will be none other than such committees who determine the parameters of the programs used by robots to select targets for destruction. The problem, then, is not with the degree of autonomy of the machines used to destroy human beings but with the first premise underlying any targeted killing campaign against suspects identified by their killers as worthy of annihilation.[276]

The official acknowledgment of the existence of a targeted killing program (in contrast to the covert and deniable black ops of the twentieth century) has served as a red herring. This pseudo-transparency distracts those who pay for the strikes from the opacity of the processes by which the names of targets for summary execution make their way onto the hit lists. Who are the people who make these decisions? What are their criteria? How could wrongful action, the murder of entirely innocent people, ever be established when the judges and executioners are also the scribes who write the official history of their very own deeds?

Concerns about these matters are hardly assuaged by a perusal of the US government's terrorist-identification rulebook, the *March 2013 Watchlisting Guidance*. Composed in bureaucratese and replete with gobbledygook and undefined terms, the 166-page document leaves much to the nominators' imagination and is destined to become a classic of confirmation bias literature. The vague and multiply interpretable 'guidelines' do not sift out terrorist suspects from obvious non-terrorists, as is demonstrated by the fact that persons as famous as Senator Edward Kennedy and Nelson Mandela found themselves unable to board airplanes, their names having been included on no-fly lists.[277] Kennedy appealed to his friends in the administration to resolve the matter. Mandela's name was removed by an Act of Congress in 2008.[278] One can only imagine how an ordinary person misidentified as a terrorist by an anonymous analyst might have his name removed.

Each Hellfire missile expended in a drone strike costs about $70,000 and is supported by a large staff. One wonders whether even a fraction of that money used to help rather than harm tribal communities would not be more effective in quelling anti-American sentiment than the execution, one by one, of people who are someone's son, father, husband and brother. Those who hunt down and destroy their targets by remote control probably seldom reflect upon the nature of the harm simultaneously inflicted upon other, entirely innocent people: the bereft survivors.

Nor is the psychological harm caused to the residents of lethal drone zones, who live in fear of their possibly imminent erasure, given any heed. Such matters are deemed irrelevant by analysts and operators who believe that their targets are dangerous terrorists with nefarious plans in the works. In reality, many of the persons killed are destitute members of tribal communities who would never be able to travel thousands of miles away, even if they harbored extreme rancor against the United States, as some of them surely do, given the ominous humming of Predator drones above their heads.

Providing tribal communities with humanitarian aid – or simply leaving them alone – would not be profitable for the military industry and so will obviously never be floated by any politician as a serious alternative to signature strikes and crowd killing. Sad to say, but the most recent entrepreneurial scheme of war profiteers is none other than the Predator drone targeted killing of thousands of people who would be alive today, but for the development of the means to eliminate them, one by one, under a pretext of national defense. The military-industrial-congressional-media-academic-pharmaceutical-logistics complex generates new millionaires as hit lists lengthen and remote territories are identified as 'battlefields'. The network of complicity implicates many different people, up to and including taxpayers, which is why institutional killing in the guise of war becomes more and more difficult to impugn as time progresses.

Predator drone targeted killing has laid bare what was true all along, that war, like black ops, offers the tyrant's solution to conflict: homicide substitutes for criminal investigation and due process, and all of this is rationalized in the name of necessity and, ultimately, self-defense. The war-making apparatus – the institution of war – is oligarchic, not democratic, and yet war is claimed to be supportive of democracy through the use of highly deceptive propaganda. At the same time, this oligarchy is decidedly plutocratic, for the contributions made to initiating, perpetuating and prolonging war by profiteers such as the associates of Halliburton, Blackwater, and many other PMCs – in addition to the countless contractors and subcontractors of military industry – help to buoy misguided marketing campaigns for institutional killing.

The only way to put a halt to what has become an industry of homicide is for people to own up to what their taxes are really paying for.[279] There must be accountability in order for risk to re-enter the military realm, the only effective restraint upon war makers. In a world in which the architects of wars are immune from their consequences, where those who pilfered billions of US tax dollars in Iraq in highly wasteful 'cost-plus' contracts are praised by warmongering pundits as patriots, only the people who pay have the power to say 'No.' But in order to be able to do so, they must be apprised of the practices carried out by the government in their name and allegedly on their behalf. Access to facts is a basic requirement of any functional democracy. When consent is coerced through deception and secrecy, then democracy itself has come under attack.

CHAPTER 11
THE DEATH OF MILITARY VIRTUE

'I want to plead guilty, and I'm going to plead guilty 100 times over. Because until the hour the US pulls its forces from Iraq and Afghanistan, and stops the drone strikes in Somalia and Yemen and in Pakistan, and stops the occupation of Muslim lands, and stops killing the Muslims, and stops reporting the Muslims to its government, we will be attacking US, and I plead guilty to that.'

Faisal Shahzad, Pakistani-American who
attempted to bomb Times Square[280]

'With the drones there is nobody on the other side. Clearly there is someone on the other side, but it's not something that can be dialoged with. And you don't know at what point you've been marked, or why you've been marked, and when you are going to meet your death. This creates incredible, acute stress among people of the area.'

Madiha Tahir, Pakistani journalist[281]

MODERN WESTERN POLITICAL LEADERS are able to wage wars with little concern for the havoc directly caused by the application of military force in places such as Vietnam, Afghanistan, Iraq, Somalia, Libya and Yemen. They may turn a blind eye to the mess left behind once bombing has come to an end. All of this is possible because leaders do not themselves face the physical consequences of their wars waged abroad. It may take a special type of strength to be able to accept the weighty burden of having been causally responsible for someone else's death, the sort of risk assumed by health professionals in carrying out procedures which sometimes lead to a patient's premature demise. But this is not the same as the courage of doctors on the ground in conflict zones, willing to treat patients even as bombs fall about their heads.

Once upon a time, every single man who agreed to participate in war, including the leader who called his troops to arms, risked making 'the ultimate sacrifice'. Long gone are the days of Gustavus Adolphus, the seventeenth-century king of Sweden who died on the battlefield with his troops attempting to thwart the takeover of Europe by the Habsburgs. The moment leaders ceased participating directly in the wars of their waging, the first safeguard against the precipitous use of military force was lifted, flinging open the floodgates to vain and even frivolous wars. The sincere belief of a commander in chief in a cause weighty enough to warrant recourse to the drastic measure of war was no longer confirmed by his own willingness to fight and even die alongside the troops being sacrificed.[282]

As civilians became the initiators of war – but spectators not participants – this prudential safeguard was supplanted by a measure of whether politicians were willing to risk *other people's* lives. In recent missions approved at least tacitly, if not explicitly, by the US Congress, nearly none of the legislators supporting military action had sons or daughters whose lives would be immediately jeopardized by the decision to wield deadly force abroad. The diminished effect of such safeguards is not limited to the people who pen policy, however. The populace on the whole appears to be far more willing to support or condone war whenever the army is said to be a voluntary, professional one. The absence of a sustained antiwar movement after the invasion of Iraq can be explained in part by the fact that the soldiers being sacrificed were not conscripted civilians, as many had been during the US intervention in Vietnam. The stifling critical climate in the aftermath of the terrorist attacks of 11 September 2001 also played a role.

Voluntary soldiers, it is often presumed, are better trained and motivated than conscripts, who have been coerced to fight against their own will, on pain of punishment for failure to comply. A closer consideration of the demographics of the US military tells a rather different story, which began to leak out as crimes were uncovered successively in both Afghanistan and Iraq.[283] The 'few bad apples' formed the better part of a bushel because only certain types of people now enlist voluntarily, an ongoing problem for recruiters, which intensified as the particularly vexed conflict in Iraq – dubious even to some patriotic Americans – dragged on.

Troops who enlist in direct response to an attack such as the mass killings at Pearl Harbor in 1941 or on 11 September 2001 do tend to exhibit extraordinary enthusiasm, especially during the initial term of their service. As a result of such monumental events, patriotic fervor may well up in prospective enlistees, as it did in former NFL (National

Football League) player Pat Tillman, galvanizing him to serve the nation in order to defend its honor and protect its people. But when a mission such as the 2003 invasion of Iraq proves to be less than honorable, the troops deployed in multiple tours of duty may become cynical and jaded. The more protracted the conflict is, the higher the toll of casualties becomes, and the less likely potential enlistees will be to don uniforms.

The notion that an army of volunteers is necessarily superior to an army of draftees rests on the premise that those who enlist believe in what they are doing. When, in reality, they are desperate for gainful employment, they may regard themselves quite simply as 'hired guns'. The types of people who agree to serve in controversial missions such as the 2003 intervention in Iraq may be more willing to kill than randomly drafted civilians would be, but for that very reason they may also be capable of committing ghastly crimes such as occurred at Abu Ghraib, Bagram, Najaf, Haditha, Fallujah and Mahmudiyah. When crimes by US troops were revealed by reporters on the ground, the role of the grunts in Iraq and Afghanistan began to seem even less honorable than before, which helps to explain the recruitment crisis during the occupations.[284]

The disconnect between the professional US military and the citizens who pay for war has been diagnosed by Andrew Bacevich in *Breach of Trust* (2013), where he argues that Americans have essentially 'signed off' on the wars since Vietnam, as soldiers are no longer drafted to serve. The civilian-soldier model has fallen out of favor, with most citizens bearing the price of war not in blood but in treasure, by paying federal taxes. As a result, war makers have been liberated from the effective constraint of personal sacrifice on the part of most of the voting public. Proliferating wars of choice, Bacevich explains, have their origins in the all-volunteer military: 'All it takes to bomb Belgrade, invade Iraq, or send Navy SEALs into Pakistan is concurrence among a half dozen people and a nod from the president. No need to secure prior congressional assent, certainly no need to consult the American people: that's what the all-volunteer force allows.'[285]

The effect of having an army of volunteers is similar to that of having civilian leadership determine when and where to wage war: those with the power to start – and stop – wars, the legislators and taxpayers, need risk nothing personally by waving patriotic banners in support of intervention abroad. Historically, the price paid for the wars of some compatriots has been the lives of others: soldiers who, being the tools of leaders, have been stripped through conscription or enlistment of their civilian right to criticize reckless deployments in wars of choice painted by politicians as necessary.

Over the course of the past century, the invention of more and more powerful weapons, which are lethal over ever-greater distances, has progressively diminished the risk to both leaders and the warriors who wield deadly force. These technological developments gave rise to the generally accepted view among the US populace that 'national defense' is something to be carried out somewhere else, preferably thousands of miles away from the homeland. In the drone age, the 'blood and treasure' equation has become far more heavily weighted toward treasure, for military missions can be carried out without risking the lives even of uniformed combatants.

One plausible explanation for the intolerance toward combatant casualties in recent times is simply that a democratic society officially condemns violence. The citizenry regards harm done to civilians and soldiers alike as a bad thing to be avoided whenever possible. The human costs of wielding deadly force abroad have been primarily tendered in the lives of non-nationals who, being so far out of sight, are equally out of mind to those funding the missions. The military self-consciously deploys euphemisms to downplay the significance of the 'collateral damage' caused by 'kinetic operations' in which targets are 'engaged' or 'employed on'. The omission of innocent victims from reports of 'successful' strikes against militants seems to have persuaded much of the US populace to believe that this technology is surgically precise and a 'silver bullet' solution to the problem of terrorism.

The progressive whittling away of risk from war, making the use of military force seem morally 'cost-free' because civilian casualties are not psychologically processed as real, leads self-styled patriots to support interventions abroad for some of the same reasons that leaders do. People feel ennobled by endorsing what history depicts as noble enterprises. Accordingly, so long as the mythic picture of soldiers and just wars is upheld, and so long as the civilians of the war-making nation are not in any immediate danger of harm, new wars will continue to be waged and supported, even by people who do not stand to profit financially from them. The blowback of such missions erupts later on down the line, and many citizens, being ignorant of history, are wholly incapable of connecting the dots between past military practice and terrorist retaliation.

The apathetic and gullible tendencies of US citizens toward foreign policy can be expected to become more pervasive as the deadly effects of wars of choice for compatriots are minimized through the use of Predator drones and other newly developed robotic platforms. Risk-aversive tendencies developed over decades will be cemented as future voters become accustomed to the 'no boots on the ground' trope so often intoned by President Obama. The very availability of Predator drones as an 'option on the table' inclines the citizenry to tolerate fewer and fewer combatant casualties. The capacity to kill by remote control has also dramatically increased the lethal power of the US executive, who uses his authority as commander in chief to dispatch suspects – even US nationals – on 'battlefields' where war was never formally waged.

Americans have for the most part accepted targeted killing as a form of 'smart war', which can be won without sacrificing troops. The prioritization of soldiers over (non-national) civilians commenced before the advent of the drone age, when in 1999 NATO pilots flew high above the terrain in Kosovo to avoid being shot down. What that policy signaled was a willingness to abandon the traditional idea that soldiers assume the risk of death in accepting their profession, while civilians are to be shielded at all costs. The readiness to cause non-national civilian deaths in order to save military pilots' lives represented a turning point in military history. The revelation in 2011 that NATO forces in Afghanistan had begun to make troop safety a higher priority than the protection of civilians illustrated the same shift in military ethos away from the code of honor historically upheld by men in uniform.[286]

Whether or not the officially stated causes of past wars actually mattered to the soldiers who fought them, there is no question that the test of courage has been deleted from the accreditation requirements of the twenty-first-century drone operator. The leaner and meaner, the more technologically advanced and lethal the military becomes, the less necessary it is for combatants to place themselves at risk of death in missions ordered by their leaders. Because weaponized drones have been wholeheartedly embraced by the military establishment and political elite, they invite reflection on the very nature of modern war. What has 'war' become when operators 'neutralize' enemy 'soldiers' quaking on the battlefield all alone, incapable of surrendering because there is no one there to hear their words?

The visceral reality of one-on-one combat using weapons such as bayonets, where the choice was to kill or be killed, made the significance to soldiers themselves of what they were doing undeniable in the past. 'Drone warriors', in contrast, are able to kill without risking any physical harm. This change flies in the face of the entire history of warfare and mandates a reevaluation of what it is that war has become. In the twenty-first century, it has become possible to kill in what are claimed to be 'wars' without coming into contact with a single drop of blood and without so much as glimpsing the faces of the persons destroyed.

Training young people to obey orders to kill for the state has always been a dubious enterprise, but training them to kill in the manner of sociopaths, with no feelings whatsoever for their victims because they are but icons on computer screens, is a frightening prospect indeed. The surreal process of killing at vast distances with the push of a button or the click of a computer mouse can only have the ultimate effect of insulating killers from the reality of what they do. Yes, they observe shadowy images of the targets on film, but humanity is shrouded by this imagistic process, as the persons 'employed on' have no voice or mind – or even a name, in most cases. That 'well-adjusted' drone operators such as Matthew Martin appear to delight in characterizing their victims as 'rats', 'rodents' and 'rabbits' to be 'hunted down' and exterminated like vermin merely underscores the emotional numbness which has supplanted courage in the drone age.

Over the centuries, hand-to-hand combat was replaced by killing at ever-greater distances with the successive invention of more and more lethal weapons. At each stage along the way, traditional soldiers balked. But the significance to Windows warriors of their acts of killing has become the weakest in history with these new, qualitatively distinct, technologies. By removing risk from the equation, the point has been reached where the very concept of the soldier is being undone. To call a drone strike – distinguishable from a paid contract killing only in the impunity and safety of the 'technician' – an act of war is to renounce in one fell swoop the entire protocol of warfare throughout history.

The logic of lethality has been pushed to its farthest limit in cases where the recourse to military force involves risk to neither leaders nor the troops under their command but only to enemy 'soldiers' (terrorist suspects) and civilians unfortunate enough to be located in their vicinity. Inhabitants of the United States have long enjoyed the protection afforded by large moats of water on both sides of their land. But with the elimination of risk, first from the role of leaders and then from that of soldiers (through the invention of high-tech soldier surrogates), wars have become easier, not more difficult, for politicians to wage. Former US Army Ranger Andrew Exum articulates the reasoning of enthusiastic war supporters in these colorful terms: 'You've got this great hammer, and, you know, why not go hammer some nails?'[287]

What has emerged with these qualitative changes in warfare is an erosion of Western civilization's mores. The banality of killing is graphically on display in proliferating and ever-lengthening hit lists, including 'evil terrorists' so little understood that the killers do not even know the targets' names. Human life has been debased in the process, with people divided into categories with greater or lesser value determined by a morally irrelevant property: where they happen to live.

In these new 'military' missions, drones 'engage the enemy' while the operators piloting them are sequestered away behind impenetrable bastions, working what are in effect desk jobs. The ability to kill by remote control represents a radical departure from the entire history of warfare, which up until rather recently required martial virtues such as courage and the willingness to risk one's life for a worthy cause. In the just war tradition, enemy soldiers are to be respected as persons capable of laying down their arms, but the targets killed in drone strikes are more like persons on death row with no right to appeal. M. Shane Riza, a conventional combat command pilot, warns: 'In no conceivable way is unmanned warfare speaking to those we are fighting in a way they understand.'[288]

What for centuries was conceived as the 'invincible ignorance' of combatants, that the soldiers of both sides are morally equivalent insofar as they are fighting at the behest of a commander whom they are not permitted to second guess, has taken on an entirely new meaning in the drone age. The victims are now 'invincibly ignorant' of the fact that they are about to die. The killers are 'invincibly ignorant' of the intentions in their targets' minds and what they would or would not have done, had they somehow survived a missile strike launched without warning and with no provision for the possibility of surrender.

Every military mission involves uncertainty, and human fallibility ensures that things will not always go as planned. When it emerges that entirely innocent people have been destroyed, soldiers may console themselves with the knowledge that nothing can be done about 'the fog of war'. That metaphor is apt when mistakes are made on the ground in the midst of smoky conflagrations, and soldiers kill their own comrades through the ironic (and tragic) use of 'friendly fire'. However, 'the fog of war' has an entirely new meaning in a world in which people are killed at a vast distance on the basis of speculative intelligence readily assumed to be actionable precisely in order that there should be some identifiable target to kill.

The business of UCAV operators is to kill. If they are not killing, if they are lying idle, then the various governmental agencies which support their work – and keep them gainfully employed – become dispensable. For these reasons, it behooves analysts to maintain a lengthy list of targets to prove that they need to be killing, to persuade politicians and their constituents to pay to keep the machine up and running and in perpetual motion. But in what sense can this bureaucratic institution of homicide be said to constitute *war*?

Predator drone-delivered Hellfire missiles incinerate the human beings closest to the impact, leaving charred remains behind. The bodies of the other persons located within the radius of destruction are ripped apart, with blood sprayed and chunks of flesh and limbs scattered about for everyone in the neighborhood to see. Such truculence has been mistaken as strength by Bush, Obama, and their supporters. But if the people paying for the carnage never witness the human cost of so-called surgical strikes, then to them it is not even real. The beheadings videotaped and disseminated by terrorist groups are indeed barbaric, but are they any more barbaric than obliterating a human body with a missile?

In truth, the reactions of war supporters to the sight of horrific beheadings appear to be not at all unlike those of persons such as Nidal Hasan and Faisal Shahzad who are radicalized by equally horrific missile strikes. Such grisly acts – committed by both sides in every military conflict – invariably motivate strident calls for retaliatory homicide in response: *violence breeds violence*. By irrevocably snuffing out dissent to their military policies, the primary source of protests both at home and abroad, US administrators have gone astray through their excessive deference to the military, whose *raison d'être*, at the end of the day, is to kill. Along the way, they have come to undermine the republican values enshrined in the US Constitution.

In October 2002 the US Congress approved the transfer of all war powers to a single man, George W. Bush. By renouncing their power as representatives of the people, Congress effectively transformed the president into a quasi-monarch with regard to foreign affairs. Because the military is required to carry out war when ordered to do so by the commander in chief, this legislative concession vested in Bush the power of a dictator to wage war whenever and wherever he pleased, in the name of national defense. Obama followed suit by expanding the Predator drone program, waging what are tantamount to micro-preemptive wars claimed to be justifiable acts of self-defense against possible future threats.

The formerly distinct legislative and executive authorities were rolled into one, removing what had been a safeguard from the awful possibility of war. Having usurped the legislators' role of advice and consent (which was renounced by the legislators themselves), the executive continued to expand, assuming next the judicial function. The details were shrouded in mystery, but the effects on the ground were as clear as they could be. A small committee of executive-appointed analysts devised criteria and nominated persons to be eliminated, all under cover of 'State Secrets Privilege'.[289] In these ways, the political structure in the ostensibly democratic United States was subverted. Far from representing the people, the US president came to represent himself and his coterie.

The historical backdrop facilitating these changes has been the prevailing cultural depiction of noble warriors and, above all, the misleading image of leaders as courageous. Once a leader has opted for the use of deadly force, this creates the illusion of representation. When many people stand in solidarity to support what a despot in democratic robes decrees, he can point to those supporters as though he were acting on their beliefs, not his. In fact, the order of explanation is precisely the reverse. The leader decides to wield deadly force. In a show of patriotism – or, in the case of foreign allies, camaraderie – others stand by the leader, and this attracts others as well. What eventually coalesces is a significant group of war advocates who serve as a deflective shield against those who dare to object.

Social and political factors have always conspired to make such gambits possible. Economic problems and the humiliating outcome of World War I helped to rouse the Germans behind Hitler. In the United States, the atrocities of 11 September 2001, still vivid in the minds of Americans, bolstered the specious idea that somehow war supporters are courageous, while war opponents are cowards. These dynamics together produced a portion of the population who were willing to stand by George W. Bush, alongside opportunistic politicians and war profiteers, no matter what he did.

The propaganda of state-funded slaughter abroad leads smoothly to a campaign of war perpetuation once the first bomb has been dropped or the first missile launched. Rhetoric and threats, such as Secretary of State Hillary Clinton's pronouncement in March 2011 that 'It is time for Gaddafi to go,' lead more often than not to military action.[290] Having once uttered such statements, figureheads become concerned with defending the integrity of the institution for which they stand and, above all, the reputation of those who spoke the words.

The feared effect of inaction upon a nation's image may itself provoke military action – whether the initiation, perpetuation or expansion of a war. In the case of Libya, how bombing could untangle the rival forces in the civil war on the ground was far from obvious, and in some ways – to those who persuaded Barack Obama to take action – irrelevant. Obama lobbed hundreds of missiles on Libya in what he claimed to be a limited engagement with a humanitarian goal: to stop what was said to be an impending slaughter of civilians. Once waged, wars propel themselves forward, demanding further commitment and an escalation of violence in order to prove that the initial action was not a mistake.

National reputation is not the only thing at stake in following through on threats. Political leaders no longer risk death by authorizing military action, but they nonetheless paint themselves as strong by ordering the deployment of homicidal weapons, as did 'drone warrior' Barack Obama. Politicians capitalize on the fact that, once upon a time, leaders really were courageous warriors. One plausible explanation for the über-hawkishness of women in power such as Condoleezza Rice, Hillary Clinton, Madeleine Albright, Margaret Thatcher and others (though not all) is their desire to prove that they are just as 'tough' as the men. In an endeavor to demonstrate that they are not 'soft' and 'feminine' – considered equivalent in nearly every society to *weak* – such women may overcompensate by banging the war drums even more loudly than their male counterparts.[291]

Variations on the same dynamic and an all-too-human concern with reputation can be seen in every era. Once President Lyndon B. Johnson had sent combat troops to Vietnam, it became necessary to send more, in order to prove that it was not a mistake to have done so before. The fact that the initial decision had been based on faulty intelligence (the Gulf of Tonkin incident) was simply 'forgotten' or ignored.[292] When some soldiers were killed, more were sent to die in order to prove that grave strategic mistakes had not already been made in sacrificing troops' lives. 'Peace with honor' is defined as ending a war without losing face, but most wars begin in misguided efforts to demonstrate the nation's 'honor'. It was only the British Parliament which caused Barack Obama to pause rather than fire missiles on Syria in 2013 to maintain his credibility after the reckless 'red line' remark.[293] As though reading a page from Yemeni president Saleh's playbook, in 2014 'no boots' Obama rebranded his intervention in Syria as a battle against Al-Qaeda-esque terrorists and thereby succeeded in galvanizing political and popular support for yet another bombing campaign.

During the wars in Afghanistan and Iraq, as in Vietnam, the distortions and lies purveyed to the US citizenry were rationalized by strategists as a necessary part of the campaign for 'hearts and minds'. Rather than face up to the fact that the war was proving impossible to win, the top brass stubbornly claimed that they would prevail. In Vietnam, the troop levels continued to be increased under the pretext that the war was being won and only needed extra 'oomph' – similar to the various 'surges' in Afghanistan and Iraq – in order to get the job done. Surely the grandest irony of all in these cases is that the prolongation of a war is so often claimed to be necessary in order to prove that the soldiers already slain did not die in vain. In fact, this twisted logic explains in large part the self-propagative nature of war more generally, at the macro level. We honor the heroes of past wars, and part of that process involves affirming the concept of a just war and the legitimacy of leaders who wage wars today. Those who died for their country are held up as examples by recruiters to lure in new troops, who are told that they can become heroes just like the men who fought and died in World War II.

The self-proliferating nature of corruption helps to explain, too, why targeted killing continues to spread into more and more territories as the killers attempt to prove to themselves that what they have already done was right. Somehow the disgraceful notion that the innocent people of other countries may be sacrificed during missions intended to protect the people of the United States has become the mainstream American view about the very nature of war. Few US government advocates appear even to register that the targeting of suspects using missiles would be vociferously denounced as unconscionable crimes of aggression if carried out by a foreign government on US soil. Strikingly, outright wars of aggression, in which the US military unleashes deadly force to secure the compliance of a foreign government with US administrators' wishes – and at the cost of non-national civilian lives – are condoned and even enthusiastically supported by many US citizens.

Weaponized drones offer politicians a way to wage war 'on the cheap' – or so it seems – for there need be no allied combatant casualties whatsoever when such aircraft are deployed. By making the use of deadly force seem less morally weighty to the taxpayers funding it, drones also reinforce the general failure to recognize that rubbing out human beings is a sign of weakness, not of strength, serving as an unmistakable demonstration that the killers are unable to convince their adversaries to renounce their position or retreat.

As difficult as this may be for some to acknowledge, the asymmetrical warriors who masterminded the attacks on the World Trade Center succeeded above all in creating their sworn enemy in their own image. The US government has reconceptualized war to include the killing by invisible attackers of unarmed persons with no means of defending themselves, the moral equivalent of the hijackers who posed as passengers on 11 September 2001. How different, really, is the delivery of Hellfire missiles via Predator drone from the use of commercial airliners as bombs? If the crimes of 9/11 were 'craven', as politicians and pundits were wont to say at the time, then what about killing by remote control?

Whatever may be said about the hijackers of 11 September 2001, it must be owned that they believed in their cause, for they were willing to die for it. Modern desktop warriors, in stark contrast, kill without risking any more serious physical harm than the workplace hazards faced by secretaries and clerks. When targeted killing is carried out or facilitated by persons who are not even a part of the military – whether CIA operatives or their private contractees – the killers, too, would seem to fit the bizarre Orwellian category invoked by George W. Bush's legal team to strip certain persons of all rights, both within civil society and on the battlefield: *unlawful combatants.*

Far from repudiating the Bush doctrine of preemptive war, Obama extended it to include 'preemptive humanitarian intervention', ironically (given his administration's signature strike policy) labeling the situation in Libya in 2011 a potential 'genocide' in order to satisfy the 'last resort' requirement of just war theory (see Appendix). But the pretext behind 'signature strikes' is itself a dangerous recipe for genocide, advocating as it does the 'status' execution of merely potentially threatening persons. Every single person in existence is potentially threatening, which is how and why this policy implies that 'everything is permitted'. Just as Bush advocated preemptive war against a nation which might in the future procure weapons which it might in the future deploy, the Obama doctrine is to execute individuals who might in the future decide to attempt to harm the people of the United States. As the map of drone strikes grew to include not only Afghanistan, Iraq, Yemen and Pakistan, but also Somalia, Libya, Mali and Syria, the entirely predictable proliferation of terrorist networks ensued.

The blood of soldiers is being protected at the expense of the lives and well-being of civilians in drone strikes against suspected terrorists and their collaborators wherever 'actionable intelligence' is more readily available than 'judicially admissible evidence' – as preposterous as that proposition might seem. The bar has simply been lowered – by executive fiat – in order to make it easier to kill than to convict suspects. Obviously, it is easier to kill people than it is to convict them of crimes. That is true within civil society as well as abroad. The fact that it is easier to carry out vigilante 'justice' than to secure a conviction in a court of law does not make it right. Indeed, vigilante revenge killing is illegal in civil society.

If the *serial* revenge killing of brown-skinned suspects whose names are not even known by their killers proves to have been ineffective, resulting in more mass attacks on the US homeland against the people paying for the practice, then clearly it was never necessary. Was it even permissible? Disturbingly, the more the hit lists proliferate and the 'battlefields' multiply, the closer this practice moves to genocide. What is it about genocide which the people of Western liberal societies revile? It is precisely the execution of individual persons not for anything they ever did but for who they are: their religion, their location, the color of their skin. In the ceaseless quest for increased lethality, all sight has been lost of what was supposed to be wrong with the wanton slaughter of human beings in the first place.

As reckless deployments of ground troops and experiments in demo-cratization such as those in Afghanistan and Iraq become progress-ively more unpopular to an already risk-averse US citizenry and the political elite, the administration will become more and more prone to deploy drones in place of soldiers in conflict zones, garnering support for bombing campaigns by parroting Obama's 'no boots' trope. Given the general tendency toward – and rationality of – risk aversion, the basic training of future soldiers will in all likelihood consist primarily in creating virtual warriors, who never come in direct contact with their victims and do not risk death as they 'fight' the enemy using as a weapon the mouse or joystick of their computer. 'The nation's finest' will come to mean the fastest clickers, with the traditional virtues associated with soldiers, such as standing firm in the face of adversity and the very real threat of death, rendered obsolete. By maximizing the safety of military killers who operate thousands of miles away from the site of their acts of destruction, the noble soldier of the past will eventually become extinct.

The high incidence of operator burnout and post-traumatic stress disorder in recent times reveals that some of the people enlisted to kill in the Predator drone program do feel compunction for snuffing out their victims. The long-range institutional effect of the fact that some among the enlistees feel badly about what they have agreed to do seems simple enough to predict. Just as morally upstanding persons with a strong sense of the inviolability of human life do not become hitmen, persons with scruples against summarily executing anonymous male suspects who happen to be located in territories designated 'hostile' by someone higher up in the command chain will not opt for the profession of drone operator. In some cases, their view of the practice will change from positive to negative through the course of 'employing on' targets, and they will abandon the vocation, leaving only enthusiasts behind.

As the drone age forges ahead, those who agree to spend their days hunting and killing 'angry poor people' can be expected to promote the program in which they have already participated. At some point, the people who agree to don a military uniform will no longer bear any resemblance whatsoever to the courageous warriors of the past. In order to feel better about what they do, drone operators may continue to compare themselves to the soldiers of World War II. Others may simply be sociopaths, having lucked out at this moment in history that they can be gainfully employed within society proper as paid assassins, what formerly was a profession found only in the criminal sector.

Perhaps some among the burgeoning military class will be people naturally drawn to the prospect of being able to kill with impunity while risking no harm to themselves. In truth, remote-control killing requires even less courage than that of the hitman, who risks severe penalties for his mistakes. But both hitmen and drone operators accept contracts to eliminate people who do not discover that their killers are killers until it is too late. With the progressive elimination of risk from what is labeled 'national defense', the fine, upstanding military 'culture' can be expected to morph into one which, for all intents and purposes, is indistinguishable from that of organized crime. The same types of people will be drawn to both kinds of enterprise. As those tasked with protecting the nation execute more and more suspects without trial – some of whom are guilty but others innocent of any wrongdoing – so, too, will newly incubated enemies proliferate.

Targeted killing by remote control strips the enemy of the capacity to fight back, by firing upon them from the sky like an angry and merciless god hurling down thunderbolts impossible to deflect. In response, violent dissidents can be expected to innovate, just as they have done throughout history. It seems safe to say that the terrorists of the future will not be strapping suicide vests onto their torsos and dying along with their victims. Instead, they will emulate their nemesis and become deft hackers in order to commandeer Predator drones and use them against the people ultimately responsible for their production: the taxpayers of Western states. Rezwan Ferdaus, who in 2011 schemed to deploy an unmanned aircraft against US targets, was only the first in what is bound to be a long list of future technology-savvy terrorists.[294]

Just as they have done in the past, persons who wish to retaliate against what they view as US war crimes will seize the opportunities afforded by the latest and greatest technologies developed by First World nations ostensibly for the purpose of national defense. Another possibility, for the keenest and most highly educated of the next generation of terrorists, will be to infiltrate the private security apparatus now conjoined with US intelligence agencies, permitting the effective commandeering of the suspect 'nomination' (selection) process itself. Eventually, the last vestige of military virtue, the courage not only to fight and to kill but also to die for a cause deemed worthy by the soldier himself, will be erased from the war picture, as the new 'evil enemy' is created in the technokillers' image.

CHAPTER 12
TYRANTS ARE AS TYRANTS DO

'I want al-Awlaki.'

US President Barack Obama[295]

'We killed a terrorist, whose hands were tied, who no longer threatened us. By what right?'

Ami Ayalon, Head of Shin Bet, 1996–2000[296]

TYRANNY IS THE RULE over people by a single person or small group who impose their will upon all of the others through the threat of punishment (often death) for refusals to accede to their demands. Tyrants snuff out human beings not as an end but as a means: to thwart potential threats to their power by eradicating dissent. 'Off with their heads,' they cry, and their lackeys obey, lopping off heads not to stop the victims from breathing, but to prevent them from speaking.

Rather than offer reasons for their actions, tyrants opt for swifter means: they muffle dissent by incarcerating or killing outspoken critics. A third, somewhat more subtle, way to quell opposition is simply to dismiss it: to discredit or marginalize dissidents so that they no longer have an effective voice. In all of these cases, the end result is the same: critics of the status quo have been rendered mute, by hook or by crook. Some critics are more difficult to suppress than others, but there are no limits, in principle, to what tyrants will do in order to neutralize threats to their imperious rule.

The surest way to secure conformity is to eliminate anyone who disagrees. More sophisticated tyrants deploy complex strategies, with carrots (bribes) for some, who are persuaded to help the tyrant to maintain his domain, and sticks (threats) for others, who are prevented from challenging the tyrant out of fear. Men such as Adolf Hitler deploy these techniques simultaneously, enlisting other people to do their dirty work while promoting the image of a great and powerful leader before the adoring masses, who come to believe that they are the true object of their leader's concern. Meanwhile, behind the scenes, a demagogic despot plots the destruction of groups of people who do not fit into his fantastical scheme. Because everything appears to be perfectly above board, the longer a leader remains in power, the more difficult it becomes to raise critical questions about what is being done.

Savvy tyrants are buoyed above all by enthusiastic supporters among the populace who blithely accept whatever their leaders say and vehemently denounce anyone who dares to speak out in opposition. Often such support derives from the benefits achieved through alliance with the powers that be. The loyalists of tyrants, who serve as zealous volunteers in defending their leader publicly against any and all detractors, are his most valuable assets. Those who truly believe in what they are doing – aside from securing their own immediate means of sustenance and survival – are highly persuasive in bringing others to comply with their leader's decrees.

The tyrant's modus operandi may seem easy to understand in the abstract, but it is far more difficult to recognize locally, in concrete practice. During their reign of power, leaders with a tyrannical bent control the perspectives of the populace to such a significant extent that even those who can call up examples of tyrants from history are blinded to the Procrustean measures wielded by the leaders of their own land. Nearly everyone today affirms that Hitler was a despicable despot, and many believe that he perpetrated evil by hoodwinking the German people. Reflections of this same tyrannical structure are incredibly difficult to identify contemporaneously, within the society in which one lives.

Deadly violence is the ultimate form of silencing. The people killed in wars cannot speak up to reveal what was done to them, and the surviving soldiers who suffer in silence with the burden of their conscience become equally irrelevant, marginalized as maladjusted 'misfits', the victims of post-traumatic stress disorder. The official story is written by the strong, surviving administrators of the system, whose primary concern is to maintain their institution in its current form. The fact that each of these spokespersons has self-interested reasons for defending the status quo is ignored by those who docilely digest the stories composed in the public relations quarters of the government.

The stories of what transpires during wartime are written by high-level officials who commence from the first premise that the institution itself is good and acts justly. This implies that any evidence to the contrary must be dismissed through explaining it away. Yes, it is owned, there may be 'a few bad apples'. Now and then 'mistakes are made'. However, the integrity of the institution itself remains for all intents and purposes publicly unassailable precisely because most of the individuals situated so as to offer substantive critiques are themselves implicated in what has gone wrong, whether directly or indirectly.

Pushed to the wall, in cases such as the abuse scandal at Abu Ghraib, when it becomes impossible to dispel the impression of atrocity, military administrators opt to charge low-level troops with crimes rather than assume responsibility for what has transpired. But even when the entire mission proves to be a fiasco – as in the US interventions in Vietnam and Iraq, and the Soviet invasion of Afghanistan – this is written off as a result of not the incompetence of those in charge but the impossibility of the mission, which comes to be characterized, in retrospect, as 'a fool's errand'.[297]

The defense establishment runs its own tribunals for the punishment of wrongdoers within the institution itself. Because the military is accorded the absolute prerogative to hand down justice in the cases under its jurisdiction, it is not possible to pose effective critiques from either outside or within. It is a closed system, in precisely the manner in which the secret meetings, dubbed 'Terror Tuesdays', during which targets were approved for execution by President Obama, cannot be penetrated. When in 2013 the president selected John Brennan, the targeted killing program 'czar', to become the new director of the CIA, he ensured that the practice would continue to dominate the Agency's efforts. The appointment served a psychological function as well: to persuade all those involved in the program, including Obama, that what they had already done was perfectly permissible and should proceed as before. It seems safe to say that Director Brennan, who commands a staggering $50 billion budget, will not be appointing as fledgling analysts anyone who regards targeted killing as a violation of international law or the moral equivalent of murder.

What is especially perplexing about the secretive Predator drone killing program is that the very people who 'make the call' at the culmination of deliberations behind closed doors are also the people who report on what is done. The police, the judge, the jury, the executioner, and the narrator of the last word on what transpired are all vested in the executive, with no possibility for a revision of the story. The target is defined as guilty of crimes with which he was never charged, except rhetorically, after his death, in a public relations pitch to the people who paid for the hit. At the opening of his thirteen-hour filibuster against the nomination of John Brennan as director of the CIA, Rand Paul aptly compared this absurd situation to the Queen of Heart's 'court' in *Alice in Wonderland. How,* Senator Paul pondered, *can persons be found guilty and sentenced* before *their trial?*

The logic of preemption – whether on the macro-level of waging war or the micro-level of summary execution without trial – is relatively straightforward: the heathens must be defeated before they make their move. The heathens waged war upon us, and now we must retaliate with crushing force and withering power, relentlessly, until at last the enemy has been defeated, in order for freedom and democracy to prevail. There are, of course, many 'pockets of resistance', areas where unenlightened leaders still exert tyrannical force within their narrowly circumscribed domains. Suspiciously, it is *only* in such forlorn places – Pakistan, Somalia, Yemen, and other poor, less-developed countries – where autocratic leaders permit the execution of the residents of their land by the US government in exchange for military aid. Needless to say, this setup serves no more obvious function than to cement petty despots' positions of power. Corrupt leaders dotting the landscape of Africa and the Middle East are essential to the US government's targeted killing program abroad. But how does a global institution of homicide support democracy and freedom? Answer: It does not.

That the practice of targeted killing has become more and more widespread and accepted by many as a standard operating procedure does not imply that it is right. Instead, it serves as a stark testimony to the existence of unscrupulous collaborators the world over who are willing to trade their compatriots' lives for foreign aid in order to shore up their own power by allying themselves with the United States, the most formidable military force on the planet to date. Savage warlords have been supported in many parts of the world, despite the fact that they rule their territories in the manner of thugs, bumping off fellow human beings at their caprice. Rigid monarchies are strengthened militarily by greasing the wheels of the US government's killing machine. Because locals furnish much of the intelligence for strikes, autocrats are able to direct US military might to the elimination of domestic political rivals.

In the countries where most US drone strikes have been carried out, the permission to do so has been granted by the central government authority. In the case of Yemen, the site of the first deadly attack openly admitted by the CIA, President Saleh in effect bartered for generous packages of military aid over the course of a decade. His successor, Abd Rabu Mansour Hadi, who became the new president in 2012, agreed to do the same.[298] Critics familiar with the terrain have argued that tribal Islamic culture and society in the peripheries of such lands – Pakistan is another example – are under siege and risk even annihilation.[299]

What is wrong with this state of affairs from the perspective of a Western liberal democracy whose citizens fund these practices? Most obviously, the Predator drone program strengthens and emboldens reigning tinpot tyrants who grant the US government permission to kill whomever the killers deem worthy of death – whatever their reasons may be. Throughout the twenty-first century, the US government has enlisted tyrants as force multipliers, while simultaneously becoming itself a force multiplier of tyrants. To sustain such leaders is not to champion but to undermine human liberty, as was exemplified in Bahrain when the United States approved a large military aid package to the government despite protests by the populace wishing to demo-cratize their land.[300]

The support by the United States of monarchies and straightforward dictators in the Middle East is not new to the drone age but a long-standing practice. No matter how miserable and oppressive the conditions of their own people may be, so long as such leaders treat US strategists with comity and provide them with access to whatever they claim to need, they are permitted to run their own nation's affairs as they see fit, even when those very places were the homelands of demonstrated enemies of the United States. Most of the hijackers of 9/11 hailed from Saudi Arabia, yet the US government remained on friendly terms with its monarchic leaders, and continues to engage in large-scale weapons trade with what is a decidedly undemocratic lot. The criterion for deciding *which* undemocratic, uncivilized countries must be invaded is obviously not their sheer lack of democracy. The question is, rather, whether the despots of the world support or challenge the authority and power of the United States and its allies at the present moment in time. Everything may change tomorrow, of course, but for today the US government will not invade its current allies. On the contrary, even when, as in Egypt, a democratically elected government is ousted by military coup, those who usurped political power by force will continue to enjoy multibillion-dollar packages of military aid, provided only that they agree to collaborate with the United States.[301]

Abd Rabu Mansour Hadi, the president of Yemen who followed his predecessor's lead in permitting the CIA to wield deadly force freely in the land, was deposed by angry militants in 2015. Yemen was supposed to be 'no boots' Obama's drone war 'success story', but the coup was arguably precipitated by the US interventions over more than a decade. In addition to the harm caused to the Yemenis themselves, the power vacuum left behind created yet another chaotic context – as in Somalia, Libya, Afghanistan and Iraq – conducive to the incubation of terrorists who wish to exact their bloody revenge. All of these fiascoes were funded by US taxpayers.

By empowering the leaders who permit targeted killing in exchange for military aid, by using tyrants as its force multipliers, the US government lays bare the tyranny of its own military practice. Tyrannical means such as the summary execution without trial of suspects do not promote but undermine liberty, democracy and peace. In prosecuting its drone wars, the United States acts unilaterally, out of state interest, not concern for humanity. Least of all do any of these interventions help the inhabitants of lands governed by iron-fisted autocrats. In May 2014, it was reported that US Special Operations forces were covertly forming elite counterterrorism units in Libya, Mauritania, Niger and

Mali.[302] What this means, of course, is that inhabitants of these lands are being armed and trained to kill. Whom will they kill? The tragic history of war-ravaged postcolonial Africa provides little cause for hope that the latest generation of First World-trained and equipped local militias will be any more discriminating or less brutal than were those of the past.

By allying itself with petty despots and providing them with the tools of techno-killing, and by training foreign soldiers to kill on command, the US government does not support but sabotages democracy. By refusing to elucidate the criteria used in producing 'hit lists' of persons to dispatch, the US administration has gone one step further, *exemplifying* tyranny. The denial of judicial process to suspects before their state execution and the use of opaque and secret decision-making procedures invulnerable to critique have always been the standard operating procedures of tyrants. The US government adduces the blanket excuse of 'State Secrets Privilege' to explain why the persons killed by Predator drone (and JSOC) are exempted from any requirements of judicial process or transparency. But that has been precisely the excuse used by tyrants throughout history. Tyrants are as tyrants do.

In order fully to appreciate the significance of remote-control killing in the twenty-first century, it is important to understand how and why modern Western democratic societies exist. What was it that the people of ancient and medieval times found so despicable about their unenlightened despots that they deemed it necessary to establish what became stable modern democracies? Nothing is clearer from history than that deadly weapons are the primary tools of tyrants, which they wield through intermediaries, usually uniformed soldiers, to control the inhabitants of their domain. Yet ostensibly democratic nations – above all, the United States – continue to deploy deadly force in imposing the will of their leaders upon the rest of the world. Throughout the Cold War, a wide array of covert, quasi-military actions using untraceable, 'unattributable' weapons were carried out by persons hired to work as private contractors. Only with the Bush–Cheney administration did the use of such private-turned-public contractors reveal to the world how far such dealings have involved practices in violation of not only the laws of civil society but also the orthodox 'rules of war'.

Before the drone age, freelance soldiers were often used in plausibly deniable ways, beyond public scrutiny and without the approval of the branch of the US government vested with the authority to wage war on behalf of the nation. The reason for the secrecy was that those who devised the missions believed either that they would not be supported by the representatives of the people, or else that the missions could not be conducted without violating the law – whether civil, military or international. The initiatives moved ahead nonetheless unimpeded, under the aegis of taxpayer-funded institutions and orchestrated by individuals who appointed themselves the arbiters of affairs beyond the domain of their proper authority under the law.

Perhaps the most celebrated such case involved the Iran–Contra scandal, during which Oliver North and others – in direct defiance of the Boland Amendment – sold arms covertly to Iran and funneled the money to the Contras in an effort to decisively influence the outcome of the Nicaraguan war.[303] Oddly enough, Oliver North ended by becoming a celebrity of sorts for violating the most basic principles of the US Constitution out of what was interpreted by many to be a heartfelt expression of patriotism. North was one among many recipients of the interpretive charity typically extended even to leaders who wage misguided wars. The prevailing assumption among military supporters is that, whatever laws such leaders may have broken, and whatever damage they may have caused, and no matter how much misery they have sown, ultimately their intentions were good. George H. W. Bush pardoned the executors of Iran Contra, and Barack Obama chose to overlook the illegal practices of the George W. Bush administration. By declining to prosecute the offenders, Obama left torture and 'extraordinary rendition', along with his signature policy – targeted killing on 'battlefields without borders' – as 'options on the table' for future leaders, both domestic and foreign.

This focus upon intentions disregards the impact on locals of 'well-intended' wars, as though the effects for the people on the ground were somehow irrelevant. Even worse, the assumption of good intentions on the part of one's own leaders and evil intentions on the part of whoever has been identified as the latest enemy, the 'Hitler *du jour*', portrays nearly every international conflict as requiring the recourse to war, since 'the evil enemy' is assumed to be beyond the reach of diplomatic means. That the persons who will suffer the most from the decision to wage war against an enemy regime are innocent bystanders – or complicit in propping up the regime only as a result of coercion of one form or another – is altogether ignored by war makers.

Among military supporters who laud the advent of targeted killing as a way of circumventing the sacrifice of troops, there seems to be a fair amount of confusion about what precisely it is that makes tyrants deplorable. All of the standard features of tyranny are present in military institutions, including, most importantly, the ability to discredit anyone who attempts to speak out in opposition to the official story of what has been done ostensibly in the name of the people. Even when dissidents such as Private Manning bravely step forward because they truly believe that their government is violating the law, the revelations are swiftly contorted into crimes by those whose policies have been challenged.

Private Manning disseminated evidence of war crimes committed by the US government. The whistleblower was indicted on a variety of charges and sentenced by a military tribunal to thirty-five years in prison.[304] Edward Snowden, a private contractor working for the National Security Agency (NSA), exposed the existence of a wide-ranging surveillance campaign on both US citizens and millions of persons abroad, including the leaders of allied nations such as Germany and France. If not for the willingness of the government of Russia to grant Snowden political asylum, he would in all likelihood have suffered a fate similar to that of Manning for having violated laws prohibiting the disclosure of classified materials accessed during his time working for the US government. Or perhaps he would simply have been found dead, the tragic victim of an automobile accident or an unexpected suicide or heart attack.

An entire wing of the US military establishment concerns itself with marketing and public relations, just as did the Ministry of Propaganda headed by Joseph Goebbels under the Third Reich. In 2009, the Pentagon was reported to have spent $4.6 billion in a single year on public relations, with 27,000 persons employed in that capacity.[305] The intellectuals who defended Hitler's mad quest for power, too, have analogues in the twenty-first century: outspoken pundits and politicians who line up to defend every single war ever waged by any US leader. A malleable president can be brought to renounce his own self-professed principles, as when persistent war promoters agitated to persuade President Barack Obama first to intervene in Libya, and later to arm the rebels in Syria, despite his claim throughout his first election campaign that he would not embroil the United States in further wars.[306] Rather than soberly assess the mess left behind in Iraq, the Obama administration deposed Muammar Gaddafi in Libya, generating yet more postwar chaos and further destabilizing the region.

Attempts to rein in military tyranny through the establishment of the UN Security Council, the *Universal Declaration of Human Rights* and the International Criminal Court (ICC) no doubt motivate belligerent leaders to work vigorously to find allies before waging war, as did George W. Bush in British Prime Minister Tony Blair and Spanish President José María Aznar. Such allies may help to evade stigmatization as a war criminal for what might seem, if committed alone, to be flagrant acts of aggression prohibited by the letter of international law. Still, the usefulness of such conventions depends crucially upon agreements by none other than the governments of nations to abide by them, and when leaders change, opinions on the validity of conventions sometimes change as well. US President Bill Clinton signed the ICC agreement, which his successor, George W. Bush, 'unsigned'.

Technologically induced changes in what people have been persuaded to accept as legitimate forms of national defense – conducted by the US government beyond the perimeters of its sovereign territory – make it difficult to see how international conventions could ever deter the strongest nations, which risk no effective sanction for their failure to comply. International institutions and declarations are wielded by the victors of armed conflicts in ways primarily designed to solidify the outcome through writing 'the last word' of the stories of glorious war, in what critics term 'victors' justice'. The war criminals tried after a ceasefire are invariably situated on the losers' side. Alleged crimes on the victors' side are said to have been committed by 'rogue' elements independently of the lofty institution which deployed them, and such criminals are dealt with through internal court-martial in military tribunals. There may be disparities between what seems to be right at a specific moment in time and what really is right, but whether or not the most powerful have justice on their side, they do write the official story of what transpired.

International conventions are crafted and agreed to by the representatives of nations, who defend their state's right to exist. The agreements apply to and are enforced only by formal states, and the UN possesses the military force only of its willing members, devoid as it is of an independent standing army. Most wars in recent times have been contests between factions to whom the conventions do not apply. Even in the case of small state belligerents, the greater power status of larger nations capable of obliterating any smaller state's military capacities likely serves as a stronger deterrent than any statement of international law.

The Geneva Conventions, too, would seem to apply only to the soldiers of states, and when they appear to be violated by so-called asymmetrical warriors, the question arises whether they are unjust warriors or simply criminals. This determination is left for political leaders to make, and because in the United States a robust military institution exists for conflict resolution between nations, it was mobilized also to contend with the problem of terrorism. Rather than interpret the attacks of 11 September 2001 as crimes, for which individuals were responsible, the US government opted to label them acts of 'war' and rationalized the deployment of the entire military in response. At the same time, US leaders have taken pains to circumvent both the Geneva Conventions and domestic law through the use of means such as extraordinary rendition and the imprisonment of persons stipulated to be 'unlawful combatants' and detained indefinitely at Guantánamo Bay, essentially a 'law-free' zone.

It is not difficult to see how and why the ready availability of a massive military establishment generated the interpretation of the attacks of 11 September 2001 as a declaration of war. Certainly, the idea that the Department of Defense should suddenly become irrelevant was unlikely to be embraced by the highest-level administrators of that very institution. Yet the striking mismatch between the means and the aims of the wars in Afghanistan and Iraq would seem to corroborate the increasing irrelevance of a defense apparatus formed during the Cold War to combat the former Soviet Union, a rival military superpower. Instead of fashioning tools apt to the task at hand, to apprehend those responsible for the 11 September 2001 attacks, the US government opted to flex its hypertrophic military muscles, using the formidable weapons of war to overtake entire nations. The efficacy of this approach in contending with terrorist groups is impugned by a 2008 Rand study according to which only 7 percent of the 648 terrorist groups studied were neutralized through military force.[307]

Being willing to kill human beings is obviously not the only thing which makes those denounced by officials as the *bad guys* bad. In the first decade of the twenty-first century, the self-proclaimed *good guys*, while inveighing against the *bad guys*, killed many times more than the number of civilians destroyed on 11 September 2001 in responding to that crime. Maximum lethality is sought by both sides of what is assumed by the adversaries mired in bloody disputes to be a Manichean divide. People who support leaders as they intentionally kill in order to achieve their political aims may become more and more emotionally attached to a technology such as the Predator drone and adamant to defend its use as just. Otherwise, they, too, will have been complicit in war crimes, since any act of killing within an illegal war is the moral equivalent of murder.

Versed in the same incredibly persuasive just war rhetoric, buoyed by the same forces of self-delusion and opportunism, all leaders who commit mass homicide do so officially in the name of abstract principles but in reality for very specific and concrete political – and often economic – purposes. They may be clad in republican clothes, but their willingness to pay for the realization of their dreams with the lives of other human beings betrays their tyrannical pretensions. Some commanders are more flagrant in their disregard for human rights than are others, but the basic willingness to end the lives of other people unites institutional killers of all stripes.

Calling drone-launched missile strikes 'acts of war' supposedly excuses the accompanying collateral damage, but UCAVs have made it possible for the executive branch of the US government also to sidestep the congressional approval required by law before the president wields military force abroad. What might be termed an 'actionable ambiguity' has arisen in the drone age because killing by remote control does not require that troops be sent to fight (and die) in the land under attack. In the past, large-scale deployments and the prospect of soldierly sacrifice mandated the approval of legislators, the holders of the purse strings to war, as specified in the *Constitution of the United States.*

Paradoxically enough, the US president now kills people all over the planet under cover of 'just war' but without officially declaring war. Simply decreeing that 'the world is a battlefield' is both too little and too much. It paves the way to profligate killing programs far and wide, while simultaneously closing off the possibility of discovering that murder has ever been committed by any Predator drone operator – or, what is more likely, by the person who supplied the killers with faulty or bogus intelligence. The victims are defined as legitimate targets (males between the ages of sixteen and fifty), and anyone who does not fit the definition is written off as the regrettable collateral damage of 'war'.

People use the word *tyranny* all the time. Tyranny is evil, and wars are fought, it is often said, to combat tyranny, without any apparent recognition that war itself is the most tyrannical of means. This contradiction complements the notion of wars fought for peace, the most extreme version of which is surely preemptive war waged to thwart the possibility of an enemy's future waging of war. A particularly stark example of this contradiction is the threat to use nuclear weapons against a regime attempting to produce the same in order to deter those who conflate offense and defense in campaigns of preemptive mass homicide.

War is incessantly touted as the means to peace, while people are annihilated in the process of supposedly defending them. The ultimate swindle in this sea of Orwellian rhetoric involves moving people to support tyrannical wars and the execution of suspects without trial all in the name of democracy. The problem is not just that the bombing of people seems an entirely ineffective way to spread democracy. Much worse, the means deployed in destroying human beings, ostensibly in the name of freedom and democracy, embody the very antithesis of the values of freedom and democracy. The people under threat of death by Predator drones hovering menacingly above are effectively enslaved. They are completely at the mercy of a group of strangers whom they never appointed as their leaders. Instead, the authority to kill in what is the victims' civil society (merely stipulated by war makers to be a 'battlefield') is granted by central authorities keen to bolster and cement their power at all costs, including the lives of entirely innocent people.

These contradictions are condoned by so many people primarily because they cling to myths with no basis in what has become the reality of modern war. War is *essentially* tyrannical, and the practice of summary execution without trial, which was arrived at by sliding down a very slippery slope, lays bare the tyranny of war in a most striking and concentrated way. Western nations claim to champion freedom, peace and democracy, but they often do so internationally through the imposition of tyrannical means upon the helpless inhabitants of other lands. Whenever missiles are launched, the powerless people on the ground find themselves trapped between the Charybdis of a local dictator and the Scylla of a homicidal self-proclaimed 'liberator'.

The person at the top of the hierarchical military structure is accorded absolute authority to wage war whenever he claims that national defense is at stake, and everyone in the chain of command beneath him is required to comply with his orders. Because the military personnel beneath the commander in chief do not decide when and where to wage war, they are absolved from responsibility for misguided deployments, and can execute dubious mission after dubious mission with impunity. When a debacle such as the US war in Vietnam takes place, no one is held accountable for the millions of lives destroyed by 'well-meaning' warriors sent by leaders claiming to be engaged in national defense. Abject crimes during wartime are brushed aside or minimized, dismissed or ignored, and when that becomes impossible they are blamed on a small number of deviant 'degenerates' said to have somehow made their way into the ranks.

The collateral damage of war, which in recent times has come to exceed the damage to combatants, continues to be regarded as acceptable, even in cases where no allied soldier's life is at stake. The overall structure of the military is affirmed to be good, even when targeted killing comes to look alarmingly similar to racial profiling, as in the case of signature strikes, which were rebranded 'terrorist attack disruption strikes' (TADS) as they began to be used in Yemen.[308] At the same time, out of sheer habit, every positive attribute of any soldier in history is ascribed to contemporary soldiers, as though they bore more than a nominal resemblance to one another. Every positive outcome of every conflict in which the military was ever engaged is regarded as a glorious victory and lauded as evidence of the righteousness of every later generation of the military.

It is not possible to pose effective objections to this structure within a regime when the head of the army and the head of the government are one and the same. In modern Western states, an effort has been made to enforce a separation of executive and legislative powers, so that a single leader cannot alone wage a full-scale war without the support of lawmakers. Still, the propaganda of war as a form of legitimate self-defense is so persuasive that it led the members of the US Congress in October 2002 to acquiesce to the president in abdicating their responsibility and effectively nullifying the separation of powers. Both the Senate and the House of Representatives granted George W. Bush permission to wage war at a time of his choosing and without securing further approval from the legislative branch. That maneuver served primarily to protect the president from skeptics about the pretexts for his 2003 invasion of Iraq. Even under the War Powers Act, it remains the US president's prerogative to deploy military force in national defense for a period of sixty days before having to seek congressional approval.

During a war waged by a foreign leader in what he claims to be national defense, the victims of bombing abroad are denied the most fundamental human right, the right to life, by a person with no legitimate political authority over them whatsoever. This is precisely what transpires, too, in drone strikes based on faulty intelligence which end by destroying entirely innocent people. The homeland of civilian inhabitants is decreed a war zone and penetrated by the massively destructive weapons of foreign political leaders. The victims are sacrificed according to the killers' timetable and for their interests, whatever they may be. The only feasible option for civilians whose land is under military attack or devoid of any semblance of security is to flee, but this, too, is typically impeded by the immigration laws of neighboring nations. Tragically, when people attempt to escape from what has been designated by war makers a battlefield, they may be mistaken for 'the enemy' and bombed, as happened to convoys of civilians leaving Kosovo in 1999.[309] When refugees take to the sea, they may not ever make it to shore.[310]

In civil society, human beings are said to possess inalienable rights to life, liberty and the pursuit of happiness. Only through the deployment of military weapons abroad, on 'battlefields' stipulated by the killers themselves, are leaders able to harm or even cause the premature deaths of innocent people with impunity. These victims have been made, against their will, the subjects of the enemy leader, even when he claims to be fighting on their behalf, for he strips some of them of their lives and terrorizes all of the rest.

Tyrannical governments are despicable precisely because they imperiously pronounce that people merely suspected of wrongdoing or evil intentions must die. Many critics objected to the Bush admin-istration's brazen deviations from international law and conventions, waxing nostalgic about 'the good old days'. Tony Geraghty captures the essence of those concerns quite well: 'The old rules, from inter-national laws of war to human rights, from the repudiation of torture to the defence of habeas corpus, were brutally rewritten so as to impose a new form of Western democracy everywhere, anywhere, any time, and to do it in Iraq with breathtaking inefficiency.'[311]

In truth, to regard what transpired since 2001 as the introduction of a 'new form of Western democracy' seems dubious, for the correct characterization of a government is not merely a matter of public relations and rhetoric. The fact that Bush-era administrators flouted the rules of war, and dismissed the UN as 'irrelevant' and the Geneva Conventions as 'quaint', shows no more and no less than that they were not a force for democracy and justice at all, regardless of what they claimed. Bush and company were simple tyrants in disguise, who perversely capitalized upon the fact that they had secured the highest positions of power within an ostensibly democratic society with a bloated defense budget and arsenals bursting at the seams.

What may have persuaded some critics to believe that George W. Bush managed to change the world irrevocably was the continuation of so many of his policies by the administration of Barack Obama, touted by many of his early supporters as the harbinger of peace. Under Obama, thousands of suspects were executed without trial, all under cover of Bush's global war, despite the fact that the practice conflicts with every principle for which the United States supposedly stands. If an administration conducts itself in the manner of a tyrant, assassinating human beings as it deems fit, using vague, secret criteria to which citizens are not privy and which lie beyond the possibility of critique, then that administration is no less than a tyrannical regime. To say that George W. Bush introduced 'a new form of Western democracy' is to give him far more credit than he deserves. Nothing that Bush did was new; he merely followed the scripts of dictators past. If the practices of a government – offensive war, torture and summary execution – are indistinguishable from those of the tyrants littering history, then the government in question, regardless of what it may label itself, is tyrannical too. Tyrants are as tyrants do.

CONCLUSION

'We couldn't find bin Laden, so we went
after anyone who looked like him.'

Michael Hastings, *The Operators*[312]

'Is AQAP [Al-Qaeda on the Arabian Peninsula] a threat to the
United States? Yeah. They could bring down an airliner, kill a
couple hundred people. But are they an existential threat to the
United States? Of course not. Of course not. None of these people
are an existential threat to the United States. We've gone crazy
over this. We had this kind of hysterical reaction to danger.'

US Colonel W. Patrick Lang[313]

Rᴇᴀʟɪsᴛɪᴄᴀʟʟʏ sᴘᴇᴀᴋɪɴɢ, the chances of being killed by a terrorist today are no greater – and probably lower – than the chances of being murdered by some solitary criminal whose only goal is to acquire whatever cash his victim may be carrying.[314] Accordingly, from a utilitarian or 'greater good' standpoint, the resources expended and the lives sacrificed in combating terrorism in the twenty-first century have been grossly disproportionate to the alleged benefits. Indeed, it is difficult to see what the benefits to ordinary people (not war profiteers) are supposed to be. Osama bin Laden is dead, along with most of the perpetrators of the attacks of 11 September 2001, but the 'Global War on Terror' has raged on, consuming people and funds and creating the conditions for the production of even more terrorists than have already been slain. People in lands far away continue to be killed on the mere suspicion of their potential for becoming active terrorists in the future.

At this point in history, it is no exaggeration to say that the administrators of the United States, the first 'Drone Nation', view their individual acts of targeted killing as though through a drone operator's 'soda straw' lens. The drone operator sees the very local and immediate consequences of his strikes, but what is going on beyond the soda straw? From the perspective of people on the ground, 'lighting up' human beings one by one using $70,000 Hellfire missiles looks not unlike what a hitman does, for the victim has nearly no chance of survival and no means for appeal before his killers. Such small 'victories' in the war on terrorism – what looks like cold-blooded murder beyond the soda straw – may not be victories at all, once the future consequences, beyond individual victims' deaths, arrive later on down the line.

The anger and frustration of US policymakers in the aftermath of the attacks of 11 September 2001 were completely comprehensible. The desire to 'do something' is also a perfectly natural one. Because assassination became both feasible and facile in the drone age, a formal institution, a targeted killing program, emerged. Premeditated homicide came to supersede other means of addressing conflict and contending with crime. However, sometimes the urge to *do something* – *do anything* – should be resisted, particularly when all evidence points to the conclusion that what is being done can only aggravate an already bad situation. The perpetrators of 9/11 and the many new terrorists who have emerged since, like their nemesis, have all felt the urge to *do something*. In the case of angry dissident groups, violent retaliation has been a direct response to what they perceive to be an assault on the Muslim people. When rival groups persist in retaliatory attacks – and Israel is a tragic case in point – then the political conflict which gave rise to the tactical use of homicide becomes more and more intractable.

A different approach is needed to stop the senseless slaughter. It is time to pause and reflect seriously upon the nature of the persons being destroyed in the name of national defense. The death toll includes not only the obviously innocent victims such as Mamana Bibi, but also the human beings defined as mortal enemies and deemed worthy of annihilation on the basis of demographics. The persons targeted by Hellfire missiles are assumed to deserve to die because, according to their killers, they are evil. How and why these people became enemies of the state is generally ignored. In many cases, they have surfaced and joined forces in direct response to policies which they themselves regard as immoral or unjust, as the members of Al-Qaeda have repeatedly claimed in rationalizing retaliatory attacks.

No reasonable person denies that the crimes of 11 September 2001 were inexcusable. But the continuation and expansion of homicidal policies which harm even more of the innocent people already explicitly identified as the very reason for many terrorist acts can and will only generate more terrorists. It is a mistake to assume that people harboring anti-American sentiments – which were formed in many cases directly by US incursions abroad – cannot be reasoned with and must be exterminated. Terrorists are not born but created through their reaction to events and people in the world. The 'solution' of killing more and more people can be expected to accomplish nothing more than to produce even more killers. That is precisely what ensued when the US military invaded Iraq in 2003, at which point the land became a magnet for violent dissidents, who traveled there specifically in order to combat the occupying forces in what they termed a 'holy war' or jihad. ISIS, estimated in 2014 to include some 30,000 members, did not even exist until after the US invasion.

Was it *necessary* to kill hundreds of thousands of people in responding to the attacks of 9/11? The bombing, invasion and occupations of Afghanistan and Iraq were perpetrated under the rubric of national self-defense, the assumption being that the US military needed to stop the evil enemy before it had the chance to attack the homeland again. By lumping together all insurgents opposed to the US invasions into a single group of 'terrorists', policymakers misconstrued the hostility met by the occupiers. The effect of these initiatives has been to cause antipathy to swell, not only within the countries attacked, but in other lands as well. The more people the US government kills, the more enemies it generates. The grisly executions and indiscriminate bombings perpetrated by violent factions in retaliation are then used as the pretext for renewed and continuous military action, generating a vortex of homicide committed by all sides.

Persons with no prior disposition to commit terrorist acts may wonder with good reason whether the hundreds of drone strikes in Pakistan, Yemen, Somalia and beyond could have been carried out with impunity within the borders of the United States. If not, then it looks suspiciously as though racism is in play. Some human beings are more equal than others. Some persons have inviolable rights to life, liberty and happiness; others do not. Some communities deserve to live without the ominous threat of death hovering above their heads; others do not. Some citizens have rights to habeas corpus and due process; others do not. People located in different parts of the world are not treated equally by the very same government, which shows that double standards are being applied, and those standards have nothing to do with the intrinsic qualities of the persons involved. Instead, the targets deemed fair game for summary execution happen always to reside in Third World countries governed by unscrupulous leaders not renowned as champions of human rights, to put it mildly.

A glaring practical objection to the 'Kill don't capture' approach is that it destroys potentially useful intelligence along with the presumed terrorist. 'Foot soldiers' and low-level members of militant groups do not possess much if any such information, which renders dubious the claim that they must be destroyed. What precisely would transpire, if they were permitted to live? Surely a sixteen-year-old male, a mere impressionable teenager who has recently been persuaded to join up with Al-Qaeda, Al-Shabaab, ISIS, or some other gang, could also be persuaded to renounce his affiliation. To suppose otherwise is to embrace a Manichean theory of human nature which is both false and nihilistic. The simpleminded division of the world into 'good guys' and 'bad guys' ignores the etiology of terrorists, as though they popped up out of nowhere spontaneously and unprovoked.

In forecasting the future effects of the new practice of killing by remote control, what matters above all is not how the perpetrators view their actions, but how those at the receiving end of missiles view them. The perceptions of the people directly affected by interventions must be changed in order for there to be any chance of quelling terrorism in the twenty-first century. Self-proclaimed members of violent factions are not categorically evil. A person targeted for obliteration by drone embodies many roles in his society beyond that of soldier. He is someone's son, and perhaps also a brother, a husband and a father. The truth is that people exhibit various moral shades of gray, and many of them will do what they deem necessary to defend those whom they love. When they perceive their entire community to be under siege, they may feel compelled to retaliate in kind, with any and all means at their disposal. Lacking Hellfire missiles and Predator drones, they will wield AK-47s, improvised explosive devices (IEDs) and knives.

The problems with the summary execution of 'angry poor people' who happen also to have brown skin are not merely matters of myopic strategy and self-defeating tactics.[315] In all of this frenzy of targeted killing by remote control, occasioned by the development of technology which makes it possible, the whole point of defending people from deadly violence has been lost sight of. Human beings possess an intrinsic and inviolable moral value, which is erased from the face of the earth when they are annihilated. 'Signature strikes' are the most extreme expression of this form of moral blindness and embody a logic similar to that of genocidal killers. Do brown-skinned males from the ages of sixteen to fifty who happen to inhabit Third World nations ruled by autocrats willing to trade human lives for military aid have fewer rights than anyone else? Are they morally equivalent to 'bugs', 'rats' and 'mice', as their killers characterize the targets? No, they are human beings.

Homicide does not lead to human flourishing nor to the democratization of society. Least of all do acts of killing promote freedom. On the contrary, the elimination of a human being is the absolute erasure of freedom, the snuffing out of a subject of consciousness who up until his death was free at the very least to think and to change his beliefs. Enemy soldiers may surrender or defect right up until the moment when they have been slain, after which all avenues to change are barred. Every single human being may possess the potential to develop into a terrorist such as Osama bin Laden, but also a very different sort of person, someone more akin to Nelson Mandela. As a young man, the future leader of South Africa inhabited a 'hostile' territory and might well have been wiped out by a Hellfire missile, had Predator drone technology existed at the time when he was locked away in a prison. Mandela emerged, nearly thirty years later, to be one of the greatest forces for peace in history.

All of this raises a vexing question: *Why should suspects be slain rather than captured, even in cases where the killers are convinced of their 'hostile intent'?* 'Angry poor people' are not the moral equivalent of vermin to be exterminated from an old house. Nor are they tiny weeds to be mowed down by a mighty 'lawnmower' machine the moment they break ground after a rain. Boundless human potential is squelched with each irrevocable act of summary execution by Predator drone. The use of Hellfire missiles to take out suspected terrorists also destroys entirely innocent people not even believed to harbor evil intentions, who might have become great leaders, artists, writers or humanitarians.

Homicide is not a means by which to persuade anyone of anything, but under certain circumstances it becomes comprehensible why weaker groups resort to violence. Consider the uprising of people against their colonial oppressors in Africa and elsewhere throughout the world. They may kill in desperation, at wits' end, in an effort to stop the tyrannical rule bearing down upon them. However, once a nation has become a formidable power with stable institutions, there is no excuse for the assassination of individual persons identified by their killers as enemies of the state. The US government *always* has the ability to capture its enemies and merely lacks the will to do so when it opts to snuff them out instead.[316]

The support of a policy by the populace is no proof of its justice, as the world learned unforgettably from the reign of the Third Reich in Germany. Many US citizens have no problem with their government 'taking the battle to the enemy', because the innocent victims have been essentially fictionalized through Pentagon public relations sanitation campaigns. The human beings mistakenly destroyed are perfunctorily labeled 'collateral damage', mentioned briefly, if at all, and then relegated to oblivion. That it has become possible to kill individual people abroad without putting 'boots on the ground' does not make it suddenly necessary or advisable to do so. US leaders have *chosen* to do this, effectively to terrorize and even sacrifice innocent civilians abroad on the supposition that the drone program protects the people back home. There are two obvious problems here. First, civilians abroad are not the property of US leaders to dispose of. Second, anyone who owns that civilians abroad are not the property of US leaders to dispose of may decide to rise up and fight back against those who fund the US military, just as Osama bin Laden did. The short-term protection of US citizens through the use of deadly force in lands far away is illusory, for it leads invariably, sometime in the future, to blowback.

A classic example of this sort of blowback occurred in Somalia in 2006, when the US-supported Ethiopian invasion backfired, emboldening militants and generating widespread sympathy among the populace for what had previously been only a minor Al-Qaeda presence in that land.[317] Thanks to classified documents made available by Private Manning, WikiLeaks was able to disclose that the Ethiopian invasion was covertly funded by the US government. Without knowledge of the connection between the US-backed Ethiopian invasion and its aftermath, the flourishing of Al-Qaeda-affiliated Al-Shabaab in Somalia would have remained something of a mystery to the US citizens effectively funding the resurgence of terrorism in the region. The picture being promulgated by the Predator drone program administrators, of a war with greatly reduced costs in soldiers' blood, does not reduce the price being paid in non-national *civilians'* blood and may well increase the harm to the civilians back home, as resentment and the urge for revenge ferment quietly in lands far from the borders of Somalia, Yemen and Pakistan.

When the US government conducts morally dubious 'signature strikes' in such places, they simultaneously produce enemy sympathizers in other parts of the world. Burgeoning terrorists are certainly not flocking to the parts of Pakistan and Yemen being mercilessly pummeled by Predator drone-delivered missiles. In Iraq, self-proclaimed warriors against the US occupation flowed to the site of postwar confusion like iron filings to a magnet. The incoming dissidents wreaked mass violence with devastating effects for the occupiers, but much more so for the people of Iraq. Jihadists incensed by US interventions have no reason to congregate in the lands where Predator drones prowl when there are no US soldiers on the ground to combat.

Across the Middle East and North Africa, Barack Obama has consistently exploited the 'actionable ambiguity' afforded by Predator drones, and also the Authorization for Use of Military Force (AUMF) passed by the US Congress during the Bush administration in 2001.

Obama has viewed the AUMF as an open invitation to deploy Predator drones around the globe and to establish more new drone stations abroad, even beyond the Middle East. By 2013, at least six African countries had drone bases, including Morocco, Senegal, Burkina Faso, Uganda and Djibouti.[318] By arming monarchic regimes and military dictators, US leaders do not promote democracy but instead maneuver in what they claim to be the nation's interest by collaborating with anyone who will grant the US government license to carry out targeted killing when and where they please.

Supporters of the new practice of summary execution by Predator drone never tire of rehearsing the refrain that 'Everything changed on 11 September 2001.' In truth, not much has really changed, at least not in any fundamental way. The United States was always vulnerable to terrorist attack – recall the 1995 bombing of the Federal Building in Oklahoma City by Timothy McVeigh, but one in a long line of homegrown terrorists. In the twenty-first century, just as in the twentieth century, the US military flies to other parts of the world to intervene in other nations' and people's affairs, often killing innocent civilians in the process, while writing off the lives destroyed as 'unavoidable' given what are said to be military exigencies.

'War is hell' continues to ring true, but now even rhetorical attempts to pretend that assaults on the helpless inhabitants of other lands are being conducted in accordance with some sort of 'rules' have been abandoned. The Geneva Conventions were dismissed by the Bush administration as 'quaint', a position tacitly embraced by the Obama administration as well. They, too, coined neologisms and redefined well-understood concepts in order to rationalize their practices. In Obama-speak, *imminence* no longer implies *immediacy*. But torture, which Obama decried before becoming president, is not the only practice forbidden by orthodox military protocol. Combatants are supposed to be the only legitimate targets during a just war, and even combatants must be provided with a warning so that they may renounce their misguided ways through surrender.

All of the traditional concepts associated with what was once considered the noble and heroic station of the warrior have been forgotten by the executors of the drone program, who assassinate suspects without warning and without regard to their active combatant status. The most glaring problem with the policy of targeted killing by drone is that there is no armed and dangerous adversary on the so-called 'battlefield' in places such as the tribal regions of Third World countries, because there are no allied soldiers on the ground to be endangered. This is why, drone advocates may say, the rules of the game must change if it is not simply to be abandoned. But that is precisely the question: *Should the 'rules' be changed to make it* even easier *to kill people than it already is? Or should the new rules not respect the inviolability of human life which serves as the very basis for the laws instituted to protect the innocent people in whose name wars are said to be waged?* The goal of 'Kill don't capture' policy is to weaken the enemy through attrition. In fact, it is a catalyst to radicalization, as the case of Anwar al-Awlaki amply illustrates.

The persons galvanized to join forces with groups such as the Taliban, Al-Qaeda and ISIS, against what they take to be the hegemonic, murderous US government, are in many cases manifesting righteous anger. Philosophers such as Aristotle would say that people who do not react with anger when they witness atrocity are morally defective. It is *rational* and indeed *right* to experience moral outrage upon the sight of obviously innocent children whose bodies have been ripped to shreds and strewn about a village by a Hellfire missile. The assassination of suspects is not a 'silver bullet' solution to the problem of terrorism. On the contrary, it is a wildly ricocheting bullet, which is bound to make its way back to US shores again, sooner or later. Supporters of the use of drones to target suspects in lands far away will reply: *What alternative do we have?*

Persuading evildoers of the error of their ways is, needless to say, quixotic in the case of incorrigible killers who have become dictators through the provision of massive amounts of Western military aid. A notorious example is Saddam Hussein, but the list of petty despots who oppress their people and have been hardened and entrenched over decades of iron-fisted rule goes on and on.[319] Such rulers have maintained their positions of power by stifling criticism and crushing nascent opposition movements. There is really no hope that they will ever be brought to appreciate the sanctity of human life.

The same, however, cannot be said of burgeoning terrorists, who are ordinary teenagers one day and the members of factions the next. If people can be persuaded to join forces with established terrorist groups, then, in principle, they could be persuaded to withdraw their allegiance. Killing is, of course, much easier than conversion, above all when the marketing claims of the enemy are continually validated by US military campaigns abroad. There is no way to deny that the US government destroyed thousands of innocent people in Afghanistan and Iraq. Instead of renouncing the sorts of practices which led directly to the revenge attack against unarmed civilians on 11 September 2001, the US administration ramped them up.

Drones are not merely the latest, most sophisticated military implement of homicide. They also provide an opportunity to reflect in a more general way upon the persistence of war in Western culture, even as so many other morally objectionable practices have been abolished or curtailed. Why has war persisted but not state-sanctioned slavery? The answer seems clear: a single-minded obsession with lethality as a solution to conflict has induced tunnel vision in politicians, policymakers and the voting public alike. Some of these parties have been adversely influenced at the same time by the lucrative economics of what has become an industry of homicide.

Aside from the locals whose lives are spared, no one profits financially from nonintervention, which requires nothing beyond leaving the people of Third World nations to manage their own affairs in peace and to adjudicate their disputes without the use of First World-sourced weapons. Many parties profit from war, which requires a huge apparatus to carry out and a massive bureaucracy to sustain. But the leaders whose prerogative it is to embroil their nation in the affairs of others often do so only because they look at conflict through a soda straw, just as the operators do at drone command stations thousands of miles away from the allegedly dangerous persons whom they destroy.

In recent years, humanitarian hawks – a particularly strident strain of just war theorists – have become vociferous but shortsighted force multipliers of war makers, agitating for military action whenever and wherever noncombatants are already at risk of death, as though the provision of yet more weapons to the warriors might somehow diminish the number of civilians slain. Genuine humanitarians would do better to limit their 'interventions' to protesting against the massive amount of military aid furnished to foreign allies who, once empowered, may proceed to victimize their citizenry, as did Saddam Hussein.

Among US administrators, lethality continues to eclipse all other approaches, under the assumption that killing is always and everywhere the solution to the problem of evil. But the narrow perimeters of the soda straw through which political leaders have been peering are largely determined by the war advocates who people their cabinets. When the 'options on the table' are drawn up by the decorated officers of wars past, who view conflict in terms of potential military engagement, the commander in chief has a constricted view of his true range of possibilities. This problem has become more marked than ever in the twenty-first century as top officials in the Central Intelligence Agency and the Department of Defense have been shuffled back and forth, with the consequence that intelligence has become not only highly politicized, as when the CIA drew up spurious pretexts for the 2003 invasion of Iraq, but also severely militarized and therefore biased in favor of the use of force as a first resort and in lieu of diplomacy.[320]

The primary lesson of the US intervention in Vietnam, painfully learned but swiftly forgotten, was that nothing positive springs spontaneously from the crater left by a bomb. The second lesson, that in order to help a people one must first understand its culture, was acknowledged briefly – albeit belatedly – by some among the architects of the Vietnam fiasco only to disappear for decades from the halls where military plans are forged. Among up-and-coming leaders such as Colin Powell, the reigning *idée fixe* of lethality continued to hold sway: 'Light and lethal is good, but you also need heavy and lethal.'[321] Lethality is a means only to death, not to anything else. Lethality is a tactic, not a strategy. When seasoned killers are called upon to advise the president and to pen policy, then death and destruction can be expected to ensue.

The catastrophic missions in Iraq and Afghanistan offer a compelling refutation of the misguided notion that lethality alone can cause democracy to flourish. The decapitation of a dictatorial regime leaves behind no more and no less than a power vacuum, anomie and chaos. Nonetheless, and perfectly in line with the 'offense is defense' outlook of his predecessor, Barack Obama, the ironic laureate of a Nobel Peace Prize, has repeatedly displayed his commitment to military force as a panacea. To his credit, President Obama signed executive orders banning torture and mandating the closure of the Bush-era secret prisons. However, the summary execution policy championed by Obama flies in the face of the most basic principles of Western liberal democratic states. It is no mere coincidence that summary executions are not being carried out (at least not openly) in First World democracies. Drones are not taking out suspects in Paris or Berlin but only in poor nations run by leaders enticed by generous military aid packages to permit such strikes to be used against the inhabitants of their land in a stunning denial of human rights.

Through four sequential US presidential terms, government administrators have conflated *terrorist suspects* and *terrorists*, as though there were no distinction between the two. Are human rights universal? Or can they be traded, à la Yemeni president Saleh, for weapons and cash? If there are universal human rights, then they protect all persons, whatever crimes they may be thought to have committed. One of the primary purposes of the *Universal Declaration of Human Rights* is to protect innocent persons erroneously suspected of crimes. In this regard, drone killing merely underscores what is wrong with the just war paradigm to begin with. The recourse to war, which assumes the permissibility of so-called collateral damage, is a flat-out denial of universal human rights because innocent people are terrorized and killed whenever and wherever military force is applied.

President Barack Obama 'made the call' to kill rather than capture the unarmed leader of Al-Qaeda, Osama bin Laden, because ours has become, regrettably, a culture of killing. This sad fact is demonstrated each time that yet another mass murder is carried out on domestic terrain by a misguided person who subscribes to ideas championed by his very own government, that force should be the first not the last resort, and that homicide is a 'feasible' way to address conflict. The use of drones in targeted killing campaigns may seem novel in history because of the technology involved. Morally speaking, however, the US government has simply slid down a long and slippery slope to the point where abject acts of tyranny – the execution of unarmed suspects without trial – are, perversely enough, carried out in the name of democracy.

In considering civil rights in the drone age, the most important question is not whether Anwar al-Awlaki was guilty of treason. The problem is that he was executed without trial. If he was guilty, then presumably this could have been proven to the satisfaction of a jury of his peers. Instead, the US executive opted to erase him from existence, along with his rights. One surmises that the killers worried that what they took to be Al-Awlaki's guilt could not be persuasively demonstrated in a court of law – but that is precisely the crux of the problem. A person has a right to be presumed innocent until proven guilty beyond a reasonable doubt, and that right was effaced along with the lives of all of the many suspects summarily executed by Predator drone. The presumption of innocence is a fundamental tenet of US law and is expressed in Article 11 of the *Universal Declaration of Human Rights*.

Unlike Predator drones, international terrorism is not new to the twenty-first century. The people of Europe dealt with many violent terrorist factions throughout the Cold War, as such groups found support among communists wishing to spread their ideology around the globe. Governments such as those of France and Germany used methods of criminal investigation and prosecution to good effect in contending with terrorists such as Ilich Ramírez Sánchez (known as 'Carlos the Jackal'), who murdered officials said to be associates of 'the imperialists'.[322] By applying tools appropriate to the problem of international terrorism, rather than simply shooting in the dark, European governments were able to bring to justice many of the culprits while safeguarding institutions wrought over centuries and designed to protect innocent people. This was a coherent approach to terrorism because it did not wreak massive and indiscriminate death and destruction in response to indiscriminate death and destruction.

Irregular warriors such as the members of Al-Qaeda and the mujahedin in Afghanistan are in basic agreement with the US government that deadly violence is an acceptable and even necessary means of venting ire and addressing conflict. That was, after all, the response of the Bush administration to the terrorist attacks of 11 September 2001: two full-scale wars and the deaths of hundreds of thousands of people. Asymmetrical warriors reject, of strategic necessity, the so-called rules of war said to be observed by formal military institutions, but they are united with their enemy in the belief that death is the solution to their differences. The insistence upon using homicide to resolve disputes is the fundamental tie binding these adversarial cultures together. When one side decides to break the rules – whether by waging surprise attacks, or by intentionally acting so as to kill civilians, or by invading a sovereign nation during peacetime – their adversaries are galvanized to adjust their strategies to match and even surpass those of 'the evil enemy'.

Former British Prime Minister Tony Blair articulated the guiding logic after the bombing of London public transport vehicles on 7 July 2005: 'The rules of the game have changed.'[323] But the willingness to diminish civil liberties and human rights in response to the enemy's commission of crimes is a capitulation to their worldview. Somehow those who support the summary execution without trial of suspects do not recognize that they are accepting the rules of the very enemy whom they denounce precisely for their violation of what were formerly thought to be the rules of the game. To renounce one's principles on the grounds that 'the rules of the game have changed' is to embrace the asymmetrical warriors' worldview.

Military institutions have always focused on lethality. The use of deadly force abroad is euphemistically termed *national defense*, but it is mass destruction, no more and no less. Through sheer habit of thought, the assumption that greater lethality will ensure victory continues to be embraced by policymakers. Yet with radical transformations in the globalized world taking place as a result of rapidly proliferating new technologies, superior lethality no longer suffices for victory – least of all over hearts and minds – as images of rapaciousness can be swiftly disseminated around the globe in the internet age. In focusing fixedly upon refining the weapons of war, making the means to death and destruction more and more lethal and precise, strategists have ignored just how much the world has changed. Image matters much more than body count in the twenty-first century.

Each time a new corner of the world is christened *hostile* and Hellfire missiles begin to rain down, yet another community's sense of security is shattered. In territories where innocent people have been destroyed and homes and workplaces cratered, the killers have been tried in the court of public opinion. Anti-American sentiment sweeps across the globe as expatriate sympathizers, family members and friends become enraged, which helps to explain the success of terrorist recruitment efforts in the West.[324] The mounting toll of innocent victims serves to bolster the enemy, effectively undermining the alleged purpose of 'Kill don't capture' campaigns. In truth, it does not matter whether 50 percent or 30 percent or 'only' 10 percent of those slain are innocent civilians. However few in number, those images will be replicated and used to recruit multiple times the number of bona fide terrorists killed.

The reason why military institutions throughout history were always equipped with the most lethal weapons available was because they were fighting against approximately equally equipped adversaries. Therefore, more men and more weapons skillfully deployed generally meant victory. But troops and weapons alone did not suffice: it was necessary also to adjust strategies so as to maximize the efficacy of the new equipment through innovative means of deployment. Now armed with far more weapons than would be needed to wipe out every living creature on the entire planet, the US government has proven incapable of leaping out of the lethality box. Victory is not guaranteed by lethality, for wars are also of ideas, not only of bullets and bombs. Winning thousands of tactical micro-battles (successful missile strikes) does not guarantee that the war will be won, above all when what is being done is regarded as grossly unjust and hypocritical by the people on the ground.

Lethality yields victory, temporarily, to a tyrant, whose private fantasy can be realized through the annihilation of anyone who happens to disagree. But that type of victory is of dubious value and generally short-lived, for all that the tyrant succeeds in demonstrating is that he is too weak to win a war of words. Instead of waging battles of ideas, the tyrant terminates the lives of anyone who does not readily accede, denouncing challengers as mortal threats, incorrigible enemies who stand in the way of whatever the tyrant decrees. Utter dependence upon military means is sure to achieve one and only one thing: the death of human beings. The tyrant's short-term ability to terminally silence anyone anywhere leads him to become smug, to exceed his means, as did Hitler in attempting to fight two major wars simultaneously, to the west against Britain and to the east against Russia. It is precisely the tyrant's previous victories which lead him to overestimate his power, giddy with delight as he is over what he has already achieved.

In the United States, the possession of more weapons and wealth than any other nation on the planet has generated complacency on the part of administrators. US leaders reach facilely for the weapons of war and attempt to prevent their development by some governments (such as Iran) while at the same time arming current allies and exerting pressure on lesser powers to condone and even participate in the latest military adventures abroad. All of this comes off as arrant hypocrisy and serves immeasurably to increase the number of enemies the world over. Factional terrorists across all borders are united in their disgust for the thinly gloved iron fist which the US government has become. US officials continue to parrot boilerplate rhetoric about democracy and peace while wielding savage weaponry and assassinating suspects abroad. Groups such as Al-Qaeda and its many offshoots conspire above all to overthrow what they regard as this hegemonic beast.

The success of Osama bin Laden and Al-Qaeda in promoting their agenda, ironically aided and abetted by the US military itself, cannot be denied. More people appear to despise the United States today than at any previous time in history. Some among even the people who truly believed that the attacks on the World Trade Center were entirely unjustified and wholly execrable have by now come to sympathize with those who continue to rise up against what they regard as a murderous military machine. In spite of the overwhelming evidence that the incidence of terrorism increases in direct response to military action, the administration obtusely persists in pretending that the crimes of 9/11 had nothing whatsoever to do with the US government's previous use of deadly force abroad. By refusing to consider the conflict from the eyes of their adversaries, by dumbly decrying them as incorrigible criminals who 'hate our liberty', while simultaneously responding to their actions as though they were a regular army, using standard military means, the United States has succeeded in fortifying its enemies both in spirit and in physical strength.

When factional terrorists and non-violent antiwar activists express outrage at the very same policies, then the time has arrived to reevaluate those policies. Insurgents who rise up in response to criminal wars differ from antiwar activists only in their tactics. They incoherently choose to emulate the killers whose crimes they decry by killing even more. In contrast, peaceful antiwar activists deploy as their weapons only words. By claiming the right to erase from the face of the earth anyone anywhere who may in the future attempt to harm the people of the United States, Presidents Bush and Obama have provided terrorists and tyrants alike – both at home and abroad – with a template by which to rationalize their own acts of homicide.

Supporters of the Predator drone program effectively affirm that war is the conjunction of thousands of summary executions carried out by the decree of the commander in chief. War makers *choose* to wield deadly force while claiming that it is a last resort. When all of the measures under consideration are lethal, drones may be selected as the seemingly lesser of a variety of evils. But drone operators themselves earn handsome salaries for suppressing their own conscience and dispatching human beings whom they have never met, and who never threatened them with death. Remote-control killers situated far from 'the battlefield' know, deep down inside, that no one would have died on that day at that place had they declined to fire on what became their victims. The brutal and merciless extermination of unwitting suspects denied the right to surrender or appeal because they are assumed to be 'vermin' destroys the bodies of the victims while corroding the souls of their killers.

POSTFACE

Under the Predator drone program, the unarmed persons targeted are said to be combatants who pose imminent threats, though not immediately so. Because they are deemed combatants, they are thought not to be protected by the laws of civil society. These specially designated combatants are considered unlawful by their killers and therefore protected by neither the Geneva Conventions nor other protocols of international law. The unnamed persons intentionally destroyed are regarded as combatants not because they are armed (they are not) but because they are allegedly guilty of unnamed capital crimes, which are said to be evidenced by 'patterns of behavior' observed by analysts from thousands of miles away. What is wrong with this picture, in which Orwellian neologism has achieved a new nadir never before seen in history, not even among the most tyrannical of regimes?

For eight years, it was easy to be distracted by the specific crimes of the George W. Bush administration, given their sheer frequency and utter flagrancy. However, against all hopes among war critics around the world – including, one surmises, the Nobel Peace Prize committee – the administration of Barack Obama has offered more of the same, which suffices to show that the problem was never peculiar to Bush. The true innovation of the Bush administration was to lay bare the reality lurking beneath longstanding US military practice, which has been shrouded by self-congratulatory moral sanctimoniousness and promoted through 'just war' rhetoric.

A closer look reveals that what was claimed to be the *last resort* perhaps never really was. What was portrayed as *defense* was far more often *offense* in disguise. What was praised as courage and patriotism was often coerced enlistment, whether literal conscription or a subtler form of economic coercion, among troops simply looking for a job. What was labeled 'heeding the call to duty' was in some cases crass opportunism, long before the advent of PMCs such as Blackwater and Aegis.

In the twenty-first century, the employees of such firms are lured to act as 'force multipliers' of the US military by the promise of generous compensation. In this way, the ranks of war profiteers, always a factor throughout the history of industrialized war, have been diversified to include also service personnel, both the veterans who find employment with PMCs and those active-duty officers who consult for private firms contracted by the Pentagon. Meanwhile, as the lucrative drone industry continues to grow, everyone seems to want 'a piece of the pie', and some of the people involved in the 'kill chain', as it is so chillingly described, now work for private enterprise and are driven to 'find, fix, and finish' human beings by the prospect of financial gain.

The Obama administration has summarily executed thousands of people, at least hundreds of whom have been children and therefore obviously innocent of any crime. How many of the *deliberately* targeted persons were unjustly killed? It remains to be seen whether what is tantamount to the inversion of the burden of proof in the secretive 'capital cases' concluded by drone strikes will withstand scrutiny. If it does not, then the US president may eventually find himself indicted for crimes against humanity at the International Criminal Court (ICC) in The Hague.

The long-term global effects of simultaneous killing campaigns in several different countries will arrive only years or decades later, by which time the policymakers whose programs caused the blowback will have retreated from public life. Will posterity characterize Barack Obama as a 'smart warrior' or yet another notorious 'assassin in chief' among so many others? Will Obama, and Bush before him, finally be aligned among the many war criminals whose bloodbaths have been documented in the annals of history? Only time will tell. Meanwhile, the short-term, domestic 'benefits' of wielding deadly force abroad under the pretext of national defense accrue immediately. Among them are surely the many mass killings perpetrated by US residents against US citizens and on US soil, in emulation of US political leaders. From Columbine and Aurora in Colorado; to Blacksburg, Virginia; to Fort Hood, Texas; to Newton, Connecticut; to the mass killing at Navy Yard in 2013, these killers have been following the lead of the US government by wielding deadly force to address whatever their specific grievances may be.

APPENDIX: DRONE KILLING AND JUST WAR THEORY

Over the centuries, many intellectuals have accepted and promoted the basic framework of 'just war' theory – the *jus ad bellum* and *jus in bello* constraints on the waging and prosecution of war. Just war theorists put forth a standard bullet-point list of 'requirements' which must be satisfied in order for a war to be christened 'just'. Typically, the list looks something like this:

Jus ad bellum (justice in going to war)	*Jus in bello* (justice in conducting war)
public declaration	proportionality of means to military objectives
reasonable prospect for success	noncombatant immunity
last resort	enemy soldiers to be respected as human beings
legitimate authority	prisoners of war to be treated as noncombatants and immune from intentional killing
just cause	
proportionality	

The just war paradigm was developed in ancient and medieval times, and its defenders were deeply religious and conservative men such as St Augustine and St Thomas Aquinas, who believed that God would rectify terrestrial injustices in the afterlife. Despite the fact that the cultural milieu of such thinkers diverges radically from the modern Western liberal democratic worldview – which is secular, not religious – the framework continues to undergird normative discourse about war.[325]

Many contemporary scholars who believe in the possibility of a 'just war' spend their time sparring over nuances such as the 'proportionality of means' to military objectives sought. The presumed *legitimate authority* of political leaders to wage wars long after the modern separation of church and state – the early just war theorists conceived of such authority as divinely dispensed – has gone for all intents and purposes unquestioned. Curious implications such as that when groups of people in places such as Ireland or Kosovo or South Sudan cleave off to form independent nations they thereby create yet another legitimate authority with the power to wage war are altogether ignored. Yet everything turns on *legitimate authority*, because in reality – beyond the rarefied halls of academia – it is political leaders' own prerogative to interpret all of the other tenets of just war theory. Leaders, not scholars, determine where, when, why, and how to wage war.

US President George W. Bush was a legitimate authority – 'The Decider', as he put it – when he ordered his troops to invade Iraq in 2003. His successor, Barack Obama, has ended the lives of thousands of human beings using Hellfire missiles launched from Predator drones hovering above Pakistan, Yemen, Libya, Somalia, Afghanistan, Iraq, Syria, and beyond. Lest we forget, the former president of Iraq, Saddam Hussein, who had been militarily empowered and sustained by the US government for years, was a legitimate authority when he ordered the Iraqi army to invade Kuwait in 1990. Even Adolf Hitler was a legitimate authority when he began his murderous rampage across the European continent in the 1930s. The soldiers of all of these commanders obeyed their orders, as dutiful troops always do.

The just war paradigm's second article of faith, the *doctrine of double effect*, builds upon the legitimate authority's power to decide when, where, and how to wage war. This doctrine derives directly from St Thomas Aquinas, a medieval religious scholar, who articulated the gist of the idea as follows:

> Nothing hinders one act from having two effects, only one of which is intended, while the other is beside the intention. Now moral acts take their species according to what is intended and not according to what is beside the intention.[326]

In a military context, the relevant 'effects' are the deaths caused by the weapons of war. If the warriors are attempting to kill enemy soldiers but accidentally harm or destroy innocent children, the morality of their action is to be evaluated by appeal to what they intended, not what they did not intend. According to the doctrine of double effect, what matters above all in evaluating the destruction of innocent persons during wartime is not the fact of their demise but the intention of the killers.

Military apologists are wont to trot out (or tacitly assume) this principle in arguing that this or that assault on a group of non-threatening civilians – assembled together at a wedding or a *jirga*, or preparing for an open-air barbecue – is perfectly permissible. The reason why it is supposed to be permissible is that, even though the killers may have reasonably foreseen the carnage to ensue (given the weapons being used), they *intended* to kill only 'the bad guys'. The doctrine of double effect is brandished (or presumed) in efforts to distinguish such actions from the intentional slaughter of civilians on 11 September 2001, by absolving the killers in the former but not the latter case. 'Just wars' may culminate in the annihilation of thousands or even millions of innocent people, but those who ordered the deployment of massively destructive weapons can still sleep at night because, according to the doctrine of double effect, they have done nothing morally wrong, provided only that they *intended* to do good.

During wartime, a legitimate authority's alleged prerogative to make quasi-divine decisions regarding the 'price' to pay in other people's lives is transferred to those delegated to kill at his behest. What are rules of engagement (ROE), after all, if not the opinions of military officers about who is and who is not 'fair game' for slaughter? Regarding the harm done to innocent noncombatants caught in a missile's radius of destruction, the question becomes not *whether* but *how much* 'collateral damage' is permissible. In reality, the first premise, that what matter morally are the intentions of the killers, leaves open the possibility for virtually unlimited carnage committed in good conscience by warriors whose leaders claim that their war is just. The proverbial road to hell – the abject misery of the psychological casualties of war, including both bereft survivors and the soldiers crippled and corrupted by what they have done – may well be paved with good intentions. Witness Vietnam, Afghanistan, Iraq ...

Most mainstream critics who oppose this or that military intervention begin by asserting that they do believe in the possibility of a 'just war' but that the particular case under examination fails to satisfy one or more of the traditional requirements. Seldom do scholars delve deeper, to examine issues more fundamental than whether this or that is a just cause, or if the use of deadly force in a specific context is 'proportional'. Needless to say, 'last resort' is no more than a metaphor in a world where US leaders continually threaten that 'all options are on the table'.

These longstanding habits of thought and rhetoric explain why, when the assassination of suspects by Predator drone was adopted by the US government as a standard operating procedure, few in the populace paused to ask whether there might be something horribly awry. The acceptance of the remote-control killing of unarmed suspects, characterized by the perpetrators as acts of 'just war', rests upon the prior assumption, deeply embedded within the just war paradigm, that what matter above all in moral assessments of wartime homicide are the intentions of the killers.

Some just war theorists have expressed concerns about the use of the new drone technology, but remote-control killing is in no way precluded at the outset by the traditional paradigm, because it is the prerogative of commanders themselves – delegated by the 'legitimate authority' – to determine which means to deploy in prosecuting what they take to be 'just wars'. In truth, the intellectual framework underlying the Bush administration's 'offensive defense' policy of preemptive attack against Iraq in 2003 was none other than the theory of just war. The Obama administration's 'Kill don't capture' doctrine is simply a further slide down a very slippery slope. Drone killing highlights the malleability of the so-called rules of just war, which are invariably interpreted so as to cohere with the interpreter's prior beliefs about the war (or practice) in question.[327]

If so-called just wars produce the same ill effects as do murder, terrorism and torture, but in far greater magnitude, then that would seem to imply that the traditional framework is sorely confused. Certainly, from the perspective of the victims, the experience of being assaulted by a uniformed soldier or a factional terrorist or an unmanned aerial vehicle (UAV) would be indistinguishable. Homicide is homicide, no more and no less, viewed from the receiving end of a Hellfire missile. Does it matter to the victims' families and community members that their assailants 'intended' to kill an evil terrorist?

The notion that a killer bears no moral culpability whatsoever for his voluntary and foreseeable acts of homicide is unique to the war context. No one upholds the analogous doctrine within civil society. In a domestic context, the accidental killing of people who stand in the way of what a criminal is trying to achieve, far from being considered a case of morally innocuous collateral damage, is interpreted as murder. Only the control by the military institution itself of the official story of what is done during wartime explains the wholesale denial of moral responsibility for collateral damage, with the warriors protected by an impenetrable shield of allegedly good intentions.

The interpretive prerogative of the killers themselves – that 'the victors write history' – derives directly from the two key articles of faith in the just war paradigm. First, legitimate authorities have the right to wage war when and where they please (given that they themselves interpret all of the so-called requirements of a 'just war'). Second, the killers' intentions determine the moral quality of their own acts of killing. One might with good reason protest that victims such as Mamana Bibi were living in civil society when they were slain, but the US government has baldly decreed that 'the world is a battlefield'. The assumption during 'wartime' is precisely the opposite of the felony murder rule, and fully encapsulated within the just war theorist's indispensable doctrine of double effect. In the just warrior's worldview, leaders may kill even innocent, unarmed persons, provided only that it is not their intention to do so, whether as a direct end or as the means to whatever good they are trying to achieve.

The doctrine of double effect is a boon for belligerent leaders: a carte blanche to wield the weapons of war in lieu of non-homicidal political tools such as diplomacy or the pursuit of suspects through orthodox means of criminal investigation. Intellectuals throughout the long reign of the just war paradigm have been rhetorical accomplices to the propagation and perpetuation of war as a preferred means of addressing conflict by militarily powerful leaders. Without 'principles' such as the doctrine of double effect, the notion of morally permissible collateral damage would be but a farce. Scholars' uncritical acceptance of the two primary articles of faith of just war theory (legitimate authority and double effect) simultaneously betrays their acceptance of the intrinsic classism of this hegemonic paradigm – a vestige of the Divine Rights of Kings.

In the wake of the terrorist attacks of 11 September 2001, the extraneous elements of warfare were cleared away by US administrators in reconceptualizing assassination – formerly denounced as illegal and forbidden – as a standard operating procedure. ROE were loosened to permit the intentional killing of all military-age males located in territories deemed 'hostile' by analysts located thousands of miles away from the 'battlefield' and in no immediate danger of harm. Many innocent people, such as the entire family of Fahim Qureshi, have been killed along with the terrorist suspects summarily executed in these strikes. Many other persons have been maimed or traumatized. All of these devastating consequences can be facilely brushed aside by military supporters under the assumption of the traditional paradigm's second article of faith, the doctrine of double effect. Former Secretary of Defense Donald Rumsfeld summed up in a pithy phrase the perspective of those who disavow responsibility for the negative consequences of wars waged with good intentions: 'Stuff happens.'[328]

It is telling that scholars do not invoke the doctrine of double effect to exonerate the perpetrators of actions such as the Rwandan genocide or the attacks of 9/11, although the killers undoubtedly believed that their victims were enemy collaborators and 'fair game' according to some fallible commander's ROE. In evaluating the acts of killing committed by their own soldiers, in contrast, war supporters regard as exculpatory the claim that they did not really intend for the 'collateral damage' caught in the crossfire of legitimate military actions to die. Such examples reveal that it is not the just war paradigm alone which explains the radically disparate attitudes of US military supporters toward the attacks of 9/11 and the 2003 invasion of Iraq or, for that matter, the 1991 Gulf War. The latter two US-led wars ultimately caused many more deaths of innocent people than did the terrorist attacks of 11 September 2001. The further crucial assumption, also invariably espoused by the architects of war, is that *the evil enemy has intrinsically evil intentions*, while our own and our allies' intentions are good.

The argument for war in such cases is circular: we know that the enemy has evil intentions because of what they do. Why do they carry out the crimes we decry? Because they are evil. Thus evil is presumed to be both the cause of and the explanation for what evil people do. In other words, the doctrine of double effect is not used to determine the impermissibility of the actions of evildoers. Rather, it serves as an interpretive apparatus for asserting what war supporters already wish to believe. The first and crucial assumption in the argument for war is the ascription of good intentions to one's own side and evil intentions to the enemy. The doctrine of double effect is an extraordinarily powerful tool not for determining the truth – whether a given act of war is just or unjust – but for cleansing the consciences of killers and those who support them, whether materially, morally or intellectually. A framework which defines a priori the intentions of the killers, depending only upon the sympathies of the interpreters, is not a serious theory at all, no matter how many embellishments may be added by well-meaning scholars. Each successive generation of just war theorists merely offers the emperor (the legitimate authority) a new set of clothes.

Neither George H. W. Bush nor George W. Bush disagreed with Saddam Hussein about the appropriateness of wielding deadly force in resolving political disputes. Similarly, Barack Obama and Muammar Gaddafi were united in their affirmation of the possibility of just war. Even Al-Qaeda leader Osama bin Laden mobilized his troops by appeal to the concept of just war. Such leaders disagree about when and where deadly force should be deployed, not whether recourse to war is justified. Such leaders also maintain that people who are complicit with what they take to be an evil enemy – the so-called *associates* – may be killed during the prosecution of a just war. The US government's 'signature strikes' and 'terrorist attack disruption strikes' (TADS) are a case in point, and a recipe for genocide.

The question is not whether the UAV operator, the soldier, the factional terrorist and the bellicose leaders of nations seek something which they themselves regard as good. The question is only what price they are willing to pay in *other people's lives* in order to achieve the object of their desire – as though human beings were their currency to spend. The doctrine of double effect no doubt makes it easier for the architects of disastrous interventions such as the Vietnam war or the invasion and occupation of Iraq to sleep better at night. It also makes it easy for people to forget about such fiascoes shortly after they transpire, which explains why the same mistakes have been repeated over and over again. The war makers in Vietnam eventually awakened to the reality that they had misunderstood the nature of the Vietnamese resistance to their presence, but only after millions of people had died. That essentially the same mistakes were repeated in Afghanistan and Iraq would appear to be a consequence of the fact that no one ever assumed any genuine responsibility for the massive violence wrought upon Vietnam and its people. Once out of sight, it was out of mind, and the US administration never made an effort nor took the time to think through the moral implications of what they had done precisely because they had already convinced themselves of their righteousness in fighting a just war. 'Mistakes were made' but the warriors were fully absolved by the just war paradigm, according to which their good intentions sufficed to wipe the moral slate clean.

Modern political leaders are elected by a fallible populace and not thought to have been appointed by an infallible God, as the early just war theorists believed. It is exceedingly difficult to see how thousands of blatantly unjust acts such as the cold-blooded execution of Mamana Bibi might add up to a just war. In truth, the utter omission from the fables of 'just war' of the plight of those whose lives are irrevocably degraded, if not destroyed, reveals that scholars take only a fraction of the consequences of war into account when they pronounce them 'just'. Thanks to the doctrine of double effect, what is assumed to be the conceptual irrelevance of collateral damage guarantees that military supporters need not be bothered by even the grossest omissions from the stories of war makers. No mention whatsoever need be made of the thousands of nameless victims, nor the corruption caused directly by war and which ramifies throughout entire societies to be transmitted from one generation to the next. The question remains: *What is this abstract 'justice' of which just war theorists purport to speak?*

NOTES

1   The alleged distinction between *targeted killing* and *assassination* is made in 'Department of Justice White Paper: Lawfulness of a Lethal Operation Directed Against a U.S. Citizen Who is a Senior Operational Leader of Al-Qa'ida or An Associated Force' (hereafter, the White Paper), which was issued by US Attorney General Eric Holder in June 2010.

2   Anti-drone groups have emerged with eponymous websites featuring frequently updated stories on victims and actions. Examples include CODEPINK's *Drone Watch, Know Drones* and *No Drones Network.*

3   Daniel Byman, 'Why Drones Work: The Case for Washington's Weapon of Choice,' *Foreign Affairs*, July/August 2013, pp. 32–43. Another popular false dichotomy among military supporters is that targeted killings are preferable to full-scale invasions.

4   William Fisher, 'UN Expert Calls on US to Halt CIA Targeted Killings,' IPS (Inter Press Service) News Agency, 2 June 2010; Philip Alston, 'Report of the Special Rapporteur on extrajudicial, summary or arbitrary executions,' United Nations General Assembly Human Rights Council, 28 May 2010.

5   Medea Benjamin offers several finely textured examples of the devastating effects of drone strikes on survivors in *Drone Warfare: Killing by Remote Control* (2013).

6   Gareth Porter, 'CIA Drone Operators Oppose Strikes as Helping al Qaeda,' IPS (Inter Press Service) News Agency, 3 June 2010.

7   President Obama cited in Mark Mazzetti, *The Way of the Knife: The CIA, a Secret Army, and a War at the Ends of the Earth* (2013), p. 228.

8   Jeremy Scahill, *Dirty Wars: The World is a Battlefield* (2013), p. 77; Gregory Johnsen, *The Last Refuge: Yemen, Al-Qaeda, and America's War in Arabia* (2013), p. 123.

9   Johnsen (2013), p. 92.

10 Scahill (2013), especially Chapters 4, 5, 6, and 11.

11 *The 9/11 Commission Report.* Online at www.9-11commission.gov/report/911Report.pdf.

12 Some just war theorists have gone so far as to argue that the use of drones is not only permissible but also obligatory. Such analyses dismiss as essentially irrelevant most of the factors discussed in the present work. Economic, political, psychological, sociological and even moral issues are generally ignored by just war theorists. Examples can be found in Bradley Jay Strawser (ed.), *Killing by Remote Control: The Ethics of an Unmanned Military* (2013). See the Appendix for more on the shortcomings of just war theory.

13 Scahill (2013), pp. 28–9.

14 It is possible that this was all part of a ploy to bolster Al-Qaeda's call to jihad by persuading the United States to invade Iraq, with predictable consequences to ensue. By providing the sought-after link between Saddam Hussein and Al-Qaeda, Libbi facilitated the invasion of Iraq, which had the effect of strengthening rather than weakening Al-Qaeda. See Paul Todd, Jonathan Bloch and Patrick Fitzgerald, *Spies, Lies and the War on Terror* (2009), p. 83.

15 In *Failure of Intelligence* (2008), Melvin Goodman relays the story of how the CIA under Director George Tenet was co-opted by the Bush administration to produce a pretext for the 2003 invasion of Iraq.

16 At the limit, the interrogators would seem to be engaging in gratuitous torture, which serves no utilitarian purpose whatsoever beyond whatever sadistic pleasure the torturers themselves may derive from their acts of cruelty. However, the value of that pleasure is effectively canceled out – if not outweighed – by the pain suffered by the victims.

17 One suspected terrorist, Muhammed al-Kazami, was killed in the 14 December 2009 action, but none of the other persons present had anything to do with Al-Qaeda. See Johnsen (2013), pp. 251–3.

18 Lloyd Gardner, *Killing Machine: The American Presidency in the Age of Drone Warfare* (2013), p. 155.

19 Reuters, 'Air Strike Kills 15 Civilians in Yemen by Mistake: Officials,' 12 December 2013.

20 In *Kill or Capture: The War on Terror and the Soul of the Obama Presidency* (2012), Daniel Klaidman relays the obstacles faced by the Obama administration, and Attorney General Eric Holder in particular, in implementing civil trials for the suspects to be removed from Guantánamo Bay.

21 Among them was then-UN Secretary General Kofi Annan, who charac-terized the invasion as a violation of international law. See BBC News, 'Iraq War Illegal, Says Annan,' 16 September 2004.

22 Johnsen (2013), p. 143.

23 Peter Bergen, 'Five Myths about Osama bin Laden,' *Washington Post*, 6 May 2011.

24 'The American Public on the 9/11 Decade: A Study of American Public Opinion,' University of Maryland Program on International Policy Attitudes (PIPA), 8 September 2011. Online at www.sadat.umd.edu/ 911Anniversary_Sep11_rpt.pdf.

25 Michael Hastings, *The Operators: The Wild and Terrifying Inside Story of America's War in Afghanistan* (2012), p. 208.

26 The case of General David Petraeus illustrates the fundamental problem with assigning military officers to head up an intelligence agency. Within a year of being appointed as director of the CIA, Petraeus was forced to resign for violating his military code of honor by having an extramarital affair. The fact that this was discovered through amateur mistakes made in attempting to camouflage his email exchanges revealed that the new CIA director was devoid of even the most rudimentary understanding of spy tradecraft. See Scott Shane and Charlie Savage, 'Officials Say F.B.I. Knew of Petraeus Affair in the Summer,' *New York Times*, 11 November 2012.

27 Greg Miller and Julie Tate, 'CIA Shifts Focus to Killing Targets,' *Washington Post*, 1 September 2011.

28 Ann Scott Tyson, 'Strain of Iraq War Means the Relief Burden Will Have to be Shared,' *Washington Post*, 31 August 2005.

29 Pew Research Center's Global Attitudes Project Report, 'Pakistani Public Opinion Ever More Critical of U.S.,' 27 June 2012. Online at www.pewglobal. org/2012/06/27/pakistani-public-opinion-ever-more-critical-of-u-s/.

30 *The Economist* reported on 19 October 2013 ('Drop the Pilots: Drones Over Pakistan') that, among twenty persons interviewed in the Federally Administered Tribal Areas, 'many' preferred drones 'to the artillery barrages of the Pakistan military'. It is very unclear what to make of such a 'statistic' given the vagueness of the claim, the choices being offered, and the size of the sample set, which of necessity selects for persons willing to talk to Westerners.

31   Mark Mazzetti and Scott Shane, 'Drones are Focus as CIA Nominee Goes Before Senators,' *New York Times*, 7 February 2013.

32   Paula Newton, 'CNN Exclusive: Al-Awlaki's Father Says Son is "not Osama bin Laden",' 11 January 2010.

33   Assassination is explicitly prohibited by Article 23b of the Hague Regulations. US President Ford issued an executive order proscribing political assassination in 1976, which was reasserted by Presidents Carter and Reagan and was never rescinded by George W. Bush, although he pronounced that Bin Laden was 'wanted dead or alive'. See James E. White (ed.), *War, Terrorism, Torture and Assassination* (2012), pp. 97–8.

34   Gordon Lubold and Shane Harris, 'The CIA, not the Pentagon, Will Keep Running Obama's Drone War,' *The Complex: Inside the National Security Maze (Foreign Policy.com)*, 5 November 2013.

35   BBC News, 'State of the Union Address: Full Text,' 29 January 2003.

36   A depiction of the story is presented in *Michael Collins* (1996), directed by Neil Jordan.

37   In *Legacy of Ashes: The History of the CIA* (2007), Timothy Weiner reveals that such facilities were used as early as the late 1940s, shortly after the establishment of the CIA.

38   Steven Spielberg's film *Munich* (2005) is based on the book *Vengeance* (1984) by George Jonas. The discussion of black ops in this chapter derives in part from Laurie Calhoun, 'Neither Masks nor Gloves,' *New Politics*, 2011, XIII/3(51), 72–78.

39   The CIA-run Phoenix program in Vietnam reportedly killed thousands of North Vietnamese soldiers and operatives. See Scahill (2013), p. 114.

40   In *Soldiers of Fortune: A History of the Mercenary in Modern Warfare* (2009), Tony Geraghty reports that 'borrowing' soldiers for covert operations has been a common practice by the British SAS.

41   The assassination of democratically elected Congolese Prime Minister Patrice Lumumba, too, was on the CIA's secret list of things to do. The CIA's plot to poison the Congolese prime minister was apparently preempted by allies of Joseph Mobutu, who, however, had been selected by analysts to lead the post-Lumumba government and were funded and armed by the United States. A version of the story is relayed in the film *Lumumba* (2000), directed by Raoul Peck.

42 Weiner (2007), Part III, 'The CIA Under Kennedy and Johnson,' pp. 195–334.

43 Geraghty (2009), especially Chapter 4.

44 Craig Whitlock, 'In Letter, Radical Cleric Details CIA Abduction, Egyptian Torture,' *Washington Post*, 10 November 2006.

45 Geraghty (2009) refers to this breed of mercenary as 'psychos' (p. 37).

46 Tony Geraghty, *Black Ops: The Rise of Special Forces in the C.I.A., the S.A.S., and Mossad* (2010), p. 201. Supporters of drone killing are wont to describe the practice as 'effective', and the meaning is equally 'lethal'.

47 Some of the most notorious deeds of the CIA during the twentieth century were drug experiments on unwitting persons selected for their marginal status: heroin addicts, mental hospital patients and prostitutes were some of the people treated by the Agency as though they had no human rights. A short film put out by National Geographic, *CIA Secret Experiments* (2008), reviews the atrocities and serves as an unforgettable reminder that the CIA has no qualms about violating human rights – whether by torture or assassination.

48 The CIA's rendition program was begun by President Clinton during the mid-1990s. In 1996, Clinton signed a presidential decision directive (PDD 39) authorizing the CIA and US special ops working with the FBI to snatch terror suspects and also to send them to Egypt for interrogation. More than seventy such renditions were carried out. See Scahill (2013), pp. 26–7, and Todd, Bloch and Fitzgerald (2009), p. 9.

49 In *Breach of Trust: How Americans Failed Their Soldiers and Their Country* (2013), Andrew Bacevich observes that President Clinton contributed significantly to the 'Israelification' of US foreign policy by normalizing the use of force (p. 173).

50 US Government, The White House, 'National Security Strategy of the United States of America,' September 2002, p. 6.

51 CNN, 'You are Either With Us or Against Us,' CNN.com, 6 November 2001.

52 Yaroslav Trofimov, 'Many Afghans Shrug at "This Event Foreigners Call 9/11",' *Wall Street Journal*, 7 September 2011.

53 The Pentagon Papers, made public by Daniel Ellsberg, were very helpful in exposing the misguided Vietnam policy and are available online at www. archives.gov/research/pentagon-papers/. See also *The Most Dangerous*

Man in America: Daniel Ellsberg and the Pentagon Papers (2009), directed by Judith Ehrlich and Rick Goldsmith.

54 Scott Pederson, 'Sudanese Factory Destroyed by US Now a Shrine,' *Christian Science Monitor*, 7 August 2012. The strike was a mistake, but its legitimacy continues to be a matter of debate in the United States.

55 BBC News, 'US Bombers Strike Civilians in Baghdad,' 13 February 1991.

56 Janet Kemp and Robert Bossarte, 'Suicide Data Report,' US Government Department of Veteran Affairs, 2012.

57 Scott Shane, 'Amid Details on Torture, Data on 26 Who Were Held in Error,' *New York Times*, 12 December 2014.

58 Charlie Savage, 'Court Releases Large Parts of Memo Approving Killing of American in Yemen,' *New York Times*, 23 June 2014.

59 *Donnie Brasco* (1997), directed by Mike Newell, is based on the true story of a hitman, Benjamin 'Lefty' Ruggiero, who was befriended by undercover FBI agent Joseph Pistone.

60 *Murder by Contract* (1958), directed by Irving Lerner.

61 Bryan Glyn Williams, *Predators: The CIA's Drone War on al Qaeda* (2013), Chapters 6 and 7.

62 Williams (2013), p. 66.

63 Shuja Nawaz is interviewed in the PBS documentary film *Rise of the Drones* (2013), directed by Peter Yost.

64 Two films about Idi Amin offer very different perspectives on the leader: *The Last King of Scotland* (2006), directed by Kevin Macdonald; and *General Idi Amin Dada: A Self Portrait* (1975), directed by Barbet Schroeder.

65 M. Shane Riza, a command pilot of traditional combat planes, agrees. He argues in *Killing without Heart* (2013) that risk is the key factor distinguishing traditional acts of warfare from drone killing and what he warns is the advent of 'autonomous' killing, with even operators taken out of the 'kill chain'. Riza maintains that warfare must remain a human activity in order to retain meaning.

66 Amnesty International, *'Will I Be Next?' US Drone Strikes in Pakistan*, October 2013 report, pp. 7–12.

67 I am grateful to Stephen Shalom for pressing me to clarify the status of active-duty combat soldiers during wartime, specifically that they need not be in the process of firing a gun in order to be considered fair game for targeting.

68 Barack Obama, 'Statement by the President on ISIL,' White House Office of the Press Secretary, 10 September 2014.

69 The document was published online in July 2014 at *The Intercept*. This sentence is found on page 11.

70 The modus operandi of hitmen is depicted in a number of feature-length films, some of which are based on true stories. Examples include *Le Samouraï* (1967), directed by Jean-Pierre Melville; and *Collateral* (2004), directed by Michael Mann. The willingness of a hitman to kill anyone who might possibly be able to connect him to any of his former victims, conceiving of the later murders as acts of legitimate self-defense, is specifically highlighted in *The American Soldier* (1970), directed by Rainer Werner Fassbinder, and *The Iceman* (2012), directed by Ariel Vromen.

71 Richard Engel, 'Former Drone Operator Says He's Haunted by his Part in More Than 1,600 Deaths,' NBC News, 6 June 2013.

72 Richard Kuklinski relays his story in a series of interviews originally aired on HBO and now available on YouTube. The story has also been made into a feature-length film heavily based on the interviews: *The Iceman* (2012), directed by Ariel Vromen.

73 Akbar Ahmed, *The Thistle and the Drone: How America's War on Terror Became a Global War on Tribal Islam* (2013), p. 22.

74 This is not to deny that economic need can itself be coercive, an issue examined in Laurie Calhoun, 'Be All That You Can Be,' *New Political Science*, 2003, volume 25, no. 1, pp. 5–17.

75 *The Killer Elite* (1975), directed by Sam Peckinpah, highlights the willingness of mercenaries to switch sides when sufficiently enticed.

76 See *Why We Fight* (2006), directed by Eugene Jarecki, and *No End in Sight* (2007), directed by Charles Ferguson. A major recruitment scandal uncovered in early 2014 revealed yet again that 'discretionary' funds are often used with indiscretion. See Jordan Carney, 'The Army's Recruiting Fraud Problem,' *National Journal*, 4 February 2014.

77 Scott Shane, 'US Said to Target Rescuers at Drone Strike Sites,' *New York Times*, 5 February 2012.

78 The fluid nature of ROE and their dependence on the caprice of mid-level commanders is highlighted in *Generation Kill* (2008), a miniseries based on *Rolling Stone* journalist Evan Wright's memoir *Generation Kill: Devil Dogs, Iceman, Captain America, and the New Face of American War* (2004),

which relays his experience traveling as an embedded journalist with the First Recon unit of the US Marines during the 2003 invasion of Iraq.

79 Jackie Spinner, Karl Vick and Omar Fekeiki, 'US Forces Battle Into Heart of Fallujah: Units Meet Scattered Resistance; Attacks Continue Elsewhere,' *Washington Post*, 10 November 2004.

80 Jo Becker and Scott Shane, 'Secret "Kill List" Proves a Test of Obama's Principles and Will,' *New York Times*, 29 May 2012.

81 Greg Miller, 'Plan for Hunting Terrorists Signals US Intends to Keep Adding Names to Kill Lists,' *Washington Post*, 23 October 2012.

82 A few different websites, including *Pakistan Body Count*, keep records of all persons killed and maimed in areas where drone strikes are carried out. Some of the victims are injured or destroyed directly by missiles, others indirectly by retaliatory suicide bombings.

83 Part of Humam al-Balawi's video clip is included in *Unmanned: America's Drone Wars* (2013), directed by Robert Greenwald. In all, ten people were killed in the attack, and several others were injured.

84 Ahmed (2013), p. 74.

85 Amnesty International, *'Will I Be Next?' US Drone Strikes in Pakistan*, October 2013 report.

86 Jo Becker and Scott Shane, 'Secret "Kill List" Proves a Test of Obama's Principles and Will,' *New York Times*, 29 May 2012.

87 Ami Ayalon and five other former leaders of Shin Bet are interviewed by director Dror Moreh in *The Gatekeepers* (2012). Shin Bet is the intelligence agency charged with defending Israel against terrorism, espionage, and the release of state secrets.

88 Andrew Exum served as an Army Ranger under General Stanley McChrystal. This citation is an excerpt from a March 2012 interview included in Scahill (2013), p. 151.

89 Some scholars have argued that anyone who rejects targeted killing must also reject war more generally and accept pacifism. See Daniel Statman, 'Targeted Killing,' in *Philosophy 9/11: Thinking about the War on Terrorism* (2005), edited by Timothy Shanahan.

90 As of 2013, covert US military operations were under way in 120 different countries. See Bacevich (2013), p. 177.

91 Lawrence B. Wilkerson is interviewed in the film *Unmanned: America's Drone Wars* (2013), directed by Robert Greenwald.

92 Brian Handwerk and Zain Habboo, 'Attack on America: An Islamic Scholar's Perspective – Part 1,' *National Geographic News*, 28 September 2001.

93 Eric Schmitt, 'US Army Buried Iraqi Soldiers Alive in Gulf War,' *New York Times*, 15 September 1991.

94 Gardner (2013), pp. 169–70.

95 Jeremy Scahill and Glenn Greenwald, 'The NSA's Secret Role in the US Assassination Program,' *The Intercept*, 10 February 2014.

96 Greg Miller and Julie Tate, 'CIA Shifts Focus to Killing Targets,' *Washington Post*, 1 September 2011.

97 Several worrying reports have been issued, including: Human Rights Watch, 'Between a Drone and Al Qaeda: The Civilian Cost of US Targeted Killings in Yemen,' October 2013; Amnesty International, '"Will I Be Next?" US Drone Strikes in Pakistan,' October 2013; International Human Rights and Conflict Resolution Clinic at Stanford Law School and Global Justice Clinic at NYU School of Law, 'Living Under Drones: Death, Injury, and Trauma to Civilians from US Drone Practices in Pakistan,' September 2012; and Center for Civilians in Conflict (CIVIC), 'Civilians in Armed Conflict: Civilian Harm and Conflict in Northwest Pakistan,' October 2010.

98 Klaidman (2012) offers a sympathetic but depressing portrait of Barack Obama as a malleable leader easily swayed by strong-willed cabinet members and others to accept already entrenched policies, including targeted killing, whether by drone or in JSOC raids. Regarding the conservative nature of belief more generally, see Gilbert Harman, *Change in View* (1986).

99 Jack Serle, 'More than 2,400 Dead as Obama's Drone Campaign Marks Five Years,' Bureau of Investigative Journalism, 23 January 2014.

100 The forces of homogenization acting on institutions are well illustrated by the CIA officers interviewed in *Pakistan Undercover* (2009), directed by Doug Shultz, who go out of their way to express their heartfelt belief that they are involved in a 'war'. The decision by the Bush administration to characterize the attacks of 11 September 2001 as an act of war continues to serve as the pretext for killing campaigns carried out by an agency established for the purpose of gathering information.

101 After the controversial killing of Abdulrahman al-Awlaki, a spokesman for the National Security Council, Thomas F. Victor, claimed: 'For over the past

year, the Department of State has publicly urged US citizens not to travel to Yemen.' (Peter Finn and Greg Miller, 'Anwar al-Awlaki's Family Speaks out against his, Son's Deaths,' *Washington Post*, 17 October 2011.) However, the young Al-Awlaki was not killed by Yemeni but by US nationals.

102 Goodman (2008), pp. 170–1.

103 Associated Press, 'Army Chief: Force to Occupy Iraq Massive,' 25 February 2003.

104 Greg Miller and Julie Tate, 'CIA Shifts Focus to Killing Targets,' *Washington Post*, 1 September 2011.

105 Scott Shane, 'CIA is Disputed on Civilian Toll in Drone Strikes,' *New York Times*, 11 August 2011.

106 Peter Baker, 'Pivoting from a War Footing, Obama Acts to Curtail Drones,' *New York Times*, 23 May 2013.

107 Mark Mazzetti and Eric Schmitt, 'US Debates Drone Strike on American Terrorism Suspect in Pakistan,' *New York Times*, 10 February 2014.

108 In late 2014, the target in question, Mohanad Mahmoud Al Farekh, was taken into custody, definitively proving that it had been possible to capture him all along. See Mark Mazzetti and Eric Schmitt, 'Terrorism Case Renews Debate Over Drone Hits,' *New York Times*, 12 April 2015.

109 Most of the 1991 Gulf War deaths occurred in the years after the bombing of water treatment facilities, when the imposition of strict sanctions prevented access to substances such as chlorine needed to purify the water, and also the medications needed to treat diseases caused by contaminated water. Many of the victims were children. See John Pilger, 'Squeezed to Death,' *The Guardian*, 3 March 2000.

110 Just war theorists have interpreted 'last resort' so broadly that the requirement is vacuously satisfied by every war waged. See Laurie Calhoun, *War and Delusion: A Critical Examination* (2013), Chapter 2.

111 Relayed by Colin Powell in his autobiography *My American Journey* (1995), p. 576.

112 Carl Boggs (ed.), *Masters of War: Militarism and Blowback in the Era of American Empire* (2003).

113 Barack Obama, 'Statement by the President on the Attempted Attack on Christmas Day and Recent Violence in Iran,' White House Office of the Press Secretary, 28 December 2009.

114 Mark Mazzetti, 'New Terror Strategy Shifts CIA Focus Back to Spying,' *New York Times*, 23 May 2013.

115 Jack Serle, 'More than 2,400 Dead as Obama's Drone Campaign Marks Five Years,' Bureau of Investigative Journalism, 23 January 2014.

116 Benjamin (2013) observes that fifteen strike attempts were made against Baitullah Mehsud before he was finally killed, with the resultant civilian casualties somewhere between 204 and 321 victims (p. 107). An illuminating study by Reprieve analyzes the number of people killed in multiple strikes intended to eliminate 41 suspected terrorists but which culminated in the deaths of 1,147 persons, most of whom were unnamed. See Spencer Ackerman, '41 Men Targeted but 1147 Killed: US Drone Strikes – the Facts on the Ground,' *The Guardian*, 24 November 2014.

117 Conservative figures on the number of deaths resulting from the US invasion in 2003 and the subsequent occupation of Iraq range from about 461,000 to more than 900,000. See Reese Erlich, *Inside Syria: The Backstory of Their Civil War and What the World Can Expect* (2014), p. 78. Millions more people, especially white collar professionals and their families, fled the land, effecting something of a 'brain drain'.

118 Hakimullah Mehsud reported by Alex Crawford, 'New Taliban Leader Vows to Carry on War,' *Sky News*, 18 September 2009.

119 Rand Paul made this statement during his thirteen-hour filibuster of the US Senate on 6 March 2013 in opposition to the nomination of John Brennan as the director of the CIA. The complete transcript is available online: www.dailypaul.com/277205/rand-paul-filibuster-entire-transcript.

120 A Waziristan drone strike survivor cited in *Unmanned: America's Drone Wars* (2013).

121 In *Shoah* (1985), a nine-hour documentary film directed by Claude Lanzmann, the Holocaust is examined through interviews with both Jewish survivors of internment, who worked in the death camps in order to preserve their lives, and Polish and German persons who benefited in various ways from Nazi policies, often by resettling in towns close to the camps (where they could hear the victims screaming) in exchange for murdered people's homes.

122 This is the picture painted by Scahill (2013), who carefully traces the trajectory from Al-Awlaki's moderate beginnings through his radicalization, strongly suggesting that the US government catalyzed the transformation through a variety of forms of harassment. Klaidman (2012) offers a very different version of the story, which is based on anonymous insider sources

from the government and echoes the administration's official statements on the case, including that Al-Awlaki was not only a propagandist but also an operational terrorist.

123 Herbert W. Titus and William J. Olson deride 'this whitewash of a white paper' as 'mimicking a judicial opinion', and shred the document in less than two pages, pointing out, among other problems, that 'When a US citizen is suspected of treason, the constitutional remedy is not to invent new crimes subject to the summary execution at the pleasure of the president and his attorneys' ('Assassin in Chief?' *American Thinker*, 7 February 2013).

124 Richard Brookhiser, 'Executive Limits,' *American History*, August 2013, pp. 22–3.

125 Only gross cases of suspected incompetence make the news. See Joseph Goldstein, 'New York Examines Over 800 Rape Cases for Possible Mishandling of Evidence,' *New York Times*, 10 January 2013.

126 One recent case involves New York City detective Louis Scarcella, who is under investigation for possible malfeasance in dozens of convictions. See Frances Robles, 'Panel to Review Up to 50 Trial Convictions Involving a Discredited Detective,' *New York Times*, 1 July 2013.

127 In a rare exception to the general rule of private contractor impunity, four former Blackwater Worldwide guards were convicted of murder or manslaughter by a federal court for their killing of fourteen unarmed Iraqi civilians in 2007. See Terrence McCoy, 'Why the Blackwater Convictions Won't Slow America's "Shadow Armies",' *Washington Post*, 23 October 2014.

128 Dana Priest and William M. Arkin, 'Inside the CIA's "Kill List",' PBS Frontline, 6 September 2011.

129 Anwar al-Awlaki's father, Nasser al-Awlaki, had filed a lawsuit in 2010 in an attempt to have his son's name removed from the US government's hit list, but his efforts were rebuffed. The judge ruled that the father could not petition on his son's behalf. Later, the father filed a new lawsuit alleging the wrongful death of both his son and his grandson. See Karen McVeigh, 'Families of US Citizens Killed in Drone Strikes File Wrongful Death Lawsuit,' *The Guardian*, 18 July 2012.

130 The theory according to which Anwar al-Awlaki was an operational terrorist and leader of AQAP was reportedly devised by John Brennan, who reasoned that the sudden appearance of US-aimed threats, in particular the attempt made on 25 December 2009 by Umar Farouk to blow up an airplane as

it approached Detroit, Michigan, was best explained by the fact that Al-Awlaki had relocated to Yemen. The hypothesis was soon cemented by the mainstream media into what the populace came to accept as objective fact. See Johnsen (2013), pp. 261–3.

131 The first American killed by a US drone appears to have been Abu Ahmad al Hijazi, a US-born Yemeni also known as Kemal Darwish. Hijazi/Darwish was not intentionally targeted in the 3 November 2002 strike in Yemen. According to some reports, officials did not know ahead of the action that a US citizen was present. See Allison McCann et al., 'The Drone War: A Comprehensive Map of Lethal US Attacks,' *Bloomberg Businessweek*, 23 May 2013.

132 Ahmed (2013), p. 83.

133 Glenn Greenwald, *No Place to Hide: Edward Snowden, the NSA, and the US Surveillance State* (2014).

134 Robert S. McNamara, *In Retrospect: The Tragedy and Lessons of Vietnam* (1996).

135 Obama was reportedly informed that 'it was only a matter of time … before the code would be pulled apart and features of it used in other cyberweapons, including those aimed back at the United States'. See David E. Sanger, *Confront and Conceal: Obama's Secret Wars and Surprising Use of American Power* (2012), p. xii. The president appears to have believed that such developments would be deterred, not spurred, by refusing to acknowledge his administration's cyberattacks (p. 265).

136 Richard Spencer, 'US Cluster Bombs "Killed 35 Women and Children",' *Telegraph*, 7 June 2010.

137 The case of Abdalilah Shaya is discussed by Johnsen (2013, pp. 265–70). Scahill (2013) went so far as to call for the journalist's release. Later, on 23 January 2013, Shaya was allowed to leave prison and serve the remaining two years of his sentence under house arrest.

138 Michael Hastings' explosive exposé 'The Runaway General', published in *Rolling Stone* magazine on 22 June 2010, led to the forced resignation of General Stanley McChrystal. Jeremy Scahill, praised by Bill Moyers as a 'one-man truth squad', published a searing investigation, *Blackwater: The Rise of the World's Most Powerful Mercenary Army* (2007), of the notorious private military company, followed up by *Dirty Wars* (2013), a wide-ranging critique of the network of killing campaigns perpetrated by the Obama administration.

139 One person in General Stanley McChrystal's entourage (a colonel named 'Jake' in Hastings' memoir) told the journalist: 'We'll hunt you down and kill you if we don't like what you write.' See Hastings (2012), p. 64. Again, while in Afghanistan, Hastings was warned that he might be in danger – not from the Afghans but from the Americans (p. 301). The circumstances surrounding the journalist's death were highly suspicious, but because Hastings had used drugs in the past, many people wrote off the conspiratorial interpretation and accepted that the automobile accident was indeed accidental. Oddly, Hastings' wife's opinion that the death was accidental was treated as significant by mainstream media outlets. Even more oddly, the LAPD (Los Angeles Police Department) declined to investigate the case.

140 Scahill (2013) has reported that he was literally threatened by a military officer not to publish a piece in the *Nation*. In 2005, it emerged that antiwar protesters were a target group for the TALON (Threat and Local Observation Notice) database. The revelations in 2013 by Edward Snowden of massive surveillance of US citizens by the NSA naturally raise the question: to what use is all of this collected data being put? See Greenwald (2014) for detailed reproductions of some of the NSA PowerPoint slides documenting invasive surveillance of US citizens and foreigners alike.

141 From an interview with Anwar al-Awlaki by Ray Suarez conducted on 31 October 2001. This excerpt can be viewed online: www.pbs.org/newshour/updates/religion-july-dec09-alawlaki_11-11/

142 Barack Obama, 'Statement by the President,' White House Office of the Press Secretary, 14 July 2013.

143 Eric Holder speaking at Northwestern University in March 2012, cited in Karen McVeigh, 'Families of US Citizens Killed in Drone Strikes File Wrongful Death Lawsuit,' *The Guardian*, 18 July 2012.

144 Barack Obama, 'Remarks by the President on Trayvon Martin,' White House Office of the Press Secretary, 19 July 2013.

145 MSNBC, 'American Drone Deaths Highlight Controversy,' NBCNews. com, 5 February 2013.

146 This disturbing hypothesis is considerably strengthened by the revelation that the fifteen-year-old boy had been encouraged by a schoolteacher to pay a visit to his father hiding out in Yemen. The schoolteacher subsequently disappeared and could not be located. See Scahill (2013), pp. 507–11.

[147] In the film *Zero Dark Thirty* (2012), directed by Kathryn Bigelow, Bin Laden's son is shot in the head by a Marine who first calls his name to lure him into peeking around the corner to look down the hall, placing his head in the crosshairs of the shooter's weapon. This version of the story is supported by Peter Bergen's account *Manhunt: The Ten-year Search for Bin Laden – from 9/11 to Abbottabad* (2012). CIA Director Leon Panetta reportedly encouraged the SEAL team members who carried out the mission to cooperate with the makers of *Zero Dark Thirty*. See Christopher Drew and Nicholas Kulish, 'Former Navy SEAL Member Investigated for Bin Laden Disclosures,' *New York Times*, 30 October 2014.

[148] As more and more men are destroyed in protracted violent conflicts, women become willing to take up arms. See Gillo Pontecorvo's classic film depiction of factional terrorism in Algeria under French occupation, *La bataille d'Alger* (*The Battle of Algiers*) (1966). Female Palestinian suicide bombers are another example. See Anat Berko's *The Smarter Bomb: Women and Children as Suicide Bombers* (2012). In 2014, ISIS began actively recruiting women as well, but primarily to partner with and serve in support roles to male combatants. Presumably this would qualify them as 'associates' in the view of drone program administrators. See Aryn Baker, 'How ISIS is Recruiting Women From Around the World,' *Time*, 6 September 2014.

[149] Christof Heyns, 'Report of the Special Rapporteur on extrajudicial, summary or arbitrary executions,' UN General Assembly Human Rights Council, 13 September 2013. Heyns reiterates many of the human rights concerns aired by his predecessor, Philip Alston. Mary Ellen O'Connell, an academic expert on international law, maintains that only the United States' veto power prevents an investigation into the illegality of its drone strikes by the UN. See Kourosh Ziabari, 'Legality of Obama's Drone Policy: A Conversation with Prof. Mary Ellen O'Connell,' *International Policy Digest*, 4 October 2014.

[150] These two forms of collateral damage are discussed in greater depth in Chapter 3 of Calhoun (2013). Second-order collateral damage is systematically neglected in projections of the likely consequences of wielding military force.

[151] Pew Research Center's Global Attitudes Project, 'Pakistani Opinion Ever More Critical of US,' 27 June 2012.

152 Usama Khilji cited in Ahmed (2013), p. 83. Other studies, also discussed by Ahmed, corroborate this report by the Foundation for Fundamental Rights in Pakistan. In the Gaza Strip, the Palestinians have been similarly afflicted (p. 298).

153 Josh Levs, 'Ferguson Violence: Critics Rip Police Tactics, Use of Military Equipment,' CNN.com, 15 August 2014.

154 There is no question that the Iraqi people had suffered under their despotic leader Saddam Hussein, but their plight was exacerbated by the crippling sanctions imposed by outside nations subsequent to the Gulf War, rendering the 'humanitarian' pretext for the 2003 invasion risible at best. See Geoff Simons, *The Scourging of Iraq: Sanctions, Law and Natural Law* (1996).

155 The pressure exerted on the CIA by Vice President Cheney's staff to produce a pretext for the 2003 invasion of Iraq is depicted in *Fair Game* (2010), directed by Doug Liman. The film focuses on the 'outing' of CIA operative Valerie Plame in retaliation for Joe Wilson's public denial that Iraq had attempted to buy 'yellow cake' (enriched uranium) from Niger.

156 Jeffrey Ethell is interviewed in the Nova PBS documentary *Top Gun over Moscow* (1996), directed by Lance K. Shultz and Lynne Squilla. The film offers an insightful pre-drone perspective on the state of aerial combat in the late twentieth century and affirms that the 'dogfight' between two rival pilots is obsolete.

157 Matthew J. Martin with Charles W. Sasser, *Predator: The Remote-control Air War over Iraq and Afghanistan: A Pilot's Story* (2010), p. 252.

158 *Flyboys* (2006), a film directed by Tony Bill, is based on the true story of a group of young American men who for various reasons wind up together in a squadron of pilots fighting on the French side against the Germans in World War I. The film conveys the sense of danger and the indisputable courage of the men who freely agreed to serve as pilots at that time.

159 The macho image of elite US pilots selected to attend 'Top Gun' training school is portrayed in the film *Top Gun* (1986), directed by Tony Scott.

160 Courtney Kube, 'Hagel Drops Controversial Medal for Drone Operators,' NBCNews.com, 15 April 2013.

161 Tom Engelhardt reported that, as of December 2013, eight weddings – in Afghanistan, Iraq and Yemen – had been wiped out by US missiles so far in the twenty-first century, with the tally of dead approaching 300. Other civil ceremonies, including funerals, have also been struck. Available online

at www.tomdispatch.com/blog/175787/tomgram%3A_engelhardt,_washington's_wedding_album_from_hell/.

162 Azmat Khan, 'Two US Soldiers Killed in Friendly Fire Drone Strike,' PBS Frontline, 17 October 2011.

163 Dan Lamothe, 'Investigation: Friendly Fire Airstrike that Killed US Special Forces was Avoidable,' *Washington Post*, 4 September 2014.

164 David Rohde and Kristen Mulvihill, *A Rope and a Prayer: A Kidnapping from Two Sides* (2010), p. 239.

165 Qadir Khan cited in Ahmed (2013), p. 93.

166 Chris Cole, Mary Dobbing and Amy Hailwood (2010) 'Convenient Killing: Armed Drones and the "Playstation" Mentality,' Oxford: The Fellowship of Reconciliation.

167 Drone operator interviewed in *Rise of the Drones* (2013), directed by Peter Yost. Surnames are not given for security reasons – presumably to protect operators from retaliation for what they do.

168 Nidhi Subbaraman, 'Drone Pilot Burnout Triggers Call for Recruiting Overhaul,' NBCNews.com, 31 July 2011.

169 Rachel Martin, 'High Levels of "Burnout" in US Drone Pilots,' NPR News, 18 December 2011.

170 An excessive concern with tallies (rather than truth and justice) can be seen also in the FBI sting operations against alleged terrorists in the US homeland. See Trevor Aaronson's *Terror Factory: Inside the FBI's Manufactured War on Terrorism* (2013).

171 Yuval Diskin is interviewed by director Dror Moreh in *The Gatekeepers* (2012).

172 Nicola Abé, 'Dreams in Infrared: The Woes of an American Drone Operator,' *Spiegel Online International*, 14 December 2012.

173 Martin (2010), p. 306.

174 Martin exemplifies the proverbial 'ugly American', as he ridicules any- and everything which deviates from 'American ways' and prides himself on his country's alleged exceptionalism. The Italians with whom Martin serves are chided as personal-hygiene challenged – suffering from body odor and halitosis. An American who eats the Korean salad kimchi bears the brunt of further charges of 'stinkiness'.

175 Martin (2010), p. 59.

176 Faisal Shahzad cited in *Unmanned: America's Drone Wars* (2013).

177 Tweet cited by Ibrahim Mothana, 'How Drones Help Al-Qaeda,' *New York Times*, 13 June 2012.

178 Martin (2010), p. 291.

179 Rumsfeld wrote this statement in a memo dated 16 October 2003 to Paul Wolfowitz, Douglas Feith, Peter Pace and Richard Myers. See Scahill (2013), p. 114.

180 Hastings (2012), p. 141.

181 Ahmed (2013), p. 82.

182 Matt Apuzzo, 'Witnesses Testify Against Ex-Blackwater Colleagues in Case of 2007 Iraq Killings,' *New York Times*, 15 July 2014.

183 Martin (2010), p. 271.

184 Martin (2010), p. 285.

185 Hastings (2012), p. 303.

186 Karen DeYoung, 'US Official Resigns Over Afghan War,' *Washington Post*, 27 October 2009.

187 Ahmed (2013), Chapter 4.

188 Martin (2010), p. 263.

189 Navy SEAL Chris Kyle, reputed to be the deadliest military sniper in US history, is credited with 160 confirmed kills (and 255 probable) over the period from 1999 to 2009. *American Sniper* (2014), directed by Clint Eastwood, is based on the former soldier's memoir, *American Sniper: The Autobiography of the Most Lethal Sniper in U.S. Military History* (2012).

190 The anonymous drone operator was interviewed by Mark Bowden, 'The Killing Machines: How to Think about Drones,' *The Atlantic*, September 2013, pp. 58–70.

191 Richard Blee cited in Mazzetti (2013), p. 319.

192 During the 2003 invasion and occupation of Iraq, for the first time in history, soldiers were able to capture on video their experience on the ground. Many soldiers produced extensive footage, some of which was later turned into full-length films. Examples include *Combat Diary: The Marines of Lima Company* (2006), *Gunner Palace* (2005), *Inside Iraq: The Untold Story* (2004), *Iraq Raw: The Tuttle Tapes* (2004), and *This is War: Memories of Iraq* (2007).

193 Nick Turse, *Kill Anything that Moves: The Real American War in Vietnam* (2013).

194 Geraghty (2009), pp. 185–212.

195 Scott Fitzsimmons and Karina Sangha, 'Killing in High Definition: Combat Stress among Operators of Remotely Piloted Aircraft,' Canadian Political Science Association Conference Paper, 2013. Available online at www.cpsa-acsp.ca/papers-2013/Fitzsimmons.pdf.

196 Ben Rooney, 'Drone Pilot Wanted: Starting salary $100,000,' CNN Money, 26 November 2014.

197 The discussion of soldier suicides and drug use in this chapter derives in part from Laurie Calhoun, 'The Silencing of Soldiers,' *Independent Review*, 2011, 16(2): 247–70.

198 Janet Kemp and Robert Bossarte, 'Suicide Data Report,' US Government Department of Veteran Affairs, 2012.

199 Such anecdotes are shared by soldiers interviewed in the film *Operation Homecoming* (2007), directed by Richard Robbins, which is based on the book of the same name edited by Andrew Carroll and published in 2006.

200 The degree to which military killers are wholly dependent upon intelligence furnished to them and which they presume to be valid is well illustrated by *Act of Valor* (2012), directed by Scott Waugh and Mouse McCoy. In this film, special operations soldiers are sent out on mission after mission to kill persons identified as terrorists in various parts of the world far beyond US borders. The film stars active duty Navy SEALs who are not professional actors and ultimately serves as a propaganda piece for the Pentagon and JSOC.

201 A disturbing example of this criminalization phenomenon has repeatedly occurred when women soldiers have attempted to report sexual abuse committed by their comrades, and in some cases (25 percent) their superior officers. In many of these cases, the women have found themselves charged with crimes such as 'conduct unbecoming a soldier' and adultery. See *The Invisible War* (2012), directed by Kirby Dick.

202 The Tillman family's efforts to ascertain what really happened to their son are relayed in *The Tillman Story* (2010), directed by Amir Bar-lev.

203 Camilo Mejía served a one-year prison sentence and became a leader of the veteran antiwar movement. His memoir, *Road from Ar Ramadi: The Private Rebellion of Sergeant Camilo Mejía*, was published in 2007.

204 The story of Zinn's life is portrayed in *Howard Zinn: You Can't Be Neutral on a Moving Train* (2004), directed by Deb Ellis and Denis Mueller.

205 Self-mutilation of soldiers to avoid redeployment also took place during the occupation of Iraq. See Tony Dokoupil, 'Soldiers' Self-Harm: Anything Not to Go Back,' *Newsweek*, 7 June 2008.

206 Mark Thompson, 'A Soldier's Tragedy,' *Time*, 7 March 2011.

207 Kelly Vlahos, 'The Military's Prescription Drug Addiction,' *American Conservative*, 3 October 2013.

208 Gardiner Harris, 'Talk Doesn't Pay, So Psychiatry Turns Instead to Drug Therapy,' *New York Times*, 5 March 2011.

209 Bob Brewin, 'Military's Policy Threatens Troops' Health, Doctors Say,' Next Gov.com, 18 January 2011. Available online at www.nextgov.com/health/ 2011/01/militarys-drug-policy-threatens-troops-health-doctors-say/48321/.

210 For one example of the magnitude of financial interests at issue, see the US Department of Defense report for the pharmaceutical contracts finalized on 31 March 2010: www.defense.gov/Contracts/Contract. aspx?ContractID=4249.

211 Guillaume Lavallee for Agence France-Presse, 'US Drone Strikes in Pakistan Linked to Rise in Depression, Anxiety,' *Huffington Post*, 7 April 2013.

212 Critics such as Al McCoy, the author of *The Politics of Heroin* (2003), report that the CIA aided Laotian drug lords by even transporting their opium crops.

213 Jeff Hargarten et al., 'Suicide Rate for Veterans Far Exceeds that of Civilian Population,' Center for Public Integrity, 30 August 2013.

214 Rachel Martin, 'High Levels of "Burnout" in US Drone Pilots,' NPR News, 18 December 2011.

215 Even President Obama was reported to be dosing himself with psychotropic medications while in office. His 'meds' of choice to combat jet lag were not made public, but some have speculated that he may have been taking Provigil, a popular performance enhancer (not a use approved by the Food and Drug Administration (FDA)). See Barbara Kantrowitz, 'The White House Mystery Drug,' *The Daily Beast*, 4 March 2010. After Obama's poor opening debate performance during the 2012 presidential campaign, one journalist referred to him as 'President Xanax'. See Charles M. Blow, 'Cool Hand Barry,' *New York Times*, 4 October 2012.

216 According to critics, the health and well-being of patients is being compromised as the drugs often work by transforming the brain, which has the ultimate effect of increasing drug dependence over time as tolerance is

developed. Patients become the equivalent of laboratory guinea pigs when they are prescribed multiple FDA-approved medications simultaneously, for the interaction effects are unknown. James Davies presents a wealth of evidence in *Cracked: The Unhappy Truth about Psychiatry* (2013).

217 Mark Corcoran, 'The Kill Chain: Australia's Drone War,' ABC.net.au, 26 June 2012.

218 Lt. Colonel Dave Grossman, *On Killing: The Psychological Cost of Learning to Kill in War and Society* (1995).

219 Former Secretary of Defense Donald Rumsfeld was the CEO of G. D. Searle & Company, a huge pharmaceutical firm, from 1977 to 1985.

220 Aaron Alexis, who killed twelve people in Navy Yard on 16 September 2013, had been prescribed Trazodone, an antidepressant used to treat patients with insomnia. The possible significance of the drug in the killer's system was minimized by VA public relations when they reported it as 'a small amount of sleep medicine'. Experts chimed in with the reassurance that the medication is 'very safe'. What is beyond dispute is that Alexis did not murder anyone before taking Trazodone. See Lena H. Sun, 'Trazodone Antidepressant, Used by Aaron Alexis, Described as "Very Safe",' *Washington Post*, 18 September 2013.

221 Nowhere was the first priority of bureaucrats better displayed than in the damage-control initiatives undertaken on multiple fronts after the December 2014 release of the Senate Intelligence Committee's report on the use of torture by the CIA. See Spencer Ackerman, 'CIA Director John Brennan Defends Agency in Wake of Torture Report,' *The Guardian*, 11 December 2014.

222 Two films critical of how the prison scandals were handled are *Standard Operating Procedure* (2008) and *Taxi to the Dark Side* (2007).

223 This declaration by Mary Cole on 1 October 2010 was made in response to a demand for information by the American Civil Liberties Union in a lawsuit about the use by the CIA of drones for targeted killing. A catalog of the administration's different, often contradictory, statements about the use of drones during 2012 can be found on Pro Publica's website: http://projects.propublica.org/graphics/cia-drones-strikes.

224 Obama was responding to a question about the efficacy of the drone program during a Google+ Hangout conversation on 30 January 2012. He was the only official in nearly a decade to acknowledge the existence

of the CIA drone killing program. The first had been Deputy Defense Secretary Paul Wolfowitz, after the strike in Yemen on 3 November 2002.

225 Micah L. Sifray and Christopher Cerf, *The Gulf War Reader* (1991), p. 178.

226 Michael Duffy, 'Interview: Monica Lewinsky Up Close,' *Time*, 15 March 1999.

227 Erlich (2014) offers a thorough investigation of the complex circumstances and controversy regarding who used chemical weapons in Syria in 2013 (pp. 101–21). He concludes that the conflicting evidence does not settle the case one way or the other. It is possible that both the Assad regime and the rebel forces used chemical weapons in Syria.

228 Ed O'Keefe, 'More than 100 Lawmakers Ask Obama to Seek Congressional Approval on Syria Strikes,' *Washington Post*, 28 August 2013.

229 'It Takes Out a Village,' *American Conservative*, 9 February 2009, pp. 4–5.

230 C. J. Chivers and Eric Schmitt, 'In Strikes in Libya by NATO, an Unspoken Civilian Toll,' *New York Times*, 17 December 2011.

231 P. W. Singer, *Wired for War: The Robotics Revolution and Conflict in the Twenty-first Century* (2009), p. 100.

232 Barack Obama, 'Statement by the President on ISIL,' White House Office of the Press Secretary, 10 September 2014.

233 Erlich (2014) reveals that arms shipments to the Free Syria Army began no later than June 2012 (p. 214). See also Phil Greaves, 'CIA Gun-running, Qatar-Libya-Syria,' *Global Research,* Centre for Research on Globalization, 9 August 2013.

234 Patrick J. McDonnell and Nabih Bulos, 'Yemeni President Flees Houthi-controlled Capital, Denounces "Coup",' *Los Angeles Times*, 21 February 2015.

235 Patrick Wintour, 'US Forms "Core Coalition" to Fight ISIS Militants in Iraq,' The *Guardian*, 5 September 2014.

236 ISIS/ISIL and Al-Qaeda had something of a falling out, but this appeared to be irrelevant to Obama, who continued to reason that because they grew out of Al-Qaeda, they could be militarily attacked under the broad authority granted by the Authorization for Use of Military Force (AUMF) passed by Congress in 2001. The tensions between the two groups persisted in 2014. See James Gordon Meek, 'Powerful Al Qaeda Group Slams Door on ISIS's Leader,' ABC News, 21 November 2014.

237 Mark Mazzetti and Eric Schmitt, 'US Debates Drone Strike on American Terrorism Suspect in Pakistan,' *New York Times*, 10 February 2014.

238 Klaidman (2012).

239 Malala Yousafzai, a Pakistani girl who survived a gunshot to the head by a member of the Taliban for promoting women's right to education, was nominated for but did not receive the Nobel Peace Prize in 2013. She was invited to the White House to speak with Nobel Peace Prize laureate Barack Obama and reported to the press that she had expressed this concern to the president during their meeting. See Philip Rucker, 'Malala Yousafzai Meets with the Obamas in the Oval Office,' *Washington Post*, 11 October 2013. In 2014, Yousafzai became the youngest Nobel laureate in history.

240 Sanger (2012) recounts the story of the Obama administration's covert cyberattack on Iran, along with the general elevation of secrecy as a means of permitting the president to exercise extraordinary power abroad, unbeknownst to the people paying for the initiatives.

241 Christopher H. Pyle, 'Barack Obama and Civil Liberties,' *Presidential Studies Quarterly*, 2012, 42(4): 867–80.

242 The Kurds in Syria are a case in point, comprising more than a dozen different political groups with varying degrees of allegiance to the many rebel factions and the Assad regime. See Erlich (2014), pp. 167–89.

243 Paul Eremenko is interviewed in the documentary film *Rise of the Drones* (2013).

244 James Pitts citation from Ed Warner, 'Freud and the Drone: Robot War Means More Killing and Less Guilt,' *The American Conservative*, June 2012, p. 10.

245 Detailed information about Hellfire missiles can be found at http://usmilitary.about.com/od/weapons/a/hellfiremissile.htm.

246 Barack Obama, 'Remarks by the President at the National Defense University,' White House Office of the Press Secretary, 23 May 2013.

247 Peter Bergen and Paul Cruickshank, 'The Iraq Effect: War Has Increased Terrorism Sevenfold Worldwide,' *Mother Jones*, March/April 2007.

248 Klaidman (2012), p. 119.

249 Dzhokhar Tsarnaev's claim to have been inspired by Anwar al-Awlaki's sermons suggests to some critics that his execution by the US government turned the cleric into a martyr of sorts. See Gardner (2013), p. 238.

250 Ahmed (2013).

251 Scahill (2013), p. 236.

252 Dan Lamothe, 'US Close to Sending Largest Ever Hellfire Missile Order to Iraq,' *Washington Post*, 29 July 2014.

253 In *The Complex* (2008), Nick Turse documents the tentacular reach of the US Department of Defense, affecting even such ostensibly far-removed areas as the fast food industry.

254 Cheney's push for the privatization of military services and logistics appears to have been part of a broader quest for unfettered expansion of executive power: 'Cheney realized early on that using private companies to wage US wars would create another barrier to oversight and could afford greater secrecy for the planning and execution of those wars, both declared and undeclared.' See Scahill (2013), p. 12. Many earlier episodes of war profiteering are discussed in Andrew Feinstein, *The Shadow World: Inside the Global Arms Trade* (2011).

255 Geraghty (2009), p. 19.

256 Sérgio Vieira de Mello, the UN Secretary General's Special Representative in Iraq, was killed on 19 August 2003, along with twenty other UN employees located outside the high-security Green Zone. ('Top UN Official Among Dead in Baghdad Blast,' *The Guardian*, 19 August 2003.)

257 Bacevich (2013), p. 127.

258 Lee Fang, 'Who's Paying the Pro-war Pundits?' *The Nation*, 16 September 2014.

259 Greg Miller, 'Increased U.S. Drone Strikes in Pakistan Killing Few High-value Militants,' *Washington Post*, 20 February 2011.

260 Salman Masood and Pir Zubair Shah, 'C.I.A. Drones Kill Civilians in Pakistan,' *New York Times*, 17 March 2011.

261 Williams (2013), p. 233.

262 These figures are from Robert Greenwald's 2013 film *Unmanned: America's Drone Wars.*

263 Matt Egan, 'Clash with Syria Could be Windfall for Tomahawk Missile Maker Raytheon,' FoxBusiness.com, 30 August 2013.

264 Bryan Bender, 'From the Pentagon to the Private Sector,' *Boston Globe*, 26 December 2010.

265 For more on this company's history, see Scahill (2007) and Suzanne Simons, *Master of War: Blackwater USA's Erik Prince and the Business of War* (2010).

266 Mark Thompson, 'Ex-Blackwater Chief Urges Hired Guns to Take on ISIS,' *Time*, 10 October 2014.

267 Aaronson (2013), p. 45.

268 Aram Roston, 'How the US Funds the Taliban,' *The Nation*, 30 November 2009.

269 Agence France-Presse, 'Billions in Afghanistan Aid Unaccounted for,' 28 October 2010.

270 Barack Obama, 'Remarks by the President at the National Defense University,' White House Office of the Press Secretary, 23 May 2013.

271 Obama's Nobel Prize acceptance speech, 'A Just and Lasting Peace', was delivered on 10 December 2009.

272 Reuters, 'Exclusive: Obama Moves to Sell Northrop Drones to South Korea,' 31 August 2011.

273 Elizabeth Dickinson, 'Business is Booming at Abu Dhabi's Great Arms Bazaar,' *Foreign Policy*, 5 March 2015.

274 Gordon Adams cited in Melvin A. Goodman, *National Insecurity: The Cost of American Militarism* (2013), p. 365.

275 *Remote Control War: The Future of Unmanned Combat* (2011), directed by Leif Kaldor.

276 Riza (2013) has expressed concerns about the coming automatization of warfare. However, he assumes that the existence of just war theory – historical restraints placed on warfare – shows that war is a moral activity. In truth, just war theory has been the belligerent leader's most dependable rhetorical weapon, used to inveigle the populace to pay for and soldiers to fight in wars. See Appendix and Calhoun (2013), especially Chapter 2: 'The Triumph of Just War Rhetoric'.

277 Rachel L. Swarns, 'Senator? Terrorist? A Watch List Stops Kennedy at Airport,' *New York Times*, 19 August 2004.

278 BBC News, 'Mandela Taken off US Terror List,' 1 July 2008.

279 The War Resisters League produces a pie chart depicting the breakdown of US federal taxpayers' money for each fiscal year budget. Available online at www.warresisters.org/store/federal-budget-pie-chart/2015.

280 Lorraine Adams with Ayesha Nasir, 'Inside the Mind of the Times Square Bomber,' *The Guardian*, 18 September 2010.

281 Paul Gottinger, 'Life Under the Drones in Pakistan: A Conversation with Madiha Tahir,' White Rose Reader, 2 October 2013.

282 The discussion of soldierly virtue in this chapter derives in part from Laurie Calhoun, 'The End of Military Virtue,' *Peace Review*, 2011, 23(3): 377–86.

283 Two of the cases of murder by soldiers are examined in *Redacted* (2007), directed by Brian De Palma, and *Battle for Haditha* (2007), directed by Nick Broomfield.

284 Bob Woodruff, James Hill and Jaime Hennessy, 'Mentally Unstable Soldiers Redeployed to Iraq,' ABCNews.com, 23 October 2008.

285 Bacevich (2013), p. 125.

286 Brian Brady, 'Afghan Civilians Pay Lethal Price for New Policy on Air Strikes: Reducing "Collateral Damage" is Seen as a "Secondary Consideration" as the Coalition Prepares Withdrawal,' *Independent*, 31 July 2011.

287 Exum was interviewed in March 2012 by Scahill (2013), p. 175.

288 Riza (2013), p. 119.

289 The impunity of the CIA became especially graphic in the wake of a scandal involving the Agency's illegal accessing of senators' computers while an investigation into the Bush-era torture program was under way. A committee selected by CIA Director John Brennan to investigate the obvious breach of US law declined to seek penalties. See Matt Apuzzo and Mark Mazzetti, 'Investigators Said to Seek No Penalty for CIA's Computer Search,' *New York Times*, 19 December 2014.

290 Andrew Quinn, 'Clinton Says Gaddafi Must Go,' Reuters, 28 February 2011.

291 A contingent of women persuaded Obama to bomb Libya. See John Avlon, 'Libya Airstrikes: The Women who Called for War,' *The Daily Beast*, 20 March 2011.

292 Errol Morris' Academy Award-winning documentary *The Fog of War: Eleven Lessons from the Life of Robert S. McNamara* (2003) examines the Tonkin Gulf incident in detail.

293 BBC News, 'Syria Crisis: Cameron Loses Commons Vote on Syria Action,' 30 August 2013.

294 Williams (2013), p. 235.

295 Obama appears to have developed something of an obsession with Anwar al-Awlaki. See Klaidman (2012), p. 261. Scahill (2013) hypothesizes that excessive attention may have been directed to Al-Awlaki for the simple reason that he wrote in English and so his words were readily accessible to CIA analysts, many of whom are ignorant of Arabic.

296 Ami Ayalon is interviewed by director Dror Moreh in *The Gatekeepers* (2012).

297 Paul Pillar, a National Intelligence Officer for the Middle East from 2000 to 2005, was interviewed by Charles Ferguson for the film *No End in Sight: Iraq's Descent into Chaos* (2007). Along with most of the other officials who agreed to be interviewed (many declined), Pillar was critical of the way the occupation of Iraq was handled, but nonetheless remarked that 'no matter how perfect the execution had been, we would have had a deep, deep difficulty to deal with. And I think on balance, that tilts the argument in favor of the fool's errand position.' The complete interviews for the film have been collected into a book: Charles Ferguson, *No End in Sight: Iraq's Descent into Chaos* (2008).

298 Faysal Makram, 'US and Yemen Step Up the Fight Against Al-Qaeda,' *Al Monitor*, 30 May 2012.

299 Ahmed (2013); and Shahzad Bashir and Robert D. Crews (eds) *Under the Drones: Modern Lives in the Afghanistan-Pakistan Borderlands* (2012).

300 Kareem Fahim, 'As Hopes for Reform Fade in Bahrain, Protesters Turn Anger on United States,' *New York Times*, 23 June 2012.

301 Ronald L. Ray, 'Were US and Israel Behind Egyptian Military Coup d'Etat?' *American Free Press*, 16 August 2013.

302 Eric Schmitt, 'US Training Elite Antiterror Troops in Four African Nations,' *New York Times*, 26 May 2014.

303 Weiner (2007), pp. 409–20.

304 Private Manning was convicted of most of the crimes with which he was charged but not 'aiding and abetting the enemy'. On 3 September 2013, Manning filed a Petition for Commutation of Sentence, along with a request for a pardon from President Obama, who had praised whistleblowers during his 2008 campaign.

305 Associated Press, 'Pentagon Sets Sights on Public Opinion,' 5 February 2009.

306 Former President Bill Clinton apparently influenced Obama's decision to begin providing weapons to the Syrian rebels. See Reuters, 'Bill Clinton Urges More Forceful US Response on Syria: Report,' 13 June 2013.

307 In 40 percent of the cases, police work was the most effective, and in 43 percent of the cases, political conciliation worked. RAND Corporation, 'How Terrorist Groups End,' 2008.

308 Peter Bergen, 'Obama's High-stakes Drone War in Yemen,' CNN Opinion, 21 April 2014.

309 Michael R. Gordon, 'Crisis in the Balkans: The Admission; NATO Admits the Mistaken Bombing of Civilians,' *New York Times,* 16 April 1999.

310 Many persons attempting to flee the chaos and insecurity in post-Gaddafi Libya have drowned. See Jim Yardley, 'Rising Toll on Migrants Leaves Europe in Crisis; 900 May Be Dead at Sea,' *New York Times,* 20 April 2015.

311 Geraghty (2009), p. 185.

312 Hastings (2012), p. 378.

313 Colonel Lang made this statement during a February 2011 interview by Scahill (2013), p. 468.

314 John Arnaldi compares the number of deaths on 11 September 2001 with those from four categories of preventable causes: child abuse/neglect; automobile-related deaths; iatrogenic deaths; and tobacco use-related deaths. See: 'Applied Ethics, Human Security, and the War on Terrorism,' in Charles P. Webel and John A. Arnaldi (eds) *The Ethics and Efficacy of the Global War on Terrorism* (2011), p. 5.

315 The Stimson Center report, 'Recommendations and Report of the Stimson Task Force on US Drone Policy,' issued on 26 June 2014, was produced by a taskforce including former CIA and military officers, academics and industry executives. The report questions the efficacy, not the morality, of the drone program.

316 In *The Shock and Awing of America: Echoing Consequences of Fear and Alienation* (2013), Ximena Ortiz diagnoses what she terms the 'Third Worlding' of the United States, as it increasingly adopts tactics – torture, summary execution, extraordinary rendition or 'disappearings' – pervasive in the Third World, but under the pretense that all of this is being done with extraordinary care and precision.

317 Mary Harper, *Getting Somalia Wrong? Faith, War and Hope in a Shattered State* (2012), pp. 171–84.

318 Gardner (2013), p. 223.

319 The story of General Zia in Pakistan is a typical case where US military aid propped up a dictator and prevented democratic reform. The billions of dollars bestowed upon the dictator can also be credited with the sprawling Pakistan intelligence agency, ISI (Inter-Services Intelligence), which now

works at cross purposes to US interests. See *Bhutto* (2011), directed by Duane Baughman and Johnny O'Hara, for a colorful portrayal of the recent political history of Pakistan.

320 The conflation of defense and intelligence by the US government was arguably hastened by the establishment of an independent intelligence apparatus housed at the Pentagon. During the George W. Bush administration, both the secretary of defense, Donald Rumsfeld, and the vice president, Dick Cheney, pushed for an independent information collection and analysis capacity at the Department of Defense. See Todd, Bloch and Fitzgerald (2009), Chapter 3.

321 Colin Powell cited in Geraghty (2010), p. 70.

322 The story of 'Carlos the Jackal' and many of his collaborators who claimed to be fighting in the name of 'the oppressed', especially the Palestinians in Israel, is portrayed in an epic film by Olivier Assayas, *Carlos* (2010).

323 Tony Blair cited in Todd, Bloch and Fitzgerald (2009), p. 100.

324 Holly Yan, 'Why is ISIS so Successful at Luring Westerners?' CNN World, 7 October 2014.

325 Michael Walzer, *Just and Unjust Wars* (1977) and *Arguing about War* (2004).

326 St Thomas Aquinas, *Summa Theologiae* (1948), Part 2-2, Q 64, Article 7, Volume 10, p. 209.

327 With regard to drone killing, just war theorists have occupied every conceivable position, perfectly in keeping with their often vigorous disagreements over which wars in reality count as 'just'. Some scholars have proposed that the classical requirements of *jus ad bellum* and *jus in bello* should be updated to accommodate drones, a prime example of molding theory to fit technologically driven policy. See Daniel Brunstetter and Megan Braun, 'The Implications of Drones on the Just War Tradition,' *Ethics & International Affairs*, 2011, 25(3): 337–58.

328 Rumsfeld's statement was made during a Department of Defense news briefing on 11 April 2003.

BOOKS CITED

Aaronson, Trevor (2013) *Terror Factory: Inside the FBI's Manufactured War on Terrorism*. Brooklyn, NY: Ig Publishers.

Ahmed, Akbar (2013) *The Thistle and the Drone: How America's War on Terror Became a Global War on Tribal Islam*. Washington, DC: Brookings Institution Press.

Aquinas, St Thomas (1948) *Summa Theologiae*. London: Burns, Oates & Washburne.

Bacevich, Andrew J. (2013) *Breach of Trust: How Americans Failed Their Soldiers and Their Country*. New York, NY: Metropolitan Books.

Bashir, Shahzad and Robert D. Crews (eds) (2012) *Under the Drones: Modern Lives in the Afghanistan-Pakistan Borderlands*. Cambridge, MA: Harvard University Press.

Benjamin, Medea (2013) *Drone Warfare: Killing by Remote Control*. New York, NY: Verso.

Bergen, Peter (2012) *Manhunt: The Ten-year Search for Bin Laden – from 9/11 to Abbottabad*. New York, NY: Crown.

Berko, Anat (2012) *The Smarter Bomb: Women and Children as Suicide Bombers*. Lanham, MD: Rowman & Littlefield.

Boggs, Carl (ed.) (2003) *Masters of War: Militarism and Blowback in the Era of American Empire*. New York, NY: Routledge.

Boot, Max (2006) *War Made New: Technology, Warfare, and the Course of History 1500 to Today*. New York, NY: Gotham Books.

Calhoun, Laurie (2013) *War and Delusion: A Critical Examination*. New York, NY: Palgrave Macmillan.

Carroll, Andrew (ed.) (2006) *Operation Homecoming: Iraq, Afghanistan, and the Home Front, in the Words of U.S. Troops and Their Families.* New York, NY: Random House.

Davies, James (2013) *Cracked: The Unhappy Truth about Psychiatry.* New York, NY: Pegasus Books.

Erlich, Reese (2014) *Inside Syria: The Backstory of Their Civil War and What the World Can Expect.* Amherst, NY: Prometheus Books.

Feinstein, Andrew (2011) *The Shadow World: Inside the Global Arms Trade.* New York, NY: Farrar, Straus and Giroux.

Ferguson, Charles (2008) *No End in Sight: Iraq's Descent into Chaos.* New York, NY: PublicAffairs (Perseus Books).

Gardner, Lloyd C. (2013) *Killing Machine: The American Presidency in the Age of Drone Warfare.* New York, NY: New Press.

Geraghty, Tony (2009) *Soldiers of Fortune: A History of the Mercenary in Modern Warfare.* New York, NY: Pegasus Books.

Geraghty, Tony (2010) *Black Ops: The Rise of Special Forces in the C.I.A., the S.A.S., and Mossad.* New York, NY: Pegasus Books.

Goodman, Melvin A. (2008) *Failure of Intelligence: The Decline and Fall of the CIA.* Lanham, MD: Rowman & Littlefield.

Goodman, Melvin A. (2013) *National Insecurity: The Cost of American Militarism.* San Francisco, CA: City Lights Books.

Greenwald, Glenn (2014) *No Place to Hide: Edward Snowden, the NSA, and the US Surveillance State.* New York, NY: Metropolitan Books.

Grossman, Lt Colonel Dave (1995) *On Killing: The Psychological Cost of Learning to Kill in War and Society.* Boston, MA: Little Brown and Company.

Harman, Gilbert (1986) *Change in View.* Cambridge, MA: MIT Press.

Harper, Mary (2012) *Getting Somalia Wrong? Faith, War and Hope in a Shattered State.* London: Zed Books.

Hastings, Michael (2012) *The Operators: The Wild and Terrifying Inside Story of America's War in Afghanistan*. New York, NY: Blue Rider Press.

Johnsen, Gregory D. (2013) *The Last Refuge: Yemen, Al-Qaeda, and America's War in Arabia*. New York, NY: W. W. Norton & Company.

Klaidman, Daniel (2012) *Kill or Capture: The War on Terror and the Soul of the Obama Presidency*. New York, NY: Houghton Mifflin Harcourt.

Kyle, Chris, with Scott McEwen and Jim DeFelice (2012) *American Sniper: The Autobiography of the Most Lethal Sniper in U.S. Military History*. New York, NY: Harper.

Martin, Matthew J., with Charles W. Sasser (2010) *Predator: The Remote-control Air War over Iraq and Afghanistan: A Pilot's Story*. Minneapolis, MN: Zenith Press.

Mazzetti, Mark (2013) *The Way of the Knife: The CIA, a Secret Army, and a War at the Ends of the Earth*. New York, NY: Penguin Press.

McCoy, Alfred W. (2003) *The Politics of Heroin: CIA Complicity in the Global Drug Trade, Afghanistan, Southeast Asia, Central America, Colombia*. Revised edition. Chicago, IL: Lawrence Hill Books.

McNamara, Robert S. (1996) *In Retrospect: The Tragedy and Lessons of Vietnam*. New York, NY: Vintage.

Mejía, Camilo (2007) *Road from Ar Ramadi: The Private Rebellion of Sergeant Camilo Mejía*. New York, NY: New Press.

Mill, J. S. (1985 [1863]) *Utilitarianism*. Indianapolis, IN: ITT Bobbs-Merrill.

Ortiz, Ximena (2013) *The Shock and Awing of America: Echoing Consequences of Fear and Alienation*. CreateSpace Independent Publishing Platform.

Orwell, George (1996 [1945]) *Animal Farm*. New York, NY: Signet Classics.

Orwell, George (2008 [1949]) *Nineteen Eighty-four*. New York, NY: Penguin Books.

Powell, Colin L. and Joseph E. Persico (1995) *My American Journey*. New York, NY: Random House.

Riza, M. Shane (2013) *Killing without Heart*. Washington, DC: Potomac Books.

Rohde, David and Kristen Mulvihill (2010) *A Rope and a Prayer: A Kidnapping from Two Sides*. New York, NY: Viking.

Sanger, David E. (2012) *Confront and Conceal: Obama's Secret Wars and Surprising Use of American Power*. New York, NY: Crown Books.

Scahill, Jeremy (2007) *Blackwater: The Rise of the World's Most Powerful Mercenary Army*. New York, NY: Nation Books.

Scahill, Jeremy (2013) *Dirty Wars: The World is a Battlefield*. New York, NY: Nation Books.

Shanahan, Timothy (ed.) (2005) *Philosophy 9/11: Thinking about the War on Terrorism*. Peru, IL: Carus Publishing Company.

Sifray, Micah L. and Christopher Cerf (1991) *The Gulf War Reader*. New York, NY: Random House.

Simons, Geoff (1996) *The Scourging of Iraq: Sanctions, Law and Natural Law*. New York, NY: Palgrave Macmillan.

Simons, Suzanne (2010) *Master of War: Blackwater USA's Erik Prince and the Business of War*. New York, NY: Harper.

Singer, P. W. (2009) *Wired for War: The Robotics Revolution and Conflict in the 21st Century*. New York, NY: Penguin Press.

Strawser, Bradley Jay (ed.) (2013) *Killing by Remote Control: The Ethics of an Unmanned Military*. New York, NY: Oxford University Press.

Todd, Paul, Jonathan Bloch and Patrick Fitzgerald (2009) *Spies, Lies and the War on Terror*. London: Zed Books.

Turse, Nick (2008) *The Complex: How the Military Invades Our Everyday Lives.* New York, NY: Metropolitan Books.

Turse, Nick (2013) *Kill Anything That Moves: The Real American War in Vietnam.* New York, NY: Metropolitan Books.

Walzer, Michael (1977) *Just and Unjust Wars.* New York, NY: Basic Books.

Walzer, Michael (2004) *Arguing about War.* New Haven, CT: Yale University Press.

Webel, Charles P. and John A. Arnaldi (eds.) (2011) *The Ethics and Efficacy of the Global War on Terrorism.* New York, NY: Palgrave Macmillan.

Weiner, Timothy (2007) *Legacy of Ashes: The History of the CIA.* New York, NY: Doubleday.

White, James E. (ed.) (2012) *War, Terrorism, Torture and Assassination.* Fourth edition. Boston, MA: Wadsworth.

Williams, Bryan Glyn (2013) *Predators: The CIA's Drone War on al Qaeda.* Washington, DC: Potomac Books.

Wright, Evan (2004) *Generation Kill: Devil Dogs, Iceman, Captain America, and the New Face of American War.* New York, NY: Putnam Books.

Zinn, Howard (2003) *A People's History of the United States.* New York, NY: HarperCollins.

FILMS CITED

Act of Valor (2012), directed by Scott Waugh and Mouse McCoy.

American Sniper (2014), directed by Clint Eastwood.

The American Soldier (1970), directed by Rainer Werner Fassbinder.

Battle for Haditha (2007), directed by Nick Broomfield.

The Battle of Algiers/La bataille d'Alger (1966), directed by Gillo Pontecorvo.

Bhutto (2011), directed by Duane Baughman and Johnny O'Hara.

The Bourne Identity (2002), directed by Doug Liman.

Breach (2007), directed by Billy Ray.

Carlos (2010), directed by Olivier Assayas.

CIA Secret Experiments (2008), directed by Nicole Teusch and Tria Thalman.

Collateral (2004), directed by Michael Mann.

Combat Diary: The Marines of Lima Company (2006), directed by Michael Epstein.

Dirty Wars (2013), directed by Richard Rowley.

Donnie Brasco (1997), directed by Mike Newell.

Fair Game (2010), directed by Doug Liman.

Flyboys (2006), directed by Tony Bill.

The Fog of War: Eleven Lessons from the Life of Robert S. McNamara (2003), directed by Errol Morris.

The Gatekeepers (2012), directed by Dror Moreh.

General Idi Amin Dada: A Self Portrait (1975), directed by Barbet Schroeder.

Generation Kill (2008), directed by Susanna White and Simon Cellan Jones.

The Godfather (1972), directed by Francis Ford Coppola.

The Godfather: Part II (1974), directed by Francis Ford Coppola.

Gunner Palace (2005), directed by Michael Tucker.

Howard Zinn: You Can't Be Neutral on a Moving Train (2004), directed by Deb Ellis and Denis Mueller.

The Iceman (2012), directed by Ariel Vromen.

Inside Iraq: The Untold Stories (2004), directed by Mike Shiley.

The Invisible War (2012), directed by Kirby Dick.

Iraq Raw: The Tuttle Tapes (2004), directed by Ryan Tuttle.

The Killer Elite (1975), directed by Sam Peckinpah.

The Last King of Scotland (2006), directed by Kevin Macdonald.

Lumumba (2000), directed by Raoul Peck.

Michael Collins (1996), directed by Neil Jordan.

The Most Dangerous Man in America: Daniel Ellsberg and the Pentagon Papers (2009), directed by Judith Ehrlich and Rick Goldsmith.

Munich (2005), directed by Steven Spielberg.

Murder by Contract (1958), directed by Irving Lerner.

No End in Sight: Iraq's Descent into Chaos (2007), directed by Charles Ferguson.

Operation Homecoming: Writing the Wartime Experience (2007), directed by Richard Robbins.

Pakistan Undercover (2009), directed by Doug Shultz.

Redacted (2007), directed by Brian De Palma.

Remote Control War: The Future of Unmanned Combat (2011), directed by Leif Kaldor.

Rise of the Drones (2013), directed by Peter Yost.

Safe House (2012), directed by Daniel Espinosa.

Le Samouraï (1967), directed by Jean-Pierre Melville.

Shoah (1985), directed by Claude Lanzmann.

The Sopranos (1999–2007), created by David Chase.

The Sorrow and the Pity/Le chagrin et la pitié (1969), directed by Marcel Ophüls.

Standard Operating Procedure (2008), directed by Errol Morris.

Syriana (2005), directed by Stephen Gaghan.

Taxi to the Dark Side (2007), directed by Alex Gibney.

The Terminator (1984), directed by James Cameron.

Terminator Salvation (2009), directed by McG.

This is War: Memories of Iraq (2007), directed by Gary Mortensen.

The Tillman Story (2010), directed by Amir Bar-lev.

Top Gun (1986), directed by Tony Scott.

Top Gun over Moscow (1996), directed by Lance K. Shultz and Lynne Squilla.

Unmanned: America's Drone Wars (2013), directed by Robert Greenwald.

Why We Fight (2006), directed by Eugene Jarecki.

Zero Dark Thirty (2012), directed by Kathryn Bigelow.

ACRONYMS AND ABBREVIATIONS

AQAP	Al-Qaeda on the Arabian Peninsula
AUMF	Authorization for Use of Military Force
CIA	Central Intelligence Agency
DARPA	Defense Advanced Research Projects Agency
DoD	Department of Defense
FBI	Federal Bureau of Investigation
GWOT	'Global War on Terror'
HUMINT	human intelligence
ICC	International Criminal Court
IED	improvised explosive device
IRA	Irish Republican Army
ISIL	Islamic State in Iraq and the Levant
ISIS	Islamic State in Iraq and Al-Sham
JSOC	Joint Special Operations Command
KLA	Kosovo Liberation Army
LOGCAP	Logistics Civil Augmentation Program
NFL	National Football League
NGO	nongovernmental organization
NSA	National Security Agency
PMC	private military company
PTSD	post-traumatic stress disorder
ROE	rules of engagement
RPA	remotely piloted aircraft
SAS	Special Air Service

SIGINT	signals intelligence
TADS	terrorist attack disruption strikes
UAV	unmanned aerial vehicle
UCAV	unmanned combat aerial vehicle
UN	United Nations
VA	Veterans Administration
WMD	weapons of mass destruction

ACKNOWLEDGMENTS

I received a great deal of encouragement during the writing of this book from a variety of people but was initially inspired by Medea Benjamin to focus specifically on drone killing. I reviewed her book, *Drone Warfare: Remote Control Killing*, for *New Politics* in early 2013. I agreed with nearly everything Benjamin wrote but worried that she would alienate readers on the other side of the divide by referring to drone killing as 'murder'. Many people opposed to drone warfare, including Benjamin and her colleagues at CODEPINK, directly perceive what is wrong with the remote-control killing of unarmed suspects and do not need any arguments. I wrote this book primarily for the people who disagree. I hope that drone program supporters will accept my challenge to read *We Kill Because We Can* and that at last we can have a long overdue public debate.

I have been writing essays about war since the 1999 NATO bombing of Kosovo. All of the people I have spoken to and interacted with since 1999 have influenced me in one way or another, but on the drone front I am especially appreciative of Daniele Archibugi, truly a kindred spirit, who first referenced my original *Peace Review* essay, 'The Strange Case of Summary Execution by Predator Drone', way back in 2004, before anyone else seemed to register that there was a problem. When I told Daniele about my drone book project, he matter-of-factly replied that targeted killing is a war crime and reiterated his surprise that so little has been written on the topic to date. In addition to offering arguments against the practice, I have endeavored in this book to illuminate factors which help to explain how the leader of the free world who campaigned on a peace platform came to be a self-styled drone warrior.

Robert Higgs, former editor of the *Independent Review* and a great champion of liberty, is one of my longest-standing allies on matters martial, having published several of my essays on soldiering, just war theory and political corruption. Marvin and Betty Mandell, the former editors of *New Politics*, published some of my relevant essays on war crimes and black ops, as well as my review of Medea Benjamin's book. I am equally grateful to the editors of *Peace Review*, who have published ten of my essays since 2000, including my ideas about military virtue, human rights and lethal centrism, which are woven throughout the present work.

The feedback of Stephen Shalom and Ajume Wingo was very helpful to me as both had read and reviewed my previous book, *War and Delusion: A Critical Examination*, which was published in 2013. Stephen Shalom read every word and footnote of the first full draft of my text (long before Obama's second call for war on Syria) and saved me from numerous errors. I initially intended to minimize discussion of just war theory in *We Kill Because We Can* because it had been the focus of *War and Delusion*. When, during the late stages of editing, I decided to add an Appendix, 'Drone Killing and Just War Theory', Ajume Wingo pored over the new text and confirmed that it should be included. Ajume and I have been talking about the logic of terrorism and tyranny since we first met. I feel fortunate to have him as an ever-willing interlocutor, moral supporter and intellectual ally.

I am grateful to Ken Barlow, my editor, for his support and suggestions. I received detailed reports from two anonymous reviewers who confirmed my belief that this book is badly needed. Two of my favorite test readers have turned out to be my parents,

ACKNOWLEDGMENTS

Charles Alexander Calhoun and Mary Margaret Brock Calhoun-Howe. My dad, a retired civil engineer whose four-decade career was spent working for the US federal government, was especially positive about my discussions of Mafia contract killing (Chapter 3), the role of politics in drone policy (Chapter 9) and the demise of military virtue (Chapter 11). My mom, a retired public relations company CEO, found the Trayvon Martin–Abdulrahman al-Awlaki analogy (Chapter 6) quite telling, and she corrected errors in my initial discussion of the case. She also offered sound advice during my search for the perfect publisher for this work, Zed Books.

I am thankful also to all of the other people – family members, friends, colleagues and acquaintances – who have patiently listened to me drone on about war, terrorism, tyranny and hitmen over the years. They are too numerous to list, but no less appreciated.

Finally, I am grateful to not only the brave whistleblowers, but also the courageous truth-seeking journalists who have risked their lives by traveling to some of the most dangerous parts of the world to find out why and how they have become so very dangerous.

INDEX

Aaronson, Trevor, 246, 351n170, 364

Abbottabad, Pakistan, 84, 110, 138, 349n147

abduction (kidnapping) by the state. *See* 'extraordinary rendition'

Abu Ghraib prison, 23, 87, 189, 202, 239, 259, 281

Academi, 244

'actionable intelligence', 21, 23-4, 73, 82, 99, 108, 122, 244-7, 272

Adams, Gordon, 251

Adolphus, Gustavus, 257

Aegis, 238, 240, 322

Afghanistan, 262
    corruption during, 248, 328
    crimes committed by US personnel, 20, 23, 39-40, 117, 181, 259-9
    drone use in, 2, 33-4, 91, 117-8, 143, 148, 161-2, 168, 174, 326
    JSOC raids, 91-2
    postwar insecurity, 175, 226, 245, 250, 257, 285
    Soviet war on, 221, 281
    US invasion and occupation of, 2, 14, 17, 25-6, 37, 40, 72, 81, 91-2, 99-100, 112-3, 117-120, 122-3, 143, 148, 161-2, 174-5, 214, 219, 240, 273, 292, 303, 311, 313

Af-Pak, 67, 91-2

Africa, 154, 283
    drone bases in, 5, 308-9
    postcolonial conflicts, 49, 125, 286, 307

African Americans, 136

Ahmed, Akbar, 67, 122, 350n152, 364

Air Force (USAF), 58, 176, 186

AK-47s, 182, 305

Al-Assad, Bashar, 211-2, 215, 217, 228, 356n227, 357n242

Al-Awlaki, Abdulrahman, xvi, 90, 138-40, 202, 343n101

Al-Awlaki, Anwar, xvi, 19, 31, 51, 84, 100, 109-11, 113-6, 119, 124-5, 129-30, 218, 221, 310, 315, 346n130, 357n249, 360n295
    public statements by, 82, 130, 348n141

Al-Awlaki, Nasser, 31, 111-2, 346n129

Al-Balawi, Humam, 71-2, 162, 342n83

Al-Bayda province, Iraq, 22

Al-Farekh, Mohanad Mahmoud, 344n108

Al-Harithi, Ali Qaed Sunian, 13

Al-Hijazi, Abu Ahmad (aka Kemal Darwish), 348n131

Al-Kazami, Muhammed, 336n17

Al-Libbi, Ibn al Sheikh, 20-1, 336n14

Al-Qaeda, ix, 6, 7, 13-5, 17, 20, 22-5, 29, 31, 34, 36, 44, 47, 59, 66, 75, 92-4, 98, 100-1, 108, 110, 113, 129, 137-8, 140, 161-2, 168-9, 172, 174, 178, 186, 207, 212-3, 221-4, 237, 245-6, 269, 299, 303-4, 308, 310, 316, 319, 334, 336n14, 336n17, 343n97, 352n177, 356n236
  on the Arabian Peninsula (AQAP), 110, 299, 347n130

Al-Shabaab, 221, 235, 304, 308

Albright, Madeleine, 96, 160, 269

Alexis, Aaron, 355n220

Algeria, 20, 35, 349n148

Alston, Philip, 142

American Civil Liberties Union (ACLU), 355n223

Amin, Idi, 59, 340n64 Amnesty International, 60, 74, 343n97

Amin, Ruhul, vii-viii

Angola, 40

'angry poor people', 167, 169, 178, 234, 274, 305-6

Annan, Kofi, 337n21

anti-Americanism, 28-9, 56, 119, 123, 138, 167, 216, 222, 252, 303, 317

anti-drone groups, xvi, 5, 58, 335n2

anxiety, 6, 71, 186, 188, 192-3, 197-9, 200, 234

Aquinas, Saint Thomas, 325, 327

Arabs, 56, 70

Argentina, 20

Aristotle, 310

assassination, 4, 7, 33-5, 38, 40, 42, 44-6, 60, 78, 84, 87, 109, 120, 141-3, 148, 173, 182, 201, 227, 302, 307, 310, 328, 331, 335n1, 338n33, 338n41, 339n47
  See also targeted killing 'associates' (of terrorist groups), 17, 50, 67, 74-5, 163, 237, 333, 349n148

Augustine, Saint, 325

Aurora, Colorado, 323

Authorization for Use of Military Force (AUMF), 308-9, 356n236

Ayalon, Ami, 77, 277, 342n87, 361n296

Aznar, José María, 290

Ba'ath party, 149, 249

Bacevich, Andrew, 259, 339n49, 342n90

'bad apples', 39, 258, 281

Bagram prison, 23, 87, 202, 239, 259

Bahrain, 217, 284, 361n300

'banality of evil', 77

battlefield, 37, 58, 61, 70, 131, 146, 258, 272, 320, 331

'no boots' battlefields, 8, 61, 147, 154, 159, 177, 185, 201, 253, 262, 273, 288, 294, 297, 310

'world is a battlefield', 27, 129, 141, 151, 293, 330

Beahan, Kermit, 158

Bedouins, 22

beheadings, 215, 228, 266

Belgrade, (former Yugoslavia), 47, 259

Benghazi, Libya, 214

Benjamin, Medea, 5, 129, 335n5, 343n116

Berlin Wall, 47

Bibi, Mamana, 60, 302, 330, 334

Bigelow, Kathryn, 245, 349n147

Bin Laden, Khalid, 138

Bin Laden, Osama, 6, 17, 25, 26, 42-5, 82, 94, 123, 177, 212-3, 221, 223, 227, 235, 299, 306-7, 319, 333, 338n33

execution of, 19, 25, 61, 64, 84, 110, 153, 221-2, 245, 314

Biya, Paul, xi

Black and Tans (British), 36

black ops, 5, 35-37, 43, 45, 47-8, 50-1, 67, 97, 143, 154, 182, 251, 253, 338n38

Blacksburg, Virginia, 323

Blackwater Worldwide, 174, 238, 240, 244, 254, 322, 346n127, 347n138, 358n265

Blair, Tony, x, 43, 290, 316

Blee, Richard, 179

Blix, Hans, 225

blowback, 96, 146, 220, 223, 226, 229, 261, 307, 323

body count (as efficacy measure), 89, 99, 246, 317

Boeing, 243, 247

Boland Amendment, 287

Boot, Max, 251

Bouchiki, Ahmed, 40, 44-5

bounty hunters, 81, 122, 245, 248

Bremer, Paul, 184

Brennan, John, 31, 92, 114-5, 127, 129, 138, 282, 345n119, 346n130, 355n221, 360n289

bribery, 15, 18, 21, 68, 82, 86, 108, 121, 130, 148, 152, 154, 201, 246, 279

Britain, vii-viii, xi-xii, 239, 318,

British Parliament, 211, 215, 269

Brown, Michael, 145

Brussels, Belgium, xiii

Bryant, Brandon, 65, 166, 178, 186, 196, 200, 203

burden of proof, 85, 99, 145, 176, 224-5, 322

bureaucracy and bureaucrats, xv, 52, 59, 69, 116, 122, 124, 183-4, 188, 209, 230, 251-2, 266, 312, 355n221

Burkina Faso, 309

burnout (of drone operators), 164, 166, 196, 273

Bush, George H.W., 47, 209, 288, 332

Bush, George W., 14-5, 19, 24-5, 34-5, 41-44, 49, 128, 148, 171-2, 190, 209-10, 213, 216, 219-20, 266, 268, 272, 290, 296-8, 326, 332, 338n33

administration, 51, 63, 79, 85, 87-8, 92, 113, 139, 151-4, 171, 199, 213, 219, 224-27, 288, 297, 308-9, 316, 321, 329, 336n15, 343n100, 363n320
See also Cheney, Dick
'Mission Accomplished', 172, 210
State of the Union address (2003), 35, 338n35

Cameron, David, vii-viii, xi, 360n293
Cameroon, xi
Camp Chapman, 71, 162
Canada, xi
capitalism, 68, 238, 250
capital punishment, vii, 50, 120, 190, 265
Carter, Jimmy, 338n33
Castro, Fidel, 38
Center for Civilians in Conflict (CIVIC), 343n97
Central Command (US CENTCOM), 193
Central Intelligence Agency (US CIA), 11, 22, 31, 36, 38, 40-2, 46-8, 67, 72, 122, 129, 162, 202, 207, 212, 216-7, 219, 336n15, 337n26, 338n37, 338n39, 338n41, 339n47, 339n48, 343n100, 345n119, 349n147, 350n155, 354n212, 355n221, 355n223, 355n224, 356n233, 360n289, 360n295, 362n315
drone use by, xv, 11, 13-4, 16-8, 27, 33-4, 46, 48, 50, 55-6, 86-8, 91, 93, 96-8, 114-5, 117-8, 122, 138-9, 147, 151, 179, 198, 217, 235, 245-7, 271, 282-3, 285
militarization of, 27, 90-3, 96-9, 181, 198
mistakes by, 16-8, 38, 40, 42, 46-8, 50, 56, 72, 87-8, 99, 122, 142, 161-2, 211-2, 216, 227, 247, 285, 313
'checks and balances', 116
chemical weapons, 47, 211-2, 215, 243, 356n227
Cheney, Dick, 15, 34, 43, 227, 238-9, 248, 287, 350n155, 358n254, 363n320
Chile, 20
China, xiii
embassy in Belgrade, bombing of, 47
Chomsky, Noam, 129
Church Committee, 42, 48
Church, Frank, 42, 48
Churchill, Winston, 64
civilians, 26-7, 92-3, 146, 194-6, 201, 213, 219, 223, 258, 260, 292, 311, 316
definition of, 52, 71, 143, 148
during wartime, 1, 4, 6, 47, 80, 58, 90, 117, 123-4, 130, 157-8, 171-3, 187-8, 202, 211, 226, 240, 242-4, 261-2, 268, 271, 309, 312, 325, 328, 346n127
effects of drone strikes on, 22, 56-7, 71, 80, 88, 92, 98, 100, 108-9, 113-5, 127, 128,

162-3, 177, 181-2, 207, 230, 232, 242, 261, 264, 272, 296-7, 307-8, 312, 317, 328, 343n97, 345n116
See also conscripts, private contractors
civil rights, 110, 115-6, 315
Clermont-Ferrand, France, 173
Clinton, Bill, 42, 47, 160, 210, 290, 339n48, 339n49, 361n306
Clinton, Hillary, 268-9
Coalition Provisional Authority (CPA), 149, 229
Order 17, 184
CODEPINK, 5, 335n2
coercion, 15, 279, 288, 322
Cold War, 38, 46, 48, 68, 124, 151, 238, 247, 286, 292, 315
Cole, Mary, 207, 355n223
Cole (USS destroyer), 13
collaborators, 68, 94, 119, 163, 272, 283, 331, 363n322
collateral damage, 1, 19, 26, 44-5, 51, 48, 60, 71, 80, 85, 87, 96, 98, 110, 113, 143-4, 147, 150, 153, 163, 181, 183, 198, 218, 234-5, 261, 293, 295, 307, 314, 328, 330-1, 334, 349n150
'Collateral Murder', 182-4, 188
Collins, Michael, 36, 338n36
colonialism, 307
Columbine, Colorado, 322
combatants, 1, 34, 42-3, 52, 70, 92-3, 98, 131, 138-9, 157, 160, 169, 173, 181, 187-9, 224, 234, 260-2, 265, 271, 295, 309-10, 321, 349n148

See also 'unlawful combatants'
commander in chief, 27, 71, 90-1, 145, 158, 165, 190, 194, 210, 213, 225-6, 257, 262, 267, 295, 312, 320
See also 'legitimate authority'
communism, 38, 48, 196, 237, 315
confirmation bias, 55, 86, 252
conscience, xvi, 89, 126, 164, 178-9, 186, 196, 280-1, 320, 328, 332
conscripts, 189, 258, 260, 333
Constitution of the United States, 41, 73, 111-2, 114, 131, 133, 266, 287, 293, 346n123
contract killers. *See* hitmen
Coppola, Francis Ford, 65
corruption, moral 38, 75, 117, 270, 334
corruption of evidence, 85
counterinsurgency (COIN), 245
counterterrorism measures, x, 23, 35, 72, 187, 199, 220, 246, 261, 285, 291, 301, 308, 310, 319, 342n87, 344n108
courage and cowardice, 5, 65, 158-60, 168, 172, 181, 188, 210-3, 229-30, 257, 262-4, 267-9, 266-7, 322, 350n158
court-martial, 39, 175, 189, 240
Creech Air Force Base, 58, 99, 167-8
'crowd killing', 63, 139, 242, 253
Cuba, 38
See also Guantánamo Bay prison
cyberattacks, 127, 347n135, 357n240

Darwish, Kemal (aka Abu Ahmad al-Hijazi), 347n131

Datta Khel, Pakistan, 22, 242

death penalty. *See* capital punishment

defense, national, 38, 49, 51, 59, 79, 84, 91, 141, 243, 248, 253, 260, 267, 274-5, 290, 295-6, 302, 316, 323

See also self-defense

Defense Advanced Research Projects Agency (DARPA), 231, 235, 250

Delta Marines (US), 37

democracy, 51, 114, 116, 119, 125-6, 149, 220, 229, 240, 254, 283-6, 284, 297-8, 309, 313, 315, 319

Department of Defense, US (DoD), 29, 33, 98, 117, 148, 159, 247, 291, 313, 354n210, 358n253, 363n320, 363n328

Department of Justice (US), 59, 112, 116, 140, 218, 335n1

Detroit, Michigan, 84, 346n130

Diem, Ngo Dinh, 38

Diskin, Yuval, 166, 351n171

'disposition matrix', 70, 139

dissent, 6, 51, 75, 111, 119, 121, 124, 126, 130, 139, 142, 173, 194-5, 200, 202, 209, 212, 220, 223, 266, 279

dissidents, 70, 126, 131, 217-8, 223, 275, 279, 302-3, 308

soldiers, 124-6, 128-9, 182, 189-90, 200, 202, 223, 288-9, 308, 353n203, 353n204, 361n304

Divine Rights of Kings, 331

Djibouti, 309

doctors, 144, 192, 197-9, 228-9, 257

See also psychiatry

double effect, doctrine of, 327-37

'double tap' strikes, 8, 69

Drone Age, 13, 24, 34-5, 52, 57, 67, 69-71, 73, 75, 82, 93, 95, 97, 109, 114, 181, 183, 203, 213, 226, 229, 260, 263, 265, 274, 293, 302, 315

drones. *See* unmanned aerial vehicles (UAVs).

Drone Watch, 335n2

drugs, 195

illegal, 192

prescription, 185, 188, 191-3

due process, 18, 50, 153, 237, 285, 303

vs. judicial process, 21, 110, 133

efficacy, 23, 27, 218, 292, 317, 355n224

Egypt, 40, 237, 285, 339n48

Eichmann, Adolf, 139

Eisenhower, Dwight D., 238

EKIA (Enemy Killed in Action), xi

Ellsberg, Daniel, 339n53

Emwazi, Mohammed (aka 'Jihadi John'), viii

'enhanced interrogation techniques', 20, 34-5, 47, 51, 87, 152, 171, 214

See also torture

entrepreneurs, war, 238, 244, 248-9, 253

See also war profiteers

Eremenko, Paul, 231, 357n243
Ethell, Jeffrey L., 155, 350n156
euphemisms for homicide, vii, xv, 44, 58, 60, 115, 129, 131, 161, 164, 176, 183-4, 198, 203, 215, 234, 246, 261
    See also collateral damage
European Union (EU), vii, 50, 190
extrajudicial execution, 18, 33, 46, 73, 83, 89, 109, 111, 142, 148, 166, 349n149
'extraordinary rendition', 34-5, 40, 42, 52, 87, 152, 213, 227, 288, 291, 339n48, 362n316
Exum, Andrew, 77, 264, 342n88, 360n287

fallibility, 22, 39, 48, 50, 162, 265
Fallujah, Iraq, 70, 169, 259
Farouk, Umar, 84, 346n130
Farouq, Ahmed, 11
fascism, 20, 124
'feasibility', 26, 67, 115-6, 218, 229, 234, 302, 314
Federal Bureau of Investigation (US FBI), 246-7, 339n48, 340n59, 351n170
Federally Administered Tribal Areas (FATA), Pakistan, 92, 337n30
Feith, Douglas, 352n179
felony murder rule, 136, 146, 150, 330
Ferdaus, Rezwan, 275
Ferguson, Missouri, 145
fighter pilots, 155, 157-8, 350n156
'find, fix, finish', xv, 49, 81, 93, 247, 322

First World countries, 67, 95, 154, 209, 275, 285, 312, 314
Florida, 27, 135-6, 139
'fog of war', 45, 52, 265
Foley, James, 215
Ford, Gerald, 338n33
Foreign Intelligence Surveillance Act (FISA), 213
Fort Hood military base, 57, 71, 112, 119, 236, 323
France, xi, 189, 289, 315
    Vichy, 35-6, 122, 148-51, 172
Free Syria Army, 356n233
freedom of speech, 121, 131
    See also dissent
'friendly fire', 161-2, 188, 265

Gadahn, Adam, ix
Gaddafi, Muammar, 214, 268, 289, 333, 362n310
Gaza Strip, 360n152
General Atomics, 243
General Electric, 247
Geneva Conventions, 3, 5, 34, 42-3, 60-1, 92, 113, 291, 297, 309, 321
genocide, 139, 14, 272-3, 331, 333
Geraghty, Tony, 41, 184, 239, 297, 338n40, 339n45
Germany, xi, 315
    Nazi, 20, 109, 122, 139-41, 289, 345n121
Ghundi Kala village, Pakistan, 60
Gibbs, Robert, 137
global positioning system (GPS), 60, 69, 161
'Global War on Terror' (GWOT), 4, 13, 45, 81, 152, 169, 298, 301

Goebbels, Joseph, 289
Goodman, Melvin, 46, 90, 336n15
Gore, Al, 209
Gotti, John, 65
Green Berets (US), 37
Green Zone, Baghdad, 82, 358n256
Guantánamo Bay prison, 5, 56, 62-3, 87, 113, 203, 213, 291, 336n20
guilt, judicial, 6, 16-9, 21-2, 51-2, 56, 62, 69, 72-3, 81, 83, 85, 95, 112, 117, 119-20, 122, 128-30, 136, 138, 143, 146-7, 152-3, 162-3, 165, 222, 225, 255, 275, 282, 315, 321
    See also burden of proof
guilt, psychological, 164, 186, 196, 202, 226

habeas corpus, 116, 277, 308
Habsburgs, 257
Hadi, Abd Rabu Mansour, 216, 284-5
Haditha, Iraq, 259, 360n283
hadjis, 170, 181
Halliburton, 68, 238-9, 254
Hamburg, Germany, 27
Hasan, Nidal, 57, 71-2, 112, 119, 236, 266
Hassan, Osama Mustafa, 40
Hastings, Michael, 27, 129, 175, 299, 347n138, 348n139
hearsay, 21, 24, 73, 121, 152, 201
'hearts and minds', 99, 245, 270, 316
Hellfire missiles, 7, 13, 15, 18, 26, 43-4, 62, 71, 96, 98, 100, 108, 123, 139, 214, 233-4, 236-7,

248, 252, 266, 271, 301-2, 305-6, 310, 317, 325, 329, 357n245
Heyns, Christof, 142, 349n149
'high-value' targets, 16, 86, 100, 148
Hiroshima, Japan, 158
Hitler, Adolf, 64, 268, 279-80, 288-9, 318, 326
hitmen, 40, 63-6, 178, 274, 301, 340n59, 341n70
Hoh, Matthew, 175
Holder, Eric, 114, 116, 133, 335n1, 336n20
Holocaust. *See* Germany, Nazi
homicide, xvi, 7, 34-5, 45, 55, 59-60, 69, 74, 80, 88, 91-2, 98, 109, 112, 116, 120, 128, 130, 148, 184, 196, 203, 244, 246, 251, 254, 266, 283, 292, 294, 302, 304, 306, 311-2, 314, 316, 320, 329
    See also murder
homogenization. *See* institutions, conservative nature of
'hostile', 3, 62, 81, 92, 108, 121, 128, 138-9, 142, 148, 161, 165, 169, 175, 220, 224, 274, 306, 317, 331
human rights, 6, 7, 20, 47, 50, 61-2, 100, 124, 152, 181, 223, 237, 245, 290, 293, 296-7, 304, 314-6, 339n47, 343n97, 349n149
Human Rights Watch, 343n97
human security, 123, 144-5, 154, 173, 187, 213, 223, 228, 240, 296, 317, 358n256, 362n310

'humanitarian hawks', 312

'humanitarian intervention', 149, 253, 268, 272, 350n154

HUMINT (human intelligence), 86-7, 188

hunting metaphor, 69, 110, 168, 212, 220, 274

Hussain, Junaid, ix-x

Hussein, Saddam, 20, 25, 47, 64, 80, 82, 168, 174, 210, 214, 219, 225, 229, 249-50, 311-2, 325, 332, 336n14, 350n154

images, 65, 68, 95, 127, 153, 157-8, 189, 268, 271, 273, 317, 350n159
  of hawks as courageous and strong, 96, 209-10, 219, 229-30, 267-9, 279
  screen, in drone killing, 99, 161, 197-8, 203, 263

'imminent threat', xvi, 3, 59, 85, 93, 112-3, 116, 129, 131, 140, 218, 224, 234, 309, 321

improvised explosive devices (IEDs), 38, 239, 305

India, 28

informants, 21, 55-6, 69, 121-2, 246-7
  See also spies

institutional killing, 2, 59, 91, 109, 131, 164, 185, 198, 203, 236, 236, 253-4, 266, 283, 293, 302
  See also capital punishment

institutions, 1, 16, 35, 41, 48, 50, 64, 73, 94, 99, 116. 123, 142, 162, 188-9, 197, 200, 202, 213,

227, 287-8, 290-2, 308, 315-7, 330
  conservative nature of, 88-9, 97, 194, 199, 268, 274, 281, 343n100

'insurgent math', 171

insurgents, 2, 33, 67, 91, 98, 100, 121, 126, 149-50, 155, 162, 167, 170, 172, 176, 187, 215, 222, 241, 248-9, 303, 319

Intercept, ix, 341n69, 343n95

International Criminal Court (ICC), xi, 290, 322

internet, 119, 130, 215, 317

'invincible ignorance', 265

Iran, xiii, 127, 175, 318

Iran-Contra scandal, 287-8

Iraq, 42, 113
  1991 Gulf War, 25, 47, 80, 82, 95, 130, 210, 228, 332, 344n109, 350n154
  2003 invasion and occupation of, ix, 15, 21, 23-6, 28, 37, 39-40, 43, 47, 51, 57, 68, 70, 72, 80-3, 117-20, 122-3, 127, 141, 143-4, 148-9, 151-2, 154, 161, 170-2, 174, 181-5, 187-9, 191, 193, 196, 209-11, 213-7, 219-23, 225-6, 228-0, 235, 238-42, 244-5, 250, 254-5, 257-60, 270, 272-3, 281, 285, 292, 296-7, 303, 308, 311, 313, 326, 328-9, 333, 336n14, 336n15, 341n78, 345n117, 346n127, 350n155, 350n161, 352n192, 354n205

drone use in, xii, 2, 33-4, 83, 118, 144, 148, 151-2, 167-8, 172, 174, 183, 237

postwar conditions, 8391, 99-100, 150, 210, 237, 245, 249, 289, 358n256, 361n297

rules of engagement (ROE) during, 83, 88, 181-2, 184, 187, 242

Inter-Services Intelligence (Pakistan), 362n319

Ireland, 326

Irish Republican Army (IRA), 36

Islamabad, Pakistan, 214

Islamic State in Iraq and Al-Sham (ISIS, aka ISIL), viii, 211, 215-7, 221-2, 224, 228, 235, 248, 303-4, 310, 349n148, 356n236

Israel, vii, xi-xiii, 3, 34, 124, 142, 302, 339n49, 363n322

Facility 1391, 36

See also Mossad, Shin Bet

Italy, xi, 20, 40

jihad, 4, 7, 8, 25, 56, 70, 72, 82, 85, 108, 111, 119, 129, 137, 142, 153, 171, 174, 186, 211, 222-3, 303, 308, 336n14

jirga, 22, 242, 327

Johnsen, Gregory, 25, 336n17, 346n132, 347n137

Johnson, Jeh, 22

Johnson, Lyndon B., 269

Joint Special Operations Command (US JSOC), 81, 91, 118, 221, 286, 343n98, 353n200

Jordan, xi, 72, 217

journalism, 4, 13, 16, 27, 46, 71, 100, 121, 128-9, 163, 175, 182-3, 188, 215, 217, 228, 240, 246, 255, 341n78, 347n137, 348n139

'just war' tradition, 5, 6, 13, 43, 45, 94-6, 123, 142, 153, 158, 177, 188, 249, 261, 264, 270, 272, 291-3, 310, 312, 314, 321, 325-334

jus ad bellum and *jus in bello*, 325

See also double effect, doctrine of

Katrina, Hurricane, 28

Kellogg Brown & Root (KBR), 238

Kennedy, Edward, 252

Kennedy, John F., 38

Kerry, John, 153, 217

Khan, Qadir, 163

Khan, Reyaad, vii

Khan, Samir, 19

Khilji, Usama, 144

'kill chain', 67-8, 122, 161, 177, 183, 201, 322, 340n65

'kill committee', 75, 116, 122, 126, 137

'kill don't capture' policy, 8, 23, 28, 52, 73, 92, 99, 153, 214, 219, 227, 304, 310, 317, 329

'killing machine', 5, 88-9, 91, 99, 109, 217, 236, 283

'kinetic operations', 27, 184, 217, 261

See also euphemisms for homicide

Know Drones, 335n2

Kosovo, 326

Kosovo Liberation Army (KLA), 37
1999 NATO bombing of, 42, 57, 160, 210, 262, 297
Kuklinski, Richard, 66, 341n72
Kurds, 357n242
Kuwait, 47, 202, 318
Kyle, Chris, 352n189

landmines, 1
Lang, W. Patrick, 300, 362n313
last resort, 5, 45, 67, 71, 81, 85, 93-5, 144, 152-3, 229, 249, 272, 314, 320, 322, 325, 328, 344n110
Latin America, 38, 124
'legitimate authority', 84, 96, 325-32
See also 'just war' tradition
'lethal centrism', ix, xiii, 28, 73, 90, 97, 145, 182, 250
definition of, 73
lethality, 17, 93, 98-9, 160, 181, 186-7, 197-201, 234, 245, 250, 264, 273, 292, 311-3, 316-8
liberty, 4, 111, 115-6, 223, 283-4, 297, 304, 319
Libya, 26, 28, 92, 143, 148, 154, 162, 250, 257, 285, 362n310
2011 bombing of, 206-9, 217-8, 226, 260, 264, 281, 318, 352n291
Benghazi, 214
Lo Porto, Giovanni, ix
Lockheed Martin, 247
Logistics Civil Augmentation Program (LOGCAP), 238-9, 241

London, England, 316
Lowenthal, Mark, 97
Luciano, Charles ('Lucky'), 65
Lumumba, Patrice, 338n41

Mafia. See organized crime
Magdzas, Matthew, 190-1
magnet metaphor, 150, 171, 303, 308
Mahmudiyah, Iraq, 259
Mali, 92, 272, 286
Mandela, Nelson, 252, 306
Manicheanism, 292, 304, 332
Manning, Bradley Edward (since 2013, Chelsea Elizabeth), 124-6, 128-9, 182, 189-90, 200, 202, 223, 288-9, 308, 361n304
martial law, 24, 120, 145
Martin, Matthew J., 155, 167-9, 172, 174-8, 183, 186, 188, 201, 263, 351n174
Martin, Trayvon, 133, 135-8, 144, 146, 202
Mauritania, 285
McChrystal, Stanley, 91, 171, 342n88, 347n138, 348n139
McNamara, Robert S., 126, 198
McVeigh, Timothy, 63, 309
media, 129
mainstream, 13-4, 51, 172, 181, 210, 212, 244, 253, 346n130, 357n139
social, 119, 121, 130, 169, 182, 198, 201, 215, 317, 341n72
medication. See drugs
Mehsud, Baitullah, 72, 100, 345n116

Mehsud, Hakimullah, 105
Mejía, Camilo, 125, 189, 353n203
mercenaries. *See* private contractors
Middle East, xiii, 4, 95, 154, 216,
    283-4, 308-9
Milan, Italy, 40
militants, 22, 56, 88, 98, 129,
    162-3, 237, 261, 285, 308
  See also insurgents, 'partisans'
military aid, 15, 18, 33, 38, 99,
    130, 151, 175, 215, 217, 237,
    245, 283-5, 303, 311-2, 314,
    362n319
military-age men, 56, 71, 92, 161,
    169, 224-5, 331
  definition of, xi, 139, 148
military-industrial complex, 238,
    241, 253
Mill, John Stuart, 19
'mistakes were made', 117, 333
  See also CIA, mistakes by
Mobutu, Joseph, 338n41
Mogadishu, Somalia, 160
Mohammed, Khalid Sheikh, 219
moral blindness, 305
morality, 12, 13, 46, 60, 117, 148,
    327, 362n315
Morocco, 309
Mossad, 35-6, 40-1, 44-5, 154
mujahidin, 221, 316
Mullen, Michael, 171
Munich massacre, 36-7, 41, 153,
    338n38
murder, 28, 34, 40-1, 44-6, 53, 55,
    57-61, 63-5, 69, 73-4, 82, 85,
    112, 145, 159, 165, 177-8, 190,
    198, 203, 236, 244, 248, 252,

    282, 292-3, 301-2, 310, 315,
    319, 329-30, 338n70, 346n127
  by soldiers, 39, 259, 360n283
  mass murder, 59, 63, 158, 178,
    248, 314, 323, 326, 345n121,
    355n220
  See also felony murder rule, hitmen
Muslims, 5, 6, 25, 82, 108, 175,
    199, 255, 302
Muslim Brotherhood, 237
My Lai massacre (Vietnam), 39
Myers, Richard, 352n179

Nagasaki, Japan, 158
Najaf, Iraq, 259
napalm, 189
Nasr, Osama Mustafa Hassan, 40
National Guardsmen (US), 28, 190-1
National Security Agency (US NSA),
    124, 289, 348n140
National Security Council (US
    NSC), 117, 343n101
*National Security Strategy of the
    United States of America*, 43
NATO (North Atlantic Treaty
    Organization), 42, 57, 160, 210,
    262
Navy SEALS (US), 19, 84, 123, 153,
    260, 353n200
Navy Yard, 323, 355n220
Nawaz, Shuja, 56, 340n63
neologism, 3, 46, 87, 96-7, 124,
    141, 148, 269, 295, 309, 321
Nevada, 58, 199, 167-8
New Baghdad, Iraq, 182, 184
Newton, Connecticut, 323
Nicaraguan war, 287

Niger, 285, 350n155

Nigeria, xiv

No Drones Network, 335n2

Nobel Peace Prize, 249, 313, 321, 357n239, 359n271

'no boots on the ground', 154, 214-5, 217, 222, 234, 244, 261, 269, 273, 285

See also risk aversion

noncombatant immunity, 94, 325

noncombatants. *See* civilians

non-governmental organizations (NGOs), 71, 128

North, Oliver, 287

Northrop Grumman, 243, 250

Norway, 40, 45

nuclear weapons. *See* weapons of mass destruction (WMD)

Obama, Barack, vii-xi, xiii, xv, 5, 11, 23, 59, 61, 80-1, 84-5, 89, 91-3, 96-8, 100, 112-3, 127-9, 132-39, 141, 143-4, 151-4, 169, 211-2, 214-8, 220-9, 237, 243-4, 250, 261, 266, 273, 282, 333, 336n20, 343n98, 347n135, 347n138, 354n215, 357n240

'drone warrior', xv, 51, 71, 75, 80, 93, 100, 139, 141, 154, 184, 199, 207, 220, 237, 250, 267, 269, 285, 322, 326, 329, 355n224, 356n236, 357n239, 361n304, 361n306

George W. Bush legacy, 44, 51-2, 87-8, 92, 96-7, 113, 139, 151, 154, 216-7, 224-6, 267, 272, 288-9, 298, 308-9, 320-3

killing of Anwar al-Awlaki, 51, 109-10, 131, 277, 360n295

killing of Osama bin Laden, 44, 153, 221-3, 314

Libya intervention, 268, 360n291

Nobel Peace Prize, 313, 359n271

Public Statements, 61, 133, 137, 207, 215, 233, 249

Syria intervention, 211-2, 215-7, 229, 243-4, 269

See also 'kill don't capture' policy

obedience, soldierly, 70, 98, 189-90, 194, 200, 240-1

O'Connell, Mary Ellen, 357n149

Oklahoma City, Oklahoma, 63, 309

Operation Desert Storm. *See* Iraq, 1991 Gulf War

operators, 142

lethal drone (UCAV), xvi, 1, 5, 22, 27, 45, 52, 57, 59-60, 64-7, 71-2, 74, 86, 83, 99, 115, 155, 158-61, 163-7, 169, 172, 174-8, 182-6, 188, 196-8, 200-3, 213, 242, 251, 253, 262-5, 273-4, 293, 301, 312, 320, 333, 340n65, 351n167

plausibly deniable, 37-40, 45, 49, 67, 69, 143, 251, 287

'options on the table', 7, 88, 90, 218-9, 224, 244, 288, 312

organized crime, 64-7, 73-4, 275

Orphüls, Marcel, 173

Ortiz, Ximena, 362n316

Orwell, George, 85, 272, 294, 321

Pace, Peter, 352n179

Pakistan, x, xii, 17, 19, 25, 28-9, 33, 45, 60, 67, 70, 72, 75, 84, 88, 91-3, 105, 110, 113, 118, 121-3, 127, 138, 143-4, 147-8, 154, 162-3, 165, 169, 176, 193, 213-4, 218, 220, 255, 260, 272, 283-4, 304, 308, 326, 337n30, 342n82, 343n97, 343n100, 350n152, 357n239, 362n319

Pakistan Body Count, 342n82

Palestinian Liberation Organization (PLO), 36

Palestinians, xii, 34, 36, 41, 130, 349n148, 350n152, 363n322

Panama, 209

Panetta, Leon, 11, 48, 86, 118, 349n147

Paris, France, xiii, 314

'partisans', 35, 149-50, 173

pathrai, 69

Patriot Act (US), xii, 213

patriotism, 6, 40, 68, 126, 172, 189, 202, 209, 213, 239, 254, 258, 260-1, 267, 286, 322

Paul, Rand, 105, 114-6, 282, 345n119

Peace Review, xv

Pearl Harbor, attack on, 25, 258

Pentagon, ix, 22, 27, 42, 88, 90, 93-4, 97-8, 162, 186, 189, 193, 197-200, 206, 238, 243, 245, 289, 307, 322, 353n200, 363n320

Pentagon Papers, 339n53

Petraeus, David, 48, 98, 337n26

Pew Research Center, 337n29, 349n151

pharmaceutical firms, 188, 192-3, 197, 199, 253, 354n210, 355n219

Philippines, 92

physicians. *See* doctors

Pillar, Paul, 361n297

Pistone, Joseph, 340n59

Pitts, James, 231

Plame, Valerie, 350n155

Plato, 39, 128

platoons, 42, 70, 194

plausible deniability, 37, 39-40, 45, 49, 67, 69, 143, 251, 287

police forces, 26-7, 57, 63, 135-6, 145-7, 282, 348n139, 361n307

Ponzi scheme, 248

postcolonialism, 124, 286

post-traumatic stress disorder (PTSD), 164, 167, 186-7, 190-1, 200-3, 273, 281

Powell, Colin, 96, 313

Predator drones. *See* unmanned aerial vehicles (UAVs).

'Predator porn', 198, 201

premeditation, xvi, 7, 19, 33-4, 38, 46, 55, 57-59, 62, 64, 69, 80, 148, 302

Presidential Decision Directive 39 (PDD 39), 339n48

Prince, Erik, 244, 350n265

private contractors, 49, 67, 125, 162, 287, 289

in Afghanistan and Iraq, 181, 239-41, 346n127

in black ops, 37-40, 45, 49, 67, 69, 143, 251, 287

in the 'kill chain', 68, 72, 271

private military companies (PMCs),
67, 184, 238, 240-1, 243-4,
254, 322, 347n138
propaganda, 96, 236, 249, 254, 268,
289, 296, 353n200
psychiatry, 191-2, 197, 354n216

Qatar, 217
Qureshi, Fahim, 88, 331

race and racial profiling, 121, 123,
136, 139, 295
RAND Corporation, 292, 361n307
Rast, Benjamin, 161
Raytheon, 243
Reagan, Ronald, 338n33
Reaper aircraft, viii, 97
See also unmanned aerial vehicles
(UAVs).
reasonable doubt, 6, 73, 85, 120,
130, 136, 153, 315
rebranding. *See* neologism
'red line' remark, 211, 217, 269
remotely piloted aircraft (RPA).
See unmanned aerial vehicles (UAVs).
Reprieve (UK), 100, 345n116
republicanism, 52, 73, 266, 272
Reuters, 182-4
revenge killing, 69, 71-2, 74, 122,
128, 241, 272-3, 285, 308, 311
revolution in military affairs (RMA),
215
rhetoric, 35, 42, 51, 97-8, 153, 196,
209, 240, 268, 282, 294, 297,
309, 319
'just war', 95-6, 249, 292, 321,
328, 330, 359n276

Rice, Condoleezza, 269
right to bear arms, 144, 165
Ring of Gyges, 39
risk aversion, 6, 98, 160, 273
See also 'no boots on the ground'
Riza, M. Shane, 265, 340n65,
359n276
robotic warfare, 251, 261
Rohde, David, 163
Ruggiero, Benjamin 'Lefty', 53,
340n59
rules of engagement (ROE), 70,
1116, 121, 164-5, 183-4, 328,
331, 341n78
Rumsfeld, Donald, 15, 43, 52, 91,
170, 198, 227, 331, 355n219,
363n320
Russia, 289, 318
See also Soviet Union (USSR)
Rwandan genocide, 331

Saleh, Ali Abdullah, 14-5, 45, 118,
129, 151, 216, 237, 269, 283,
314
San Bernardino, California, xiii
San Diego, California, 27
Sánchez, Ilich Ramírez, 315,
363n322
Saudi Arabia, 25, 217, 284
Scahill, Jeremy, 129, 345n122,
347n137, 347n138, 348n140,
360n295
Scarcella, Louis, 346n126
secrecy, 17, 22-3, 31, 36-41, 49-52,
55, 63, 69, 109, 113, 117, 122,
125-6, 128, 137, 143, 214, 230,
246, 249, 251, 254, 282, 286-7,

298, 313, 322, 338n41, 339n47, 342n87, 347n135, 357n240, 358n254
See also State Secrets Privilege
security agents, 68, 87, 117, 124-5, 199, 217, 238, 275, 289, 351n167
Security Council (UN), 79-80, 148, 290
self-defense, xii, 6, 8, 59, 63, 74, 123, 131, 136, 150-1, 160, 165, 181, 184, 242, 341n70
economic and political, 49, 209, 213, 220-2, 225
legitimate, 45, 57-8, 70-1, 80, 84-5, 135, 152
national, vii-viii, xi-xii, 140-2, 249-50, 253, 267, 296, 303
re-defined, 59
self-mutilation, 189, 354n205
Senegal, 309
sensors (of laser-guided missiles), 165, 176, 196-7, 200
See also operators, lethal drone
September 11 attacks, 4, 6, 13, 25, 28, 34, 36, 42, 47, 49, 63, 72, 81, 84, 92-4, 109-10, 119, 123, 130, 138, 146, 153, 162, 171-2, 177, 182, 187, 209, 212-3, 220-1, 223-4, 226, 258, 268, 271, 291-2, 301-5, 309, 311, 316, 327, 331-2, 343n100, 362n314
Seychelles, xi
Shahzad, Faisal, 168, 236, 255, 266
Shaya, Abdalilah, 129, 347n137
Shiites, 216, 237

Shin Bet, 77, 166, 277, 342n87
Shinseki, Eric, 91
Sicily, Italy, xi
SIGINT (signals intelligence), 86
'signature strikes', xi, 63, 70, 86-7, 121, 139, 164, 219, 242, 253, 272, 295, 305, 308, 333
'silent killing', 37
SIM cards, 23, 86
Sinn Féin, 36
'smart war', ix, xi 141, 262, 323
'smart weapons', 161
Smith, Jeremy, 161
snipers, 142, 181, 352n189
Snowden, Edward, 48-9, 124-8, 223, 289, 348n140
sociopaths, 247, 263, 274
soldiers, 1, 2, 3, 13, 66, 148, 150-1, 189, 212-3, 262-3, 269-70, 286, 295, 306
crimes committed by, 39, 117, 183-4, 360n283
ground troops, 8, 45, 120, 148, 174, 176-8, 181, 187, 242, 310, 352n192
mercenary, 237, 67-8, 184, 186, 239-40, 244, 259, 287
traditional concept, 5, 27, 34, 61, 70, 80, 82, 91, 94, 99-100, 157-60, 164, 173, 177, 194, 258-65, 273-4, 291, 325-29, 340n67
See also combatants, conscripts, partisans, Special Forces, 'unlawful combatants'
Somalia, xiii, 26, 45, 92, 113, 118, 143, 148, 154, 162, 216, 221,

226, 235, 255, 257, 272, 283, 285, 304, 326
Black Hawk Down incident, 160
2006 Ethiopian invasion of, 249-50, 307-8
Sotloff, Steven, 215
South Africa, 306
South Sudan, 326
Soviet Union (USSR), 247, 292
Spain, xi, 20, 290
Special Air Service (British SAS), 338n40
Special Forces (US), xi, 17, 26, 36-7, 41, 153, 184
Spielberg, Steven, 37, 338n38
spies, 37-8, 108, 163, 201
    double agents, 68, 162
    intelligence agents depicted in films, 39, 245
    See also informants
'squirters', 164
'Stand Your Ground' policy, 136, 145
State Department (US), 96, 153, 160, 171, 214, 217, 268
State Secrets Privilege, x, 87-8, 118, 126, 267, 286
state security, 39, 43, 49, 51, 59, 117-8, 132, 199
Stimson Center Task Force, x, 362n315
Sudan, 42, 47
suicide, 289
    bombings, 72, 162, 172, 275, 342n82, 349n148
    soldier, 28, 185, 187, 190-2, 195-6, 203, 211, 213

summary execution, xv-xvi, 3, 34, 42-3, 48, 50-2, 59, 88, 93-4, 97, 99, 111, 113, 129, 131, 138, 147, 152-3, 201, 252, 282, 285, 294, 298, 304-6, 309, 313-4, 316, 318, 346n123, 362n316
Sunnis, 216, 229
Sweden, 25, 257
Syria, viii, 26, 92, 154, 212, 215-7, 221, 228-9, 234, 243-4, 248-9, 269, 272, 289, 326, 356n227, 356n233, 357n242, 361n306

tactics vs. strategy, 6, 14, 41, 47, 91, 97-8, 118, 142, 172, 199, 221, 246, 302, 305, 313, 318-9, 362n316
Tahir, Madiha, 255
Taliban, 7, 14, 22, 72, 100, 105, 161, 163, 175, 186, 222, 236, 242, 310, 357n239
targeted killing, xv-8, 23, 26-7, 29, 33, 35, 44-6, 48, 51-2, 55-75, 80-1, 83-9, 91, 94-8, 109, 113-4, 120, 123-4, 127, 131, 138, 140-2, 148, 152-3, 162, 166, 176, 184, 199, 215, 216, 220-1, 224, 229, 235, 241, 242-3, 246, 251, 253, 262, 270-1, 275, 282-3, 285, 288, 295, 301-2, 305, 309-10, 314, 335n1, 342n89, 343n97, 355n223
    See also assassination
Tausend, Helmuth, 173-4
taxes, 128, 231-54, 259
technology, xv-4, 13, 19, 44, 65, 75, 120, 139, 143, 157, 159, 175,

185, 187, 220, 229, 234-5,
250-1, 260
Tehrik-e-Taliban Pakistan (TTP),
672, 105
Tenet, George, 336n15
'Terror Tuesdays', 75, 101, 137,
142, 282
terrorism, 6, 22, 26, 29, 48-9, 72,
111-2, 114, 119, 164, 167-8,
171, 220, 235, 305, 315, 319,
29, 349n148
definition of, 177
terrorist attack disruption strikes
(TADs), 295, 333
See also 'signature strikes', 'crowd
killing'
Thatcher, Margaret, 269
Third Reich. See Nazi Germany.
Third World countries, 18, 27, 141,
151, 240, 304-5, 310, 312,
362n316
Threat and Local Observation Notice
(TALON), 348n140
Tibbets, Paul, 158
Tillman, Pat, 188, 259, 353n202
Times Square, New York, 168, 236,
255
Tomahawk missiles, 7, 90, 234
Tonkin Gulf incident, 269, 360n292
Tora Bora mountain range
(Afghanistan), 17
torture, 19-23, 34, 40-1, 48, 52, 87,
97, 113, 154, 214, 227, 288,
297-8, 309, 313, 329, 390n16,
339n47, 355n221, 360n289,
362n316
See also 'enhanced interrogation
techniques'

totalitarianism, 86, 124
transparency, 18, 31, 42, 153, 252
treachery, 65, 124, 163
treason, 79, 111, 116, 129, 315,
346n123
tribal communities, 70, 73, 92, 105,
247, 253, 284, 310, 337n30
'troop surge', 99, 270
Tsarnaev, Dzhokhar, 236, 357n249
Twitter, 169
tyranny, 6, 35, 52, 59, 110, 131,
251, 280, 284, 293, 297-8, 315,
318, 320
definition of, 279
military, 190, 253, 284-6, 288, 294
Tzu, Sun, 24

'unlawful combatants', 3, 61, 80,
113, 148, 224, 272, 291
unmanned aerial vehicles (UAV),
viii, xi-xii, xv-8, 13, 16, 18, 23,
26-9, 33, 35, 43-6, 48, 50-1, 55,
59-60, 62-3, 65, 68, 72, 74-5,
84, 86, 89-91, 93, 95-8, 100-1,
108, 115, 117, 119, 122-3,
129-31, 137-9, 141-4, 146-7,
150, 152-3, 158, 165-9, 174,
178, 181, 184, 197, 201, 203,
212, 214, 218-21, 230, 233-7,
241-50, 253, 261, 266-7, 271,
274-5, 282, 284, 286, 292-4,
305-6, 308-9, 315, 320-1, 326,
328
Uganda, 59, 309
United Arab Emirates (UAE), 218
United Nations (UN), 24, 80, 212
Charter, 5, 7, 61, 79, 142

Security Council, 79-80, 148, 290
Special Rapporteurs on extrajudicial executions, 142
Universal Declaration of Human Rights, 7, 61, 124, 290, 314
Article 11, 62, 315
utilitarian reasoning, 19-21, 24, 26, 110-1, 301, 336n16

vermin metaphor, 155, 167, 169, 175, 263, 306, 320
veterans, 37, 47, 90, 146, 159, 184, 186-8, 190-3, 196-7, 200, 243, 322, 353n203
Veterans Administration (VA), 187, 193, 198-9, 202
Victor, Thomas F., 343n101
'victors write history', 146, 290, 330
video games, 160, 164, 201
Vieira de Mello, Sérgio, 358n256
Vietcong soldiers, 181
Vietnam, 20, 37-9, 42, 46, 57, 122, 126, 181, 187, 193, 196, 226, 257-9, 269-70, 281, 295, 313, 328, 333, 339n53
Phoenix program, 338n39
vigilante killing, 82, 109, 272
Virginia, 167, 323
virtue, 264, 273, 275

war crimes, 7, 8, 60, 119, 125-6, 128-9, 149, 168-70, 188, 202, 236, 275, 289, 292
war profiteers, 68, 74, 193, 225, 230, 236, 238, 241, 243-4, 247-8, 250, 253-4, 261, 268, 301, 312, 322, 358n254

War Resisters League, 359n279
warlords, 14, 122, 247, 283
Washington, DC, 130, 243, 355n220, 357n239
Watchlisting Guidance manual, 62, 252
Waziristan, Pakistan, 109, 163, 234
weapons, xv-7, 27, 38, 45, 95-6, 144, 150, 158-61, 177, 184-5, 197, 215-6, 226, 262-3, 269, 272, 286-7, 292, 296-7, 327-8, 330, 358n245, 361n306
chemical, 211-2, 215, 243, 356n227
exportation, 248-51, 284, 312, 314
of mass destruction (WMD), xv, 3, 25, 46-7, 79, 127, 149, 158, 168, 209, 225, 294
production, 75, 236, 238, 241, 243-4, 246, 248, 260, 318
weddings (disrupted by missile strikes), 22, 161, 327, 350n161
Weiner, Timothy, 46, 338n37
Weinstein, Warren, ix
Western civilization, 25, 35, 50, 63, 80, 123, 131, 190, 195, 212, 234-5, 257, 264, 273, 284, 286, 294, 296-8, 311, 314, 326
whistleblowers, 124-7, 223, 289, 361n304, *See also* Manning, Bradley; Snowden, Edward
White, Andrew, 192
White Paper (US Department of Justice), 59, 75, 86, 110, 112, 115-6, 124, 131, 140-1, 218, 335n1, 346n123

Wikileaks, 182, 308
Wilkerson, Lawrence B., 81, 342n91
Williams, Bryan Glyn, 55-6
Wilson, Joe, 350n155
Wolfowitz, Paul, 14-5, 352n179, 355n224
World Trade Center (New York), 94, 271, 319
World War I, 157-8, 189, 268, 350n158
World War II, 36, 57, 79, 109, 148-50, 154, 157-8, 172, 174, 178, 189, 238, 270, 274

Xe Services, 244

'yellow cake', 350n155
Yemen, x, 22, 25-6, 28, 33, 45, 51, 72, 75, 84, 90, 92, 113, 115,
118, 122, 129-30, 137, 139, 143, 147-8, 151, 154, 162, 169, 176, 216-7, 220, 226, 235, 237, 250, 255, 257, 269, 272, 283, 285, 295, 304, 308, 314, 326, 343n97, 343n101, 346n130, 348n146, 350n161
November 2002 drone strike, xvii, 13-6, 18, 34, 51, 347n131, 355n224
Yousafzai, Malala, 220, 357n239
YouTube, 121, 182, 198, 201, 341n72

Zazi, Najibullah, 236
Zia-ul-Haq, Muhammad, 362n319
Zimmerman, George, 135-9, 144, 146
Zinn, Howard, 189, 353n204